DIALECT AND ACCENT IN INDUSTRIAL WEST YORKSHIRE

Varieties of English Around the World

General Editor:

Manfred Görlach
Englisches Seminar
Universität zu Köln
Albertus Magnus Platz 1
D-5000 KÖLN 41
Germany

GENERAL SERIES
Volume 6

K.M. Petyt
Dialect and Accent in Industrial West Yorkshire

DIALECT AND ACCENT
IN INDUSTRIAL WEST YORKSHIRE

by

K.M. Petyt

JOHN BENJAMINS PUBLISHING COMPANY
AMSTERDAM/PHILADELPHIA

1985

Library of Congress Cataloging in Publication Data

Petyt, K.M.
Dialect and accent in industrial West Yorkshire.

(Varieties of English around the world, ISSN 0172-7362. General series; v. 6)
Abbreviated and slightly modified version of the author's thesis (doctoral) -- University of
Reading, 1977.
Bibliography: p.
1. English language -- Dialects -- England -- West Yorkshire. 2. English language -- Eng-
land -- West Yorkshire -- Accents and accentuation. 3. English language -- Social aspects
-- England -- West Yorkshire. 4. West Yorkshire -- Social life and customs. I. Title. II.
Series.
PE2084.W45P4   1985   427'.81   85-20136
ISBN 90-272-4864-8 (alk. paper)

PREFACE

This book is an abbreviated and slightly modified version of my doctoral thesis, which was submitted to the University of Reading in 1977. I have omitted some of the preliminary material which discussed earlier work in the field, and some of the less interesting descriptive parts - a thesis is required to demonstrate how it relates to other studies and to present all its results, but a book should not give a potted version of what has been better covered elsewhere (and my own book *The Study of Dialect* has now made available an outline of the development of dialectology), and need not report the least fruitful parts of a project. Beyond this, I have made few changes, apart from correcting obvious flaws of presentation.

The book, and the methods on which it is based, may appear somewhat dated. It largely follows the approach of Labov (1966a), and planning and fieldwork were carried out in 1970-71, within a few years of the appearance of that pioneering work. Analysis of the data and writing-up were done during my spare time over the following five years or so (I was employed full-time during the whole period of my work). Other commitments have delayed this publication until 1985, and much has changed in the fields of sociolinguistics and dialectology during the fifteen years since I began work. Criticisms have been made of 'Labovian' studies (see for example Hudson, 1980), and other approaches have been attempted in social-urban dialectology (for instance, Milroy, 1980). If I were to take account of all these developments, and of everything I learned by experience and all the second thoughts I have had, I would probably tackle the subject quite differently. But since I cannot start again, I feel that it would be better to present the material almost in its original form, rather than trying to amend or reinterpret it in the light of subsequent research. It is one of very few thoroughgoing Labovian studies carried out in Britain, and it was intended to be primarily descriptive rather than theoretical. I publish it now in the hope that, though the theoretical framework and some of the conclusions have been shown to have flaws, many of its descriptive findings may still be of interest and value - and may be interpreted according to whatever theoretical viewpoint is adopted.

CONTENTS

Appendices: 359

TRANSCRIPTION

The system of transcription employed in this book is basically that of Gimson (1970).   I use the same symbols as Gimson when referring to RP;   for specifically Yorkshire sounds or phonemes some additional symbols are required: these can be found in Gimson's 'List of Phonetic Symbols and Signs', but I employ them with the value I describe in the text.   When dealing specifically with phonemes and phonetic contrasts, I employ the usual slants: otherwise transcriptions are enclosed in square brackets.

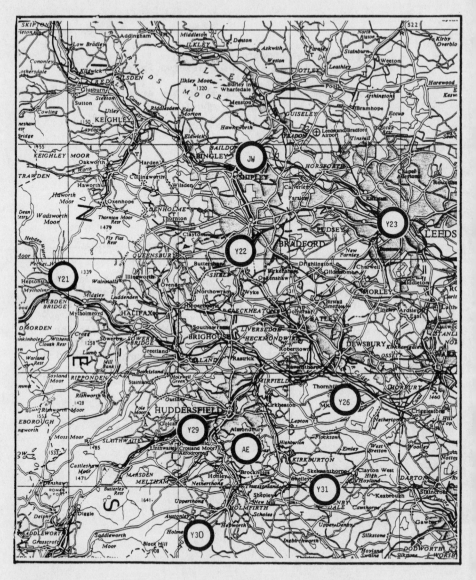

Map showing Bradford, Halifax, Huddersfield and surrounding areas,
including Windhill (JW = Joseph Wright), Almondbury (AE = A. Easther),
and the locations at which the Survey of English Dialects conducted
investigations (Y21, Y22 etc): these works are described in Chapters
1 and 5.

INTRODUCTION

The dialects spoken in Yorkshire have probably received more attention than those of any other region of Britain. Many of the publications of the English Dialect Society were concerned with this area, and the great Joseph Wright, editor of its massive *English Dialect Dictionary* and the *English Dialect Grammar*, was a native of a village near Bradford. Soon after the winding up of that Society, Wright was largely responsible for the founding of the still-flourishing Yorkshire Dialect Society, which has encouraged work both on and in the dialects of the area: serious descriptive studies, and both serious and light-hearted works in poetry and prose, such as have appeared not only in his own publications, but also in numerous almanacs[1], newspaper columns, and so on.

But great numbers of Yorkshiremen, like myself, know these dialects only from such sources - or perhaps we have heard them from a few old people or some country folk. Certainly we do not speak like that ourselves; some of us may be able to imitate dialect-speakers to some extent as a party trick, but in our everyday speech we do not say [fɪnd] for *find*, [niːt] for *night*, [nɪvə] for *never*, [fʊɪt] for *foot*, [varɪ] for *very*, [mak] for *make*, [nʊə] for *no*, and so on; we pronounce these words, in our opinion, very much as does the man on the BBC. Nor do we use many unusual vocabulary items, or past tense forms like *telled* or plurals like *een* or *childer:* in lexicon and grammar we are not far from StE. The forms of speech described as 'the dialect of' Bradford, Leeds, Huddersfield, or wherever, are generally those considered to be the 'genuine', 'pure', 'traditional' speech of those localities - but they do not seem to be used by the great majority of town-dwellers today.

And yet nearly all of us, in spite of having a mode of speech probably closer to StE and RP than to 'real' Yorkshire dialect, have had the experience of being recognised as Yorkshiremen (see p. 253). What is it, if we do not speak what is usually described as 'dialect', which continues to give us away? To attempt to answer this question was my main aim: to examine which kinds of features persist, and which have been or are being modified.

Abercrombie (1951) once said that English people divide into three groups according to the way they speak: 1) RP speakers of StE, 2) non-RP speakers of StE, 3) dialect speakers. Now these divisions are probably too sharp: for instance, many people from time to time use lexical or grammatical items that could not be considered to be StE, yet they could hardly be described as 'dialect speakers' - they are closer to the second group than to the third; but generally this is a reasonable summary picture. The first

---

1   See Dyson (1975) for examples of these.

group, users of RP and StE, has of course been extensively described;
and the third, dialect speakers, has received a good deal of attention, especially in Yorkshire. But the second group (including those
I have just mentioned) has been relatively neglected - though it is
quite possible that it includes the majority of the population of
Britain, and almost certainly it includes very many urban Yorkshiremen. I decided that this was the group I should make sure of covering; I would examine the speech of a good number of native Yorkshiremen from my home area, the 'wool' district of industrial West
Yorkshire. I wanted to see what sort of regional features had now
given way to StE and RP, and what sort still persisted in the towns -
what is it that continues to make most Yorkshiremen recognisable as
such, and how is it that some seem more 'Yorkshire' than others?

        I had been thinking along these lines when I came into contact
with Labov's work on New York City, and also with the first study
within the same framework to be carried out in Britain, that of
Trudgill on Norwich. I soon decided that it would be profitable to
carry out a major part of my own investigation along the same lines,
for a number of reasons. For instance, this would involve the study
of a sizeable sample of the population, selected by sound random
procedures, rather than an attempt to find particular types of
speakers as had been usual in most previous studies: this should help
to reveal the actual extent to which 'dialect' is still spoken, and
indeed to which any non-standard feature is used. Also, it would
make 'variation' central,₂and it was obvious to me that variation in
the degree of 'broadness'² was very noticeable in the area: some
people clearly had more or 'stronger' Yorkshire features than others,
and it would be profitable to measure this more objectively, and to
see whether it tied in with social status, say, or age, or with some
other factor such as 'situation' (for the same person seemed sometimes to speak more broadly than at others).

        Other reasons for my deciding to test the Labov approach on new
material related to some of the claims made on the basis of findings
in New York or Norwich. For instance, Trudgill had not found
evidence of the 'hypercorrection' (in an idiosyncratic sense of the
term) of the next-to-highest class claimed by Labov to be an important factor in linguistic change - would my findings support the
former or the latter? Trudgill had claimed that the working class/
middle class division was revealed to be important linguistically -
could this be shown to be the case by an examination of different

---

2   The term 'broad', though not a scientific one, is common in
the area, and I shall employ it from time to time in its popularly
accepted sense. I shall also, unless otherwise indicated, use
'dialectal' and 'dialect speaker' thus, rather than in terms of my
own definition of 'dialect' which is proposed in Chapter 8.

British data, or might it be the result of placing too much emphasis
on certain findings, or of the method of measuring social class?;
Labov had claimed that his work showed that there was a 'New York
speech community', united by certain norms at which its members
aimed, and Trudgill had gone even further: every member of the
'Norwich speech community' had the same 'diasystem' as some sort of
psychological reality - these seemed to me to be very strong claims.
There are important differences between New York or Norwich on the
one hand and my area on the other, and this is one important reason
why it is worthwhile to test the Labov approach on different data;
one such difference relates to this question of a 'speech community':
West Yorkshire contains a large industrial conurbation, and Bradford,
Wakefield, Leeds etc. are not 'isolated' large towns such as Norwich,
but rather they all shade into one another.   In what sense could
there be a 'speech community' in such a situation?

Another important difference in the West Yorkshire situation from
that in New York or Norwich may concern the 'prestige' of an area or
its speech.   Labov said that New York speech had 'negative prestige',
whereas I have found quite a number of Yorkshire folk claiming to
like their form of speech (see p.246) probably because they are proud
of their origins: Yorkshire is one of the most 'identity conscious'
parts of Britain; there is more pride in being a Yorkshireman (see
p. 381), and the British in general have more idea of what is a
'Yorkshireman' than a native of say Surrey or Berkshire - and it
could be that this difference relates to different attitudes to modifying regional speech.   On the other hand, unlike the American
situation, there is a generally-recognised 'prestige pronunciation'
of British English, and speakers in West Yorkshire like those in
Norwich must to some extent come under the influence of RP.

This study then examines the speech of a random sample of
speakers from part of West Yorkshire, with the aim of answering
questions such as:

How far does Yorkshire dialect survive among the populations of
the industrial towns?

What sort of changes have occurred or are taking place in the
speech of the area?

What sort of features tend to be more subject to pressure from
StE and RP?

How is it that many people, though they would not be considered
dialect speakers, are still recognisable as Yorkshiremen?

What accounts for the fact that some speakers sound more
'Yorkshire' than others?

Are people really proud of their Yorkshire speech?

and so on. The theme which links all these questions is 'persistence': some regional features are more persistent, some have been
more subject to modification.

The sample is drawn not from one town, but from three: Bradford,
Halifax and Huddersfield. These are all sizeable centres, inspiring
local loyalties, but they have in common that they are the three chief
towns of an identifiable part of West Yorkshire: the wool district.
The reasons for examining speakers from three towns are a) to provide
a link with traditional studies of the area which have treated geography as the dimension of primary importance and have shown different
dialects in the different towns; do such differences persist, or has
there been a drawing together towards some sort of regional standard,
and if so, has the most important of these towns, Bradford, exercised
more influence than the other two? and b) to tackle the related
question of whether it is realistic to talk about 'speech communities'
in such a situation.

Whereas previous studies in the area have been mainly concerned
with geographical differences, and with the historical axis of study,
this work concerns itself more with social differences and with the
synchronic axis; though of course the apparent changes from traditional dialect to the present are a main topic, it is primarily a
descriptive study of the facts of the speech situation in the area,
with a structural rather than a historical viewpoint - with systems
of items and systemically-different types of items being examined,
rather than with individual items being traced back to their origins
in Old or Middle English[3]. A major part of the study is set in a
Labovian framework[4]: certain 'variables' are examined from the view-
points of 'social differentiation' and 'evaluation'; but a considerable number of other features are examined too, since they are also

---

3   My knowledge of Old and Middle English is minimal and I would
not be capable of treating such points systematically; such snippets
as I have picked up and seem to be relevant will be confined to the
notes.
     Also in the notes will be most of the incidental remarks of or
about particular informants. A study of this 'statistical' type can
appear impersonal, whereas speech is something produced by individuals
and their peculiarities are interesting and often revealing - but too
many such references would disrupt the main flow of discussion.

4   I decided to keep fairly close to the methods of investigation
and analysis employed by Labov, since a) in 1970 these did not appear
to have been discredited by expert criticism, and b) I have not been
trained in survey and statistical techniques myself, and the number

presumably among the 'persistent' items which may continue to make
the Yorkshireman identifiable.

The work is primarily descriptive rather than theoretical: it
seeks to examine the facts, which I consider to be interesting for
their own sakes. However, because Labov's method has not been used
in many large-scale studies, any new attempt to employ it may well
produce useful lessons about various aspects of it, and this has been
the case. Also, of course, descriptive data is almost bound to
suggest some new theoretical conclusions, however minor, and these
have been drawn in a number of places; perhaps most important here
is the somewhat different distinction I suggest between *dialect* and
accent, and *Standard English* and *RP*, from that generally accepted.

The work is arranged on the following plan. The first part
(Chapters 1 and 2) 'sets the scene': it examines the background of
previous studies against which this one is set (Chapter 1), and some
important notions basic to this study (Chapter 2). The second part
(Chapters 3 and 4) describes the methods employed: the method of
sampling and the characteristics of the sample (Chapter 3), and the
fieldwork and analysis (Chapter 4). The third part (Chapters 5-7)
is the central section: against the background of a sketch of
aspects of the 'traditional' dialects (Chapter 5), the present situation is described in Chapters 6 and 7: the former describes
'performance': a) a number of variables are examined in a Labovian
framework, and b) other non-standard features observed are recorded;
the latter deals with 'evaluation' in terms of a) openly-expressed
opinions about speech, and b) two Labov-type experiments designed
to elicit less overt feelings. The final part (Chapter 8) attempts
to draw some general conclusions and to answer our initial questions.
A number of interesting but less central findings are reported in
the Appendices.

---

of new subjects I could study in the time available was limited.

I do not necessarily reject the various proposals that have
been made in more recent years for refining Labov's approach in
certain respects, but in the first place many of these were not published at the date I commenced my work, and in the second those which
were had mostly not been subjected to the same testing as Labov's
1966 methods.

THE AREA

Of the eighty per cent or so of the population of England who
live in towns, half are in seven 'conurbations' - great tracts of
built-up land, where several towns and cities have spread, engorging
previously independent small towns and villages, till they merge
into one another. Among these the 'West Riding' conurbation, with
approaching two million inhabitants, is a somewhat unusual case:
due to the fact that it is partly in the Pennines, the hills and
rivers have ensured that there remain certain breaks in the density
of habitation, and that some of the old nuclei retain their individ-
uality.

The old West Riding as an administrative area was in fact broken
up by local government changes in 1974. Wakefield had been the
administrative capital, Sheffield the largest city, and Leeds in many
ways the real capital. But within the conurbation there has long
existed an identifiable sub-unit: the 'wool area', and here Bradford,
centre of the world's wool trade for over 100 years, is the capital.
The wool trade was one of the first in England to be mechanised, and
the centres of the trade are among the oldest industrial towns; they
increased in size rapidly following the Industrial Revolution.   But
in more recent years the trade has contracted, and the wool towns
have shown less population growth than most, and in some cases even
a loss.

The three main centres, Bradford, Halifax and Huddersfield,
have much in common.   All were built beside good streams, because
water is very important in the wool industry.   All three were, until
recent times at least (when there has been much rebuilding, especially in the centres), dominated by solid and often ugly Victorian
factories and warehouses, turned black with grime, and there were
rows upon rows of terrace (often 'back-to-back') houses.   All
became county boroughs in the mid-nineteenth century.   All have
similar social, economic, and demographic characteristics (see
Moser and Scott, 1961): lower than the national mean in housing
standards, proportion with higher education, social class index (the
relation of those in Classes I - II to those in III - V), jury index
(the percentage qualifying to act as jurors), and commuting ratio -
but higher than the mean in terms of the proportion of the population
employed in manufacturing industries.   Yet all three towns are on
the edge of wild and relatively unspoiled country, and the hilly
terrain means that from many parts of the towns open country can be
seen.

Bradford, which lies on a beck which is a tributary of the nearby River Aire, was granted its charter in 1947, and was in fact
smaller than the other two until the 1830s, but it is now over twice
the size of Huddersfield and three times that of Halifax.   It

prospered on the wool trade, and the Wool Exchange (built, like the
Town Hall, after an Italian model) and the Conditioning House, where
wool is tested for water and grease content, strength, etc. were
focal points of the district. Bradford itself is predominantly a
'worsted' town, producing fine cloth from the 'tops' or longer strands
of wool, with 'woollens', from the 'noils' or shorter strands, being
made largely in other centres such as Batley and Dewsbury. In a town
of such a size there are of course other industries: a large English
Electric works, several sizeable engineering firms, and so on - but
wool is still important.

Yet the town has made its name in other areas too: its methods
of waste-disposal, both the tipping of refuse to make foundations
for playing-fields and to fill old quarries, and the sewage-works
which make a large profit from by-products, have drawn interested
parties from all over the world; and several welfare services within
the educational system have been pioneered: nursery-schooling,
school dinners, medical services, child guidance clinics, and so on.
The Technical College was started mainly for practical purposes: to
provide training in various aspects of the cloth trade, and only
since the War has part of it hived off and developed into a university.

Cultural activities are well provided for: regular concerts by
the Halle Orchestra, two choral societies, two art galleries, a large
theatre and a thriving amateur theatre, and so on.

The population has received several influxes of immigrants:
some of the largest wool firms were founded last century by Germans
(there is still a German church); after the last war a considerable
number of Poles, Ukrainians, Lithuanians, and Latvians arrived, and
have largely been absorbed into the population (though retaining their
own churches, cultural activities, and clubs); and since the 1950s
a very large number of Commonwealth immigrants, mainly Pakistanis and
West Indians, have come and by 1970 made up over 10% of the population, often concentrating in certain parts of the city.

Bradford draws in some workers from distances up to twenty-five
miles or more, but the great majority live within the immediate
vicinity. The 'urban field' (see Smailes, 1966: 130 sq), the area
for which the town acts as a centre for employment, shopping, entertainment etc., stretches mainly Northward: the Pennines are to the
West, Leeds to the East, and in the South, though Halifax and
Huddersfield look to Bradford for some things, they are in many ways
their own centres. The distribution of the local Bradford paper,
the 'Telegraph and Argus', tends to confirm this - as does the area
now designated the 'Bradford Metropolitan Area', created in 1974.

Halifax, which gained its charter the year after Bradford, lies

some seven miles South-West, and about the same distance from the
Lancashire border.   It is a town of very steep hills, lying mainly
between the Rivers Calder and Hebble which join at its southern
boundary.   It has been a centre of wool manufacture for over 800
years, and like Bradford it is mainly involved with worsteds, though
less exclusively so.   But it is unlike Bradford in that the wool
trade has been less dominant among its industry: it also contains
Crossley's, the largest carpet factory in the world;   Mackintosh's
the largest toffee factory in the world;   the Halifax, the country's
biggest building society;   and it had the first Yorkshire Penny Bank
in 1851 (the middle word has been dropped in recent times), and
produced the inventor and manufacturer of 'cats' eyes' (he was still
alive at the time of my survey, and was a good example of a successful Yorkshireman still having a 'broad' accent).

The town has, among other cultural activities, a fine choral
society, a dramatic society, and an authors' circle.   It has its
own evening paper, the 'Halifax Courier'.   Though it is quite a
good shopping centre, many people go to Bradford for a bigger day
out.

Huddersfield lies some ten miles South of Bradford and about
six miles from Halifax, at the junction of the Rivers Colne and Holme,
which then join the Calder.   The town was not granted its charter
until 1868, though the Colne valley has been a stronghold of the
cloth-making industry for over 600 years, and Huddersfield and
Almondbury (now just a suburb) were the markets of the valley and
are even mentioned in Domesday Book.   The area played a major role
in the development of the wool industry last century, especially in
designs and colours, and led the way in dyeing.   Again mainly a
worsted town , Huddersfield has, like Halifax, a great variety of
other major industries: chemical works, engineering factories,
dyeing and metal works etc.

Among her cultural activities, the Huddersfield Choral Society
is the leading such body in the country and is world famous.   There
is a local evening paper, the 'Huddersfield Examiner'.   The
Huddersfield Polytechnic has developed out of the Technical College.
Though the wool industry looks to Bradford, for shopping and entertainment people often go also to Leeds, and some to Sheffield, which
are bigger centres and easy to reach.

CHAPTER ONE

DIALECT STUDIES OF WEST YORKSHIRE*

'Yorkshire dialect', in the sense of a regionally identifiable variety of English, has of course a considerable history (see Waddington-Feather, 1970), and Yorkshire dialectology too goes back quite some time. For instance, of particular interest for our study is a work by Rev. John Watson published in 1775: *Remarks on the Dialect of Halifax Parish*, a glossary of some 250 words plus 17 'Rules for Pronunciation'. A section of Peacock (1869), one of the earliest special publications of the Philological Society, also contains points of interest; so too do such 'glossary and gossip' types of book as Dyer's (1891) *Dialect of the West Riding of Yorkshire.*

It was in the latter half of the nineteench century that a greater interest in dialect on the part of serious scholars was beginning to be shown, and in 1873 this resulted in the foundation of the English Dialect Society. The Society embarked on an ambitious programme of publication, and put out 80 works over the next 20 years or so. Among these are a number of works on Yorkshire dialects, and of special relevance to this study are those of Easther (1883) and Wright (1892). Easther's *Glossary of the Dialect of Almondbury and Huddersfield* is a work by a local headmaster who was not a native of the area; nor was he phonetically trained, so his transcriptions are not always of obvious interpretation. The book is primarily concerned with vocabulary, and includes a good number of everyday words which have a different form in the area. Easther gathered his material from very old inhabitants who recalled forms used by the previous generation, so he claimed that his material must go back to the 1770s. Wright's *Grammar of the Dialect of Windhill* is a very different and much more scientific work. Joseph Wright grew up in the village of Windhill, about 3 miles from Bradford, and spoke the local dialect. He was illiterate until his teens, and was largely self-taught. Eventually he went to Germany and trained as a philologist under the Neogrammarian influence.

---

* The map on p.viii may be referred to for the location of various places referred to in this chapter.

On his return to England he went to Oxford, and was soon appointed
Deputy Professor of Comparative Philology. *Windhill* was the first
major work for which he is famous; later came several now standard
texts on Old and Middle English - and of course his most famous
production, the *English Dialect Dictionary*.

Windhill was later described as 'the first really scientific
historical grammar on an English dialect, thus marking a new era',and
it became the model for a considerable number of dialect monographs
over the next half century. A very thorough and systematic treatment of Wright's native dialect, it has a long section on phonology,
which traces the development of the sound system from its Old English
(or French) origins, and a solid treatment of the morphology. There
are also a number of illustrative 'specimens' and a large index;
though this certainly could not represent a speaker's total repertoire (as Wright seems to suggest in the Preface), it does include
many Standard English items in their local pronunciation, rather
than just concentrating on those peculiar to the area.

During the period when the English Dialect Society was flourishing, A.J. Ellis was working on his monumental volume, *The Existing
Phonology of English Dialects (1889)*, which was the fifth and final
part of his *On Early English Pronunciation*. This is not the place
for a general discussion of the merits or otherwise of this work
(see Petyt, 1980:70 sq); suffice it to say that among his 1145
localities for which data is provided are a good number in Yorkshire.
His 'District 24', the 'Eastern North Midland', includes 'the whole
of South Yorkshire, comprising the great industrial centres of
Huddersfield, Halifax ... Bradford...' He distinguished nine
'varieties': Huddersfield (var 1) and Halifax (var 2) comprising
the Western Group, and Bradford (var 4) along with Keighley, Leeds,
and Dewsbury making up the North Central Group - though he noted
that in fact 'the real dialect is heard in the surrounding villages'.
But his mention of 'a great manufacturing population rejoicing in
their dialect' seems to indicate that the urban Yorkshiremen were not
ashamed of their speech. In spite of Ellis's obvious inadequacies
and mistakes, there is much useful information to be extracted about
the phonology of our three towns.

In order to help collect material for the *English Dialect
Dictionary*, Wright suggested the setting up in 1894 of the Yorkshire
Committee of Workers. This body provided much useful material on
the dialects of the county, which was incorporated into the
Dictionary (published in six large volumes between 1898 and 1905).
As part of Volume VI, Wright also produced the *English Dialect
Grammar*. About half of this work is the Index, which Wright compiled
first: it is an alphabetical list of words (most of them Standard
English rather than dialectal), together with their various dialect
pronunciations and the region where these are used. From the Index

Wright drew the material for the two main sections: 'Phonology', which gives a historical description of the development of sounds in their various combinations from West Germanic to the modern dialects; and 'Accidence', which details various peculiarities of dialect grammar, mostly inflectional morphology. From the *Dictionary* and the *Grammar* it is possible to extract a good deal of useful information about our area, but the locality references are unfortunately imprecise: 'W. Yks' or 'S.W. Yks' are the closest we can get to our three towns.

Once the major project of the *Dictionary* was launched, the members of the English Dialect Society seem to have felt that their job was done for all time, and in 1896 the extraordinary decision was taken to wind up the Society! However, Wright helped to see to it that the gap thus left was at least partly filled: in 1897 the Yorkshire Committee of Workers turned into the Yorkshire Dialect Society, which is still flourishing. Its aims are to promote both the study and the use of dialect, and its annual *Transactions* reflect this dual aim. The following are a number of papers published in that journal which are of particular relevance to this study. Crossland (1899) on 'The Vowel Sounds and Substitutions of the Halifax Dialect' is a brief, and as the title suggests, rather naive article: see for instance his statement about *oo*: 'in certain words, as 'wood', 'cook', 'poor', this *diphthong* has apparently not been *subjected to any deviation from, or extension of its ordinary English sound*' (my italics). However, it is possible to extract a picture of the vowel system, and there are some interesting remarks, such as that there is 'no definitive and uniform dialect' of the parish of Halifax: on the outskirts there are traces of say Huddersfield and Bradford features, and there are incursions from the standard language. Marsden (1922) 'Two Essays on the Dialect of Upper Calderdale', though concerned with the area including Halifax, unfortunately offers little linguistic information; but Sheard (1945) 'Some Recent Research on West Riding Dialects' is better. Principally concerned with Calderdale (though his research on Upper Calderdale was not so advanced and he confined himself to a commentary on the 17 'rules for pronunciation' of Watson: see above) his remarks on the lower part of the valley, the 'Heavy Woollen District', contain several points of interest. His more general discussion of West Riding dialects is also relevant: while noting that the Border between Northern and Midland dialects crosses the area, he went on to predict that as 'recent urbanisation ..... has tended to destroy the finer shades of pronunciation .... the influence of these dialects one upon the other will probably result in the production of a standard West Riding dialect'. Unfortunately however, though saying he intended to investigate this, he went on to describe how he was collecting pronunciations of *'genuine dialect speakers* ... from villages and small towns rather than from large towns and cities, where *real dialect* has ceased to exist' (my italics).

In 1928 there appeared a work by W.E. Haigh entitled *A New Glossary of the Dialect of the Huddersfield District* (the word 'New' is employed because Haigh saw his work as a successor to Easther's: see above). His glossary contains over 4000 words, with an Appendix of some 500 Standard English items in phonetic transcription to show their local pronunciation. He also sets out a vowel system, though this has some obvious deficiencies (see p.93 below), in which he says he uses Wright's phonetic symbols; unfortunately he made some confusing changes (e.g. au = not [aʊ] but [ɔ:]). His discussion of pronunciation is in terms of Old English vowels and their developments, and he sought to obtain the oldest material available - from elderly speakers and his memory of old relatives born around 1790.

Unfortunately, this primary interest in historical development rather than present-day structure, and this concern to find 'real dialect' in the sense of the oldest and least 'corrupted' speech is also to be seen in most of the work produced by students and researchers from Leeds University, probably the main centre of dialect study in England. Among the more relevant of these are Rohrer (1950), who investigated the border between Northern and North Midland dialects, from which we may conclude that the Bradford-Halifax-Huddersfield area is North Midland, though some Northern features are to be found; and Jones (1952) who examined the distribution of the different forms of the definite article in Yorkshire. An article by a former member of the group is Sykes (1961), dealing with the vowels 'in and around the town of Huddersfield'; unfortunately, while noting that the area has seen 'a great breaking down of the older dialect', he persisted in describing 'the traditional dialect' and tracing its development from Middle English. Though he claimed that this is 'still vigorous', in my own investigation just ten years later I did not find a single speaker in my random sample of 30 or so who used this dialect in 'pure' form - yet almost all spoke with a recognisably West Yorkshire accent.

Sykes had earlier been one of the fieldworkers for the *Survey of English Dialects*, which was based on Leeds University. This important major project has been discussed elsewhere; here we may simply recall that it went for 'genuine dialect' - the traditional vernacular as spoken preferably by elderly males of little education, agricultural workers if possible; while it claimed to be 'linguistically comprehensive', over half its questions aimed primarily for lexical information, and such phonological effort as there was sought to trace historical developments of Middle English sounds rather than to find the present-day 'system'. However, all responses were taken down in an impressionistic phonetic transcription, and much relevant material can be extracted from Orton and Halliday (1962), Kolb (1966), Orton and Wright (1975), and the *Linguistic Atlas of England*, edited by Orton, Sanderson and Widdowson (1978), (which of course appeared after my thesis was completed). SED investigated 34

localities in Yorkshire, seven of them in the South-Western quadrant
within which our three towns are situated.   Y21 Heptonstall (about
8 miles West of Halifax), Y22 Wibsey (2 miles from Bradford centre,
on the West side), Y23 Leeds (about 10 miles East of Bradford), Y26
Thornhill (about 7 miles ENE of Huddersfield), Y29 Golcar (less than
3 miles from Huddersfield centre, on the West side), Y30 Holmbridge
(about 6 miles SW of Huddersfield), and Y31 Skelmanthorpe (about 6½
miles ESE of Huddersfield).   Y23 and Y31 were investigated by
Stanley Ellis, the rest by Peter Wright.   Y22, and to a lesser
extent Y23, are of interest for Bradford;   Y29 for Huddersfield (and
Y26, Y30, and Y31 to a lesser extent);   no locality is particularly
close to Halifax, but Y21 is in the same valley and is perhaps
closer in speech to Halifax than any other.

The works referred to so far in this chapter may all be classed
as examples of 'traditional dialectology'.   From the 1950s this
type of approach to the subject came under criticism from various
quarters (see Petyt, 1980: Ch 4).   Scholars in the field of linguistics felt that the orientation was too historical: dialectology
seemed to have stuck in the days of comparative philology (from which
the subject had received great impetus in the late nineteenth
century), whereas modern linguistics was less concerned with tracing
historical developments and was more interested in structural relations within a dialect as spoken at one point in time.   Also, dialectologists usually recorded just the 'purest' forms, and ignored
the fluctuation between these and other forms which is to be
observed in almost any locality, and which may on the one hand show
interesting correlations with aspects of social structure, and on
the other have important things to teach us about linguistic change.
Scholars from the field of social science have other criticisms:
the methods of investigation employed by many dialectologists were
defective, and the concentration on 'pure' dialect meant that only a
very small and unrepresentative sample of the population was studied.
What was described as 'The Dialect of X' was, especially if X was a
large town, a form of speech used only by a tiny minority of the
inhabitants;   the rest of the population used quite different varieties, which might be very interesting but which were neglected.

Largely as a result of these criticisms, different approaches
to dialect study began to appear.   'Structural dialectology' was
much discussed in the 1950s and 1960s, and many dialectologists
began to examine features in the context of their system.   Variation between different forms, both within the community and within
the individual, was studied, and produced fascinating findings.
And instead of concentrating on elderly rural speakers, scholars
began to examine the towns and cities and to draw larger and more
representative samples of informants.   These approaches came together in the important work of the American linguist William Labov
(1966 and numerous related publications).   In Britain, a number of

scholars began to work on similar lines: for example, Trudgill
(1974) and Heath (1971 thesis, published as a book in 1980). And
in fact one of the first British urban investigations planned on
sound sociological lines was carried out in West Yorkshire: C.L.
Houck took a 'multi-stage' random sample of about 100 informants in
the city of Leeds (see Houck, 1968; Ellis, 1976). Unfortunately,
the rest of the investigation was not as advanced as this: Houck
did seek to investigate phonemic systems rather than historical
phonetics, but he set about this with a traditional type of questionnaire designed to elicit one-word responses such as *bill, pill*
etc., which would give him minimally-contrasting sets of words;
and he rather naively believed that this very artificial situation
would yield 'isolated approximations to *casual speech*' (my italics).
Few of Houck's results have been published; it is disappointing
that all we have learned from what seemed to be a very promising
investigation is that the vowels of *bud* and *bath* serve as social
markers in Leeds.

Apart from Houck's work, no 'modern' dialect studies had been
undertaken in West Yorkshire, and this was the gap I wished to start
to fill. I had a large amount of material from which I could
extract a picture of the 'traditional' speech of my area; by attempting a study along the lines laid down by Labov in America and
followed by Trudgill in Britain, I could obtain a more representative
picture of the present situation, and then see which features of
Yorkshire dialect appeared to have persisted, and which had been
modified under the influence of the standard language.

CHAPTER TWO

METHODOLOGICAL MATTERS

In this chapter I shall examine a number of important matters which are central to this work; I shall discuss each of them briefly in general terms, and then consider the ways it has been handled in studies of this type. (The specialist reader could probably omit this chapter, since it covers ground which may well be familiar).

1   SAMPLES AND SURVEYS

As I noted above, traditional dialectology came under fire in the 1950s from social scientists as well as from linguists: their criticisms were directed against its survey methodology in general, and in particular its selection of informants.

Let us refer for illustration just to two of the main surveys: those of England and the United States. SED (see Orton 1962:15 sq) selected its localities carefully - they were preferably agricultural communities with a stable population of some 500 (only half-a-dozen towns or cities of any size were investigated) - and within these the best informants were felt to be males over 60 with limited education and social contacts. American dialectologists made some attempt to investigate a wider range of speech: they sought speakers of three educational types and of two age-groups within each of these; towns and cities made up about one-fifth of the communities investigated (see Kurath, 1939:39 sq).

The sort of criticisms sociologists would level at these ways of choosing informants are well represented by Pickford (1956)[5]: such methods, she stated, are subject to grave errors of *reliability*, which is a matter of obtaining a representative unbiased selection of data. Though the American scholars made some effort to gain information about different social classes and age-groups, both surveys

---

5   Wright (1966) gives a useful later summary.

were in fact preoccupied with geography at the expense of other
dimensions of linguistic variation: they were mainly interested in
the 'pure' or 'genuine' dialect speaker whose speech reflected
regular historical developments, patterns of settlement, and so on.
But how representative is such a speaker? The 1951 UK census, which
was taken early in the period of SED's investigation showed that only
4% of British workers were employed in agriculture (and this figure
has continued to fall), and those over 60 and non-mobile were only a
fraction of these. The study of such speakers is a legitimate
pursuit, but it is *not* legitimate to entitle a description of them
'The Speech of Blankshire'. The American survey's attempt to describe social class differences was rather naïve because the social
classifications were not adequate: first, they were not objective
but depended on the fieldworker's judgement, and sometimes were
obviously circular; second, they were based largely on education
which is only one of the factors relevant to social class (see below);
and third, the social classes were not proportionately represented.

The preoccupation with rural dialect, whereas in both America
and Britain the majority of the population is urban, was clearly a
major shortcoming of much of traditional dialectology. But the
descriptions of urban speech were little better. For example,
DeCamp for his work in San Francisco (1958, 1959) selected 25 informants, all long-time residents, of three educational classes
(making sure to include one Negro and one Jew of each type). Leaving aside the question of whether 25 was a reasonable number for a
city of this size, and the fact already mentioned that education is
not the only factor in social class, it is clear that his method of
choosing informants suffered from 'hand-picking' and considerations
of availability; he admitted himself that random sampling would
have yielded greater reliability. In Britain, Sivertsen's *Cockney
Phonology* (1960) is a typical example of too broad a title: she
studied only a very restricted selection of Cockneys (working-class,
with minimal education and social contacts; for intensive study she
concentrated on four old ladies from Bethnal Green!) and confined
herself to what she considered to be 'off-guard' speech. Viereck's
(1966) methods in Gateshead were very similar: in spite of a chapter
on the population of Gateshead (over 100,000) and how it divides
into social classes, age-groups, sexes, and so on, his main informants were 12 men with an average age of 76, most of them resident
in old peoples' homes and formerly manual workers. Surely an
analysis of such a sample hardly warrants the title *Phonematische
Analyse des Dialekts von Gateshead-upon-Tyne*.

One of the main sociological criticisms of much dialectology, then
concerns the reliability of its findings: they cannot be considered
representative of the population as a whole because of deficiencies
in sampling. Concentration on rural-dwellers and particular age-
groups and social classes (the whole notion of social class has

generally been very naively treated anyway), has led to very considerable biases - as have also considerations of availability and
willingness to cooperate. Let us turn then to a brief examination
of more 'reliable' methods.

There is of course a considerable sociological and statistical
literature on the subject of sampling[6], and I shall only summarize
some of the main points relevant to this project.

One of the earliest examples of a sample survey, Bowley's work
on the condition of the working-class in Reading, illustrated how a
properly-conducted sample can save time, labour, and money, and
still achieve a high and calculable degree of precision: he showed
that, provided every unit had an equal chance of being selected,
samples of 30%, 10% and 1% produced very much the same results (and
he claimed that 0.1% would probably do the same).

Samples are used to investigate two main types of things (both
of which are involved in my survey): a) attributes - how many
individuals possess a certain property, do a certain thing etc.,
and b) variables - how much of a certain property they have, how
much do they do a certain thing etc.[7]   In either case, one of the
main aims is to avoid *bias* - the difference between the 'expected
value' i.e. the average from a sample (e.g. average age = 45) and
the 'true population value' (e.g. average age = 40).   Bias can be
introduced 1) if sampling is by a non-random method, i.e. human
choice is involved; 2) if the sampling frame, the population
record used, is inadequate or incomplete in some way[8]; 3) if some
sections of the population cannot be found or refuse to cooperate.

Broadly, there are two main types of sample: 1) *judgement
samples*, where selection is by human judgement (*quota samples*, by
which one attempts to find informants to fit certain slots, are a
particular example); and 2) *random* samples (in America *probability*

---

6   E.g. Moser (1958), Yates (1960 3rd Ed), Grebenik and Moser
(1962) etc.

7   We shall be much concerned with the latter: e.g. *how much* do
informants 'drop their h's'?, but in some cases we are interested
in the former: e.g. *how many* speakers use reduced forms of the
definite article?

8   The age bias of the example quoted could be introduced by using
the electoral register, which contains no names of people under 18,
as a sampling frame.

samples), where each member of the population to be covered has a calculable non-zero probability of being selected.   It should be noted that 'random' thus defined is not synonymous with 'haphazard': a human selector may be haphazard but will hardly ever be random – he will tend however unconsciously to favour some of the population. Truly random procedures of selection are by lottery or random numbers.   It should also be noted that randomness characterises the method rather than the result: the sample selected may, if one is unlucky, be unrepresentative since members of certain groups just have not turned up; the likelihood of this is related to the size of the sample.

'Simple random sampling' is where every member of a population has an equal chance of being selected; a 'quasi-random sample' would result if one took a random member to start with, then say every twentieth name: strictly, not all members would have an equal chance of selection.   More radical modifications are 'stratified samples', where a certain number of say each sex, age-group, social class etc. is chosen at random; this can only be done if these particulars are known for every member of the population, when this knowledge can be used to make the sample representative of all these strata; and 'multi-stage samples', where for the sake of economy one can concentrate the sample by introducing intermediate stages: e.g. within a city taking a random sample of wards, then polling districts, then individuals.

The result of random sampling should be a selection which is *representative* of the population as a whole in the sense that it contains the same proportions of people in all the different categories (sex, age-group, occupational and educational class, etc.) as the total population from which it is chosen.

The record or list of the population from which a sample is drawn is known as the *sampling frame*.   A sampling frame should be 1) adequate: i.e. cover the whole population; 2) complete: i.e. everyone is on the list who should be; 3) accurate: i.e. no-one is listed who is not there; 4) convenient.   In Britain the electoral register is frequently used, and certainly is one of the most convenient frames; it is also relatively complete and accurate since it is compiled annually (though numerous changes can occur in a year); its main inadequacy is that it contains no-one under the age of 18: these members of the population have to be approached in other ways, with care being taken to preserve randomness.   The electoral register would of course be of little use for stratified sampling, since it contains no information about personal character-istics except sex.

The representativeness of the sample may be considerably affec-ted by failure to contact some of those selected because of such

facts as removal, unsuitability (e.g. senile, deaf, ill etc.), not
being at home, or refusal to cooperate. Two things should be done
about such non-response: it should be kept as low as possible, e.g.
by making several calls on those not immediately available; and
its bias should be estimated, e.g. by noting characteristics of
refusers such as sex, age, social grouping etc., and then seeing
whether this group differs significantly in these respects from
those interviewed. In some surveys, where social characteristics
are known, *substitutes* who match the non-responder may be chosen.

The avoidance of bias is one major principle of sampling.
Another is to achieve maximum precision: the probable accuracy of
the sample findings when compared to the population as a whole.
It is here that the question of sample size comes in: this is determined by the degree of *sampling error* it is decided to permit, not
by the size of the total population. It may be noted that if the
method of selection is unsound (e.g. non-random), increasing the
size of the sample will not compensate for this.

After this brief discussion, let us examine the sampling
methods employed in earlier projects of the type of this work.

In New York City, Labov was faced with an area with much immig-
ration and emigration, where a random sample would obviously pick
up many subjects not native to the area; but he was fortunate in
having available the results of a sound survey with a high success-
rate carried out only two years earlier by Mobilisation for Youth.
Detailed demographic data was available on all their subjects, and
so Labov decided in effect to use this as his sampling frame. By
eliminating all non-native speakers of English he reduced the 'pool'
from 988 to 617; from the remainder (all classified on a 10-point
scale for a combination of occupation, education, and income) he
took a stratified sample, reducing the figure to 553; then he
eliminated those who had not come to New York before the age of eight,
leaving 312. Over 100 of the remainder had removed, died or become
incapacitated since the MFY survey, leaving 195 of whom he succeeded
in interviewing 122[9]. Labov also approached by telephone 16/27
refusers and 17/46 of those not reached, pretending to be researching
reactions to TV programmes; he concluded that the speech patterns
of these 'failures' did not differ in any important respects from

-----

9   This 63% success-rate looks good, but in fact it was of course
63% only after subtracting removers, non-natives etc. Like for
like, my own success-rate compared favourably with this.

those of his 'successes'[10]. He also reached important conclusions about sample size: he and his assistant had not been able to aim at as many interviews as MFY, but this did not matter because he found that 'numbers which might be totally inadequate for the study of attitudes say towards racial segregation ... are quite adequate for the study of phonological variables': groups of 10-20 readily gave a value for say a social class, which fitted into an overall pattern (1966a:181); and in fact he concluded that a random sample of only about 25 informants is large enough to show the stylistic and social structure of variation (1966b:107).

One apparently less sound procedure employed by Labov was the way he 'adjusted' the numbers in certain groups on discovering that only 84 of his 122 had actually been born in New York: for example, on finding he had only 8 natives in his top class he asked one informant to name 'community leaders', which yielded 2 more, and he also used one of MFY's research assistants. The worst bias remaining was one of 2:1 in favour of women; examining his 70 or so non-respondents (refusals and no-contacts), Labov found that the 40-59 age-group were disproportionately highly represented among these; so were the lower classes; men tended more often to be unavailable, while women and younger informants were more likely to refuse.

The later survey by Labov et al (1968) used somewhat different methods. Their main aim was to investigate 'natural peer-groups' of lower-class Negroes and Puerto Ricans in the 10-17 age range: obviously these had to be picked through knowledge of the local culture and situation rather than at random. Contacts through Vacation Day Camps were obviously biased in favour of those likely to attend such; relations with groups were built up and eventually every individual connected with them was interviewed. Only with the 'background' sample of 100 negro adults was selection more random, but here too there was a sizeable 'judgement' factor: a stratified random sample (Males/Females, under/over 40, 'higher'/'lower' areas) selected by a multi-stage procedure of 'apartment house', 'building unit', and 'dwelling unit', was taken from three selected Harlem areas - selected impressionistically by the state of the houses; a success rate of 50% was supplemented by a number of informants from drug rehabilitation centres chosen because they appeared to be of the same type as some of the failures.

In the Detroit survey, Shuy's team (1968a,b) were also able to work on the basis of an earlier survey, of religious affiliations.

---

10   Of course this finding could be said to be biased in favour of the type of informant likely to have a telephone; but since other characteristics were known it is probably not important.

They divided the city into ten religiously homogeneous areas, then
selected at random one public and one parochial school in each;
from the middle grades of these 30 pupils were chosen at random, and
their parents and siblings were added to this sample.   15 informants
from 'under-represented areas' were added (admitted to be an element
of judgement sampling); the total sample came to 702.   Wolfram (1969)
for his sub-study of Negro speakers in Detroit used a stratified
sampling procedure to select 48 informants using the 702 as his sampling frame: he took 12 from each of 4 social classes, 4 of these 12
from each of three age-groups, with equal representation of the sexes.
He also selected for comparative purposes 12 Upper Middle Class
Whites, equally divided for age and sex.   All informants had to have
lived in Detroit at least 10 years, and those under 17 had to be
natives.   Wolfram admitted that his criteria 'somewhat restricted
the randomness of the sample'; but as he and Fasold (1974) point
out, simple random sampling may yield a representative sample but it
may produce say very few Class I informants and many of Class IV[11],
and since less than 5 informants in each 'cell' may skew the results,
it is legitimate, they claimed, to follow procedures like theirs.

A review article by Baubkus and Viereck (1973) was much more
critical of Shuy's and Wolfram's departures from strict sampling
methods: sampling from schools violates a basic principle in that
all members of the population do not have an equal chance of selection (unmarrieds and those without school-age children cannot be
chosen, while those with several schoolchildren stand a more-than-
equal chance).   Wolfram's sample suffered *a priori* from Shuy's
faults, and also revealed the classical judgement sample approach of
traditional dialectology, since apart from the stratified procedure
and other restrictions already noted, he also limited himself to
those interviews with a 'reasonable amount of discourse' and good
quality taping.   The reviewers claimed that for these and other
reasons Wolfram's conclusions could not be trusted.

Turning to Britain, Houck's work in Leeds (1968) represented a
considerable advance on the selection methods employed by Leeds dialectologists in the SED[12].   He used a multi-stage random sampling
procedure, the first stage consisting of dividing the map of Leeds
into squares of a certain size and population-density, and the second
of selecting one house at random in each square;   the actual informant was then chosen at random, from those members of the household

---

11   As my own sample did: see p. 54-56

12   We may note that SED ideas for future work on urban speech
envisaged seeking out lower-class artisans and labourers of restricted social contacts and mobility;   this would not of course be a
representative sample of the urban population.

eligible.   Houck achieved a 75% success-rate, and it seems a pity
that so little was produced by such a well-conducted survey.

In Norwich Trudgill divided the total population (100,000) by
the number of informants required (50) to obtain a 'sampling
fraction' of 2000.   A number less than this was chosen at random
(46), and the selection was then quasi-random: the 46th, 2046th,
4046th etc. informant on the electoral register was taken.   Trudgill
actually departed from a simple random sample in another way too:
he drew his sample not from the whole city but from 5 wards chosen
because they had on average the same socio-economic characteristics
as the city as a whole.   25 were taken from each ward, and approaches
made to a random 10 of these; in the event of failure, replacements
were drawn from the rest of the 25.   95 approaches were made in
order to secure 50 interviews.   Because the electoral register at
that time contained no-one under 21, Trudgill selected 10 schoolchildren; his method here was less sound, since he drew his informants from 2 grammar schools.   Apart from not reaching speakers
between leaving-age and 21, this had the obvious danger of biasing
selection towards the upper end of the social scale; but Trudgill
felt his sacrifice of strict procedures was justified in terms of
time saved and results achieved (the children selected were not
markedly distributed towards the top of the scale).

My own method of sampling is described in detail in Chapter 3.
Like Trudgill, I decided that, though it would be desirable to
examine the whole population (and this would have been essential had
my main aim been to discover what features are diagnostic of a
Yorkshireman, a Bradfordian etc.), considerations of time made it
necessary to define as 'my' population those I classed as natives
(or those who had come to the area early) - though not of course
only those with 'pure' Yorkshire speech.   Stratified sampling was
not possible since I did not have details of the social characteristics of potential informants, so I employed a 'simple random sample'
method for the population aged 18 or over.   Unlike Trudgill, I did
not have available information on the characteristics of different
wards, so I drew my samples from the whole towns (I could of course
have employed a multi-stage procedure - wards, polling districts etc.
- but I thought that in towns of the size in question and with the
number of informants needed I could probably group my calls and
interviews in such a way as to avoid waste of time and effort[13]).
For informants under 18 I selected comprehensive schools and then
chose pupils at random within these[14].

13   This turned out to be only partly true, but my interview-rate
of about 13 per week was about the same as Labov's and compared
reasonably with Trudgill's 16.

14   This was the case in Bradford and Huddersfield; in Halifax the
Director of Education asked me to use the FE college, which catered
for a similar ability range but the pupils were all 15 or over.

Besides criticisms about *reliability*, sociologists (see Pickford, 1956) also cast doubts on traditional dialectology on the grounds of *validity*, which concerns matters such as asking the right questions, and how to draw out this information. Here too dialectologists had not made use of the expertise available, and interviews sometimes failed to get valid information partly because of questionnaires that were faulty in respect of length, question-phrasing etc, and partly through inadequate interview technique: fieldworkers varied in skill and training. Again there is a considerable literature on interviewing and questionnaires, and as it is not the main concern of this work, I shall only briefly rehearse a few of the main points to be found in e.g. Harris (1950), Moser (1958), Grebenik and Moser (1962) etc.

Questionnaire-design is one of the most important tasks in a survey, since faults here could invalidate certain 'findings' before work even begins. The aim of the survey must be clearly defined: is it to collect facts, say, or is it to gauge opinions? In the former case the framing of questions is not too difficult, and they can be further 'explained' without danger, but in the latter the precise wording may be important. Questions must always be in simple language, yet they have to be sufficiently specific; they must not 'lead' an informant and influence his answer. Sometimes 'pre-coded answers' may be used - and what comes under each category must be made clear; in other cases 'open' questions are best. The order in which questions appear can be important: a different order may elicit different responses - so, once fixed, the same order should be kept to; the order of sections of the questionnaire should also be considered: factual questions may be the best to ask first, with discussion questions kept till the ice is broken. Finally, the length of the questionnaire is important: if too long, it might increase the refusal-rate or affect the quality of responses. A testing of questionnaires in 'pilot' surveys is desirable.

The interaction of interviewer and informant, the 'rapport' they achieve and the degree of cooperation by the informant can obviously affect the responses. The interviewer has to be very careful about his attitude, lest he influence the response, either by suggesting an answer, or by seeming to be an authority, or by making the informant feel embarrassed about a 'don't know'. He must be careful to get permission from the authorities to conduct interviews, if appropriate, and should assure informants that information given will be anonymous and confidential. He should be honest about the purpose of the enquiry, and should explain why it is necessary to know certain personal details - and he should allow the informant to ask questions about the survey. A faulty interview technique - because of the character and opinions of the interviewer, the degree of probing, any kind of 'cheating', the wrong coding of responses etc. - can be a major source of *response error;* in fact

it is a more likely cause than an informant deliberately giving
wrong answers.

     In my questionnaire design and interview technique I endeavoured
to follow these principles, though doubtless faults remained.   In
presenting my findings I have tried to combine tables and graphs of
aggregates with reference to individuals, for speech is primarily an
individual rather than a group phenomenon.   Finally, though I have
tried to use modern methods I trust I have not fallen into the trap
pointed out by Grebenik and Moser (1962:22):   'some surveys are
more distinguished for technical virtuosity than for the contribution
they make to knowledge'!

2   SOCIAL CLASS

     This subject has received the attention of several of the social
sciences for many years.   It is not of course a main theme of this
work, but since 'Labovian' studies pay a good deal of attention to
the correlation of linguistic differences with social class, we must
briefly examine the notion here.

     'Social stratification studies are concerned with the placement
of people into social categories ... on the basis of some one or
several characteristics they possess' (Owen, 1968:1).   Social
stratification a) involves the evaluation of particular factual differences;   and b) results in grading the population into superior and
inferior strata;   c) this system persists over time;   and d) it has
consequences in terms of different opportunities.   In general, then,
social stratification is the stabilisation of social inequality.

     Obviously important are questions such as 1) which character-
istics are made the basis for stratification?;   2) what relationships
exist between such strata and other social differences such as education, income, property ownership etc?;   and 3) what are the means
of recruitment to the different strata?

     Though there are other types of stratification - such as *caste*
or *estate* - the one which generally operates in modern western cap-
italist society is that known as *social class*.   Some would claim
that for various reasons there is in these societies a gradual move
towards classlessness;   but such changes as have taken place certainly do not amount to an abolition of social class.   On what then
is the social class system based?

     Social classes are generally agreed to be basically economic;

unlike caste or estate, therefore, which are supported by specific
religious or legal rules, classes are not precisely defined and their
membership is less stable.   This produces a weakness in certain
theories of social class, such as the best known - that of Marx: he
saw social class in terms of the relation to the means of production,
and claimed that there were just two classes, the owners and the
operators, between whom the gap would widen, which would produce a
greater class consciousness.   This has not in fact happened: the
gap has not widened and there has been a diminishing of the polarisation through the growth of the 'new middle classes' - a growth which
reflects the greater complexity of social stratification in modern
industrial societies, and introduces another important factor pointed
out by Weber, the first theorist to offer a comprehensive alternative
to Marx: 'social prestige' or *status* based on occupation, education,
style of life, and so on.

Weber held that class and prestige stratification coexist in
modern society, and the latter affects the former by 1) interposing
between the two major classes a bridging range of status groups, and
2) suggesting an entirely different conception of the whole social
hierarchy, by which it appears as a continuum of status positions
determined by a variety of factors rather than simply by property-
ownership.   Since 'some recent sociologists have concluded that
status groups have now become far more important than social classes
in the system of stratification' (Bottomore, 1965:26), it is largely
in this sense that I shall be continuing to employ the old term
'social class' (as appears to be common practice).

What are the factors which appear to determine which social
class a person belongs to?   Though economic considerations are still
important to some extent,and a person with a high income will, all
things being equal, command more prestige than one with a lower, all
things are frequently not equal, and some people are still considered
to be of an inferior class in comparison to others with a lower
income, e.g. miners compared to teachers.   For though in general
greater rewards are given to the 'better' jobs, occupation, which
is clearly one of the main indicators of social status, is evaluated
not solely in terms of financial rewards but also of such factors as
training, educational qualification, responsibility, and so on.   In
Britain one well-known system of grading jobs is the Registrar
General's *Classification of Occupations*[15], which classifies virtually
all occupations named in census returns in terms of five classes:
I Professional, II Intermediate, III Skilled, IV Partly-skilled,
V Unskilled.   It is pointed out that 'each category is homogeneous
in relation to the basic criterion of *general standing in the*

_____

15   I used the 1966 edition.

community ... but it has *no direct relationship to the average level
of remuneration...*' (my italics).

That this division of occupations can be justified was shown by
two studies. Hall and Jones (1950)[16], (who in fact used a seven-
grade system with each of the Registrar General's Classes I and II
divided into two) found a high degree of agreement among 1400 subjects when asked to allocate 30 occupations to classes. They also
found certain correlations with characteristics of the subjects:
e.g. the young tended to upgrade white collar jobs, the older skilled
manuals; and some groups tended to 'upgrade themselves', as it were.
Thus in spite of the fact that different people probably gave weight
to different factors: e.g. pay, conditions, responsibility, educational qualifications etc., the overall totality of judgements, which
make up social status distinctions and prejudices, showed general
agreement. A later study by Young and Wilmott (1956), basically
a repeat of the above experiment with 82 subjects, showed that rating criteria were of five broad types: ability, education, remuneration, social milieu, and social contribution; but it also serves
as a warning that agreement on grading is not complete since they
found 22 subjects who were in a sense 'deviant'[17].

We noted that the system of social classes is not supported by
specific religious or legal rules; a person is not therefore restricted to the class of his birth, i.e. that of his father.   There
are possibilities for *social mobility;* for a woman marriage is an
important means to this, while for a man it is largely a matter of
getting a 'better' job than his father - and sociologists have
pointed out that in complex industrial societies there are more
opportunities for upward mobility.   Research in Britain (see Glass,
1954: Lockwood, 1962; etc.) has shown that the greatest rigidity
is at the 'top' and the 'bottom', where the social and economic
effects of parental status and attitudes are most likely to outweigh
sheer ability; and that mobility is commonest between adjacent
classes, especially 'skilled manual' and 'routine non-manual' (Glass,
1954:19).   It has also been pointed out that there are differing
degrees of 'social distance' between classes: there is for example
a more pronounced jump between manual 'working class' and non-manual
'middle class' (Lockwood, 1962:510).

Various factors are important for social mobility besides

---

16   See also Moser and Hall (1954).

17   The key to this was provided by the fact that their reasons for
rating as they did, and the way they rated themselves, depended largely on the last criterion named: social contribution - with the result
that say a miner was ranked higher than many white collar workers
because he was seen as more 'essential'.

occupational structure: e.g. different fertility rates of strata,
distribution of innate ability, distribution of occupational opportunities and motivation to achieve - and, very important, the
structure of the educational system.   In Britain, before the 1944
Education Act the level of education one could achieve depended to
some extent on the social status of one's family, in terms of occupation and income; after that Act the opportunities for education,
obviously a key to a better job and therefore upward social mobility,
became greater.   But in fact, as sociologists of education have
pointed out (e.g Floud, 1962), the changes in mobility have been less
than might have been expected: there is clearly a significant relationship between home background and educational success (partly
because of differences between classes in respect of aspirations for
their children and motivation to achieve), and it is the middle class
rather than the working class who have benefited more from the
greater educational opportunities.

Besides occupation and education, another important factor in
social status (though for the reasons noted it is not as crucial as
in the past) is income - and various matters related to this such
as residence: the type of house one inhabits and the sort of area
in which it is situated[18],[19], and one's style of life in general:
material standards, leisure activities etc. There are also less
measurable factors such as language itself - though social differences in accent seem to be felt to be of less importance now (see
p.244 below); and less tangible, but possibly also indicative of one's
position in a status hierarchy, are differences in attitudes and
aspirations.

A particular instance of the importance of attitudes is a person's own view of himself in social class terms: if he considers
himself to be middle class, for example, he may strive to develop
middle class characteristics.   An example of the type of work done
by sociologists in popular conceptions of social class and subjects'
own assessment of themselves is Martin (1954), who asked 500 informants how many classes they thought there were and which class they

---

18   The Index of Social Characteristics' developed in America by
W.L. Warner and others produces ratings based on four factors including those just mentioned: 1) occupation, 2) source of income (wages,
salary etc.) 3) house type, 4) area. Each was rated on a seven-point
scale from 1 (low) to 7, and 'weighted' by multiplying by 4,3,3,2
respectively - yielding scores ranging between 12 and 84.

19   Hoggart (1957) in his readable account of working-class life in
northern cities, says that even in working-class areas there is often
'a fine range of distinctions of prestige from street to street'.

considered themselves to belong to[20].   He found that the majority
distinguished between upper, middle, and working class; and when
assessing themselves it was mainly the 'middle groups', especially
the lowest non-manual workers, who were divided as to whether they
were middle or working class.   Other findings included a tendency
for women to upgrade themselves, confirming the common observation
that women are more status-conscious than men[21], and the facts that
those whose objective class clashed with their subjective assessment
tended to emphasise indicators such as income and standard of living
besides occupation, and that the middle class tended to 'shift the
boundaries' to fit their own assessment of themselves as working or
middle class.

The conclusion of this general discussion must be that social
class in Britain today is a complex and somewhat arbitrary notion.
Status groups do not depend on a single criterion such as occupation;
though this is an important factor, various others are given different amounts of weight by different people.   There is no clear
demarcation between the different classes, and indeed the division
into a particular number of classes (whether it be the seven employed
by Hall and Jones, or the Registrar General's five - or his alternative scheme of seventeen 'socio-economic groups') is a fairly
arbitrary procedure.   'Only in rigidly stratified societies would
one expect to find a single stratification system to which all in
the society would agree and in which all would be accommodated' (Owen,
1968:88).   And clearly Britain is not such a society.

Let us turn now to the way social class has been defined in some
recent linguistic studies.   For it has been claimed that social
class of some sort is probably the most frequent non-linguistic correlate of linguistic variation.   Some scholars, like Wells (1973)[22],
have employed a simple notion, based solely on occupational class.
But, as Labov demonstrated (1966a: Ch VIII), the single factor of
occupation does not correlate as clearly with linguistic variation
as a more complex notion of social or socio-economic class (thus confirming the findings discussed above that there are various factors
involved in social class today); Labov himself therefore used three
factors: education, and the occupation and income of the breadwinner
- each scored on a four-point scale (0 - 3), so that informants ranged
in class from 0 to 9.

_____

20   See App. E for my own simplified replication of this experiment.

21   Chapters 6 - 7 below give numerous examples of women approaching
closer to the 'better' form of speech.

22   Wells' class-system was as crude as anything could be, being
divided simply into 'manual' and 'non-manual'.

Trudgill followed Labov in employing a composite notion: he
used six factors, each with a six-point scale (0 - 5), so that informants received scores between 0 and 30. Besides occupation, education, and income, he also took into consideration housing, locality,
and father's occupation. This last I regard as irrelevant from a
synchronic point of view: as a child one's social standing is usually
determined by that of one's father, and the latter may of course
affect one's achievement in terms of education, and therefore also of
occupation, income, standard of living etc. - but once one is independent one is judged in terms of these factors themselves if (as is
most often the case) one's father's occupation is not known. Housing and area of residence are doubtless relevant when allocating one's
fellows to particular social classes[23], but it seems to me that Trudgill had to stretch things somewhat in order to produce his neat six-
point scale for each factor. For locality he used his subjective
assessment based on experience of living in the town; certainly one
does get to know that some areas are 'respectable', 'classy', and
'poor' etc., but it is surely doubtful whether a subjective rating
on anything finer than a three or four-point scale should be given
equal weight with more objectively measurable factors like education
or income. For housing, his method of assessment seems even more
dubious. He subdivided first into three sub-factors: ownership,
age and type of house - each of which was marked on a three-point
scale. Ownership was own/privately rented/rented from Local Authority; age was pre-1914/pre-1939/post-war; type was detached/semi/
terrace or flat. But since marking 0 - 2 on each of these would

---

23   We have already noted that these are included in the Index of
Social Characteristics developed in America by Warner and others -
which was employed by Putnam and O'Herne (1955), one of the earliest
linguistic works based on an objective measure of social status.

Bickerton (1975) complained that Trudgill, following Labov,leaned
heavily on Warner-like 'status-based'theories, and that there seemed
to be no awareness that there were other possible approaches, such as
those of Marx or 'attitudinal studies'. Two points may be made in
reply to this: 1) Trudgill did in fact discuss other views of class
in his original thesis (1971), and decided in favour of status-type
approaches. I agree with him, on the grounds that a) approaches such
as that of Marx have suffered much criticism; b) my questions to informants about social class seemed to indicate that a majority saw it
in this way (see App. E); 2) Labov's source in fact distinguished
between 'class', which he held to be based on 'productive' factors and
measurable in terms of occupation, income, and education - and
'status', based on 'consumptive' factors (style of life, where one is
educated, how one spends one's money etc.): see (1966a:212). Labov
decided that housing and standard of living come into the second category, and so he did not use them in setting up his 'socio-economic
classes'.

yield a seven-point scale (0 - 6), in order to maintain neatness he
reduced ownership to private/rented.   So the extremes were a post-
war detached privately-owned (5) and a pre-1914 rented terrace/flat
(0)[24].   But surely this does not always make sense: is age, for
example, so simple a measure - surely some old houses (0) are much
'classier' than modern boxes (2).   And the general prestige-scale
of terrace or flat/semi/detached must permit exceptions: there are
some high-class terraces or flats that carry more status than a common
semi.   One is tempted to conclude that the score would sometimes
have to be doctored in order to bring it into line with what one felt
should be the right answer - and therefore one may as well simply use
subjective assessment from the start, as Trudgill did with locality.

        I decided to follow Labov and Trudgill in employing a complex
notion of social class, for the following reasons: 1) much previous
sociological work seemed in favour of this, as we have seen; 2) I
introduced the topic of social class into my questionnaire, and from
the various responses it became clear that my informants did have
some feeling of social class differences, but there was no one factor
that all agreed to be the basis of these differences: they mentioned
all the criteria I have employed in deciding on social classes, and
others; 3) there seemed to me to be even more cases of 'status-
incongruence' of speech (i.e. the performance of an informant on the
variables did not fit into the expected pattern) if one considered
say only education or only occupation than when the complex concept
was employed, and on no one parameter are there any more objective
(non-arbitrary) divisions anyway.   I accept that there is an increase
in subjectivity if one departs from a simpler system such as the
Registrar General's *Classification of Occupations;* but I think that
the above considerations outweigh this one.

        I decided that all of Labov's factors were relevant, but I rejec-
ted parts of Trudgill's approach.   My social class 'scorings' are
based on five criteria (all employed by some previous investigators
and all mentioned by my informants as relevant).   I have not attempted to reduce them all to the same scale, say of four points;   I
employed as many points as seemed appropriate to each.   The five
factors are occupation (0 - 4), education (0 - 5), income of main
breadwinner (0 - 5), housing (0 - 3), and style of living (0 - 4).
The total possible range of scores is thus 0 - 21 (as compared to
Labov's 0 - 9 and Trudgill's 0 - 30), and the actual range in the
sample was from a lowest of 2 to a highest of 19;   I shall discuss in
Chapter 3 how this continuum may be divided into social class groups.
Let us now examine the five factors in more detail.

_____

24   Note that a number of the possible cells in this neat scheme
were in fact empty (1974a:42).

There are two grading-scales of occupations well known in
Britain: the five-point scale of the Registrar General, as used in
national censuses, and that employed by Hall and Jones and others who
produced a seven-point scale by dividing the Registrar General's
Class I 'Professional' into 1) Professional and High Administrative,
and 2) Managerial and Executive, and his Class II 'Intermediate'
into 3) Inspectional, Supervisory and other non-manual (higher grade)
and 4) ditto (lower grade). I allocated informants scores on each
of these scales (0 - 4 and 0 - 6 respectively),and though I preferred
the Hall and Jones scheme on intuitive grounds and also because it
gave more weight to occupation in the total social class scores, I
eventually decided to use the Registrar General's scale for the
following reasons. Firstly, since Hall and Jones do not give a cat-
egorisation of all possible occupations in these terms it is necessary to use one's subjective judgement, and there is certainly room
for doubt especially in the area of Classes 2 - 4. The Registrar
General's *Classification of Occupations* on the other hand gives a list
of almost every conceivable job with a label referring to the five-
point scale[25]; secondly, by using the Registrar General's scale I
arrived at a set of total scores for subjects on the combined ratings
for social class which seemed so convenient for division into class-
groups that were so intuitively right that I decided to stay with it
(see Ch. 3.ii). In the case of men the occupation of the informant
himself was always used; women and children were rated according to
the occupation of their husbands or fathers, unless a woman was un-
married, in which case her own occupation was used.

    I decided that two factors were important in the social stand-
ing of one's education: whether it was paid for privately or obtained
free under the state system, and how long it continued. Private
education (boarding school or occasionally private day school)
certainly has 'snob value' whether the teaching is good or bad - so
here I scored one point for private education as against 0 for state.
I felt that Trudgill's six-point scale for length of education
(0 = left at 13, 1 = 14, 2 = 15(+),3 = O Level/CSE, 4 = A level,
5 = university/college) was too detailed at the lower end and not
sufficiently so at the upper. My own five-point scale is as follows: 0 = minimum required by law (in 1971, at the date of the survey,
the minimum leaving-age was 15, but older informants had left earlier
- at 12, 13, or 14, depending on the law at the time. Basically
then a score of 0 indicates education at 'elementary' or later
'secondary modern'schools - or by 1971 in some cases at 'comprehensive'

---

25   The RG's scheme included all the specialised jobs within the
textile industry which some of my informants had worked in (including
a number I had to have explained to me: for instance, a 'piecer' is
quite different from a 'piecener'!); but there was no entry for one
informant, a cattery proprietor!   Since he had spent much of his
life in journalism, I scored him on that basis.

schools); 1 = either success at 11-plus or staying on to O-level
(in the area in question to have 'passed one's scholarship' and gone
to grammar school certainly had some prestige; a score of 1 applies
mostly to such informants, but was also given to some who had attended comprehensive schools but stayed on beyond the minimum leaving-age
to take O-level or CSE, and a few who had spent some time at a further
education institute after leaving at say 15); 2 = stayed on voluntar-
ily beyond O-level age (i.e. those who stayed on to the age of 17 or
18, usually taking A-level); 3 = college or professional training
(those who had attended teacher-training college or polytechnic);
4 = university (I felt that Trudgill's 'university or college' category should be divided thus because university does seem to carry
more prestige - parents being careful to distinguish it from mere
teacher-training or technical college!)[26]. In the case of children
still at school one might not know the final educational grade.
Trudgill scored all his as 3 because they were at Grammar Schools;
several of mine were in their final grade (e.g. taking O/A level,
then leaving; or about to enter university), so were rated accordingly. The few remaining were rated according to their 'probable'
level, bearing in mind the type of school, the form they were in,
and their expressed intentions.

Income groupings are bound to be somewhat arbitrary and subjective - and of course they soon look very out of date! My six-
point scale appeared reasonable in the autumn of 1971. It was:
0 = under £20 pw/£1000 pa; 1 = £20 - £30 pw/£1000 - £1500 pa;
2 = £30 - £40 pw/£1500 - £2000 pa; 3 = £40 - £50 pw/£2000 - £2500 pa;
4 = £50 - £60 pw/£2500 - £3000 pa; 5 = over £60 pw/£3000 pa[27].
This scale was applied to the informant himself, or to the husband
or father in the case of a married woman or child.

With housing, two factors were considered important: ownership
and type of property. The first divides simply into tenant (0)
and owner (1), but the second must permit some subjective assessment.
Basically I adopted the same scale as Trudgill: flat or terrace (0),
semi (1), detached (2). But a large good-class terrace house or a
pair of cottages tastefully converted into one dwelling must surely
rank at least as high as many semis; likewise some large fashionable semis are as prestigious as some modern detached houses; so
adjustments were made where this seemed appropriate. (In the case
of children interviewed at school, I had to get this sort of information discreetly - but this was usually possible).

26   My rating-scheme is not very different from that of the Education Tables used in the 1961 Census Reports: 'terminal education age'
= under 15/15/16/17-19/20+.

27   Trudgill's six point scale for 1968 (from '0 = under £9 pw' to
'5 = over £2000 pa') was as outdated by 1971 as mine was within
another few years.

In attempting to score for style of living, I rated two factors, each on a five-point scale. However, since both were matters of my own subjective assessment, and I did not wish to give too much weight to such non-measurable factors, I divided the total score by two: a scale of 0 - 8 was thus reduced to 0 - 4 (with a half-mark rounded up in the one or two cases where this occurred). For 'standard of home comforts', I used the scale 0 = poor, 1 = moderate, 2 = good, 3 = very good, 4 = outstanding; with 'locality of residence' I scored as follows: 0 = poor (i.e. deteriorating/slum/demolition area etc.), 1 = council estates and 'not good' areas of private housing, 2 = 'medium' areas (i.e. respectable, but not reckoned as 'good'); 3 = good: mainly desirable area in the suburbs; 4 = exclusive. As I noted, both these are matters of subjective judgement, but I think no-one would widely disagree with my scoring in any particular case. For children interviewed at school, whose homes I did not enter, I had to give an estimated grading for 'standard of home comforts'; 'locality' I could judge from their addresses.

3   VARIATION

In our area 'h's are sometimes dropped' and 't's are sometimes missed'. The word 'sometimes' is important: *hand* and *letter* for example, may be pronounced [hand], [betə], or they may be [and], [be2ə] - there is variation. We should note that such variation may occur either within the community: i.e. some people 'sound their h's' while others do not; or it may occur within the individual: i.e. a particular speaker sometimes pronounces [h] and sometimes does not; or both these phenomena may occur.

This sort of thing has long been recognised within linguistics, at various 'levels': for example, phonetics: the /a/ phoneme may be phonetically closer to Cardinal Vowels 3 or 4; phonemics: the word *economics* may begin with either /i:/ or /e/; grammar: words like *none* and *neither* may be followed by either a singular or a plural verb; and so on. The term *free variation* has often been employed, 'free' implying that there is no discernible pattern to this variation - as distinct from the *conditioned variation* we find with allophones, allomorphs, etc. whose occurrence is predictable from their environment. But in more recent years the extensive use of the term 'free variation' has been questioned: as Fischer (1958) pointed out, further investigation of linguistic and non-linguistic factors often shows that the variation is not free; rather, it correlates with certain determining factors that had not hitherto been recognised.

Labov found that one of the main failings of previous studies of New York was their treatment of variation. They recognised the

existence of variation, and sometimes gave elaborate lists of variants, but they hardly considered the frequency and the possible
correlates of these variants. A work by Hubbell, for example, gave
quite detailed descriptions in qualitative terms (i.e. what the
variants were) but as to quantity (i.e. frequency of occurrence) he
used only labels like 'rarely' or 'occasionally', and came to conclusions such as that the pattern of postvocalic-r 'might most accurately be described as the complete absence of any pattern'. A
later work by Bronstein recognised that there were differences of
pronunciation between social groups, but his description too was
mainly in terms like 'seems', 'frequent', 'fluctuation' etc. In
his own preliminary studies Labov himself found that at first sight
there did appear to be a chaotic situation, with a wide range of
variation even among the working class. But free variation on such
a scale was hardly consistent with the idea of a coherent inter-
related system (one of the main tenets of structural linguistics).
He decided that instead of impressionistic description of variables
a *quantitative* treatment was necessary: actually counting what variants occur, how often, and in what circumstances. When this was
done it emerged that:

'The amount of randomness in the system is relatively small:
behaviour that seemed at first sight to be 'free' or 'random'
is discovered on closer examination to be determined by factors
accessible to the linguist'. (1966a:49).

In fact, he held, variability is far from randomness or absence of
pattern: it is an integral and inherent part of the linguistic
system.

Labov (1969:737) makes an important point about the treatment
of variation which is worth quoting in full: there is 'a general and
important principle of accountability which is required in the
analysis of linguistic behaviour: *that any variable form should be
reported with the proportion of cases in which the form did occur
in the relevant environment compared to the total number of cases
in which it might have occurred.* Unless this principle is followed
it is possible to prove any theoretical preconception by citing isolated instances of what individuals have been heard saying. Speech
is perceived categorically, and linguists who are searching for an
invariant homogeneous dialect will perceive even more categorically
than most. The problem is most severe in the study of non-standard
dialects. Unwanted variants will first be set aside as examples of
'dialect mixture', and only the forms most different from the standard will be reported. Gradually even the linguist perceives only
the marked or exceptional form, when in fact these forms may occur
with vanishingly small frequency. The principle of accountability

is motivated by a conviction that the aim of linguistic analysis is
to describe the regular patterns of the speech community, rather
than the eccentricities of any given individual'.

The criticism of dialectologists for ignoring 'unwanted variants'
applies particularly to those who have worked on British dialects; as
was noted above, there has been a preoccupation with 'genuine dialect'
which has led scholars to concentrate on the most non-standard features, and to end up by describing as 'The Dialect of ----' something very artificial and unrepresentative of the general situation.

The method developed by Labov for examining variation involved
choosing certain features showing variability for special study:
these he termed *variables*.   His earlier study on Martha's Vineyard
(1963) had examined the variation in centralisation of the /aɪ/ and
/aʊ/ diphthongs: he abstracted a number of *variants* or 'values',
worked out the total occurrences of these as proportions of the total
occurrences of the variable as a whole, and found interesting correlations with certain social characteristics or groups of informants.
His procedure in New York was essentially the same.

In a number of places[28] Labov has suggested criteria for the
selection of variables.   An important one is 'frequency': whereas
a handful of occurrences might show a fairly random distribution of
variants, a larger number soon reveals some basic patterns of correlation.   For this reason, phonological segments are generally
easier to handle in this way than say grammatical constructions:
the former are likely to occur fairly frequently within a few minutes'
speech[29].   Another desirable criterion is 'saliency': if speakers
can be made consciously aware of different variants, it is possible
to explore their subjective response to them.   On the other hand
variables should have some 'immunity from conscious suppression',
i.e. speakers should not be able to avoid using them (this criterion
again favours phonological over some types of grammatical features),
though there is no need for 'immunity from conscious distortion',
since the way speakers 'distort' their use of different variants
(assuming such distortion can be identified in some valid way) can
be an important clue to their prestige value.   It is also desirable
that a variable should be an 'integral part of some larger structure':
the consequences of variation in one part of a system for the rest
of that system are an important aspect of the whole picture. Finally,
a variable should be 'easily quantified': it should be possible to

---

28   E.g. (1963), (1964), (1966a), (1968).

29   Some grammatical features have been tackled in this way: see
Shuy et al (1968b), Labov et al (1968), Trudgill (1974a), and the
present work.

distinguish variants sufficiently clearly for the actual occurrences to be allocated to them.

Labov in fact chose five main phonological variables for detailed study in New York, and examined several others as well.
Trudgill followed him fairly closely; he felt that the majority of
segmental phonological elements in Norwich English are involved in
variation of some social significance, but selected 16 by his own
criteria of the amount of apparent social significance in the pronunciation of the segment, and the amount of phonetic differentiation
involved.   (The former of these seems almost to presuppose the
results of the investigation, though Trudgill says he employed 1) his
native-speaker knowledge of the area; 2) a small pilot survey; 3)
the results of previous dialect work in East Anglia).

A quantitative study obviously involves counting; but even the
simplest kind of counting raises several subtle problems (see Labov,
1969:728 sq): we have to decide just what to count.   First, we
must identify the total population of utterances in which the feature
actually does vary.   Thus if we are interested in the variation
between the forms [aɪ] and [a] for the pronoun _I_ (see p.203 below),
and if in fact [aɪ] is obligatory in prevocalic position, then these
environments must be excluded since no variation is possible; if we
did not do this the frequency of the [a] variant in those environments where it can occur might appear to be much lower than it is.
Second, we must decide how many variants can be reliably identified,
and we must exclude those environments where say for phonetic
reasons the difference cannot clearly be heard   For example, with a
variable (eɪ) we may be able to identify monophongal [e:], diph-[30]
thongal [eɪ], and the 'impure diphthong'[30] [e·ɪ]; but in pre-/l/
environments the [ɪ] element may be absorbed in the glide to this
consonant (see Gimson, 1970:128), so we should exclude such occurrences from our total.   Third, we must try to identify all the factors
that might influence the frequency of variants: the phonological or
grammatical characteristics of adjacent elements or the grammatical
status of the larger form within which a segment is embedded.   For
example, though _with_ may be pronounced [wɪð] or [wɪ] in any environment, the frequency of these forms may be closely linked to whether
a consonant or vowel follows, and though unstressed _-ing_ may always
vary between [ɪŋ] and [ɪn], the frequency of these variants may depend
on whether the larger form is a participle/gerund, a word like
shilling or _during_, or a compound of _thing_ like _something_[31] .

---

30   I adopted this term as a student from J.L.M. Trim.

31   In this connection we may also note the 'ranking of constraints'
in Labov et al (1968),Labov (1969) etc.on say the frequency of deletion
of a final dental stop: following C or V is most important, then
whether the syllable is accented or not, then whether the dental is
part of the Past formative or not.

The above are all linguistic matters; we have also to decide
what possible correlations with non-linguistic factors should be
examined[32].   Labov found in his exploratory work, for example, that
a professor varied considerably in pronouncing postvocalic-r at
different stages in a lecture: apparently then 'formality' or *style*
was a significant factor.   Similarly, much variation appeared to
link to social factors such as status, sex, age, or race.   His main
investigation was therefore designed in such a way as to permit an
examination of the correlation of such features with the frequency
of particular variants.   Social class or status has generally been
found to be one of the most important correlations: many variables
are 'socially diagnostic'.   Wolfram and Fasold (1974) found it
possible to divide these into three sub-categories: *social
indicators* where there was correlation with class but not style,
presumably because speakers are not aware of the social significance
involved; *social markers,* where a regular correlation with both
style and class indicates some awareness that certain variants are
'prestigious' or 'stigmatised'; and *social stereotypes* such as
'h-dropping' which are overt topics of social comment.   It should
be emphasised that though several studies in Britain have shown that
in general there is a relation between position on the social class
hierarchy and the frequency with which certain variants are used by
a particular group, it is not claimed that variables are in any real
sense 'diagnostic' of social class.

Labov developed the following notation, which was largely
adopted by Trudgill.   A variable was indicated by parentheses: e.g.
(r) = the presence or absence of postvocalic-r.   Each variable had
two or more 'values' or variants, indicated thus: (r-1), the
occurrence of [r] in the environments in question; (r-2), the
absence of [r].   Each value was associated with a particular score
e.g. (r-1) = 1, (r-2) = 0; an informant's score on a section of an
interview could then be shown as say (r)-25, which in this case
indicates that he pronounced [r] in 25% of those contexts where it
might have occurred.   Similarly, the score for a whole group of
informants, say those of Social Class 3 or those aged 40-50, can be
obtained by averaging the scores of individuals.

My study had the investigation of linguistic variation within
an urban society as a major objective, and my sample was selected
in such a way as to obtain a reasonably representative cross-section
of the population, so that I could examine variation in relation to
such factors as social class, sex, age, area and so on.   My inter-

---

32   Wolfram and Fasold (1974) discuss the influences on variability
in two quite separate chapters: 'The Linguistic Variable' and 'The
Social Variable'; though this terminology seems somewhat confusing.

view was designed to show up variation with changes in style or formality, and I also attempted with a number of variables to investigate
the influence of linguistic as well as social factors: e.g. the
occurrence of [2] for (t) was divided into environment classes.

My choice of variables was determined by my aims of trying to
discover which regional features had persisted in the speech of the
general population, which were undergoing change at the present time,
and which were responsible for the fact that some speakers sound more
'Yorkshire' than others. I therefore picked on features which, as
a native speaker and an observer of regional accents, I thought
probably came into this category. But I was also concerned to
embody some of the insights of structural dialectology, and ensure
that I examined examples of various categories of phonological difference between dialects.

The most obvious 'inventory variables' concerned whether /h/
existed in the system; whether there was an /ʌ/ to contrast with
/ʊ/; whether there was a possibility of contrast between /ɛɪ/ and
/e:/, and similarly with the corresponding back pair /ɔʊ/ and /o:/,
or whether as in RP there were only /eɪ/ and /əʊ/; and how many vowel
phonemes existed in such sets as *paw, pore,* and *poor.*

In the matter of distribution the two variables that suggested
themselves were the occurrence of /əʊ/ or /ə/ in unstressed positions
in words like *window, borrow;* and the occurrence of /tʃ/ or /ʃ/
after /n/ in words such as *inch* and *branch*[33].

Under incidence, obviously the typically Northern use of /æ/
in words like *grass, path* should be examined; so too should the
common /ɪn/ in *-ing* forms; somewhat more regionally restricted are
/u:/ in words like *took, look,* and /e/ in a few words such as *take*
and *make.*

In most of the above, determining the number of variants and
the decision as to what one hears is relatively straightforward:
/h/ is either present or not, *borrow* ends perceptibly in/əʊ/ or /ə/,
took has either /u:/ or /ʊ/, and so on. But some difficulties can
occur with a number of these variables, such as (ʌ), and (ɔʊ/o:) and
(ɛɪ/e:), because questions of realisation arise as well as those of
inventory.

---

33   It occurred to me later that the occurrence of stressed /e/ or
/ə/ before /r/ in words like *very, Terry, derelict* etc. would have
been more interesting (since there are almost certainly geographical
differences within the area), and also a more typically Yorkshire
feature and one yielding a more satisfactory amount of data (since
it probably occurs more frequently than the second of the above).

Realisation is the fourth type of phonological difference, and here we are further into the less clear area of impressionistic phonetics. With the one consonantal variable of this type, (t), it is usually fairly clear whether one hears [t] or [2], but with vowels there is more room for doubt: just how front is /ɑː/; how diphthongal are /aʊ/ and /aɪ, /ɛə/ and /ɔə/, and where are their start-points; can we really hear a glide with [eːɪ] and [oːʊ]? There are two problems: deciding on how many variants we can recognise with some confidence, and dealing with those instances that admit of some doubt. Trudgill (1974a:84) admitted that his 13 vowel variables had 'no or very few auditorily distinct variants', and division of the continuum admitted of some arbitrariness and also caused difficulty for the analyst with border-line pronunciations. He decided that the arbitrariness was unimportant provided the transcriber was consistent in the allocation of border-line cases, and concluded: 'In the present study it is felt with some confidence that this has been achieved'. It must be nice to be so self-confident (especially when the variants are as detailed as some of his are!); I have no great opinion of myself as a phonetician, and confess that though I have striven to be honest and consistent, I have less confidence in the validity of my findings in respect of these variables than with others, and they will not therefore be presented in as much detail as those in other categories. (It would be a useful future project to have some of my material of this sort analysed by a trained phonetician who is not a native of the area).

Though the above were the main variables that satisfied most of the criteria outlined above, there were a number of others which seemed worthy of investigation because they are certainly relevant to the question of the 'persistence' of regional features, and I decided to try to examine them in the same way. The further modification of two classes of contracted negative forms (1 *doesn't* etc., 2 *don't* etc.) is not readily categorised as either phonological or grammatical variation. The same may be said of the occurrence of [wə] for *was* and the reduction of the definite article to [t ~ 2].[34] A couple of grammatical variables that were reasonably frequent were the use of *us* for *our* in unstressed positions, and the singular noun forms in certain phrases of measure like 'twenty-two year'; and a number of common single 'grammatical words' may have typically regional forms which probably contribute to the total picture of a Yorkshireman, so I decided to keep a note of them: I picked on three pronouns: *I, us,* and *they;* on two words where there is a possibility of both phonological and grammatical variations: *than* and *that;* and two where variation is only phonological: *with* and unstressed *too.*

---

34   It may be noted that they were more like the one such examined by Trudgill than some of those of Labov et al (1968).

Having listened to all my data I decided that I had probably
been reasonably justified in my choice of variables - but as often
happens, I felt that if I were starting again I would do some things
differently: abandoning some variables in favour of others I had
noticed, and looking at some others in a different way.   There certainly are many other variables - phonological, grammatical, and
lexical - which occur in the area, but most of those not examined
in this 'quantitative' framework appeared to do so too infrequently
for this type of treatment.

As regards notation, I have adopted the use of parentheses to
symbolise a variable: e.g. (h), but I do not use either the term
'value' or the symbolisation (h-1) to indicate these - I consider
the latter too taxing on the memory and think it is preferable to
refer directly to the 'variant', say [h] and [Ø].   Nor have I given
scores in the form (h)-50 etc.

4   STYLE

I noted above that by the late 1950s linguistics had realised
that much of what had been called 'free variation' was in fact
related to hitherto unrecognised linguistic or non-linguistic factors.
The latter may be either relatively permanent characteristics of the
user (his geographical or social background, his sex, his age-group,
and so on), or relatively temporary differences in *use* - and it is
for this last factor that I shall be employing the overworked term
style.

'Style' has been used in various ways in language-study;   I
shall be following Labov in using it for 'level of formality'.
There would seem to be at least three factors involved in the choice
of style in this sense.   First, the relationship between speaker
and addressee: different levels are clearly appropriate say to
one's family and to one's professional superiors.   Second, the
'occasion' or situation, though this factor is not always independent of the preceding one: for example, the superior may in a sense
'define the situation' by his choice of style, whereas the inferior
is more likely to adopt the style that suits the situation.   Third,
the degree of attention paid to the way something is said: in more
formal styles the speaker is likely to be interested in 'the sound
of his own voice', whereas in casual styles the degree of 'audio-
monitoring' is much less.

Formality is of course a continuum: there are no clear
'stations' such as those referred to in one of the best-known approaches to style in this sense, that of Joos (1959,1962) who recognised five 'levels' of usage.   But it is necessary to select a
number of points on the continuum, however arbitrary these may be,
if we are to make comparisons between different groups of speakers

in a particular style, or between the performances of the same group
in different styles. As his starting-point, Labov assumed that with
a randomly-selected sample one would have an interview between
parties previously unknown to each other and working in a fairly
structured framework; this ('context B') would probably result in
a style Labov called *careful speech*. (However, Trudgill's term
formal speech is more easily distinguished in abbreviation from
'casual speech', so I have adopted this.)

Formal speech, then, is defined as what normally occurs when
answering questions which are part of the prepared interview.   To
shift style in a more formal direction, Labov asked informants to
read a set passage 'context C': *Reading Passage Style)*. He in-
structed informants to 'read this as naturally as possible', but
this had little effect; however, the fact that the text was obviously a teenage boy's narrative did help to reduce formality somewhat.   But neither of these factors brought reading style into
confusion with formal style: only a few upper-middle class speakers could make their reading fairly conversational. The next step in
a formal direction was to do something similar to traditional
dialectologists: i.e. obtain a 'single-word style' ('context D':
Word List Style).   But instead of eliciting single-word responses,
Labov asked informants to read unrelated lists of words, where
obviously their pronunciation would be less modified than in the
context of a text, even a written one.   Finally, the situation
likely to produce the highest degree of attention to speech, i.e.
the most formal speech, was another word list, of minimal pairs
('context D^1': *Minimal Pairs Style)*, where informants were also
asked to say whether a pair sounded alike or different.

The most difficult problem concerned moving in the opposite
direction along the formality continuum from the starting-point: i.e.
obtaining 'casual speech' of some sort.   This is the sort of style
which occurs in everyday informal situations; how then was it possible to get this in an interview situation?   Labov in fact devised
ways of getting what he termed 'spontaneous speech': speech that
because it was excited and emotional overrode the constraints of the
interview.   Comparing this with 'real' casual speech (recorded
from teenagers playing games in the street) Labov claimed that the
two could be treated as to all intents and purposes the same -
'spontaneous speech' being the counterpart of 'casual speech' occurring in formal situations but as it were in spite of them - so the
label *casual speech* was used.

Two types of factor were considered necessary for speech to be
labelled 'casual', First, those we might class as 'occasion' -
times when the formality of the interview situation is as it were
forgotten. Labov recognised five such occasions ('context A'):
1) outside the formal interview itself, e.g. before or after the

actual questioning, during a break for a cup of tea or an interruption, and so on[35]; 2) speech with a third person: e.g. a child running in, another member of the family making a comment, or an unexpected visit or telephone call; 3) speech not in direct response to a question: some informants, especially the older, quickly move off, either unintentionally or deliberately, onto some subject close to their hearts; 4) and 5) responses to questions specifically designed to elicit spontaneous and emotional speech: Labov asked about childhood games, and situations where the subject had been in danger of death.

The fact of these situations occurring is not in itself sufficient to guarantee that spontaneous speech will occur - a speaker *may* continue to use formal style.   There must be some evidence that he has switched; but the usual signals of this are linguistic ones - the use of certain phonological or grammatical features - and since the investigator is seeking to isolate styles and then see what linguistic features occur in them, to use these customary signals would be circular.   Labov therefore decided that the second necessary factor for calling something casual speech would be paralinguistic 'channel cues': 'modulations of voice-production which affect speech as a whole'.   Again he set up five such: changes in 1) tempo, 2) pitch range, 3) volume, 4) rate of breathing, and 5) laughter (which could be considered a variant of the last).   Any of these could be taken to indicate casual speech, provided it occurred in one of the five situations discussed above; outside of these contexts (where they still *might* indicate casual speech) Labov's rules forced him to treat the speech as formal.   But the distortion resulting would be less than would occur if some formal speech were included as casual (as might happen if there was no insistence on context AND channel cues), since there was generally found to be over twice as much formal as casual speech in an interview.

Labov rightly admitted that his division of conversation into formal and casual was arbitrary: 'it is not contended that...(these) ...are natural units of stylistic variation: rather they are formal divisions of the continuum set up for the purposes of this study... (1966a:112).   The division may of course be an oversimplification: Crystal and Davy (1969:87) suggested that perhaps six categories of formality might be needed.   On the other hand, the difficulties frequently encountered in distinguishing casual and formal speech lead to a more or less opposite criticism: that the division is impracticable.   Wolfram (1969) and Wolfram and Fasold (1974) pointed out that workers on the Detroit survey had great difficulty in distinguishing the two and so treated all conversation as one style.

---

35   Unfortunately an interviewer often feels that the best such speech occurs either before or after the tape-recorder is running!

The reasons given for rejecting Labov's distinction were:
1) the 'channel cues' could indicate not only casualness but also
say nervousness and increased awareness of the artificiality of the
situation; 2) channel cues are subjectively interpreted, and so
the interpretation of casual speech may be biased even though these
cues are supposed to be independent of the measurement of the variables: 3) for some informants there was so little casual speech that
it was difficult to base statistics on such data[36].

The major investigation by Labov et al (1968) aimed at a more
sophisticated approach to the problem of obtaining casual speech.
The individual interview was still designed to elicit a range of
styles, and for adults this was the main tool of investigation; one
important difference was that only a single channel cue was recognised as indicating casual speech: change in intonation pattern[37].
For the younger informants, who formed the main object of the study,
more emphasis was placed on obtaining interaction between informants,
in the form of a 'double interview' of two close associates, or more
importantly a 'peer group session'. Contacts had been built up
with 'peer groups' (i.e. gangs!), with minibus trips and other meet-
ings; eventually quite lengthy group sessions were arranged (with
games, refreshments, singing, video-recordings of boxing-matches
etc), with each member equipped with an individual microphone and
recorder, which would pick up invaluable data from asides, interior
monologue etc., as well as the general interaction. The effects of
remaining constraints on spontaneity, e.g. presence of non-members,
use of university premises, tape-recording etc., were minimised by
the staff joining in the games and using taboo words!

Trudgill (1974a) consciously sought to follow Labov's earlier
methods for constructing a series of contexts within the formal

---

36 Against these points it could be argued 1) that a sensitive observer can distinguish nervousness and spontaneity, and that anyway
nervousness may not mean the speech will be careful; 2) while interpretation of channel cues *is* subjective, it is only if certain values
of variables influence interpretation that the two become not independent; 3) Labov admitted that some informants may not produce the
full range of styles, and some individuals may not be sufficiently
relaxed to produce casual speech - but statistics are generally worked
out for groups of speakers rather than individuals, and it is thus
that regularities emerge. Finally, it could be pointed out that
Wolfram himself was guilty of subjectivity in that he said he used
'narrative passages as comparable as possible' (1969:59).

37 Labov (1969:731) seems to say this was only for Negroes, where
increases in pitch range are relatively much more important than for
Whites, for whom the (1966a) cues were used.

interview situation.   The bulk of the interview was assumed to
yield 'formal' speech;   this of course varied in formality according
to each informant's degree of constraint, but the *relative* position
of this basic style was felt to be more or less the same for all.
The Reading Passage aimed to be as informal as possible, and informants were asked to read as naturally as they could - but Trudgill
was surely optimistic in claiming that the result was 'to *standardise*
the style for all speakers towards the informal end of the range of
possible styles in this context' (my italics).   The more formal Word
List aimed to get information on all phonetic segments in Norwich
English, especially the variables studied, and also to seek the pronunciation of a large number of words which might not arise in conversation but could be written into this and the Reading Passage[38].
Most formal was the Pairs Test, where Trudgill correctly noted that
informants might produce the most 'correct' form, but also possibly
might give a 'dis-corrected' one, in order to find some difference
between the minimal pairs.   For casual speech Trudgill followed
Labov's '5 channel cues + 5 contexts' method, with questions about
East Anglian expressions and 'a very funny incident'[39] replacing
Labov's contexts 4) and 5).   He noted that using 'speech not in
direct response to a question' could bias the casual speech obtained
towards the more talkative type of informant, often the older ones.

    Trudgill noted (1974a:46) that his work was carried out too
early to benefit from the new methods developed for obtaining casual
speech by Labov et al (1968).   But surely there would have been big
problems in adopting them: first, the expense in money, labour, time,
and resources if they were carried out in the same manner as Labov's
team employed - obviously such an approach is more appropriate to a
larger-scale operation;   second, peer-group sessions presuppose prior
identification of groups, which is hardly consistent with a random
sample approach, and if cheaper and quicker methods were employed one
would be faced with a different set of problems, as I outline below.

    In the West Yorkshire survey, I followed Labov and Trudgill for
the most part.   Formal style was assumed to be basic in the interview
situation;   the Reading Passage was of a fairly informal nature and
informants were asked to read 'in a normal conversational manner' -
though the effect of this was of course variable;   the Word List was
quite long and made no attempt to concentrate any categories (except,
incidentally, with beginning with /h/) since words were in roughly

---

38   Trudgill also had some Rapid Word Lists, e.g. days of the week,
but he found little difference in pronunciation from the main list.

39   Trudgill said he adopted this from Houck (1968).

alphabetical order - both of which facts may have helped to avoid
too careful a style; there was also a 'Minimal Sets' word list.
Casual style was sought via the 'channel cues + specific contexts'
approach[40], with various topics attempted corresponding to Labov's
contexts 4) and 5): (see Section IV of Interview).

One general misgiving I have applies to all these styles; just
how comparable are different informants' styles?   Trudgill said 'all
informants are placed in a series of 'contexts' which are, relatively
speaking, the same for each of them...' (1974a:46).   Relatively
speaking, maybe: generally any informant will become more formal in
passing along the casual - formal - reading - word list scale, but
some informants may have a much faster, more casual-like style in
formal situations than some others, and in the reading passage and
word list too there are considerable variations in speed and fluency[41].
It seemed possible that the reading style of one or two very relaxed
informants was hardly more formal than the formal style of some of
the more careful and dignified ones.   So in totalling the scores
of informants for a particular style one is not always strictly adding like to like.

But casual style obviously presents the biggest problems.
Crystal and Davy (1969:96) said it could be demonstrated that most
people will behave differently if they are aware of being taped -
even if they appear to have forgotten this fact; the only valid
data then is that obtained through surreptitious recording.   However there are at least two problems here: first, the ethical one
of recording without the informant's permission; and second, if
this is done in the most 'natural' surroundings, e.g. the street,
or a pub, one is faced with further difficulties: either one does
not know much about the social characteristics of informants (and
the various bits of the conversation are difficult to allocate to
speakers anyway) and so it is more difficult to assemble comparable
data on various sub-groups; or, if one does know this sort of thing

---

40   I stuck to the five channel cues of Labov (1966a); though there
are problems sometimes in deciding what constitutes a 'change' in
these, I have more confidence in my ability to recognise such changes
than those in 'intonation pattern', as in Labov et al (1968).

41   In the reading passage I noted 7 informants who seemed to read
considerably faster than the norm, and 2 a good deal slower (for the
word list the corresponding figures were 5 and 4, and I made a particular note about one man who speeded up after a very slow start
when I said he could do so if he wished: he showed a considerable
increase in non-standard variants).   A hurried correction of a mis-
reading by one woman is particularly interesting: [aɪ θɔ:t aɪd daɪ
lafɪŋ]... No! [a θɔ:t "ʃi:d daɪ lafɪn].

about the speakers, it is presumably because they have been in some
sense hand-picked rather than chosen by a more reliable random procedure.

Earlier in this section I referred to three factors involved in
the level of formality.   Within the interview I attempted to man-
ipulate these as far as possible in order to reduce the basic
formality-level and to make casual speech more possible.   The 'relationship' problem was met by my revealing myself to be a native
of the area with a fair knowledge of the local situation and a local
accent (which in fact varied according to the informant - see
App. B);   that of 'occasion' was met by virtually always holding the
interview on the informant's 'home ground' and where he was often
in a majority (family or friends being around), and my trying to
make him feel that he was the authority who was helping me;   that
of 'the amount of attention paid to speech' was most difficult for
me to have any control over - apart from making the recording-
apparatus inconspicuous and paying as little attention to it as
possible.

It is quite likely that the casual speech I obtained was not
the *most* casual.   Probably such casual speech as occurs in an
interview situation is usually some way from the end of the formality continuum - and surreptitious recording may elicit something
'further along'.   In fact two pieces of evidence from my interview
experience suggest that some examples of 'casual' speech may be more
or less casual than some others.   First, quite a number of informants seemed to produce 'more casual' speech as the interview progressed, i.e. the channel cues were more obvious in what was taken
to be casual speech, and there were more non-standard features than
earlier[42].   Second, in several good interviews where there had
been a number of outbursts of what fitted the criteria for casual
speech a visitor or member of the family suddenly interrupted the
proceedings - and the speech of the informant became noticeably more
casual than what I had been counting as such.   But this does not
invalidate the formal/casual distinction I had drawn;   what I had
taken to be casual was certainly more so than the surrounding formal speech - it simply confirms that our notion of 'casual style'
is a simplification embracing several levels of informality.

In listening to my tapes I constantly had to resist the temptation to identify the formality of the situation from the language,
i.e. to respond to certain phonological or grammatical features and

---

42   Labov (1966a:113) also found that 'In the course of the interview there is a steady process of familiarisation which diminishes
the formality of the context' - and thus such casual speech as occurs
might move further along the continuum.

to identify the speech as formal or casual from these.   As a native
speaker sensitive to the significance of particular variants this
temptation was probably greater for me; but I was aware of the circularity of such a procedure and (usually, I think) forced myself
to stick to the definition and only count as casual speech that which
fitted the 'channel cues + contexts' criteria.   In the last resort,
however, I am forced to admit that I have less faith in this stylistic division than in the others employed in this study[43].   I have
to grant that there were a number of cases where I was not confident
that I had drawn the casual/formal distinction correctly.   I noted
several speakers with whom, due to their being naturally very talkative and speaking quickly at almost any time, no matter whether
the context was one of those recognised as likely to produce casual
speech or not, I was frequently in some doubt about where to draw
the line.   On the other hand several, mainly older speakers or those
high on the social scale, seemed generally to have a relatively slow
and careful style.   Now it may be that most of what this latter
group said was in 'formal' style, and most of what the other set
said was in 'casual' - or it could be that neither group has as marked
a difference in these respects as do most informants.   Perhaps some
informants do not vary very greatly in everyday life.

---

43   I had reached similar conclusions long before reading Bickerton
(1975) who said it was a pity Trudgill followed 'established sociolinguistic tradition of taking a body of text and dividing it into
two mutually exclusive categories...while anyone who is honest and
has spent any length of time listening to speech outputs must surely
admit that speech does not work like this.   While one does occasionally encounter sharp shifts of style, speech variation is far
more often characterised by a series of minute graduations which
constitute a true continuum'.

I am not sure however that I follow the logic of Bickerton's
claim that 'any linguist who divides speech into 'formal' and 'casual'
ON ANY BASIS WHATSOEVER and then averages percentages of variables...
MUST come up with marked differences'.   These are held to be an
'artefact of the methodology and therefore uninteresting'.

CHAPTER THREE

THE WEST YORKSHIRE SAMPLE

1   SAMPLING METHOD

A simple random sample of the populations of Bradford, Halifax, and Huddersfield was selected in the following way.   The electoral register of each town was employed as a sampling frame;   this was arranged in wards (AA, AB, AC, etc.), and voters in each ward were numbered 1,2,3,4 etc.   In Bradford for example, ward AA contained 2532 names, AB 755 names, AC 2245 names, and so on.   In order to give each person in the city an individual number, those in AA kept their original numbering (1 - 2532), those in AB were renumbered 2533 - 3287, those in AC became 3288 - 5532, and so on.   The last person on the register was thus numbered 210,472, and so this was the total population aged 18 or over from which the sample was to be drawn.

Selection was by means of random numbers taken from the *Cambridge Elementary Statistical Tables*.   Table 8, Random Sampling Numbers, gave columns of digits independently sampled, in which digits 0 to 9 were equally likely.   As the total population of Bradford was a six figure number (210,472) numbers were taken on a six-column basis: thus the table began:

20	17	42	28	23	17	....
74	49	04	49	03	04	....

Taking the first six columns, my first number was 20 17 42, i.e. 201,742;   the next was 744,904;   and so on to the bottom of the page. Then starting again at the top, 282,317;   490,304;   and so forth. Of course, any number in excess of 210,472 was useless, so only those from 000000 to that figure were noted.   In fact the figures used ranged from 001127 (obviously within ward AA) through to 210467 (only five from the end of the electoral register).

The numbers thus drawn were matched with names in the electoral

register renumbered as described above, and the names and addresses
of these potential informants were noted.   In Bradford I was aiming
for a sample of 46 informants from this source (plus 4 schoolchildren to be selected as described below - a total of 50 seeming
reasonable for a town of this size as compared to the numbers decided
on for Halifax and Huddersfield).   Initially I took 80 names from
the register, thinking I should thus have sufficient reserves in case
of various types of failure;   when it became clear that this was over-
optimistic (since the 80 names in fact yielded only 32 'successes'),
I took a second sample of just over 30 names, which yielded the balance of my informants.   One minor departure from simple random
sampling occurred in Bradford: the first 80 names contained considerably more women than men, and the next 30 appeared to be doing
so too.   Because I wished to have roughly equal numbers of each
sex, and I believed that a 'stratifying' adjustment could reasonably
be made here without introducing a non-random element, for the last
dozen numbers I took the corresponding name from the register only
if it was a man: otherwise I took the next man below on the list.

Because the electoral register only included those members of
the population aged 18 or over, and I wished to have a number of
younger[44] informants, I selected a few children from a secondary
school[44].   In Bradford this was done as follows: there was by 1971
a 'non-selective' system of secondary education, so I chose two
comprehensive schools from different sides of the city, telephoned
the Director of Education, and with his permission approached the
headmasters.   (One was completely cooperative, the other only allowed me to approach pupils in the upper half of the school, i.e.aged
14 or over, believing that younger children would think they were
being 'picked on' for some reason.)   With four-figure random numbers
I took two children from each school as follows: 3415 meant, for
example, the 3rd year, 4th form, 15th pupil.

Essentially the same methods of selection were employed in
Halifax and Huddersfield.   The total populations on the electoral
registers were 66,291 and 94,409 respectively, and so of course
five-column random numbers were used.   In Halifax I was aiming at
23 informants (plus 2 school children).   60 approaches ultimately
yielded 25 successes.   In Huddersfield I wanted 28 (plus 2);   75
approaches yielded 29.   These samples, though larger than those
studied in traditional dialectology, would not of course be sufficient if one were wanting to have a representative sample for all the
various sub-groups within the area (see below).   The total sample

---

44   I.e. those aged 11 or over;   I felt that the questionnaire was
probably not appropriate for younger children.   This feeling was
justified in that the youngest informants though not uncooperative
were somewhat shy and overawed.

size of around 100 was decided on because this was probably as large
as could be managed by a single worker in the time available for the
project, and also because I wished to test in the two smaller towns
Labov's claim that a sample of 25 would probably be enough to show
the basic patterns of linguistic stratification (see Labov 1966b:107).

The total number of approaches was thus almost 250 (excluding
school-children) and the total number of successes 98.   The total
sample of 106 was produced as follows[45] .

	From register	From schools	Total
Bradford	44	4	48
Halifax	25	2	27
Huddersfield	29	2	31
Total:	98	8	106

2   CHARACTERISTICS OF THE SAMPLE

An initial hypothesis for this study was that there would be
variation in speech among members of the community in the area under
investigation, and that this would not be 'free variation':   rather,
it would correlate with various sub-groupings within the community.
One of the functions of the interview was therefore to provide personal information about the informant which would enable me to group
together informants with shared characteristics, and thus test this
hypothesis.

It was thought, on the basis of previous studies elsewhere, that
among the most probable correlates of linguistic variation, apart
from 'style' or formality, would be the following: the age and sex
of the informant, the geographical district from which he came, and
his social class.

---

45   My aim of 46 for Bradford was frustrated by two last-minute
changes of mind.   The totals for each town were slightly modified
as outlined below: Note 47.   Of course the total in the 10 - 19
age-group was a good deal higher than the 8 from schools because the
electoral register yielded several informants under 20.   (At the
time of Trudgill's survey the register listed those aged 21 or over,
so his higher number of schoolchildren was appropriate, though he
presumably had no-one in the 18 - 21 range.)

The *sex* of an informant leaves no room for debate! However,
none of the other factors admit of such clearcut division: they
are all 'continua' which have to be divided at some more or less
arbitrary points, and in each case it could be debated whether one's
divisions are too fine or too crude. With *age* Wells (1973) for
example divided simply into 'young'/'older' (on arrival in UK), with
the division set at age 20; this is surely too crude if one wishes
to get a clear picture either of age-grading or of linguistic change.
Here I follow Labov (1966a) and Trudgill (1974a) in breaking the
continuum into 10-year divisions, and classing informants as 10+,
20+, 30+ etc. (though of course such divisions are also arbitrary).
As regards geographical *locality* within the area, neither Labov nor
Trudgill considered this[46]: they were investigating just particular
parts of one city. I deliberately decided to select informants
from three separate towns: all are manufacturing towns within the
'wool district' of West Yorkshire and share the great majority of
their linguistic features, but some people insist that they can
still recognise differences between the speech of these towns (see
p.256), and it was to investigate whether differences do exist that
I decided to draw my sample from the populations of these towns and
to compare the performance of informants from each[47]. Occasionally
it might be useful to have more precise and narrow geographical
divisions, since speech patterns may of course vary even within one
town; the questionnaire therefore attempted to discover the area
within the town where the informant had been to school and passed his
formative years (though in fact little use has been made of this
information in this study).

Social class is of course the most complex of these parameters.
I have discussed the general question and my own approach above; the
questionnaire sought information on the various factors on which I
base my use of the term. Obviously my method of 'scoring' informants yielded 22 possible classes, (i.e. people had a points total

---

46   In fact, though Trudgill did not investigate different towns
he did occasionally compare different parts of the city, and Labov
did concern himself with differences between natives and 'out-of-
towners'.

47   It should be noted that if an informant, in spite of being
drawn from the electoral register of say Bradford, was found to have
spent most of his life including his formative years (i.e. up to
the age of end of secondary schooling) in say Huddersfield, then he
was grouped with the informants of the latter. This occurred in
some half-dozen cases.

between 0 and 21)[48], which for most purposes of analysis, as well
as according to the subjective judgements of the population (see
App. E), is too many.   I was therefore (like Labov with his 10
possible classes, and Trudgill with his 31) faced with the problem
of dividing up the continuum into a smaller more workable number of
classes.

Labov had tackled this by utilising a division into social
classes in the USA on the basis of educational, occupational and
income characteristics developed by Kahl, who set up five classes -
V upper, IV upper middle, III lower middle, II working, I lower -
and gave an estimate of the size of each class in the USA: thus V
was said to comprise only 1% of the population, IV = 9%, III = 40%,
II = 40%, I = 10%.   Labov found that if he divided up his ten-point
social scale as follows: 0 - 1 lower, 2 - 5 working class, 6 - 8
lower middle class, 9 upper middle class (the upper class one would
not expect to be represented in the area he was investigating),
then the proportions of those in each of these four classes in his
sample would not be widely discrepant from Kahl's estimate for the
nation as a whole.   The sample was somewhat biased towards the
lower end of the scale, but the only serious weakness appeared to
be the shortage of lower middle class speakers (only 23%);   however
he decided that this group displayed 'relatively consistent behaviour' and so the numbers available should 'yield clear insight into
the linguistic pattern characteristic...(of them)'.

The British social scale would probably not be divided up in
this way, either in terms of the proportion of the population in
each class or in the labels which would be applied to them, so some
other method has to be employed.   Trudgill said that he sought 'to
divide the continuum into larger more discrete groups relatively
unified in their linguistic behaviour and reflecting the class structure of society as a whole' (1974a:58).   He did this by grouping
his informants according to the way they scored on the use of a
grammatical variable in casual speech, supplemented where necessary
by formal speech: for example, his lowest class (V) used the non-
standard grammatical form over 80% of the time, while his highest
never did so.   But other supplementary criteria had to be used too,
since both I and II never used non-standard forms and so could not
be distinguished by this variable.   His resulting classes were
Class I (middle middle) = over 19 points;   II (lower middle) =
15 - 18;   III (upper working) = 11 - 14;   IV (middle working)
= 7 - 10;   V (lower working) = 3 - 6.   Two criticisms seem appropriate: first, his investigation sought to examine the correlation
of linguistic and non-linguistic features, including social class:

---

48   In fact I had only 18, since no-one scored less than 2 or more
than 19 (all the intervening scores were occupied).

it therefore seems circular to use linguistic data when setting up
classes - surely such are not merely 'social classes' but rather
'sociolinguistic classes', to which his labels are less appropriate[49]. Second, the fact that four of his five classes occupy
under two-thirds of the total scale might seem to indicate that his
31-point scale is faulty. However, Trudgill felt his classes did
reflect the general social structure, since the members of each
shared certain characteristics: e.g. his middle middle class were
all professional or at least white-collar workers - while the lower
working class were all labourers or unskilled workers (but it should
be noted that this is only a classification by occupation, which was
of course supposed to be only one of six determining factors).

My own method of dividing into classes was as follows. Figure 1
shows the number of informants on each point of my 22-point scale;
there is a 'peak and trough' configuration. If we assume that the
major peaks are as it were the 'focus points' around which the
members of a class cluster (we have such peaks at the lower end at
4,6, and 9), and if we also assume that the scale should be cut into
more or less equal sections, we find that cuts every four points
produce five classes each to some extent grouped around a focus:
cutting after points 4,8,12 and 16 gives the following classes:
Class V (0 - 4), IV (5 - 8), III (9 - 12), II (13 - 16), I (17 - 21).
Besides falling in with the 'peak and trough' configuration and
dividing the scale more equally than did Trudgill, this method also
resulted in informants being placed, with few exceptions in classes
which coincided with an intuitive classification (on more factors
than just occupation) of the people involved. For example, Class
I contains only 3 members (a number far too small for any findings
to be considered reliable - though only rarely was it out of the
'expected' position in relation to the other classes), but one would
intuitively have bracketted them together and considered them to be

---

49   And Trudgill's claim (p. 91) that 'The social class index has
provided a successful basis for the establishment of *discrete social
classes* as these classes are reflected in their linguistic behaviour,
since...the scores rise consistently from MMC to LWC' (my italics)
surely means very little: the 'discrete' classes result from lumping together numbers of individuals who in fact form a continuum
(see his Fig. 4) and then working out average scores - there are
bound to be differences, i.e. apparent discreteness. I recognise
of course, that my own method produces a similar illusory 'discreteness'. However, my classes were not established linguistically in
any way: since Trudgill divided into classes on the basis of one
linguistic variable it is not surprising that the pattern is repeated
with others. See Labov (1966a:226) on the need for caution in
drawing conclusions from 'a division of classes that was quite arbitrary'.

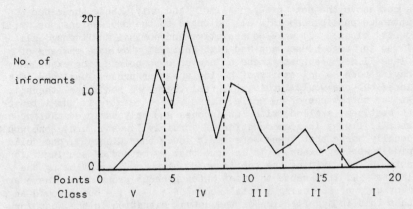

Figure 1: Social Class scores and groupings

The total 'points' scores in this figure result from a combination of
points in a) - e) below: page 30 .   In each of a) - e), points are
represented by the horizontal axis and number of informants by the
vertical axis; f) shows the number of informants in each age group.

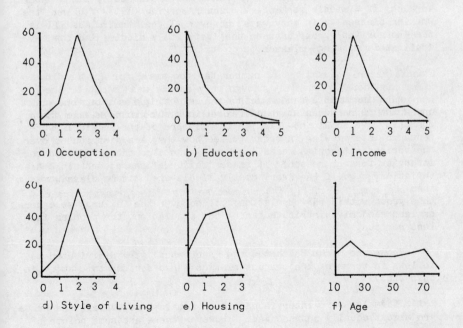

a cut above the next group: all of (and only) these three had
attended public schools; all belonged to the professional or 'mill
owner' class; all were conservative and nominal Anglicans; all
lived in large houses and had high incomes. Now some members of
Class II might surpass these on one or more points, for example by
having been to university of having superior professional qualifications, but one would intuitively feel they were not quite 'there'.
At the bottom end of the scale, Class V were nearly all unskilled or
at best semi-skilled, with low incomes and only basic education, and
usually living in accommodation of a fairly low standard; one would
usually agree that these were a bit lower than Class IV, the solid
middle working class.   It is true that my method of scoring informants and of dividing the continuum results in Class IV being the
largest *and* in a sense the most heterogeneous group (i.e. there are
many ways of achieving a total score of 5 - 8) - but I would argue
that this is a reflection of the actual situation in the West Yorkshire community: the middle working class is the largest in the
population, and it is a status achievable by various characteristics.

These then were the classes I decided to operate with for the
purposes of analysis.   At times I shall use the same labels as Trudgill: I = middle middle class, II = lower middle (I and II will sometimes be referred to together as 'the middle classes'), III = upper
working, IV = middle working, V = lower working (III - V being 'the
working classes'); in many ways, however, I feel that Class III is
the 'borderline' group between the 'definitely middle' and the
'definitely working' classes.

Assuming that a random method of selecting a sample will yield
one which is representative of the various sub-groups within the
community, we should now examine the members of the sample I succeeded in interviewing in order to see how they are distributed over
the various categories we have set up - and also those I failed to
interview for any reason: if these 'failures' shared certain characteristics, e.g. if they were mostly middle-aged middle class women,
then *the sample actually interviewed may not be representative* of
this group within the population; if however the failures were more
or less randomly distributed among the population, the problem is
less serious.

Those who might be termed the 'successes' were distributed as
follows in terms of the characteristics I had decided to examine in
this study.

Sex: 56 males were interviewed and 50 females, so overall the sexes
are almost equally represented.   However there are some points of
weakness when sex is combined with some other characteristics.

Locality: The numbers of informants from each town are very roughly
proportionate to their total populations. The sexes are equally
represented in Bradford (24 M - 24 W) and Halifax (14 M - 13 W), and
even in Huddersfield where the figures (18 M - 13 W) reflect a higher
number of failures among women during the last few days of the fieldwork, the sexes are not far out of balance. Individuals who could
really be said to belong to one of the other two towns rather than
where they were at present resident were counted with the former's
informants when a correlation with locality was being examined (see
note 47); this made little difference to the numbers for each town:
Bradford's total dropped by 2 to 46, while Halifax and Huddersfield
each gained one, to give 28 and 32 respectively.

Age: The total sample appears to contain reasonable numbers in the
various age-groups, apart from the 80+ group which has only three
informants[50]. With age + locality, in a sample of this size there
will obviously be weak spots (e.g. there was only one Huddersfield
informant in the 40+ group); we cannot therefore attempt to correlate variation with the age-groups in each town. With age + sex
there are also some weaknesses, mainly in the middle-aged groups
(men in their 30s, women in their 40s, and men in their 50s appearing to be under-represented): with such possible biases care must
be taken in drawing conclusions from age + sex figures. Age + class
can hardly be expected to yield reasonable-sized groups, and in fact
only in Class IV are there a fair number in each age-group; no
attempt will therefore be made to correlate linguistic variation with
age + class groups.

Social Class: First let us examine how informants are distributed
according to the five factors I have combined to produce my composite
notion of social class. *Occupation:* about 60% of the sample came
midway - in the Registrar General's Class III; there is a sharp fall
on either side of this peak. Intuitively, I should probably have
made the lowest two classes larger at the expense of III, but I followed the grading assigned in the *Classification of Occupations*.
Education: about 60% belong to the lowest group, reflecting the
fact that the majority of the population have had no more than the
legal minimum of education. At the other end of the scale, only
one informant was scored the highest possible: he was a public
schoolboy about to start at Oxford (the 1% of my sample he represents
is somewhat higher than the national average). *Income:* the majority
of the sample (about 55%) belong to the next lowest income group,
earning £20 - £30 pw in 1971. Seven earned less than this; at the
top of the scale only two had an income of over £3000 pa. In 1971
the national average wage was under £30, so these figures are probably

---

50   As compared to the other groups this may be 'representative' of
the population at large, but it is too small for reliable statistics.

reasonably representative. *Housing:* most informants scored 1
(i.e. private terrace/rented semi) or 2 (private semi); 17 scored
0 (rented terrace or flat) and 5 were on 3 (private detached).
Style of Living: over 55% were on the medium score of 2, reflecting
say a good standard of home comforts and a fairly good neighbourhood; at the extremes, three informants scored 0, reflecting near-
slum conditions, and two (both ex-mill bosses) scored 4, i.e. very
classy home conditions and exclusive neighbourhoods.

As I noted above, none of these factors on their own would
yield a system of social classes that seems intuitively right in
terms of 'who goes with whom' or in the proportions of the population
in the various classes. But with the combined scores, and the scale
divided as outlined, there are 19 informants in Class V (LWC), 43 in
Class IV (MWC), 28 in Class III (UWC), 13 in Class II (LMC), and 3 in
Class I (MMC). Since these are my own constructs there is no way
of measuring whether the numbers in the sample reflect the population
as a whole, but intuitively they seem about right: the solid working class (Class IV) are doubtless the biggest group, followed by
those on the borderline of middle and working class (Class III);
the professional and management set (Class II) seems about right at
12%, and the 'nobs' do not account for more than 3%.

Apart from Class I, a similar distribution of class groups is
found in the samples from all three towns - though it may be noted
that the average score of Halifax informants (8.64) is appreciably
higher than those for Bradford and Huddersfield (7.57 and 7.67 respectively). Combining sex and class, we note that Class I in my
sample contains only men, Classes II and IV have about the same
number of each sex, Class III has 17 women and only 11 men, and
Class V 6 women but 13 men. If sex appears to be an important factor in some linguistic variable it will then be advisable to examine
class figures separately for each sex; (this was in fact always
done, but reference will only be made to the findings if they seem
to be of particular interest).

As we noted in an earlier section, a properly conducted random
sampling of a population should yield a sub-set which is representative of the whole: it should not contain any bias either towards or
against any particular group in the community. In a survey such as
this, however, where participation is completely voluntary and where
the time and resources available are limited, one cannot expect to
achieve anything like a 100% success-rate in actually interviewing
the subjects selected by the sampling. If there is a considerable
number of 'failures', it is quite possible that certain groups in
the community will be heavily represented in this number, with the
result that the sample actually contacted may be unrepresentative

of these groups: i.e.the sample may be biased against them.   It is
therefore advisable to examine the failures to see whether this is
the case, so that when one starts to consider one's findings one may
not draw unwarranted conclusions.

The number of failures in my survey was high: out of a total
of 251 contacts or attempted contacts only 106 (i.e. 42%) were
actually interviewed.   It is then imperative that we should examine
the reasons for the failures and their social characteristics.
Those not interviewed fall into three broad groups, for the first of
which the label 'failure' is hardly appropriate.

Non-natives

Though a comparison between the speech characteristics of
natives and outsiders would be a useful exercise - and would have
been essential if the main objective of my project had been to discover the 'identifying' features of the area rather than to examine
the persistence or modification of non-standard features described
in the traditional studies - I decided that because of considerations of time and manpower I must reject all those I classed as 'not
native to the area'.   My criteria were these: 'the area' for my
purposes was taken to be anywhere within a radius of ten miles from
the centres of Bradford, Halifax, and Huddersfield; and 'native'
was taken to mean that an informant had come to live in this area
before reaching the age of secondary schooling (i.e. about eleven)[51].
Both of these limits may be too generous, and any limit will be
arbitrary, of course.   However, the great majority of those interviewed had been born and had lived virtually all their lives considerably nearer than this to the centres of the towns (the electoral
register of course covers a very much smaller radius).

Of the 251 people whose names were selected, 45 (i.e. 18% were
non-native in the sense defined; some were from elsewhere in Yorkshire, but most were real 'off-cummed uns' (the Yorkshire term for
outsiders), as the following table shows.   The most surprising thing
to observe is the small numbers of 'Commonwealth immigrants', who
certainly made up a bigger percentage of the 1971 population than
these figures would suggest[52].

---

51   A lady who had come from Glossop (18 m SW of Huddersfield), the
only non-Yorkshire-born informant, at the age of 12 was taken as just
qualifying.   She said she was always taken for Yorkshire/Lancashire
and was conscious of speaking differently from those in Glossop.   And
a man from Norton (about 20 m East of York) who had come at the same
age was also accepted; his speech was not obviously different from
that of Bradford, though he said he sometimes had a more Norton 'twang.

52   Perhaps an explanation is the fact that they tend to congregate
in certain areas (i.e. wards) rather than being evenly spread around
the towns.

Discounting all non-natives makes my success rate look a little healthier (106 out of 206), but it is still only just over 50% of those who might be eligible on grounds of nativeness[53].

Origin of Non-natives	Bfd	Hfx	Hudd	TOTAL
Elsewhere in Yks	1		4	5
North: North-East	4	2	2	8
North-West			1	1
Lancs	2		1	3
Midlands		2	2	4
South	1	2		3
Scotland	4		1	5
Ireland		2	3	5
Europe: West		1	1	2
East	1			1
Commonwealth:				
India/Pakistan	3	1	1	5
West Indies			1	1
Not known	1		1	2

Unable to be interviewed

The 54 in this category (21%) are a mixed bag; they include 23 who had removed since the register was compiled and were unable to be contacted, 3 who had died[54] , 5 who were too ill or senile to co-operate, and 10 with whom no contact was made. (Every effort was made to keep this last figure as low as possible. I usually called at least three times at an address before abandoning - though in the last few days of fieldwork this was not possible, which is part of

---

53   I say 'might be' because, as we see below, in a fair number of cases no contact at all was possible: if there had been contact some may well have turned out to be non-native.

54   I thought I must be jinxed when the first address with someone at home in both Bradford and Halifax yielded deceaseds!

the reason why 6 of the 10 were in Huddersfield, where I worked last).
The remaining 13 were for a variety of reasons: e.g. one woman was
ill on the day fixed for interview; one old man was illiterate and
obviously did not understand what I wanted; some were away on holiday or said they worked unpredictable hours. It is of course possible that some of these were really 'refusals', but did not like to
say so outright.

Refusals

Those who refused to cooperate totalled 46: expressed as a
percentage of 'those eligible, capable, and available' (i.e. successes
+ refusals, total 152),this is almost exactly 30%: in other words
almost one in three of those able to help was unwilling to do so.

With a proportion as high as this it is quite possible that bias
might creep in. We must therefore examine this group in some detail
in order to decide whether this is likely to have been the case.
Since I was aware of this possibility at the time of fieldwork, I
tried with each refuser to note down one or two facts: sex was of
course obvious; age was something I could estimate roughly (to the
extent of placing someone in their 30s, 40s etc.). Social class is
of course more difficult; but by calling at the home, seeing the
neighbourhood, type of house, and perhaps a little of the conditions
inside, sometimes picking up information about occupation or education (I rarely got a simple 'No' without any other conversation),
I was able to form a rough classification of people into groups more
or less corresponding to Classes II - III/Classes III - IV/Classes
IV - V above. I usually also got some idea of their reasons for
refusing. Three refused by letter, but even here I could form some
estimation for everything but age.

The following table shows that while the proportions of refusers
in each of the towns is the same (Totals - Bfd: 29.4%, Hfx: 32.5%,
Hudd: 29.5%), the picture for sex is not so equally balanced: 36%
of women refused to cooperate as compared to 25% of men.

	Bfd M	Bfd W	Hfx M	Hfx W	Hudd M	Hudd W	TOTAL M	TOTAL W
Refusals	8	12	8	5	3	10	19	27
Cooperators	24	24	14	13	18	13	56	50
TOTAL:	32	36	22	18	21	23	75	77
Ref as %	25	33	36	28	14	44	25	36

With regard to estimated age the refusers are again unequally spread:

	10	20	30	40	50	60	70	80	dk
Refusals	0	6	2	16	8	5	4	2	3
Cooperators	14	22	13	12	12	13	17	3	-
TOTAL:	14	28	15	28	20	18	21	5	3
% Refusing	0	21	13	57	40	27	19	40	-

If these figures were further broken down, according to sex, it would appear that the worst 'black spots' are women in their 40s (82%) and men in their 50s (64%): but since the ages of refusers are only estimated it is probably more reasonable to observe simply that the middle-aged groups seem about twice as likely to refuse as any others (apart from the 80+ group, which is much smaller anyway and where reasons such as illness are more likely to be involved).

As to estimated social class, where categories are deliberately somewhat blurred since the detailed information furnished by the interview was not available, the numbers of refusers were as follows:

	Classes II - III	Classes III - IV	Classes IV - V
Men	6	3	10
Women	9	5	13
TOTAL:	15	8	23

In proportion to the numbers involved, people in Classes II - III perhaps show a somewhat high disposition to refuse. When this table is broken down by age-groups the middle-aged groups show a higher proportion of refusers in these social classes.

The main weaknesses in my sample appear then to be among the middle-aged, the women especially, and those of the lower middle and upper working classes. The impressions I got were that housewives of this type, often with children and a job, tended to be or claim

to be too busy to participate in the survey; men in their 40s and
50s also seemed to be more difficult to persuade: they seemed to
be between the more active and interested period of youth (virtually
no men under the age of 40 refused to cooperate) and the later years
when the interview offered them the chance of a change (only 13% of
those over 60 refused).

Finally, the reasons given (if any - 18 of the 46 gave no clear
reason) for refusing to take part in the survey.   The main reason
was undoubtedly apathy, though both this and 'suspicious of the whole
business - probably some sort of elaborate sales exercise'[55], tended
to be covered by the proffered excuses of being too busy or unwell.

Reason alleged	Men	Women	TOTAL
Not interested/don't want the bother	4	4	8
No time	5	6	11
Not well	1	5	6
Opposed to project	2		2
Nervous of tape-recorder		1	1
No reason given	7	11	18
TOTALS:	19	27	46

---

55   Never actually put into words by a refuser, but certainly an
impression given: see following note.

CHAPTER FOUR

THE FIELDWORK AND ANALYSIS

In this chapter I shall briefly describe the procedures followed during the two-month period in the autumn of 1971 when I was
conducting fieldwork in Bradford, Halifax, and Huddersfield, and
over the following two or three years when I worked over my material.

1   FIELDWORK

A circular letter had been prepared, with the heading 'An investigation of West Riding Speech - will you help?'[56]. The letter
talked about popular ideas of 'correctness', and the fact that these
may have little real basis; it mentioned previous work on Yorkshire
dialect and on the speech of urban areas, and said that the present
survey was aiming to study the actual speech of the area (without
any judgements about 'good' or 'bad'), and to see how differences
in speech might relate to age, sex, occupation, and so on.   I sent
a copy of this letter, or explained my aims, to the local newspapers,
so that people receiving the letter might recall reading about the
survey and be assured that it was all above-board.   The letters

---

56   I later came to realise that the letter had at least one big
drawback: it was duplicated on paper headed simply 'University of
Reading', with 'Department of Linguistic Science' typed below;   I
also added, when inserting the addressee's name, the address and
telephone number of my local base, in case the recipient wished to
reply.   Experience proved that, whatever the additional expense,
it would have been preferable to use better paper with the full address of the Department and University: the reason was the possible
ambiguity of 'Reading' - a recipient glancing at the heading, seeing
some ordinary address in a Yorkshire village, noting the local post-
mark and the fact that the letter referred to language, might be
forgiven for taking 'Reading' as [riːdɪŋ], and concluding that this
was some new gimmick for selling encyclopaedias and so throwing the
letter away.   That this was the case was clear from the reception
I got on more than one occasion: 'Oh, is this about that reading
job?   No, thanks; we're all right here'.

were posted in batches of about a dozen.   I had plotted on a map
the location of the various members of the sample, and I sent out
letters to groups in a certain part of the town.   Within two or
three days of posting the letter I called in person at the address.
The results of such calls fell into three categories:

1)   Nobody in: if this was the case I left a duplicated note on the
same headed paper[57] explaining that I had been and would call again
within a few days.   Whatever time of day I had paid the first
visit, the second always took place in the early evening, which was
the best time for finding people at home.   If that visit was also
fruitless I called at least once more: apart from a few cases in
the last week of the survey I always made at least three calls before
abandoning the person as a case of 'no contact'.   I am sure that
if I had not followed this policy, the number of failures would have
been much higher, and therefore there would have been a risk of
greater bias in the sample actually interviewed; certainly, some
very interesting informants were only recruited at second or third
attempt.

2)   'Failure': Several times, the first words uttered as the door
was opened made it obvious that this was a non-native.   In these
cases I simply checked where they came from and thanked them.   Other
failures, due to removal, death, senility etc., were also noted.

    Sometimes I was recommended to 'try Mr. so-and-so at Number 10';
where this was in a genuine effort to help, I thanked them and said
perhaps I would.   But I did so only once or twice: the reason for
not following such suggestions was that I was often being steered to
a person of a particular type: e.g. 'a real old Yorkshireman' or
'a schoolteacher - he'll tell you what you want to know', and it was
important not to allow such non-random informants to affect the overall picture.   So I only contacted such people where I was able to
establish that the person in question might be a reasonable 'substitute', i.e. he was of similar social characteristics either to the
person who was the original failure or to someone in that area who
had recently been a refusal: not more than two or three informants
were contacted thus.

    A considerable number of failures were refusals.   I had read
in the literature on surveys that a refuser can often be persuaded
to change his mind if the objects of the survey are carefully explained; I tried this for some time, but with only one exception it
did not work (and the exception was probably less of a refusal than

---

57   Sometimes of course it was a case of 'prospective informant not
in - and no indication given to wife/mother of whether he would be
willing to take part': if so, I asked when he would be likely to be
in and called again.

a 'dubious' - in these latter cases persuasion sometimes was effec-
tive).   If a person said he did not want to take part, therefore,
I did not press the matter; I simply made a note of such information as I could gather so that I might later be able to work out
what sort of people had refused to cooperate and see whether this
might have introduced bias into my sample.

3)   Success: The prospective informant was in and agreed to help.
A convenient time for an interview was fixed.   On only a handful of
occasions was it convenient to hold the interview there and then:
usually a time within the next few days had to be arranged[58].

     With the exception only of the school-children, who were inter-
viewed in a staff-room or a vacant classroom, all informants were
interviewed in their own homes.   This was felt to be important,
partly for the sake of convenience, but mainly because they would
there be on their home ground: they would be the hosts who were
giving me their help, and in these surroundings they would be most
likely to feel relaxed.   Several informants asked whether a relative or friend could stay in the room during the interview, and this
I always encouraged in the belief that if the informant subconsciously felt himself to be 'in the majority' he might be more confident
and relaxed.   In fact 39 of the interviews were conducted in the
presence of third parties[59].

---

58   My timetable during the eight weeks of the survey usually followed this pattern: the morning was generally the least useful time
of day - people were often not at home, so I only called then if I
happened to be in the district for other reasons; only a relatively
small proportion of the interviews took place in the morning (these
were of schoolchildren, and a few pensioners and married women). The
afternoon between 2 and 4.30 pm was quite often a convenient time for
interviews; from 4.30 to 6.30 seemed to be the best time for visiting; and the period between 7 and 9 pm was when a large proportion
of the interviews took place. Naturally, though I tried to arrange
a schedule convenient for myself, the informant's preferences came
first - which meant I sometimes had to interview say on a Sunday
afternoon.

59   Often these people joined in with comments or discussion at some
stage, and in a few cases made a considerable contribution. So I
decided, when listening to the tapes, to 'score' these supplementary
informants also - though I did not count them when reckoning up the
totals, since I was often not sure of their precise 'social characteristics'.   What was possible was to estimate these and then see
whether these speakers showed similar trends to the main informants:

I sought from the start to develop a relaxed atmosphere, and
generally succeeded in doing so. I had a number of advantages, the
main one being the fact that I was a native of the area: I had mentioned this in the introductory letter, and soon referred to it
either when visiting or in the interview. I was often able to talk
about something of interest to the informant - a possible mutual
acquaintance, the local football team, his school or place of work,
plans for new roads or redevelopment in the area, and so on - and
this helped to create some 'rapport'. My own accent must also have
been important at times: I had spent my formative years quite near
the centre of Bradford, and had developed a local accent; and though
this has of course undergone some modification in recent years, I
tend to 'slip back' into it with people who use it themselves. When
listening to the tapes I realised that I had unconsciously been
adopting a similar degree of 'broadness' to the informant of the
moment (see App. B), and I imagine this must have been a help in
eliciting natural speech.

All interviews were taped at $3\frac{3}{4}$ ips on a UHER 4000L reel-to-
reel machine, and the recording obviously constituted a threat to
the informality of the interview. Only one person refused to be
interviewed specifically because she did not want to be taped, but
I am sure it was a contributory factor in several other refusals,
and also a number of those interviewed expressed some concern about
it at first. Of course I made no effort to record secretly (which
would have been next to impossible as well as unethical), but I tried
to make as light of it as possible. I avoided 'ideal' recording
situations such as having the informant and myself facing each other
across a table with the microphone between us; rather, I preferred
to be sitting in easy chairs with the recorder almost out of sight[60]
by my side and the microphone standing somewhere on the carpet .

---

for example, with (ing) the Class scores were I 0, II 33, III 65,
IV 92, V 100 - and the general picture of class differentiation in
conversational speech is confirmed. However this would be possible
only with one or two very common features since a) the occurrences
of most variables in such 'accidental' data are very few; b) the
sample of such informants was by no means a representative one.

60   Sometimes, of course, the room conditions meant that the repro-
duction was not all that could be desired: for example, one informant took me into the 'best' room where heating was by means of a fan-
heater which I could hardly ask him to switch off; children crying,
interrupting or trying to contribute, noisy gas-fires, televisions
in neighbouring rooms, etc. were other difficulties - and one man at
quite a late stage of the interview said: 'Ee, I'd've been better
wi' my teeth in'! But there were no completely inaudible passages
on the tapes.

At the start of the interview I tried to keep up a general conversation while setting up and testing the apparatus, and once it was
running I told the informant to forget about it and tried to appear
to do so myself - apparently only remembering it when it was necessary to reverse the tape.   If, after the more formal part of the
interview was over, the informant seemed to be willing to continue
chatting, I did not touch the machine, hoping in this way to pick
up the most natural speech[61].   Each interview was recorded on a
separate 5" spool, which was labelled with the informant's name and
the date of the interview, and then filed away for future analysis.

The questionnaire was designed with several purposes in mind.
The main aim was of course to elicit speech of various styles or
degrees of formality.   Certain sections consisting of fairly specific questions were expected to produce formal speech, while the
other more conversational topics were introduced in the hope that
they would elicit a more casual style.   The reading passage and
word lists would of course tend to result in less spontaneous, more
careful styles of speech.   The second aim was to discover certain
things about the informant (though of course these parts of the
interview would also produce data in the form of formal speech - or
occasionally casual speech, as the speaker rambled off the subject).
One sort of information elicited was personal details, i.e. facts
about the informant's education, occupation, areas of residence,
family background, age, religion, politics, etc; this information
would enable me to group informants according to certain shared
characteristics, and to see whether there appeared to be any correlation between these and certain aspects of linguistic behaviour.   I
also sought to elicit the opinions of an informant, particularly
about the part of the country we were in and about the way people
speak in that area (both in general terms and with regard to certain
specific details).   Labov (1963:304) had discovered that one's
attitude to the area could make an important difference to the degree
to which one conforms to the typically-local speech patterns and it
is also likely that one's opinions about local speech will influence
one's own linguistic behaviour, especially at times when one is more
conscious of how one is speaking; for example, in reading passages
or word lists.

The questionnaire was arranged as follows. First, there were
a few questions about the informant's life and background; these
were factual questions to which everyone knew the answer, so they

---

61   Some excellent casual speech was recorded by leaving the machine
on when one young man was called to the telephone and engaged in
quite a lengthy conversation with a friend.   And it quite often
happened that a stream of beautiful informal speech would occur
after I had packed up the equipment and was getting ready to leave!

were a better way to get things started than 'opinion questions',
which could leave an informant 'speechless'.   This first section
sometimes led to some general conversation, and anyway always took
several minutes as I expressed interest in some of the answers and
asked supplementaries, and by the end the ice was usually broken.
Then I tried for a few opinions: I briefly introduced the topic of
social class[62], attempting to see how conscious people were of this
institution, and also perhaps whether their views on class-differ-
ences and their assessment of their own position on the class-scale
might correlate with aspects of linguistic behaviour.   My idea was
gradually to introduce more linguistic tasks as the interview progressed and the informant became more relaxed, so the next section
was the first of these: a simple word list designed to elicit the
vowel-systems in the environments 'bilabial C dental C' and
'bilabial C _ #'[63].   The words were written on different cards which
I showed in rapid succession - this was done so the informant would
not see minimal pairs together and so attempt to produce a difference he would not normally make.   This section took only a very
short time, and I then returned to asking the informant about his
past or his opinions on topical issues: the subjects in this
section were selected with the aim of getting free conversation, in
the hope that some quite informal speech might result.   I did not
ask all the questions of every informant;   as long as one or two
gave something to talk about, that was sufficient.   Some questions
produced little response;   others elicited strong opinions or vivid
memories, expressed in speech so riddled with 'channel cues' and
other 'performance features' that it was almost certainly casual
conversational style[64].   I did not even always keep to the questions
listed: if the informant mentioned a hobby or interest this often
provided an excellent opening - I had detailed and interesting con-
versations about fishing, wood-carving, the St. John Ambulance
Brigade, speedway, Rugby League, and buying a few shares!

     After this came the main word list: sets of cards, each with
a dozen words, in roughly alphabetical order (to obscure the points

---

62   This section was omitted with the younger schoolchildren, since
the notion was usually unfamiliar to such.   See App. E for the
findings of this section.

63   One aim of this word list was to obtain data for detailed phonetic analysis of the vowels of this area at some future date.

64   Of the topics listed in the questionnaire that concerning immi-
gration was the most successful in producing some response;   the
'accident' question and the 'hated teacher' (adopted from the
Detroit survey) were reasonably so;   and the 'humorous incident'
(taken via Trudgill from Houck) was least useful.

I was listening for).   There were over 200 words in all, and this
large number was included for several reasons.   First, I wanted a
fair number of examples of the particular variables I had decided
to examine.   Second, I wished to see how frequently a pronunciation
described by the traditional studies of the area occurred among the
general urban population[65].   Finally, the large number usually dis-
couraged an informant from reading too slowly and carefully.

Next came some light relief in the form of a section of the
sort more expected by those who thought that what I wanted to know
about was 'real Yorkshire':   it concerned the pronouns *thou* and
thee ; my aim was to see how familiar these forms are today, how
many of the sample claimed to use them, and what connotations they
might have (see App. C).   Another linguistic task came next: sets
of minimal pairs or groups appearing together on cards;   this was
expected to produce the most careful speech - if an informant ever
distinguished two forms he would probably do so here.   Also of
course it might produce the most unnatural forms, since the speaker
might try to produce distinctions that did not really exist.   A
further set of opinion questions followed, this time specifically
relating to language: I wanted to see what regional features informants might be aware of, and what their attitudes to them might
be.

Before the most difficult linguistic task, the reading passage,
came the first of two 'evaluation' sections[66].   I told the informants I would read some words to them with two or more pronunciations
- usually the common local form and an RP-like one, but sometimes
another local version or a 'hyper-RP' form was given too;   I asked
informants to indicate which they used, and also whether they preferred one of the others or regarded it as more correct.   I hoped
to discover, by seeing how often they picked the local or RP forms
and how far this corresponded to their actual usage, how much
'linguistic insecurity' there was among various groups.

The reading passage followed.   It contained virtually all the
words from the main word list, and so aimed to examine both the
special variables and also other words which might have typically-

---

65   A large proportion of these words are now pronounced in a
roughly standard form (e.g. 'head' is in traditional dialect [ɪəd]
or [jed] but now usually [ed]).   A few informants said they could
not understand why I was asking about these 'ordinary' words instead
of 'real Yorkshire' ones.

66   I was aware that this section could draw attention to certain
features and so affect later performance, but experience during the
testing-period of the questionnaire suggested that this was not a
serious problem.   See Ch. 7 ii) for the findings of this section.

regional forms, in another and less artificial style[67].   Finally,
and provided there was time, came another evaluation section: a
recording of a short story consisting of a number of sentences in
which some of the variables were concentrated, each sentence being
read at least twice by male readers of varying degrees of broadness.
After each reading of a sentence informants were asked to grade the
reader on an occupational scale; my aim was to see how judgements
of a reader varied according to his performance on particular variables.   Some informants, particularly older ones, found this task
difficult and so it was sometimes abandoned.

The formal part of the interview ended with a few more questions
about the informant; these were more personal than those of the
first section, and so it was better to ask them after the ice was
properly broken and when any objections taken would not affect the
quality of the interview.   Last of all I invited the informant to
ask me any questions; quite a high proportion responded: some
asked after the relevance of particular questions or sections, while
others wanted to know in more general terms what I was hoping to
achieve.

The sections of the questionnaire were usually administered in
the order described, though this was very occasionally varied if
appropriate.   The order and wording of the questions were finalised
during the first week or so of fieldwork: I found it helpful to
make slight modifications to my original design[68].   It will be observed that in general the interview took the form of an interming-
ling of linguistic tasks and more conversational sections; this I
felt to be advisable both in order to make things more interesting
and informal and also to prevent fatigue on the part of the informant.

With the occasional exceptions of Sections II and/or XII the
whole questionnaire was used in every interview.   Only one interview was incomplete, the informant being called away to work about
two-thirds the way through Section XI.   The time taken naturally
depended on the talkativeness of the particular informant and
whether any sections were omitted; the shortest time taken by the
questionnaire itself was about 35 minutes, the longest around an

---

67   A handful of informants remarked that they had noticed that the
same words kept coming up and probably others realised it too without mentioning the fact.   I doubt whether this had any effect on
their pronunciation.

68   I must confess to agreeing with the great pioneer of dialectology,
Gilliéron, who remarked with regard to questionnaires: 'in order to be
considerably better, it ought to be compiled after the investigation'!

hour - though the interview often lasted longer, as we chatted before
or after the formal part.

The final version of the questionnaire is reproduced as App.A.

2   ANALYSIS

The tapes were examined using a Tandberg Model 15-21 tape-
recorder linked to a Model 1325 loop-repeater, which continually
recorded the last five seconds played on the main tape; when the
main machine was stopped, the loop of this last five seconds played
over and over, enabling me to listen as often as I needed to a particular point of interest.   Each hour of tape took about four to
five hours to examine in this way[69] .

For each informant I had an envelope of papers on which to
record my findings.   Part of the 'Questionnaire Record' was completed first, by going through each tape fairly rapidly and extract-
ing factual answers and opinions in the sections dealing with such.
Then I started again, working much more slowly as I listened to the
actual pronunciation and grammar, and noted points of interest either
on appropriate pages of the Questionnaire Record or on one of the
more specific supplementary papers.

These included sheets for Word List I (vocalic contrasts) and
Word List III (minimal sets); a sheet for each of the 'evaluation'
sections, on which the informant's responses could easily be noted;
a sheet for recording what particular variant was used for every
occurrence of words containing RP/eɪ/or/əʊ/, with separate columns
for each style; and, most important, four sheets (one for each of
the four main styles: casual, formal, reading passage, and Word List
II) on which the thirty or so variables to be examined were noted
down the left hand side, and then there were 'boxes' across the page
for each of the variants; for example:

(h)	h		∅		(-h-)	h		∅
(ʊə)	ɔ:	ɔə		oə		ʊə		uə

At each occurrence of a word containing a variable, a mark was placed

---

69   The much shorter time Labov claimed to have taken to listen to
each hour of tape (see 1966a:153) seems almost incredible, since he
said he was examining, in addition to the five main variables he
discussed in his book, 'a great many other linguistic variables'
(p.380).

in the box representing the variant that had occurred.   Finally, in
the case of a few informants who used a considerable number of unusual forms (i.e. 'dialect speakers') I included complete texts of the
reading passage and Word List II on which I marked their pronunciations (for other informants who produced occasional such forms, I
simply noted these on the appropriate page of their Questionnaire
Record).

     After I had completed my examination of the tapes I went through
all the 'score sheets' and totted up the numbers of marks in each box.
This information was then recorded on a 'summary sheet' for each informant;   here the total number of occurrences of each variant in
each style was noted for every variable, together with the total for
all styles (except minimal sets) added together;   on the other side
of the sheet, for ease of reference, were noted the summary bio-
graphical details and opinions expressed in answer to the various
sections of the questionnaire.   These summary sheets could easily
be re-sorted into social class sets, age-group sets, (subdivided
into Males/Females, or natives of Bradford/Halifax/Huddersfield) and
so on.   It should be noted that I made no attempt to add up totals,
or even to work out the informant's social class, until after I had
finished listening to all the tapes: this I hoped would help to
ensure that I did not 'hear' things I felt I ought to hear from an
informant of this type!

     Then I added together the scores of individual informants in
the various class, sex, age, style, or town groupings, and worked
out the scores for each category.   This I did for each variable in
turn, recording these scores on a set of tables: I Class + Style
groups, with totals for all classes and all styles;   II Sex, Class,
and Style (and totals);   III Town, Class and Style (and totals);
IV Age and Style (and totals);   V Age, Sex and Style (and totals).
From these tables I then drew graphs, on which noticeable differences and trends often showed up more clearly.

3   INTERPRETATION

     'It is immediately obvious to the sophisticated statistician
that tests of significance are irrelevant...even if a particular
case were below the level of significance, the convergence of so
many independent events carries us to a level of confidence which
is unknown in most social or psychological research'.   Trudgill
(1974a:91) quoted these words of Labov in support of his not carrying out significance tests, and I have adopted this position also[70].

---

70   Not, however, because I regard such tests as 'otiose' (see
Bickerton, 1975:302), but because restrictions of time have forced me
to cut down the number of subjects I might wish to follow up. Wells

This attitude may be justifiable, but having adopted it, it is
surely then *not* reasonable to base arguments on minor details of
single figures or graphs, and to draw theoretical conclusions from
findings which may well be below the level of significance - or,
even worse, to choose which facts to use and which to ignore without
such tests.   Some, perhaps many, of the sub-groups in my sample are
certainly too small to be considered representative (e.g. Class I or
the 80+ age-group), so I do not base any important arguments on their
scores.   But one must be ware of ascribing too much 'significance'
to findings in several other cases too[71].

Trudgill seems to me to be guilty of faults such as those just
referred to.   For example, referring to his Figure 21, he claimed
that the UWC had a score 'significantly higher' than that of the
MWC in casual style.   Now, a) there are obviously dangers in placing too much reliance on performances in casual style, since the
casual/formal division is one which depends on the analyst's judgement and where decisions are most debateable; surely therefore it
is unsound to base arguments on an 'irregularity' in this style (and
the MWC does show such an irregularity here when compared to formal
style) or on things that only show up in this style (as Trudgill did
with his Figures 35 and 36, arguing that 'two originally distinct
vowels have gone past each other in phonetic space' - but only in
CS; and, for his Figure 38, observing that 'MMC is quite clearly
distinct from the other classes in CS' - though their score here
produces a violent and unusual reversal of the general direction
of the graph).   Also, b) the use of the word 'significantly' in
this claim, apart from any doubts of its justifiability in the absence of significance tests, seems very odd, especially as Trudgill
went on to say that 'the LWC score approaches those of the (L)MC
very closely': now the latter two scores appear to be about 72 and
30, whereas those of UWC and MWC are about 130 and 90; how can the
first pair be 'very close' and the second 'significantly' different?
Yet it was on such statements that Trudgill based one of his main
arguments about linguistic change.   Several other examples of
doubtful conclusions can be found: for instance, he 'explained' a
minor irregularity in the lower-line of his Figure 30 (which did
not fit his hypothesis) in terms of 'pressures in phonetic space',
but the greater amount of 'up-and-down' in his Figure 29 was ignored;
the same 'pressures' were alleged to explain minor movements in the
positions of FS in his Figures 35-36 (though he had ignored much
bigger fluctuations in other graphs).   But why should such pressures
operate only in FS, permitting a 'cross-over' in CS - particularly

---

(1973) and Heath (1980) were exceptional in this type of study in
that they did carry out such tests.

71   See p.189 on the position of Class III.

when in his Figure 37 the same cross-over occurs in FS?   In Chapter
3 he argued that the break between the middle and the working-classes
was a fundamental one and therefore likely to be 'a very important
factor in......linguistic characteristics';   he found this hypothesis
borne out by his grammatical variable and also by (a:) and (ð) - but
he apparently ignored the situations with (ā), (ī), (er) etc. where
the main break appears to be between the MMC and the rest (including
the LMC).   Some of Trudgill's most important claims concerned apparent linguistic changes and were based on figures for age-groups,
but here too his reasoning is sometimes suspect: for example, with
(e) he claimed that the high figures for the under 30s show a change
in progress to a more regional form;   this may be so, but since the
scores in question are

10	20	30	40	50	60	70
173	100	67	88	46	58	81

he ought to explain the 40+ and the 70+ figures, since otherwise
there could be other reasons why the 10s and 20s scored highly on
regionalisms and why the 30s scored lowest[72].His arguments about the
(a) variable seem particularly strained: a) he says the 10s use 'a
high percentage' of (a)-3 and the 70s of (a)-4 but the respective
figures are 44% and 25% and this latter group scores 28% and 26%
on two other variants; b) the 25% score is supposed to show that
older people use more of certain regional variants - but the graph
is irregular, and if (a)-4 and (a)-5 were totalled, both being regional, it would be even more so; c) he claims that the 'demise of
(a)-1' is clearly indicated by the very low score in the 10s - but
the score for the 20s is the second *highest* and again the graph
shows no clear trend; d) he totals the scores for (a)-3 and the
least common (a)-5, both being diphthongs, and then claims that diphthongal forms are on the increase since only the under 30s have 'more
than 31%' (the 20s have just 32%) - when in fact the 30s have 30%,
the 60s have 31%, and even the 70s have 29%.

I have made these criticisms of Trudgill because I think it is
important to realise that one cannot expect to 'have it both ways':
one cannot use a sample which is too small for a statistician to
regard as representative, and also decide not to bother about significance tests, AND treat any little up-and-down on a graph as potentially important, and decide that it can be used as evidence in

---

72   See my own conclusions on p.212; on the other hand, as Bickerton (1975:302) suggested, the explanation could lie in the class-
composition of the groups.

support of some hypothesis - or that it has to be explained away if
it does not 'fit'.   Trudgill of course examined a good many more
variables than Labov, and in certain ways his work was a necessary
corrective to the latter's, since his 'style-class arrays look much
messier than Labov's', who showed 'variable index figures majestically
and symmetrically falling or rising from left to right' (Bickerton,
1975:301), which may have suggested that the patterns of sociolinguistic variation are much more regular than is in fact the case.   I
also examined a much larger number of variables than did Labov, but
I do not feel that my figures and graphs can be taken as providing
detailed evidence for certain views - rather, they can only be used
to show up general trends and patterns.

CHAPTER FIVE

THE TRADITIONAL DIALECT OF THE AREA

Since the main aim of this work is to examine the persistence or modification of dialect features in the West Yorkshire towns, a picture of the traditional dialect of the area must form our starting-point. Against this background my own random sample of the present-day population can then be examined. In order to obtain my picture of traditional dialect, I decided not to adopt the time-consuming and somewhat dubious procedure of seeking out people considered to be 'real old Yorkshire speakers'; instead, I chose to rely on what is presented in the traditional dialect descriptions of the three towns examined. Assuming that what is described there was indeed the form of speech commonly used at one time, we shall be in a position to see what sort of changes have occurred to produce the English normally heard in the area today.

It would of course be a very big task to present a full picture of traditional dialect: there is a wealth of information on vocabulary, grammar, and phonology, and obviously I cannot deal with the whole of this. Grammar and vocabulary are areas too big to be covered systematically, and so they are excluded from this chapter: traditional evidence will be summarised where appropriate when points of non-standard grammar and vocabulary observed during my survey are referred to. Here I shall seek to give a flavour of traditional dialect by concentrating on just one aspect of phonology. It is a well-established fact that within phonology dialects differ more in terms of vowels than they do in consonants, and it is clear from the descriptions that the difference between West Yorkshire dialects and RP is more a matter of vowels than of consonants; so, while noting that there are some minor consonantal differences (e.g./tl,dl/ for /kl,gl/) and some more extensive ones (e.g. the frequent absence of /h/ and the common use of /-ɪn/ rather than /-ɪŋ/, we shall concentrate on the vowels. Taking the various works concerned with our three towns in chronological order, I shall attempt to extract a picture of the vowel system at the period they purport to describe. I shall mainly be concerned with vowel inventory, but I shall also note a number of points of interest in connection with distribution and realisation, and I shall give a specimen list of vowel incidence in a few hundred everyday words: all these are matters of vowel 'system', and are part of the changing picture of regional speech which I am investigating.

A number of important problems should be noted at the outset. Firstly, modern sociolinguistic research (including the present work) has shown that such 'systems' are only convenient generalisations and abstractions from a situation that was almost certainly more heterogeneous.   In particular, they do not cover the full range of styles, and they take no account of those members of the community who alread use features of a later system.   This problem is more acute in many traditional works because they deliberately ignored some features which they considered to be 'corruptions' of the 'genuine' dialect.

Secondly, several of the writers of earlier works were phonetically naive, and it is often difficult to interpret both their descriptions and their transcriptions.   Even those with a knowledge of phonetics can give a very confusing picture: Ellis's 'palaeotype', for example, is fiendishly complicated, and without doubt caused difficulties both for those attempting to employ it, and for those responsible for typesetting and proof-reading (its mixture of lower case, capitals, italics, inverted letters, etc. must have been bewildering to those who did not know what it was supposed to be representing anyway), and also for those of us who have tried to interpret it.

Thirdly, none of the earlier works, even SED, is basically 'structural': they are all concerned more with showing the historical developments of individual sounds than with giving a description of a system of functionally distinct units at a point in time. Only in Wright (1892) and Haigh (1928) is there a clear attempt to set out the vowels of the dialect (and there is at least one obvious mistake in the latter which makes it clear that Haigh was thinking in terms of sounds rather than of distinctive units).   It was therefore necessary, after noting all the various portrayals of vowel *sounds*, to attempt to find, on the basis of my own knowledge of the speech of the area, in each work a full set of 'key words' that would show up the vowel *phonemes*, and to decide, in doubtful cases, whether certain forms written differently were likely to have been phonemically distinct or not - this meant, among other things, checking on the frequency and distribution of the various vowels recorded.

The Bradford Vowel System

Joseph Wright (1892) sets out the vowels of the Windhill dialect in the following symbols, and he is clearly giving something at least very close to the vowel phoneme system:

	Short			*Long*	
i̩		u		ī	ū
	e ə o			ə̄	
	a			ā	

		Diphthongs				*Triphthongs*	
ei	ui	iu		iə	uə	iuə	ouə
ai	oi	eu	ou	eə	oə	aiə	
				ā̄ə			

A very similar picture can be extracted from the 'Comparative
Specimen' of Ellis, published at about the same time (1889): Ellis
says that Wright gave him help, so it is not surprising that more
or less the same system emerges. The main difference between the
two is that the /ā̄ə/ diphthong and the three triphthongs do not
appear in Ellis, largely because they occur finally and Ellis records the linking [r] which occurs before an initial vowel.

However, it should be noted that there are points of doubt and
difficulty when attempting to interpret such 'pre-phonemic' accounts
and some of these should be mentioned. With Ellis's account, among
the short vowels, the symbols o and ɔ (= [ɒ] and [ɔ], according to
my interpretation of Ellis's descriptions on pp. 76-88 of his work)
both appear; it seems most unlikely that if intentional this difference represents more than one of phonetics and I have grouped them
together as /o/.   Also the symbols i and u occur in addition to *i*
and *u*, italicised (Ellis's usual transcription of [ɪ] and [ʊ]); if
not simply a mistake, these would indicate a shortened form of [i:]
and [u:], but again it seems unlikely that there is a significant
distinction. With the long vowels the symbols ee and oo (representing rather open front and back long mid vowels) occur, but
only rarely, and apparently as variants of eɐ [ɛə] and oɐ [ɒə];
AA as in *saw* looks like another non-distinctive variant of the
latter.   əə [ə:] does not occur in the specimen, but is in the
'Collected Word List' in the word *girn;* with this exception, Ellis
records [ə] in all words where Wright has the long vowel. With
the diphthongs, there is a lot of variation of symbols: /ʊə/ for example occurs as uɐ, *u*ɐ, uuɐ; these I assume not to be distinctively
different. Likewise I group together as /ʊɪ/: oi [ɒɪ] as in
afternoon, good, foot and *u*i [ʊi] as in *school, soon.*

The points of doubt in Wright are far fewer since he was probably a better phonetician (he tells us he was helped by Sweet), and
he was also an unconscious phonemicist: whereas Ellis tried to
record a mass of fine phonetic detail, Wright's is essentially a
broad or phonemic transcription. But I do have doubts about one
aspect of the above system: the mid-centring diphthongs /eə/ and
/oə/. Whereas Ellis could be interpreted as showing variation
between [e:] and [eə], and between [ɔ:] and [ɔə] in Bradford, and
certainly the later evidence shows the existence of [e:] and [ɔ:],
Wright has perhaps gone too far in 'regularising' and eliminating
unimportant differences: he ends up by in effect denying the possibility of a significant difference between words such as *pay* and
pair.

As examples of the incidence of the above vowels, I give here
for each of them, i) instances where this vowel occurs as in RP, and
ii) a number of everyday words where this is not the case:

/i/   i)   him, it
       ii)   much, such; find, blind; hang (strong verb); ever,
            never; week

/e/   i)   egg, tell
       ii)   have, hang (weak verb); break; among, wrong; wash

/a/   i)   hand, that
       ii)   make, take, game late; father; settle, very

/o/   i)   John, ox
       ii)   chance dance; broken, open, over; any, many, yellow;
            for, always, water

/u/   i)   bull, butcher
       ii)   butter, husband, some, come, one...; found, ground

/ə/   i)   a, of
       ii)   berry, bury, worry; Sunday etc; yesterday, yet;
            spirit; borrow, window etc.

/ī/   i)   field, see
       ii)   bright, night, die, eye, fly, mild; well

/ā/   i)   cart, harvest
       ii)   doubt, house, now, town...; room; servant; warm,
            work(N), worst

/ū/   i)   -
       ii)   book, cook; pull, wool; shoulder

/ə̄/   i)   bird, work(V), world

/ei/   i)   eight, straight
       ii) fight, right; eat, speak, teach

/ai/   i)   dry, fine, write
       ii) pick

/ui/   i)   ruin
       ii) boot, noon, school...; good, foot; blood

/oi/   i)   boil, voice
       ii) close, hole, coal, coat; lose; lane

/iu/   i)   new, suit
       ii) blew, grew, through; hook, look, took; enough

/eu/   i)   –
       ii) few, strew; shew

/ou/   i)   colt, old, roll, soul...; folk, coke; bowl, flow,
            grow...
       ii) bought, daughter, thought

/iə/   i)   clear, here
       ii) beat, meal, sea...; bread, deaf, head; again; heard,
            learn; swear, there

/eə/   i)   care, share
       ii) bake, spade, nail, rain, day, way; spoke(V), stole;
            master, rather; weak

/oə/   i)   –
       ii) order, saw, all, bald; either, neither; calf, half;
            know, slow, throw...

/uə/   i)   moor, poor
       ii) door, floor, before, more, board, thorn...; go, home,
            both, nose, loaf...; who

/ā̄ə/   i)   –
       ii) far, star; dare; sour, tower

/aiə/ i)   fire
       ii) –

/iuə/ i)   cure, pure
       ii) sure

/ouə/   i) -
         ii) four

Sixty years after the publication of Wright's work, in 1952,
fieldwork for the *Survey of English Dialects* was conducted at Wibsey,
which is about two miles south-west of the centre of Bradford and
thus about 4½ miles from Windhill, which is three miles to the north
of the town.   Though both concern areas of Bradford, there is therefore a difference in both time and locality between these two descriptions, either of which may be responsible for any linguistic
differences emerging.   In fact these turn out to be few; the most
noticeable ones concern the long vowels and the centring diphthongs:

	Wright				*SED*		
i:	u:	ɪə	ʊə	i:	u:	ɪə	ʊə
ə:		eə	ɔə	e:	ɔ:	ɛə	
a:		a:ə		a:			

At first sight there appears to have been an addition of two long
vowels /e:/ and /ɔ:/; a loss of /ɔə/ and a very considerable reduction in the load of /ɛə/; /a:ə/ seems also to have gone, its
incidence being taken over partly by /a:/ and partly by a 'new'
triphthong /aʊə/.   The following differences of incidence from
Wright's list illustrate these 'changes':

/eə/⟨   /e:/   spade, nail, way; spoke, stole; weak (i.e. items
                such as those under (ii) in the above list)
        /ɛə/   care, hair

/oə/ —— /ɔ:/   bald, corn, wall; know, snow...; calf, half;
                either, neither (i.e. items listed under (ii) above)

/a̅ə/⟨   /a:/   dare, far
        /aʊə/   flour

But are these differences due to phonetic change or geographical
distance - or are they matters of phonemic interpretation?   It was
noted above that Ellis recorded both /e:/ and /eə/, and /ɔ:/ and
/ɔə/; it seems quite possible that Wright 'standardised' in favour
of the diphthong, and that the SED system more accurately shows the
phonemic contrasts, including that between /e:/ and /ɛə/, e.g. *way -
ware* (as well as that between /e:/ and /ɛɪ/ e.g. *way - weigh*).

The following points are worth noting also:

SED agrees with Ellis rather than Wright in recording /ə/ in most
cases where the latter has /əː/.

The /ɛʊ/ diphthong looks to be very marginal; it is recorded in
show and *sew*, but *few* is shown to have the RP-like /iu/.

There are some differences of incidence:

> in *take,make* SED has /e/ as well as /a/ forms;
> in *look, took* SED has /ʊ/ ~ /uː/, Wright /iu/.   There is no SED
>   evidence of /iu/ in any *-ook* words;
> in *shoulder,*SED has /ɔʊ/, Wright /uː/;
> in *water,* SED has /a/, Wright /ɒ/;
> in *ground,* SED has /aː/, Wright /ʊ/.

(in these last three examples, both forms can be heard in the Bradford area, but probably there was a geographical difference between
the two sides of the town, and the Windhill and Wibsey speakers
reflect this.   The other two differences of incidence noted here
are more probably matters of linguistic change.)

There is then little substantive difference between the accounts of Wright and the SED.

The Halifax Vowel System

Ellis (1889) again provides our first picture, extracted mainly
from his 'comparative specimen'.   It is as follows (according to my
interpretation of his transcription):

	Short				*Long*	
ɪ		ʊ		iː		uː
e	ə	ɒ		eː	ɔː	
	a			aː		

	Diphthongs				
ɛɪ	ʊɪ	ɪu		ɪə	ʊə
aɪ	ɔɪ	ɛʊ	ɔʊ	eə	

Again, a number of points of interpretation should be commented on.
Among the short vowels, the symbols corresponding to both [ɒ] and
[ɔ] again occur, but I have grouped them as /ɒ/ since their distribution makes it unlikely that the difference is distinctive.
Also the symbols *o* and u appear in addition to the expected o and *u*
([ɒ], [ʊ]), but since Ellis himself says (p.385) 'On the difference
of o and *o* it is needless to dwell: they may be merely an accident
of writing or memory', thus admitting the fallibility of his description, we are justified in taking them as simply /ɒ/ and /ʊ/.

With long vowels, the symbols ee and *ee* ([ɛ:], [e:]) both occur, but
have been taken as /e:/ in the light both of the above and of the
unaccountable 'pattern' of distribution and of later evidence. Likewise oo and *oo* ([ɒ:], [o:]) have been grouped as /ɔ:/, even though
today /o:/ and /ɔ:/ contrast; this is because *oo* is written only in
call and *talk*, where it must surely be a mistake.   AA occurs once
([ɒ̄:]?) but only in an exclamation so I have not distinguished it
from /ɔ:/.   When we examine the diphthongs, we find that there are,
as with the Bradford specimen, numerous variations of transcription,
but leaving aside the probable mistakes and merely phonetic differences, the above system emerges.   The /ɛɪ/ diphthong does not occur
in the comparative specimen (the words *straight* and *speak* being
written with ee [ɛ:] which looks like a mistake of some sort), but
it is confirmed in the 'dialect test' reading passage for Elland,
on the outskirts of Halifax.

Comparing this with the earlier Ellis/Wright picture of the
Bradford system, the most noticeable difference is the 'extra' pair
of long vowels /e:/ and /ɔ:/, and the absence of /ɔə/ and the different load of /eə/: thus

Bradford		Halifax
/ɔə/	all, law, talk...; know, crow...	/ɔ:/
/eə/	name, safe, case...	/e:/
	care...	/eə/

However, it is worth remembering that Ellis did note some cases of
[ɔ:] and [e:] for Bradford, and that it was largely Wright who supplied the 'regularised' picture; and that the SED system for Bradford
(see above) does match this one in these respects.

But there is an important difference of incidence in respect of
/eə/ between Halifax and Bradford: Ellis writes this sound in *now,
ground, bound, house, down, out* etc. and *hearken, yard*, all of which
have /a:/ in Bradford.   This is a feature which is also found in
Huddersfield, as we shall see below.

Other differences of incidence (omitting a number for which I
can find no evidence, and which look like mistakes) include:

/e:/	father	(this form is attested from not very far away by SED)
/a:/	learn	(EDGr shows [lɪən~la:n] in this part of York-shire)
/ɒ/	one	(readily confirmed).

Crossland's paper (1889) is short and rather naive linguistically;
it is however possible to extract a picture of the vowel system for
a date very close to Ellis's, and thus to use it partly as a check
on the latter. The fact that his 'transcription' is in terms of
the orthography makes for certain difficulties, as does the use of
terms such as 'deviation from...the ordinary English sound', and so
on.

The inventory of short and long vowels extracted from Ellis is
largely confirmed, though few examples are given of some (e.g. only
lope for *leap* confirms the existence of /ɔʊ/, the word being thus
transcribed by Wright), because they are mostly 'as in ordinary
English' rather than what he is pleased to call 'substitutions'.

The main difference from Ellis appears in what is also the most
difficult passage to interpret: 'The local pronunciation of *ī* in
words like *mine, thine, time, mice* is difficult to define in writing
by either a single or combined letter symbol. We do not see any
sign in Professor Wright's equivalents to fit this sound. In our
local dialect writings the diphthong *aw* has generally been told off
to represent it, but it does not fulfil the duty to our satisfaction;
it is not exactly representative. To our mind this sound is more
accurately expressed by that of the *o* in words like *cork, stork* or
fork...' This of course suggests [ɔ:], but since Crossland has
already said 'in *balm*, *calf* and *half* we retain the old *aw* or long *o*
sound of the *al*...' i.e. [kɔ:f] etc., he presumably means something
slightly different from this, and I would suggest he is talking
about something like [ɑ:] (as contrasted with the [a:] which he has
in *learn* etc.). Now some of the early works on Huddersfield had
similar difficulties over the sound in some of what are today RP/aɪ/
words, and recent works such as SED have recorded [ɑ:]. Presumably
the isogloss for this set of words between an [aɪ] diphthong in
Bradford and a long vowel [ɑ:] in Huddersfield must be close to
Halifax, for though we saw above that Ellis recorded [aɪ] he noted
that a few miles away in Elland his prolific amateur fieldworker
Hallam had found ɑɑ ([ɑ:])in these RP/aɪ/ words, contrasting with
aa ([a:]) in certain RP/aʊ/ words - and Crossland seems to be portraying a variety of Halifax dialect following the latter pattern.

If this reasoning is correct, the following long vowel and
diphthong system emerges from Crossland's paper:

i:	u:		εɪ	ʊɪ		ɪu			ɪə	ʊə
e:	ɔ:			ɔɪ		(εʊ)*	ɔʊ	εə		
a:	ɑ:									

(* no examples are given of /εʊ/, but it has a light load at the best
of times in this area).

On matters of incidence it may be noted first that Crossland agrees with Ellis in recording /ɛə/ in many words that in Bradford have /a:/: '... *taan, raand, caa* (All the foregoing *aa*'s are pronounced like the *a* in *care* = eə).' He also seems to hear something like this sound in *part* and *master* (as did Wright) though his wording is confusing: 'in *master* and *part* we get an *ai* sound, *maister, pairt,* the *a* as in *care* and the short *i*'- he surely cannot mean [ɛəɪ]?

As in Ellis, /ɔ:/ is recorded for Wright's /ɔə/, and /a:/ for his /āə/. The following additional matters of incidence also emerge:

/e/   sat

/a/   water, want (both recorded by others than Wright for
               Bradford), watch, among, belong;

/ʊ/   yesterday

       cook, look, took, nook, book

       Referring to *oo* Crossland says 'a short *i* is added in
       good, flood, foot, school, noon' (i.e. [ʊɪ] as in
       Wright), but 'in certain other words, as *wood, cook,
       poor,* this diphthong (sic) has apparently not been
       subjected to any deviation from, or extension to, its
       ordinary English sound... *book* we should certainly
       classify in the latter group...' and 'in *look, nook,took*
       and a few others, the *oo* is like short *u*: *luk, nuk,
       tuk* not *lewk* or *newk*...' Crossland is certainly deny-
       ing the /ɪu/ of Wright, but also seems to be denying
       the /u:/ pronunciation, unless he thought the latter
       was 'its ordinary English sound'.

/e:/   decent, late, got

/u:/   come (as past tense)

/ɛɪ/   day, way

       'In *day* and *way* the *ay* is pronounced something like the
       eig in *eight* or *weigh*...'. SED finds [we:] for *way* in
       this part of Yorkshire, but Patchett (1981) records
       [dɛɪ] and [wɛɪ] in Upper Calderdale.

Marsden (1922) offers far too little phonological information for us to extract a vowel system for the Halifax area, but he makes

it clear that the a:/ɛə isogloss in words like *house down* etc. does
cross this area,with /a:/ said to be commoner in eastern parts and
/ɛə/ in western.   He also thinks there is a difference between the
vowels in *day, master* and *name, face* etc.

SED unfortunately did not investigate any locality as close to
Halifax as Y22 is to Bradford or Y29 to Huddersfield;   indeed these
two are probably the SED points closest to the centre of Halifax.
But Y21, though some eight miles away, would probably regard Halifax
as its nearest town (which Y22 and Y29 obviously would not), being
situated near a good route of communication through the Calder valley.

The vowel inventory to be extracted for Y21 is similar to that
described above for Y22, the main difference being the existence of
/aʊ/ in words like *about, ground, cow, house* etc. rather than /a:/
(or /ɛə/ as in the earlier works on Halifax);   Y21 is also closer to
the Bradford situation in having /aɪ/ in certain words rather than
the /a:/ discussed above.   There are a number of differences of
incidence, but these will not be discussed since this locality is of
more marginal interest.

The Huddersfield Vowel System

Easther (1883) is the first source we shall examine.   Being
only a glossary, coming from a 'pre-scientific' period of dialectology, and employing simply ad hoc modifications of the orthography
by way of transcription, it is difficult at times to interpret in
terms of a vowel system. But the following picture, using Easther's
own symbols for the present, seems to emerge:

	Short		*Long*		
i		u	ee		oo
(ə implied)			ai/ay	er	ō
e		o	aa		au/aw
	a				

Diphthongs					
aCe	ooi	eoo		ēă̆	ooă̆
iCe	oi	ayoo	ow	ā̆ă̆/ai(r)	

There are no problems of interpretation as far as the short
vowels are concerned: the same system is implied as in the other
works examined here.   But with long vowels and diphthongs, there

are two main areas of difficulty, both concerning typically local
features:

i) Easther seems to distinguish ō and au, saying *Paul* becomes *Pōle*
and *calf, half* are *cōfe, hōfe* OR *cauf, hauf;* I find no evidence
for [o:] in such words, but plenty for [ɔ:], as the *au* spelling suggests.   Now, with the *au* or *aw* transcription Easther
has what I see (from other evidence) as two separate sets of
words: first, words like *either, slow, no,* for which there is
evidence of [ɔ:] pronunciation; but second, a more interesting
set:

> 'Long *ī* I vocalised as *aw:* this was objected to, and *ah*
> (in *father*) proposed instead.   No doubt both these sounds
> are heard for *ī*, but I am of the opinion that *aw* most
> nearly represents the *ī* as generally heard from the least
> refined talkers'.   (In support, Easther tells us that 'an
> antiquarian and scientific friend' rejected the *ah* trans-
> cription, and gives a couple of anecdotes, suggesting that
> *wife* could be misunderstood as *warp,* and *bible* as *bauble*).

Thus Easther seems at first sight to be saying that words like
wife and *time* have [ɔ:] in Huddersfield, for which I can find no
other support.   Perhaps the explanation, granting that the
'incidence' picture is confused in Easther, could be as follows:
he was not happy about representing this set of words with *ah*
because the sound was different from the usual 'long A' of this
area ([a:] as in *laarn* = *learn*), being low and back, i.e. somewhere in the phonetic area [ɑ:/ɒ:].   But it was different too
from the vowel in say *calf* which was also roughly in this area.
He therefore tried as it were to 'shift' the latter to ō
(though he was not entirely consistent) in order to have *aw*
available for these words.

  (It may be noted that Easther implies that [aɪ] also occurs,
by his 'iCe' transcription in forms like *pike* (*pick*), but it is
of limited incidence.)

ii) Easther also gets into difficulties with words of the *mouse,
mouth, cow* set.   He transcribes *out, about* etc. as *aat,
abaat,* and says 'the first *a* as in *father,* the second as in *fat'*
which seems to imply something like the [a:] pronunciation
common in much of West Yorkshire.   But he also uses a transcription *āǎ* in some of these words, e.g.*mouth, mouse, south*
etc.   Now he may simply have been inconsistent, but his remark
that *paark* or *paerk* is the pronunciation of *park* could suggest
[ɛə], which is also heard in many of these words in the area.
But this sound also seems to be suggested by *ai* in *airm, kaird*
for *arm, card* etc., which other evidence suggests had [ɛə]

pronunciations. All that we may conclude is that Easther has
heard both [a:] and [ɛə] forms somewhere, but he is unclear
about their geographical distribution and lexical incidence,
and inconsistent in how he transcribes them.

Easther's description of words in which we should have expected
[ɔʊ] e.g. *grow, fought* etc. is also somewhat unexpected: the former
is said to rhyme with *cow, now*, and in the latter *ou* is described
as 'as in *sound*'; clearly something like [aʊ] seems to be indicated,
but perhaps he is just trying to show that the diphthong is not one
of 'the ordinary vowel sounds of English' which he constantly takes
as a basis of description.

I suggest that Easther's system can be interpreted as:

	Short			*Long*	
ɪ		ʊ	i:		u:
e	ə	ɒ	e:	ə:	ɔ:
a			a:		ɑ:

Diphthongs

ɛɪ	ʊɪ	ɪu		ɪə	ʊə
aɪ	ɔɪ	ɛʊ	ɔʊ	ɛə	

As regards differences of incidence from the Wright list given
earlier, in addition to examples of [e:] and [ɔ:] for Wright's [eə]
and [ɔə] a few others may be noted.

/ə/   spirit

/a/   long, wrong, among; water

/ʊ/   yes, yesterday

/i:/   right (~/ɛɪ/)

/u:/   hook

Ellis (1889) is our next source. The vowel system emerging
from his 'comparative specimen' for Huddersfield is one of the most
confusing. The inventory appears to be as follows:

Short   *Long*

ɪ   ʊ   i: u:

e   ə   ɒ   e: ɔ:

a   a:

Diphthongs

ɪɜ   ʊɪ   ɪu   eɪ   ʊə

ɔɪ   ɔʊ   ɛɜ   (ɔə)

There are a number of problems of interpretation here.   Among
the short vowels, the symbols ɔ,i,u, appear as well as o,*i,u*   -
but the difference is either a mistake or a matter of unimportant
phonetic variation.   With the long vowels, I have also discounted
the variation between *uu*, ee, *oo* and uu, *ee*, oo.   The main differences from Easther's implied system are the absence of /ə:/ (possibly
the result of the fairly small amount of data) and of /ɑ:/ (see
below).   As regards diphthongs, there are the usual probably phonetic variations (*iɐ ~ iiɐ, ooɐ ~ oɐ* etc) and an obvious confusion
over o*i* and o*i* [ɔɪ] and [ʊɪ].   I have bracketted /ɔə/ since it
seems to carry very little load.   The absence of the uncommon /ɛʊ/
may be due to paucity of data.

The main difference, both from Ellis's own pictures of Bradford
and Halifax, and from the situation just extracted from Easther,
concerns what we may call '/aɪ/ words'.   Ellis notes that in nearby
localities, including Marsden (just a few miles up the Colne valley)
for which he prints a 'dialect test' passage, there is an a:/ɑ: contrast, with *down/dine* being [da:n]/[dɑ:n].   But in Huddersfield
itself he portrays the pronunciation of words such as *bright, child,
dry, fine, like, my, mine, nine, why, whine* as diphthongal - and
what is most surprising, chooses the same symbol o*i* [ɔɪ] as he gives
in *boil, voice, point* etc.   Now there is evidence that in some varieties of English in the nineteenth century there was an /aɪ/ variant
for some or all /ɔɪ/ words, but I know of no other evidence for this
area.   It could be that Ellis's assistant who produced the Huddersfield transcription (one C.C. Robinson) was rather confused in this
low back area, but was trying to express something like [ɑ·ɪ] or [ɑɪ]

Ellis also gives a confused picture with words where there is
variation within West Yorkshire between /a:/ and/ɛə/; he writes the
former in *doubt* the latter in *how, out* and *hark*, but in *ground, now,
house* he unaccountably gives a closer start-point, resulting in his
writing this group with the same /ɪə/ vowel as in *where, least,
beast.*

Omitting a number for which I can find no support and which are
therefore probably mistakes, the following differences of incidence

from our initial list are worth recording (all are readily confirmed
in other sources)

/a/   want, wrong

/ɒ/   one, whole ([wɒl])

/ə/   word, world

/e:/   reason, lane

/a:/   certain, learn

Haigh (1928) saw himself as producing a new version of a Huddersfield glossary such as Easther had provided, and there are certain
interesting similarities between the vowel systems deducible from
the two works.

Haigh sets out what appears at first sight to be a 'system' of
vowels, but on closer examination it seems to be more of a 'trans-
criptional arsenal'. For instance, among the 'short vowel sounds'
we find the familiar six (though *her* as a key-word for /ə/ is misleading) but also ǫ (alongside o in *not*): this is not in fact a
separate short vowel, but the first element of the /ɔɪ/ diphthong
which Haigh presumably considers to have a more open start-point.
Among his diphthongs, most are given key-words, but four are not:
ou, uə , əu and æu - and though for the first three of these (presumably /ɔʊ/, /ʊə/, /ɛʊ/, though Haigh obviously considers the last
to have a fairly central start-point) examples can be found in the
glossary, I could not readily find any words with æu, which presumably indicates /aʊ/ (though the whole business is confused by his
using au to indicate one of his long vowels: /ɔ:/ - a most unfortunate departure from his professed policy of using Wright's symbols).

The system that seems to emerge is very similar to Easther's;
at first sight is appears to be:

Short				*Long*		
ɪ		ʊ		i:		u:
e	ə	o		e:	ə:	o:
a				a:		ɔ:

Diphthongs

ɛɪ	ʊɪ	ɪu		ɪə	ʊə
ɔɪˑ	ɛʊ	ɔʊ		ɛə	(ɔə)

The short vowels are the familiar set (Haigh makes it clear that
/ə/ occurs in the second syllable of *barrow, swallow* etc); with the
long vowels, more than once Haigh points out that /e:/ and /o:/ are
'level' i.e. monophthongal, 'without final uplift'; the quality of
ō is indicated by the key-word *note*, which today would have [o̞:]
(other present-day /o:/ words are given with /ʊə/ e.g. *road, both,*
as in Wright).

But Haigh too seems to be confused in the low back area.   For
instance, under the ō vowel he gives mostly words with an *ow* spelling: *blow, crow, row, slow* etc; but also with this vowel are *talk,
Shaw,* etc.   Now other traditional works have given all these words
with [ɔ:] - but Haigh gives the latter, transcribed au, for the set
of words including *dry, fine, find, hide, like, my, mine, pike,
sky, time, while, why, write* etc.   Like Easther, Haigh does not
seem to have reached what was probably the correct solution: that
there are two different types of 'long A' - so he assigns the words
in question to/ɔ:/, which means that he has to 'shift' most 'real'
/ɔ:/ words to /o:/ (some as it were 'escape': e.g. *half* and *neither)*.

As regards diphthongs, /ɔə/ is bracketted here, since the only
example I noticed was *four*, where /ɔə/~/ɔʊə/.   With /ɔʊ/ Haigh has
mainly a neat etymological picture: i) *ought, thought, caught* etc;
ii) *ol* words like *old, cold, folk, roll, sold, shoulder* etc;   iii)
some *ow* words such as *grow, row, low, own, blow,* (N and expletive)
etc; iv) *no, coke* (with historical [l]).   But he notes that *own*
and *blow* can have /o:/, so the neat picture is becoming confused.
He also says that *hold* and *folk* can have /ɒ/, *folk* and *no* can have
/ʊə/, and *shoulder* can have /u:/; some of these may be, or may
have been originally, matters of geographical difference.

Haigh gives a clearer picture of the /ɛə/ situation: it occurs
in i) *fair, swear* (~/ɪə/) etc; ii) *can't, yard, room* etc; and iii)
about, down, ground, house, how, loud, now, out, round etc. - in the
latter two groups, of course, /a:/ occurs in other parts of the area.

The following other differences of incidence from our initial
list seem to be worthy of note:

/ɪ/   fell*ow*

/e/   hand; spirit; waken (~/a/).

/a/   water; among, long, wrong; chance (~/ɒ/)

/ɒ/   one, love

/ʊ/   yesterday

/i:/   right (~/ɛɪ/)

/u:/   book, look, cook, etc; come

/e:/   decent; straight, laik (~/ɛɪ/)

/ɛɪ/   break, drain

/ʊɪ/   boil, voice (there is no other recent evidence of this
pronunciation, but Gimson (1970:132) says that in Middle
or Early Modern English some words which now have /ɔɪ/
were pronounced with [ʊɪ])

/ɪə/   feel

Sykes (1961), as one might expect from an SED fieldworker
(though he did not investigate this area for that survey) concentrates on the genuine traditional dialect, though admitting that
this is 'very much under pressure from other forms of English', and
on tracing the development of Middle English sounds.

The following vowel system can be deduced:

Short				Long	
ɪ		ʊ		i:	u:
e	ə	ɒ		e:	o:
	a			a:	ɑ:

Diphthongs

ɛɪ	ʊɪ	uɪ		ɪə	ʊə
	ɔɪ		ɔʊ	ɛə	

Of the short vowels, Sykes does not specifically mention /ə/, but
from his transcriptions of *harrow, window* etc it is clear that it
occurs at least in unstressed position. With long vowels, he
gives *calf* and *palm* as examples of /o:/; it could be that his use
of this symbol is due to a desire for symmetry with /e:/, or to the
feeling that there must be more distance from /ɑ:/ than the [ɔ:]
symbol would suggest. As examples of /a:/ he gives *starling,bark,
certain, deserve*; while under back /ɑ:/ he has i) *fall, walk, thaw*
etc;   ii) *dike, mice, knife* etc;   iii) *wire, iron*.

Among the diphthongs, Sykes has /ɛə/ in i) *fair, stare;*   ii)
arm, yard, warm etc;   iii) *mouth, foul* etc;   iv) *flour, shower.*

Other points of incidence include:

/a/   wrong, among; wasp, swap

/ɒ/   man; work, first, nurse, turn

We may conclude that broadly, and while substituting /ɑ:/ for
/ɔ:/ (probably inaccurately in the set including *fall*, *thaw*, *walk*
etc: see below) Sykes presents an essentially similar picture to
that of Haigh.

SED (published in 1962, though the fieldwork probably antedated
Sykes) investigated several localities within a 10-mile radius of
Huddersfield: Y26, Y29, Y30, Y31.   Of these, Y29 Golcar, a village
on the outskirts of the town, is the nearest, so we shall concentrate on it, though all four appear virtually identical in vowel
inventory and also in most matters of incidence (the main exception
being that at Y26 /ɛə/ occurs in words of the *arm* set, but does not
do so in *ground*, *mouth* etc. which have /a:/).

The vowel system at Y29 is as follows:

Short				*Long*	
ɪ		ʊ		i:	u:
e	ə	ɒ		e:	ɔ:
	a			a:	ɑ:

Diphthongs

ɛɪ	ʊɪ	ɪu		ɪə	ʊə
aɪ	ɔɪ	ɛʊ	ɔʊ	ɛə	

The words written with /ɔ:/ are those appearing with ō/o: etc.
in previous works; my own ear suggests that the quality implied by
the SED symbol is more accurate.   /a:/ occurs in words such as *barn*,
shan't, *worse*, *dare* etc, /ɔ:/ in *walk*, *thaw* etc., /ɑ:/ in *time*, *write*,
Friday, *find*, *blind* (except at Y26), *I* (at Y30, 31), *sky* (at Y31) -
but all have the diphthong /aɪ/ in *nine*, and all but Y31 have it in
sky, so we are justified in including this diphthong in the system.
/ɛʊ/ is only a marginal member of the system, occurring e.g. in *sew*
at Y29 and 30.   /ɛə/ occurs in i) *care*, *hair*, *chair*, *swear* etc;
ii) *arm* etc. iii) *about*, *cow*, *ground*, *house*, *mouth* etc. (in this last
set Y26 has /a:/).

A few points of incidence are worth noting:

/e/   take (~/a/; cf. make at Y30,31)

/a/   among; water

/ɒ/   one (~/ʊ/); bird (Y30,31)

/ʊ/   yesterday

/ə/   bury (/e/ at Y30, Y31); first

/e:/   break (~/ɛɪ/)

/u:/   look, took

/ɛɪ/   neighbour (~/e:/), break (ditto), drain

Summary

Let us attempt to summarise the picture of traditional vowel systems that has emerged from the works examined in this chapter.

It would appear that there are two main vowel-systems within the area. First, that for the Bradford district, which we shall represent as:

		Short			*Long*		
ɪ		ʊ		i:			u:
	e ə ɒ				e: ə: ɔ:		
	a				a:		

		Diphthongs			
ɛɪ ʊɪ	(ɪu)			ɪə ʊə	
aɪ ɔɪ	(ɛʊ) ɔʊ			ɛə	

Phonemes of rare incidence are bracketted. This is substantially the picture deduced from the SED material for Y22 (and, incidentally, that for Y23, Leeds, some ten miles East, differs only in minor respects - matters of either phonetics or fieldworker). It is to be noted that this differs from Joseph Wright's picture for Windhill, mainly in that his long vowel system does not contain /e:/ and /ɔ:/ - words containing these vowels are written by him with /eə/ and/ɔə/, the system of centring diphthongs being thus more 'symmetrical'. This difference could simply be a matter of interpretation (Wright taking certain variants as 'canonical'), or of geography (Windhill is several miles from Wibsey), or possibly of phonetic change. If this last is the real explanation then we must conclude that Bradford has moved in the direction of systems elsewhere in this area.

Second, there is the system for the Huddersfield area, which
we take to be:

	Short				*Long*	
ɪ		ʊ			i:	u:
	e ə ɒ				e:	ɔ:
	a				a:	ɑ:

Diphthongs

ɛɪ	ʊɪ	(ɪu)		ɪə	ʊə
(aɪ)	ɔɪ	(ɛʊ) ɔʊ		ɛə	

This is largely the picture to be deduced from SED Y29.   Apart
from the question of whether there is /ə:/ or not (on which writers
are divided, as they are in Bradford too), there are two main differences from the Bradford system.   First, the long vowel system of
'quadrilateral' rather than 'triangular':   this is because in the
'open' area there is an extra back vowel: the exact quality of the
back vowels has caused confusion among earlier writers, but SED
shows the main difference from the Bradford-type system to be the
/a:/-/ɑ:/ contrast.   This /ɑ:/ vowel accounts for many words that
have /aɪ/ in the other system, the latter carrying a light load
here.   The other major difference concerns incidence: a large set
of words with /a:/ in the Bradford system have /ɛə/ in Huddersfield,
the former having a much lighter load here.   Other differences
between the systems concern less weighty matters of incidence e.g./e/
or /a/ in *wrong, long* etc;   /ʊ/ or /ɒ/ in *one, love* etc;   /e:/ or
/ɛɪ/ in *break, drain* etc;   or distribution e.g. /ə/ in stressed
syllables: cf. /ə/ or /e/ in *bury, worry, spirit* etc;   /ə/ or /ʊ/
in *yes, yesterday* etc.

     The picture to be extracted for Halifax depends on less detailed
and less accurate works of a fairly early date.   The impression is
that Halifax lies fairly near to the isoglosses in respect of both
major features referred to above;   with the /ɛə/ incidence difference it seems more likely that Halifax resembles the Huddersfield
system, whereas on the question of /ɑ:/ there is no unanimity.

     Of course the question must be asked 'How representative of the
speech of the population at the period in question is any of the
systems extracted?'   The SED material was gathered around 1950, and
one suspects that they may have had to look hard to find the 'right'
informants - and even the SED material shows signs of the encroach-
ment of RP-like or RP-influenced pronunciations in everyday words

such as *among*, *any*, *boot*, *sow*, *daughter*, *deaf*, *die*, *eye*, *horse*, *lane*, *look*, *make*, *many*, *spokes*, *swear*, *then*, *time*, *very*, *what*, *where*, *with*, *worse*, *yellow* etc.   In the next chapter we shall see what sort of picture emerged from quite a large 'non-hand-picked' sample of the urban population, and i n Chapter 8 we shall be in a position to draw some conclusions about what sort of changes have occurred in the vowel systems of the area.

CHAPTER SIX

THE PRESENT SITUATION: PERFORMANCE

This chapter will describe what appear to be some of the most
noticeable non-RP and non-Standard English features in the speech
of my sample: the persistence or modification of such features is
the main focus of this study.   The major part of the chapter will
be concerned with the examination of a number of *variables*, after
the manner of Labov (1966a) , Trudgill (1974a) etc: variation
within a community offers clear indications both of the prestige or
otherwise of certain features and of the course of linguistic change.
Some thirty features will be examined as variables; other non-standard features observed among my informants, but not with sufficient
frequency to permit this kind of treatment, will also be recorded
since they too are an important part of the picture of the persistence or modification of regional features.

1   AN EXAMINATION OF SOME LINGUISTIC VARIABLES

The variables to be examined were chosen at one of two stages.
An initial selection was made on the basis of my study of previous
works on the area (such as are described in Chapters 1 and 5 above):
certain features appeared to be worth investigating since they were
regarded as traditional to this area (for example, the absence of
/h/ and /ʌ/ from the phoneme system; the existence of both /ɛɪ/ and
/e:/; the 'front' quality of /ɑ:/; the reduced form of the definite article; and so on).   Other features were chosen in order to
have examples of different linguistic types: phonological variables
involving inventory, distribution, realisation, and incidence, and
also grammatical variables.   All these were selected before the
investigation, and the questionnaire and interview were designed
with these variables in mind.   However, I realised that I might not
have selected the most interesting or most important variables in
this way, so I was prepared to examine others which turned up in the
course of my work.   This did in fact occur: certain features which
traditional studies had not led one to expect showed up either
through my own observation (for example, it soon became clear that

a possible /ɔʊ/ - /o:/ contrast, parallel to the traditional /ɛɪ/ - /e:/, had come to exist), or from the remarks of my informants about features typical of the area or those they disliked or would correct in their children (for instance, the glottal stop was obviously the subject of much feeling). In order to allow for the possibility that other variables worth examining in detail would emerge during the investigation, I had included in the reading passage and word list examples of all phonological segments, so that I could study them in these styles as well as the conversational ones.

     The following arrangement will be adopted in the discussion of each variable. First, the picture emerging from traditional dia- lect descriptions of the area will briefly be outlined, and con- trasted with the RP or Standard English situation. Then I shall discuss what appears to occur in the area today. The quantitative findings i.e. the possible correlations of the use of non-standard variants with linguistic and/or non-linguistic factors will next be presented and discussed. Finally, certain conclusions will be drawn. It should be noted that though scores were worked out and graphs pro- duced for all the variables examined in respect of I Class and Style groups, with totals for all classes and all styles; II Sex, Class,and Style (and totals); III Town, Class, and Style (and totals); IV Age and Style (and totals); V Age, Sex and Style (and totals), these findings will not all be presented. For each var- iable I shall reproduce only those figures where some interesting pattern seemed to emerge.

     In the case of the phonological variables the particular lex- ical items involved will not usually be spelled out: for instance, when dealing with (h) we shall be discussing all those items where initial /h/ would occur in RP, which turned up in informants' speech during the interview. Except in the case of the variables (ɛɪ/e:) and (ɔʊ/o:) no record was kept of which particular items occurred, and with which variant; the items which were employed in the read- ing passage and word list are of course known, but again no detailed record was kept of which had [h] and which did not. So, like Labov and Trudgill, I shall not be considering whether *happy* is more sub- ject to 'h-dropping' than *hilly*: they will be lumped together and an overall 'score' produced. This is not because I believe such lexical differences are totally irrelevant (indeed in one of the first studies of this type, Fischer (1958), it seemed to emerge that there were differences between everyday and more 'learned' words in respect of /ɪŋ/ vs /ɪn/ variation), but because such a treatment would raise a host of other problems (e.g. how does one decide what words are everyday/learned? etc.), and my impression is that, while some such differences do sometimes appear, this is not by any means

always the case[73], and the vast amount of detailed investigation
needed is beyond the scope of this work.

However, this rather crude lumping together of all words involving a certain variable was modified in two ways. On the one hand,
I discounted all occurrences where there was no possibility of variation (for example, before an initial velar only the /ɪŋ/ variant
of (ing) occurs, so such instances cannot be counted as the use of
one variant rather than another), or where RP might be expected to
have a form similar to the non-standard (thus, weak forms of *him*,
his, *have*, etc. may be pronounced without /h/). On the other hand,
I have introduced a refinement not seen in some earlier work in that
I have broken down certain lexical sets according to the environment
of the variable. This may be the phonological environment: I investigated the glottal stop in four separate positions[74] - or the
grammatical/lexical environment: with (ing) I distinguished between
1) participles and gerunds and 2) the rest, and felt that I might
usefully have further broken down the latter set.

PHONOLOGICAL VARIATION

1   Inventory Variables

In this section I shall examine the most striking cases of variation which seem to involve the number of phonemes in the system or
systems to be found in our area - as opposed to say merely the pronunciation of the 'same' phoneme. My pre-survey observations had
indicated that the RP system has exercised some degree of influence
on many speakers in this area, in that the 'traditional dialect'
appears to have been modified in the direction of RP to varying
extents, so I shall be looking at the main points of difference between the inventories of these two systems.

Of course, though our interest is in the *phonemic* system, what
one hears is *phonetic* data, and the interpretation of this often
leaves room for debate, since few speakers appear to be 'pure'
examples of either of two competing systems. For instance, RP contains the phoneme /h/ in its inventory, whereas the traditional
dialect does not; now, if we hear a speaker say [haus], does this

---

73   For example, one might have expected that more 'learned' lexical
items would tend to co-occur with more standard grammar as well as
phonology - yet I recorded the statement 'Them are my honest contentions'!

74   Trudgill (1974a:96) suggested that glottalisation of syllable-
final /t/ is more frequent word-finally than medially, but his 'index-
scores' lumped both together.

necessarily mean that he has /h/?   What if we hear ten instances
of [aʊs] for every one of [haʊs]?   Or, even more crucial, what if
he appears to have [h] in about 50% of items where it would be expected in RP?   Is it realistic to say that a speaker has /h/ in
his inventory, but in everyday conversation he just happens to omit
it on 99% of occasions?   And so on.

In many linguistic studies, 'minimal pairs' have been taken as
the deciding factor: if we hear a person pronounce *hotter* as [hɒtə]
and *otter* as [ɒtə], then he has /h/.   But if the minimal pairs
'test' is used, it can yield a result quite untypical of other situations, in that either more people appear to 'have' the phoneme
than might have been expected from the other evidence (see p.107
below), or sometimes fewer (see p.115).   On the other hand, if we
decide to search for minimal or near-minimal pairs in 'normal' speech,
this will often be an enormous task and they may well just not happen
to turn up in the data available.   And even if they do, the problem
previously referred to remains: if a speaker happened to pronounce
both the above words as [ɒtə] does this mean he has no /h/, even
though he might have recently said *happy*, *Hello*, *hip* etc. with [h]?
I do not think any convincing answer has been offered to these
problems; so all we can do here is to examine some of the phonetic
facts that bear on such questions of competing phonemic inventories.

The Variable (h)

We are concerned here with the large lexical set which in RP
has initial /h/ e.g. *how*, *hat*, *who*, etc.etc. and the smaller set
with medial /h/ e.g. *behind*, *behave*, *anyhow* etc.   The descriptions
of traditional dialect in West Yorkshire are almost unanimous in portraying the non-existence of this phoneme: thus, Wright and SED,
two of the most reliable, show no trace of it; the less 'professional' paper of Crossland (1899) makes a statement which at first
sight appears naive and amusing: 'The aspirate, as an initial, gives
little trouble to speakers of our dialect; they rarely, if ever,
use it, either in place or out' - but it might possibly be taken to
indicate that some [h] was to be heard, which the more 'purist' descriptions have discounted[75].

The absence of /h/ is common in many other non-standard varieties

---

75   It may be noted that most sources on Huddersfield and some on
Halifax give numerous examples of initial /j/ where RP has /h/ e.g.
head, heard and some where RP has /ɸ/ e.g. *Elland*.   This /j/ on-
glide is not connected with /h/ (it developed before initial vowels
in several varieties of English) except in that loss of initial /h/
was a precondition for it in some words.   No examples were recorded
during my survey.

of English, and it rarely leads to difficulties of communication.
But for some reason 'h-dropping' is widely stigmatised: Strang
(1970:81) says that condemnation of this feature began around the end
of the eighteenth century, and was then reinforced by the spread of
education; the responses of my informants, both spontaneous and elicited (see Chapter 7) - as well as my personal experience in the educational system - make it clear that this stigmatisation is prevalent
in West Yorkshire, and consequently speakers are mostly 'aware' of /h/,
however much or little they actually employ it[76].

Though RP is an 'h-dialect', there are some words in which, in
fluent speech, h-dropping is normal and quite acceptable, e.g. the
verb-forms *have*, *has*, *had* (especially when auxiliaries), the pronouns
and pronominal adjectives *he*, *him*, *his*, *her* etc: providing the form
is unstressed and not sentence-initial it is quite usual to omit /h/
e.g. [aɪ wʊd əv hɪt ɪm ɒn ɪz tʃɪn]; similarly, with medial /h/, some
words are normally 'h-less' e.g. *Birmingham, Southampton.* There are
also one or two words, such as *hotel* and *historical* where some RP
speakers quite acceptably have no /h/, but this appears to be becoming less common). When analysing the speech of my informants I only
counted as h-dropping those cases where /h/ would be expected in RP
speech.

The quantitative findings of my survey for (h) are expressed in
terms of the percentage of non-standard forms i.e. [Ø] where [h] would
be expected in RP.   The pattern of class and style variation for
word-initial /h/ is seen in Figure 2.   A similar picture emerged for

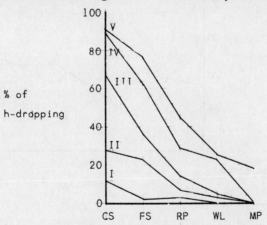

Figure 2:   (h) - Class and Style

/h/ in medial (or more strictly 'morpheme initial') position;   since
relatively few examples of the latter were recorded, and since
it does not appear to pattern differently from word-initial /h/, we
shall discuss it no further.

When the class groups are broken down by sex, the picture of
h-dropping (initial only, hereafter) is as in the following table:

	CS		FS		RP		WL		MP	
	M	W	M	W	M	W	M	W	M	W
I	12	-	2	-	3	-	0	-	0	-
II	36	19	36	4	10	4	5	0	0	0
III	80	58	46	30	24	9	9	3	0	0
IV	91	86	68	57	31	28	32	18	0	0
V	93	90	76	77	56	25	34	6	23	9

With the informants grouped according to age, figures for the
80+ group should in this case be treated with caution since they will
obviously be biased because there were only three informants of this
age and all belong to Class V - and it is obvious from the above
that social class and performance on (h) are related.   The age-group
scores are in Figure 3.

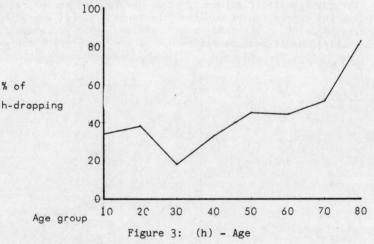

Figure 3:   (h) - Age

---

made a conscious effort to sound [h];   one woman exclaimed 'Oh' when
she found she was failing to do so, and a man said 'That's the thing
- the h's...I'm not used to pronounce 'em'.

Grouping together all the informants in each town, the total
scores for h-dropping, in each style except minimal pairs, are as
follows:

	CS	FS	RP	WL
Bfd	81	45	25	16
Hfx	72	46	17	11
Hudd	74	53	27	10

Figures for class and style variation present an extremely
'regular' picture, with h-dropping increasing down the social scale,
and with all classes pronouncing more and more [h] with increased
levels of formality.   It is noteworthy that the scores range so
widely - both between classes,e.g. in casual style the range is from
93% h-dropping in the lowest class to only 12% in the highest, and
between styles within the same class, e.g.Class IV range from 89%
in the casual style to 23% in the word list and 0% in the minimal
pairs; we may contrast this with Trudgill's findings for (h),
(1974a:131), where all classes had considerably more [h], presumably
because /h/ is present in traditional Norfolk dialects.

The results of the minimal pairs test call for comment.   Informants were presented with the pair *hotter* and *otter*, and only four
failed to produce [h] 'correctly'[77].   If decisions about whether
informants 'have /h/' were to be based on the results in this highly
artificial situation, they would obviously be quite unrepresentative
of what happens in everyday speech.   But the figures for this style
are 'in line' with the rest of the style graph, which presumably
reflects the conscious stigmatisation of h-dropping, resulting in
even those who are naturally 'h-less making an effort to use [h] as
they speak more carefully.

The consistent difference between the sexes, with women almost
invariably using more [h] than men of the same group, is a pattern
that has been observed in previous studies (see Trudgill (1972) etc):
women tend to show more prestige forms or fewer stigmatised forms,
whichever of these situations obtains with a particular variable.

Another result of the stigmatisation of h-dropping is to be

---

77   One of these in fact pronounced the two forms the wrong way round
and then corrected herself and so perhaps should not be counted;   another informant laughed as if he realised what he had done, i.e. he
was conscious of /h/ though not producing it.

observed in the phenomenon of 'hypercorrection' (I employ this term
in the traditional sense rather than that of Labov, (1966b)): the
addition of [h] to a vowel-initial word.   Often in fact this takes
the form of 'h-spoonerism', e.g. one woman said [haɪ ɪə] for 'I hear'
which should perhaps not be counted as the same thing.   I recorded
only 13 instances (from 12 informants) during my interviews, so this
is clearly not a common practice - for there were many thousands of
words where this could have occurred.   It appears that: a) all
those who showed any hypercorrections were fairly substantial
h-droppers, who were presumably conscious of their 'problem'[78];   b)
hypercorrection is not a feature of casual speech: of the 13 instances, 7 occurred in formal style and the rest in the reading passage - which again seems to indicate that speakers were 'trying hard'
in more formal situations; c) all but two instances were from inform
ants of Classes IV-V (the two exceptions coming from schoolchildren
scored as Class II by parental characteristics but, as often with
youngsters, showing a higher proportion of regionalisms than might be
expected in that class): this reinforces the point about this phenomenon being more likely among the h-dropping groups.

The figures for age-groups in Figure 3 show some signs of a
decrease in h-dropping, with informants over 50 scoring a little
higher than those younger, but the most noticeable feature of the
graph is the 'dip' to the score of the 30+ group.   With a sample of
this size, the 'class composition' of the group could have been responsible for such a graph in the case of a variable which shows clear
signs of a correlation with social class; but a similar pattern
emerges if separate figures are produced for the age-groups within
each class.   Possible reasons for this low score among the 30+
group will be discussed at a later stage.

The following conclusions seem possible in respect of the (h)
variable.   If the traditional dialect descriptions are assumed to
be correct in portraying a situation some years ago where [h] was
rarely if ever heard in this area, then the influence of 'h-dialects'
particularly RP, and the stigma that has become associated with
h-dropping, has led to the present situation where h-usage constitutes a variable for the great majority of speakers.   [h] has become
a mark of 'better speech', h-dropping of 'substandard speech', and
thus (h) constitutes a 'classic' stratifying feature: more [h]
exists the higher we look on the social scale, and everybody, even
in the lowest class, makes some effort to use [h] as formality of

---

78   An interesting example of a hypercorrector was a woman of Class
V in her 30s: she dropped only 21 out of 110/h/s overall, but
almost all were in conversation, i.e. she was aware of her difficulty
and tried hard in the more formal styles - to the extent of hypercorrection on one occasion.

style increases.   Women, for whatever reason, appear to be more
'speech-conscious' than men, and this is reflected in their greater
use of [h].   'Town', or locality within our area, does not appear
to be a significant factor in h-usage; the influence of h-dialects
and the stigma of h-dropping affects the whole h-less area (the
slightly lower overall figures for h-dropping in Halifax may just
possibly relate to the fact that Halifax has a slightly higher average
social class 'score' than the other two towns: see p.58.
Figures for the age-groups cannot be taken to indicate any rapid
change in progress at the present time, but we may note that a) the
fact that they show a fair degree of h-usage even among the older
seems to suggest that the start of this practice in the area was probably during the period supposedly described in the traditional descriptions; b) the 'unexpectedly' high degree of h-usage in the 30+
group, which does not appear to be class-related, shows a pattern
that will be repeated below with a number of other variables.

Interlude: Group Averages and Individual Scores

        Having now examined a set of figures of the type we shall be
presenting throughout this treatment of variables, it may be salutory
to consider a matter which should make us hesitant about drawing certain too sweeping conclusions.

        The figures presented above are 'averages' for a group of inform-
ants - a grouping by class, age, sex, town, or whatever.   Such
figures give an impression of 'discreteness' that does not really
exist: the social classes, for example, may appear to be spread out
in terms of percentages of h-pronouncing, but the 106 individual informants in fact form almost a continuum over the scale from 0 to
100%, with well over half the slots being occupied.   Examining each
'10% band' rather than individual scores, we find the following
numbers of informants in each category:

	0	1-10%	11-20%	21-30%	31-40%	41-50%
Conversation (CS + FS)	7	28	13	8	9	4
All styles	0	5	8	10	11	11

	51-60%	61-70%	71-80%	81-90%	91-99%	100%
Conversation CS + FS)	2	10	6	6	8	5
All styles	11	8	8	16	13	5

Clearly there are no 'discrete groups which are relatively unified in their linguistic behaviour', as Trudgill (1974a:59) described his classes.   The apparent discreteness is a product of this
method of analysis.   Not only are individuals on a continuum linguistically as well as socially (see Figure 1), but the classes are
not entirely composed of speakers more or less adjacent to each other
on this linguistic continuum: the average scores may incorporate
widely disparate individuals.   For example, with h-pronouncing in
conversation (i.e. casual plus formal speech) the range of individual
scores in the class groups was as follows:

    I   81 - 100%
    II   7 - 100% (40-100% if one very 'incongruent' individual
                        were excluded)
    III   2 - 100%
    IV   0 - 86%
    V   0 - 80% (0 - 37%   - do -   )

Besides reminding us of the artificiality of average scores,
though it must be granted that there is more sign of a 'clustering'
in some cases than I have suggested here, these facts about individual speakers are also relevant to the question posed at the start of
this section: which of the 106 informants have /h/ in their phonemic inventories, and which have not?   Where do we draw the line?

Rejecting the minimal pairs test, which showed that at least
102 of the total *can* make the distinction, because this is so untypical of the general situation, what criteria can we use?   Obviously the 5 who never once dropped [h] can be said to have the
phoneme.   Perhaps the 7 who never pronounced [h] in conversation
could be said *not* to have it - but all of them produced some examples in the more 'artificial' styles;   are these to be ignored?
And it may be noted that 23 informants used 100% [h] in these contexts (reading passage and word list);   surely it is reasonable to
conclude that they have /h/ at some 'level'.   But then, by this
argument, so do at least 102 of the 106.....

The variable (ʌ)

We shall be concerned here with the large set of lexical items
which in RP contain the phoneme /ʌ/.

Traditional dialect descriptions of our area are unanimous in
portraying a situation where this phoneme does not exist: the RP
contrast /ʌ/ - /ʊ/ as in *but*/*put* etc. is not found, both sets of
words having /ʊ/;   and this is in fact the major regional difference
in short vowel inventories in Britain - the Northern half of England
traditionally having one phoneme fewer than the South.   Historically

the North preserves the older situation, i.e. it is not the case that
/ʌ/ and /ʊ/ have merged in the North, but rather that /ʊ/ has split[79]
in the South.   The change has puzzled scholars of English[79], but it
seems that most Middle English /ʊ/ developed to [ʌ] in the South,
with [ʊ] being retained in a number of words e.g. *full, bull, pull,
put, butcher, push, woman, wolf*, possibly because of the preceding
labial; however, any allophonic pattern disappeared with the change
to [ʌ] in some labial environments, e.g. *but, bud, butter,pulse* etc.
Perhaps the complementary distribution became spoilt, and confusion
resulted, through the development of [ʊ] in a new set of words (mostly
without a preceding labial) spelled *oo* e.g. *good, foot, stood-* and
this development itself led to more 'confusions': *good* /ʊ/ - *blood*/ʌ/
-*food* / u:/[80] .

Whatever may have been the development in the South, the North
did not split /ʊ/, and the result is that in the region today /ʊ/
corresponds to both /ʊ/ and /ʌ/ in RP - but with two groups of possible exceptions: 1) *book, took, look*, etc. where in parts of the
North, including our area, /u:/ may correspond to RP /ʊ/ (see p.
below); 2) a number of words spelled with *o*, which in RP have /ʌ/,
but in the North may have /ɒ/: the commonest include *among, monger,
nothing, none, one* - again, in these words the North preserves the
more 'regular' situation historically: see Ekwall (1975:42)[81] .

Unlike h-dropping, the use of /ʌ/ in words where RP has /ʌ/ is
not a feature which, in my experience, is widely stigmatised in the

_____

79   See Strang (1970:112): 'one of the most unaccountable things
that has happened in the history of English'.

80   The historical development in these words may have been as
follows: ME [o:] > EModE [u:]; the latter generally underwent shortening to [ʊ], which in the case of *flood, blood, done, month, glove,
mother* etc. was in time to join the [ʊ > ʌ] change, but a) in some
words the long [u:] was retained e.g. *food, moon, shoot*, and b) in
others such as *good, foot, stood* the shortening came too late to join
the change to [ʌ]: see Ekwall (1975:11).   Alternatively it has been
suggested that in the first group ME [o:] was shortened to [o], which
then underwent the change to [ʌ] along with [ʊ] to which it was
similar in quality: see Gimson (1970:109).

81   Strang (1970:83) also notes that 'there has been a steady growth
of /ɒ/ replacing /ʌ/ in such words as *dromedary, bomb, bombast;*
compare the present divided usage in *combat, conduit, constable,
comrade, Lombardy, accomplish.*'   In all these, except the last, where
there is some /ɒ/ ~ (ʌ) variation, there is no 'divided usage' in our
area: /ɒ/ seems to be virtually universal.

schools[82].   However, it is something of which some people are aware:
see p. 254 below[83], and is a characteristic on which comedians and
others pick when imitating a 'stereotype' Northerner.   The result
of this seems to be that the RP/ʌ/ and /ʊ/ = Northern /ʊ/ situation
portrayed in traditional descriptions no longer applies universally:
some speakers have introduced [ʌ] into their speech.   It was because
I had become aware of this phenomenon in my pre-survey observations
that I decided to examine this as a variable.

        There are considerable problems, both theoretical and practical.
The theoretical ones concern the phonetics/phonemics distinction:
though /ʌ/-/ʊ/ as in RP is obviously a matter of phonemic contrast,
for the Northerner it seems to 'start' as one of phonetics.   A
person becomes aware that some 'better' speaker has different 'U's[84],
and so he imitates this in varying amounts, depending how aware of
the feature he is and how carefully he is speaking.   Eventually,
he may do so in every word where RP has /ʌ/, and then of course he
has added this phoneme to his inventory; but at what point in his
increasing use of [ʌ] can we say that this has occurred?   The
practical problems involve the decision as to what the investigator
believes he has heard: West Yorkshire /ʊ/ does not appear to me to
be as back and round as I have heard in some areas, and some speakers who on all the evidence are trying to produce an /ʌ/-/ʊ/ distinction do not make the latter as different phonetically from the
former as in other parts of Britain (and as in two of my informants
who would almost certainly be accepted as RP).   The result was that
I was sometimes in doubt as to whether I heard [ʌ] or [ʊ][85].   I am
not referring here to rapid unstressed forms of words such as *but*,
some, *just*, *us* etc. where the vowel is often reduced to [ə]; these
I simply ignored.   For other (ʌ) words I adopted the following
policy: if in my opinion an occurrence was definitely [ʊ], it

---

82   In my childhood at least, children learning to read were taught
to call the five vowel letters [a,ɛ,ɪ,ɒ,ʊ], whereas in the South they
are [a,ɛ,ɪ,ɒ,ʌ], with [ʊ] being reserved for *oo*.

83   Besides introducing discussion of the feature at some stage in
the interview, several informants giggled or hesitated over certain
items in the word lists.

84   Remarks to this effect were made by various informants.

85   With about half-a-dozen informants I find that I noted when listening to the tapes that I was in several instances unsure whether to
record [ʌ] or [ʊ]; some of these speakers were obviously 'ʌ-conscious',
and seemed to have modified their /ʊ/ as well as aiming for a distinct
/ʌ/.

scored 1, if definitely an attempt at [ʌ], it rated 0; if the quality was obscure (and this was so in only a fairly small minority of
cases), I noted it, but did not count it.   If I had rated it as say
½ , it would probably have given a distortedly high score in the
case of informants who normally had [ʌ] and may well have been aiming at this, and on the other hand it would have given the impression
of [ʌ]-usage among informants who in virtually every clear occurrence
had [ʊ][86].   Words such as *among*, *-monger*, *nothing*, *none*, *one* were
ignored if they had [ɒ], but scored accordingly if they had (ʌ).

     The quantitative results are expressed in terms of the percent-
age of [ʊ] in (ʌ) words.   Figure 4 shows the scores by class and
style, and the following table breaks these down by sex:

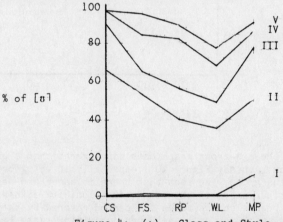

Figure 4: (ʌ) - Class and Style

	CS		FS		RP		WL		MP	
	M	W	M	W	M	W	M	W	M	W
I	0	–	1	–	0	–	0	–	11	–
II	78	50	66	32	55	24	46	22	63	36
III	97	83	76	57	84	37	69	37	88	71
IV	98	96	89	78	92	72	77	60	92	79
V	97	99	95	96	93	81	84	63	90	92

---

86   If I have erred, it is almost certainly on the side of being
over-generous with [ʌ], but since the informants involved were spread
across the sample the relative positions of the different groups are
probably little affected.

Figure 5 shows the total scores (i.e. CS, FS, RP, WL) by age-groups;
if we took only the conversational data, all figures would be app-
roximately 10% higher.   Figures for the towns do not appear to show
up any interesting differences, and are not given here.

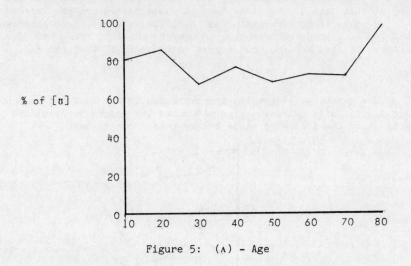

Figure 5:   (ʌ) - Age

Though the age-group graph does not suggest that a change is in
progress (contrast say Figure 10), especially if we ignore the class-
biased 80-plus group, the fact that there is a certain degree of [ʌ]-
usage in various parts of the sample must indicate either that there
has in fact been a change since the period covered by the traditional
descriptions, with not only the young 'acquiring' some [ʌ], or that
these works ignored the beginnings of this phenomenon.

Figure 4 shows that there must be some feeling either for the
prestige of [ʌ] or for the 'unculturedness' of [ʊ]: as is common in
such cases this affects the social classes 'in order', with the
highest class showing the highest use of the 'better' variant, and
also there is a relation with formality, all classes showing progressively more of these variants with increasing carefulness of speech.
There are two particular points of interest in this graph: first,
only Class I uses [ʌ] regularly; in all other classes [ʊ] variants
are commonest in conversation.   There is thus quite a difference
from the corresponding graph for (h), and presumably this is partly
due to the fact that there is with (h) more overt stigmatisation of
one variant.   But another factor could be that whereas with (h)
people are generally in no doubt, largely because of literacy, about
where /h/ 'should' occur, with (ʌ) it seems fairly arbitrary whether

one has /ʌ/ as in *but* or /ʊ/ as in *put*[87].   And this arbitrariness
may help to explain the second interesting feature of Figure 4: that
whereas with (h) almost all informants could make the distinction in
a minimal pairs context, and scores dived towards the bottom of the
graph, with (ʌ) all classes showed a considerably higher proportion
of [ʊ] in (ʌ)-words in the minimal pairs than in the word list and
the reading passage.   Which words will have /ʌ/ is unpredictable,and
one simply has to learn them individually (contrast the other major
Northern feature - /æ/ corresponding to Southern /ɑ:/ in *grass*, *path*,
laugh, etc., where there is some 'regularity' in terms of the phonological environment); and the pairs I chose to use probably illustrate the confusion in many people's minds.   These were a) *put/putt*
- very many informants (including the most 'Yorkshire' member of
Class I) were foxed; there is no clue in the spelling of course, and
most people pronounced both with [ʊ] - though a few, feeling that
there ought to be a difference, had [ʌ] or [ə] in *put*! b) *luck/look*
- here a frequent response was to seize on the obvious difference in
spelling and pronounce the latter with the obsolescent form [lu:k],
leaving the first as [lʊk]; c) *should/blood* - this was not strictly
a minimal pair, of course, but it was the most likely to produce a
'correct' response.   In the less artificial situations informants
behaved more naturally, and produced a higher percentage of [ʌ]
variants.

Another result of the unpredictability of the incidence of /ʌ/
and /ʊ/, and also probably of the prestige/stigma attaching to the
variants, is the phenomenon of hypercorrection.   I noticed only 59
definite instances in my data, but some interesting points emerge.
First, there are clear signs that hypercorrection is more likely in
careful styles: only one instance was recorded in casual style, 12
in formal, 25 in the reading passage, and 21 in the word list (the
reading passage contained more instances of (ʌ) than the word list,
which may explain the higher score).   Second, a slightly higher
proportion of women than men showed hypercorrections.   Third, and
less expected, almost all hypercorrections came from the older half
of the population, as the following table shows:

	10	20	30	40	50	60	70	80
No.of informants	1	1	2	1	7	6	3	0

Fourth, there is a clear relation to social class: Figure 6

---

87 Two informants, both intelligent professional people in Class II,
expressed surprise when they noticed that in Word List I they pronounced *put* and *but* with different vowels.

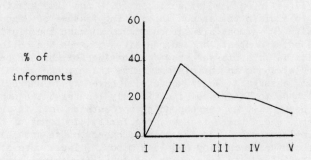

Figure 6: (ʌ) Hypercorrecters - by class

showing the proportions of informants making some hypercorrections,
indicates that this is commoner in those classes where there is more
effort to use [ʌ] variants (Class I showed no hypercorrection, but
there was less 'effort' involved there); the position with (h) was
that hypercorrection occurred at the lower end of the scale - where
again however, it could be a matter of more 'effort' being involved
in the use of [h].   Finally, hypercorrection appears to occur more
commonly a) in certain words: the majority of instances in my interview material, especially in the word list, concerned the word
butcher (the fact that in the word list the preceding word was *butter*
may have contributed to this); the next commonest hypercorrections
were of *pull* and *push*;   b) where /ʌ/ occurs inclose proximity to /ʊ/:
for example, one man said [lʌk/ʌp] - and I have often stumbled over
good luck.

     The table referring to differences in respect of (ʌ) between
the sexes tends to confirm that prestige/stigma is involved here: in
such cases women tend to use more 'better' variants, and this appears
to be the case especially in Classes I and III[88] ; in the more careful styles even women of Classes IV and V show more [ʌ] than men of
the same group.

---

88   The fact that the figure for Class III men in FS is unexpectedly
low compared to that in RP is largely due to there being one 'status-
incongruent' informant with whom I had a very long interview, during
which most of his speech was 'formal' according to our criteria; he
thus had a marked effect on the average in FS, whereas in the RP he
would have less impact on the score because he had no more to say than
anybody else.   This could be held to be a defect of my method, and
taking say the first 25 examples of a variable from each informant
(see Wolfram, 1969:135 etc.) might produce more valid results.   Labov
(1966a:248) discusses the fact that the odd 'deviant' individual could
disturb an otherwise regular structure.

To return to the age-graph: ignoring the 80-plus group (as we must, since class appears to be an important factor with (ʌ), and all three informants of this age were Class V), we see that the highest scores are among informants in their teens and twenties: perhaps the explanation is that the younger age-groups are most 'regional' in their pronunciation because they have had less contact with and aware-ness of the wider English-speaking world; later, there is some ten-dency to pick up [ʌ].

What conclusions can be drawn?   The West Yorkshire vowel system has, with increasing facility of communication and the greater in-fluence of the mass media come into more extensive contact this cen-tury with Southern dialects, and especially with the prestigious RP, which several centuries ago split /ʊ/ into /ʌ/ and /ʊ/; due to the influence of these dialects and/or a feeling of inferiority about their own speech, some speakers have tried to acquire the 'foreign' vowel.   The degree to which this occurs varies with social class, style, and sex in the way commonly found when prestige or stigma attaches to some variant.   But because the conditioning factors of the split are no longer evident, there is a degree of unpredictabil-ity about which words should have /ʌ/ or /ʊ/; this probably results in greater hesitation about attempting to use [ʌ], and so a smaller amount of [ʌ] than say [h]; a greater amount of hypercorrection; and perhaps a less ready stigmatising of [ʊ], which of course in turn reinforces the slowness in acquiring /ʌ/.   My results suggest either that this process has been taking place for many years, and con-sequently the traditional descriptions are over-simplified, or that speakers of all ages have attempted to acquire [ʌ] (and figures for hypercorrection could be interpreted as indicating that the older have made less sense of the 'pattern', such as it is, which they have only recently had more contact with through broadcasting etc). How far we can say that there is a phoneme /ʌ/ in this area is a problem we have already encountered with (h), and to which, in a situation where again individuals form a continuum in the degree to which they use [ʌ], there is again no easy answer.

As a postscript to this discussion of the (ʌ) variable, let us briefly examine a related phenomenon: variation between (ʌ) and /ɒ/.

It was noted above that in certain words, of which the common-est are *among*, *-monger*, *nothing*, *none*, *one*, either /ɒ/ or /ʌ~ʊ/ may be heard in this area.   From less systematic investigation and dis-cussion I had reached two interesting conclusions about these words. First, though the form with /ɒ/ is non-standard, it does not carry such stigma as may attach to /ʊ/ in (ʌ) words - and so it is quite

common for speakers who could quite definitely be described as having added /ʌ/ to their inventory to continue to use /ɒ/ in these
items[89].   Second, there are geographical differences over which of
these words have /ɒ/ and which are (ʌ): to a colleague, *among* and
nothing are (ʌ), whereas *none* and *one* are /ɒ/; for me, *among* and
none are /ɒ/, *one* is (ʌ), while *nothing* can be either; for many
people, all these words are /ɒ/; and so on.

Keeping a record of occurrences of three of the words in question while listening to my tapes enabled me to find some confirmation
of both these points.   *One* shows an interesting geographical pattern
in the area: in Huddersfield 94% of speakers said [wɒn], in Halifax
89%, but in Bradford only 35% (there were a number here who varied
between [wʊn] and [wɒn], but the majority were consistent); it would
appear that an isogloss crosses the area, with Huddersfield and Halifax definitely on the [wɒn] side, and Bradford more or less astride
it - some speakers, like myself, acquiring [wʊn], others [wɒn].
Among and *nothing* occurred in the reading passage and word list;
figures suggest that [nɒθɪŋ] is almost the universal pronunciation in
the area, but beyond this the numbers involved are too small to draw
firm conclusions, though there are signs of a tendency towards a situation similar to that which exists with *among* : here it would seem
that [əmɒŋ] is the commonest form,[əmʌŋ] has 'better' connotations,
and - perhaps surprisingly, since [əmɒŋ] too is non-RP - [əmʊŋ] worse
(though it is true that it was much more frequent in the WL than in
the RP).   The numbers of informants using (ʌ) rather than/ɒ/ in
among and *nothing* were:

	RP		WL		RP		WL	
	əmʌŋ	əmʊŋ	əmʌŋ	əmʊŋ	nʌθɪŋ	nʊθɪŋ	nʌθɪŋ	nʊθɪŋ
I	2		3		1		2	
II	1							1
III		1	2	6	1	1	3	
IV	1	1		6				
V		2		6				2

The Variable (ɛɪ/e:)

All the traditional dialect descriptions of our area are agreed
that there is a distinction between /ɛɪ/, occurring in a lexical set
which usually includes *eight*, *weigh(t)*, *straight*, *right*, *fight*,
speak, *steal*, *eat*, *meat*, *teach*, etc and /e:/ which occurs in *bake*,
cake, *place*, *rain*, *day*, *clay*, *neighbour*, *master*, *rather* etc.   Various
minimal pairs can be found in the dialects, including *weight/wait*,
rein/rain , *speak/spoke*, *steal/stole* (see SED etc.).

Such a phonemic distinction was in fact to be found generally
in English some centuries ago, when pairs like *ail/ale* were differentiated;   but in RP/ɛɪ/ and /e:/ have merged in /eɪ/, and pairs such
as this have become homophonous (as they are in fact in West Yorkshire dialects, where the lexical incidence of these phonemes is now
somewhat different).

From the above it is clear that West Yorkshire dialects differ
from RP in this 'phonetic area' not only in inventory, but also in
incidence and realisation.   The influence of another dialect may
affect all of these, though not necessarily simultaneously: people
may become aware that they have a different sound in *teach* (i.e. they
have different incidence);   or that their '/eɪ/' sounds different
(i.e. their realisation is different);   perhaps they may become aware
that they differentiate RP homophones (i.e. they have a different
inventory) - and they may modify their speech for any of these reasons.

In order to investigate in detail this area of difference between the West Yorkshire and RP systems, records were kept of every
item which occurred with [ɛɪ], [e·ɪ] or [eɪ], and the following words
were deliberately incorporated in the reading passage and word list:

from the traditional /ɛɪ/ set - *eight, straight, fight, right, eat,*
                                  steal, speak

from the traditional /e:/ set - *case , late, made, name, nail,*
                                  neighbour , spade, day, may, way

from traditional /ɛɪ/ or /e:/,
      depending on area   - *break , drain*

words with other phonemes
      in dialect but /eɪ/ in RP - *again , make, take*

In this section we are primarily concerned with inventory;   details of 'unusual' incidence are given in section 2 of this chapter,
and the realisation of (eɪ) will also be discussed separately (see
p. 161 below);   but since the three factors cannot be kept entirely
separate some reference must inevitably be made here to incidence and
realisation insofar as these are relevant to the matter of inventory.

Briefly, the position as regards incidence was found to be that /ɛɪ/ and /e:/ are common nowadays only in those words where RP has /eɪ/.   Thus /ɛɪ/ occurs only in *eight, straight, weight* and one or two more (including in part of the area, *drain* and *break.*   These two items tend to confirm that it is the correspondence to RP that is important rather than the phonemic environment: thus *gh* indicates a historical palatal or velar fricative - and in *eight, straight, weight* etc. /ɛɪ/ is usual throughout the area; but the fact that *right* and *fight*, which have this historical environment, do not now usually have /ɛɪ/ also argues against this being the most important factor[90]).   Other words in the traditional /ɛɪ/ set now usually have the RP phoneme: thus *eat, speak, teach* etc. have /i:/, *fight, right* have /aɪ/, and so on.   The same applies to /e:/: very many words in the traditional set correspond to ones with /eɪ/ in RP, and so these 'survive'; but *stole, rather master spoke* etc. have now been 'transferred' to the same phoneme as in RP, and *make, tale, again* etc., which in traditional dialect have other phonemes, have been brought into the /e:/ set to correspond to RP /eɪ/.   The result of these incidence changes is that the 'load' of /e:/ has remained much the same overall: it has lost some items and gained others; but that of /ɛɪ/ has been considerably reduced, and it only survives throughout the area in a small set of items including *eight, weight(s), straight, Speight* etc.   Besides these [ɛɪ] was observed on odd occasions:

a)   in one or two 'dialectal' occurrences of *teach, eat, fight, right*

b)   in a number of words which in the great majority of occurrences had [e:]: in some, probably the odd [ɛɪ] form resulted from some confusion or mistake: *labour, explain, gate, late, brake, occasion, Wakefield, same*; some monosyllables in *ay* had some instances of [ɛɪ] e.g. *say, day, play, pay* etc. in prevocalic position, whether before *-ing* or word-finally.

c)   in a few words where there appears to be an ɛɪ/e: isogloss cross-ing our area.   Let us briefly examine my findings in these cases:

(i)   with the nominal termination *-ation* and the associated verbal *-ate*, the percentages of informants producing [ɛɪ] or [e:] forms were as follows:

	Bfd	Hfx	Hudd
[ɛɪ] only	12.5	-	4
both	20	5	
[e:] only	67.5	95	96

(these figures only include informants pronouncing the words in question with [ɛɪ] or [e:]; a few using only [eɪ] are excluded)

90   Note that *neighbour*, though it has the *gh* spelling, does not belong to the /ɛɪ/ set in traditional dialect, presumably because of

Bradford appears to stand on the isogloss, with Huddersfield and Halifax to the South of it.

ii) Only in Huddersfield do *break* and *drain* belong to the /ɛɪ/ set, according to traditional sources. This I confirmed; neither word turned up in conversation, but in the reading passage and word list they were pronounced with [ɛɪ] by some Huddersfield informants; but the following percentage figures for this make it clear that /ɛɪ/ is by no means universal in the town now, and suggest that it decreased somewhat with increased formality:

	break	drain
RP	58	22
WL	52	14

It appears then that /ɛɪ/ is now for most urban speakers very restricted in incidence, and so is likely to be in a precarious position as far as its phonemic status is concerned.

But besides incidence, contact with RP and other dialects may also affect realisation: informants may become aware that [strɛɪt] or [geːt] sound 'Yorkshire' compared to [streɪt], [geɪt] etc., and so they modify their pronunciation. Obviously a merger of /ɛɪ/ and /eː/ as [eɪ] then becomes likely, and this has occurred completely with some speakers; others produce some instances of narrow diphthongal [eɪ] alongside others of [ɛɪ] or [eː], the amounts varying in different sections of the population and in different styles. In this situation it is difficult to say how far the /ɛɪ/-/eː/ distinction is preserved, but a few interesting facts may be noted:

a) quite a number of speakers who have diphthongised their /eː/ to [eɪ] quite extensively still seem to retain, on some occasions at least, a wider diphthong in /ɛɪ/ words: thus they may say [weɪt] *wait* but [wɛɪt] *weight*.

b) On the other hand, there are odd bits of evidence that [ɛɪ] seems more regionally 'marked' to some speakers than [eː]: thus 1) the figures for *break* and *drain* above reflect the fact that in the more careful word list style some speakers 'transferred' these words from [ɛɪ] to [eː] (besides of course some who narrowed [ɛɪ] to [eɪ]); 2) we noted that changes from 'dialectal'

___

a different historical vowel: see Kolb (1966:165) etc; in my data it belonged, as in dialect, to the /eː/ set.

incidence in words like *again*, *take*, *make* etc. brought them to
th e /e:/ class, i.e. they were pronounced with [e:] or [eɪ],
never [ɛɪ]; 3) data below on the word *straight* reflects a
similar increase in [e:] with increased formality to that with
drain and *break* in Huddersfield; 4) one informant wavered between [strɛɪt] and [stre:t] with this word, and seemed to say
that he felt the latter to be more 'correct'; 5) the use of
[ɛɪ] in *-ate/-ation* noted above was recorded mainly with speakers
of Classes IV and V.   It must be admitted however that not all
this evidence is weighty, and some of it could simply be a reflection of the fact that /e:/ is the 'stronger' phoneme now,
rather than that [ɛɪ] is more 'regional' than [e:].

Let us turn to the minimal pairs test, though we have noted
above that its evidence has to be used with caution.   By the stage
informants were presented with the pairs for (ɛɪ/e:) they were probably used to finding that some words spelled differently did not
sound differently.   I offered them *ate/eight* and also the non-
minimal *late/straight*[91].   The first pair was always distinguished
as [e:t]/[ɛɪt][92], except by a very small number who pronounced both
as RP [eɪt]; but with the second, perhaps partly because a contrast
already existed in the initial consonant, quite a few speakers pronounced both with [e:].   Whether the /ɛɪ/-/e:/ distinction is made
in the minimal pairs test seems to show some relation to social
class: Fig. 7 (opposite) shows that the middle classes are more
likely to produce mergers than are Classes III-V.   It should be
noted that the impression of a similar amount of merger in Classes
III and IV is deceptive: in Class III there were somewhat more
mergings in the RP-like [eɪ] than in Class IV, where [e:] was almost
always the merger form.   As regards sex, there was no constant
picture from class to class, but overall 77% of men preserved a distinction compared to 64% of women.   With age, there was no clear
picture.   Among the towns, the overall figure of 87% in Huddersfield
is markedly higher than in the other two, both in the 60-65% range.

It is very difficult, as we have seen, to say how far inventory
as opposed to realisation varies with style, because informants may

---

91   I decided this would be better than *strait/straight*, since the
first word might not have been familiar to some. For some unaccountable reason the pair *wait/weight* did not occur to me when I was
designing the questionnaire.

92   The usual past tense form of *eat* in the area today is /e:t/,
rather than /et/ as in RP; incidentally, traditional dialect also
has /et/ for *ate* - while *eat* is /ɛɪt/.

produce forms with [ɛɪ], [e:], [e·ɪ], and [eɪ] in any style.   But
looking for a moment at the commonest /ɛɪ/ words (*eight, weight,
straight*), and ignoring indeterminate pronunciations like [e·ɪ] and
[eɪ], I found no instances of *eight* or *weigh(t)* being pronounced
with [e:], i.e. merging with /e:/; but *straight* did show some variation with style in Bradford: Figure 8 s h o w s the percentage
occurrences of *straight* in that town with [e:];   and all towns
showed some increase between word list and minimal pairs of [e:] in
this word, as is seen from the following percentages of [e:] pronunciation:

	Bfd	Hfx	Hudd
WL	17	4	3
MP	27	16	6

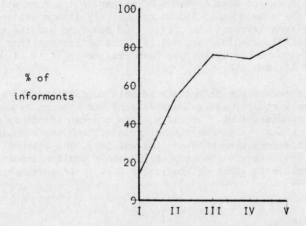

Figure 7:   /ɛɪ/-/e:/ distinct in MP-by Class

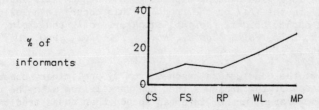

Figure 8:   [e:] in *straight* in Bradford - by style

This is then a small amount of evidence, provided by only one particular word, that /ɛɪ/ decreases with increased formality in favour of
/e:/ - either because the latter seems less 'regional', or because
as the commoner phoneme it is more likely to be the merger form as
the dialect distinction disappears.

    What conclusions are we to draw from this rather confused pic-
ture?   It would seem that the influence of other systems, especially
RP, had its first and most widespread effect on the incidence of
/ɛɪ/ and /e:/:   virtually all cases of these phonemes occurring
where RP does not have /eɪ/ have now disappeared.   The result of
this has been a weakening of the /ɛɪ/-/e:/ distinction: the former
has now lost much of its lexical load, and few contrasts remain.
This in turn seems to have produced some confusion over the incidence of /ɛɪ/ and /e:/, with odd examples of /e:/ words occurring
with [ɛɪ], and also some evidence of merger in the more widespread
/e:/ (and there is a small amount of not very strong evidence that
[e:] seems less 'marked' than [ɛɪ]).   RP has also had its effect
on realisation: when/e:/ becomes [eɪ] the difference from [ɛɪ] is
slight, if indeed the latter has been retained;   if it is narrowed,
the merger is complete.

    Some speakers can definitely be said to distinguish /ɛɪ/ and
/e:/;   they virtually always keep sets of words apart by using [ɛɪ]
and [e:] pronunciations.   Equally, some others definitely have
only /eɪ/, using the narrow diphthong in all the words in question.
But other speakers vary between [ɛɪ] and [eɪ], and between [e:],
[e·ɪ] and [eɪ] even in the same style, and I would maintain that it
is not possible to state categorically what their inventory is.

The Variable (ɔʊ/o:)

    Descriptions of traditional dialect in our area make it clear
that there is a wide closing diphthong on the back axis /ɔʊ/,
'parallel' to the /ɛɪ/ on the front.   This occurs in a lexical set
including *ought, bought, thought, daughter, roll, soul, old, cold,
gold, sold, colt, folk, blow(N), bowl, flow, glow, grow, owt, coke,
no* etc. etc.

    One of the conclusions reached from my preliminary observations
of the speech of the area was that the parallelism with the front
axis has developed further in urban speech than these traditional
descriptions imply: there is now a long monophthong in a mid-back
position, which we shall symbolise /o:/, matching the long mid-
front /e:/.   (Also as in the case of /ɛɪ/-/e:/, there is some

evidence in favour of there having been a /ɔʊ/-/o:/ distinction in
English elsewhere at an earlier date - though with a different
incidence[93].)

    In order to investigate the situation in detail, records were
kept of every item pronounced with [ɔʊ], [o:], [o·ᵁ], [oʊ], [əʊ] -
and also of any other pronunciation of items usually pronounced with
any of these.   The following relevant items were included in the
reading passage and word list: *borrow, both, broken, cloak, closed,
clothes, coal, coat, cold, daughter, don't, fellow, folk, go, grow,
hole, hold, know, no, old, open, ought, own, road, shallow, shoulder,
show, snow, so, window, won't, yellow.*

    My findings regarding the incidence of /ɔʊ/ and /o:/ were that
for the majority of instances the lexical sets were as follows:

/ɔʊ/ occurs in two main groups of words, identifiable to a large
extent by their spelling:

1   those with *ol* or *oul*: in my data this category included *Bolton,
    cold, Colne, control, fold, folk, Golcar* [gɔʊkə], *gold, hold,
    Holme, mould, Moldgreen, Newbould, old, Oldham, patrol, roll,
    Rolls, sold, soldier, soul, shoulder, stroll, told, upholster,
    Volkswagen, whole*.   The majority of these would also have /ɔʊ/
    in traditional dialect (*whole* is one exception - and it was cer-
    tainly not always pronounced with [ɔʊ] in my data: it was comm-
    only, like *hole*, pronounced with [o:].)

2   those with *ow*: this included *blow, bow, bowl, Bowling, below,
    crow, flow, glow, know, Knowles, low, owe, own, tow, sew, show,
    slow, snow, throw, nowt, owt* (the last two being local words for
    'nothing' and 'anything'); but not those words with *-ow* in un-
    stressed positions: *window, fellow* etc.   Some of these e.g.
    blow, bowl, flow, glow, etc. also have /ɔʊ/ in traditional dia-
    lect; but some have /ɔ:/ e.g. *blow(V), crow, know, mow, own,
    slow, snow, sow, throw* etc, and *show* has /ɛʊ/.

/o:/ occurs in a very large set of words with various 'sources' in
traditional dialect:

_____

93   Strang (1970:168) believes such a contrast may have arisen for
some speakers in the late 16th Century through their having a diphthongal pronunciation in such words as *hold* and *bold*; see p.177:
'both /l/ and /x/ tended to produce dipthongisation of ... /ɒ/ in
late ME'.   (Note the /ɔʊ/ before historical velar fricative in
bought, daughter, etc. in the traditional dialects in our area.)

1 *both, clothes, cloak, go, goat, hope, no, load, road, so, whole,*
  etc. etc. - which are usually recorded with/ʊə/ in dialect. This
  group forms the majority of /o:/ words; the variants I recorded
  in these words suggest that there might have occurred a succession
  of phonetic changes: [ʊə > oə > o: (> o·ᵘ > oʊ > əʊ)].

2 *coat, closed, coal, hole* etc. - with/ɔɪ/ in dialect.

3 *broken, open, over,* etc. - with /ɒ/ in dialect.

4 *borrow, fellow, window, yellow* etc. - with /ə/ in dialect.

5 *won't* - which is [wɪənt] in dialect, and other miscellaneous items
  e.g. *spoke,* for which the dialect form is [speːk].

     At first sight it might seem obvious to conclude that /o:/ has
arisen through some sort of 'structural pressures' within the system,
and the result is a greater symmetry in the vowel system, with /ɔʊ/-
/o:/ on the back axis parallel to /ɛɪ/-/e:/ on the front.   But there
is evidence that at least partly responsible has been the influence
of RP/əʊ/.   The following details are relevant.   First, while /ɔʊ/
has gained some items - e.g. *know, own, slow* etc from /ɔ:/ - it has
also lost some: *bought, daughter, ought* etc. now have /ɔ:/.   Both
these changes bring the items in question closer to RP: the latter
group also have /ɔ:/ in RP, and the former now have a vowel somewhat
closer phonetically to RP/əʊ/.   Second, all the groups of words
with/o:/ described above now have a vowel phonetically nearer to RP
than they had in dialect; and more important, they all represent
just a subset of those items which had a certain dialect vowel: for
example, besides the above words which have given urban/o:/, dialect
/ʊə/ also included *door, floor, before, more, sort* etc. which give
/ɔə/~/ɔ:/ today (see below) and *poor, moor* etc. which usually retain
/ʊə/; similarly, dialect /ɔɪ/ also included *boil, voice* etc where
/ɔɪ/ remains today, and *loss, lane* etc which have undergone other
changes.   What can account for this 'breaking away' of some items
to produce /o:/ except the incidence of /əʊ/ in RP?

     Viereck (1968:79), referring to a point first made by Orton,
states 'Before traditional sounds are lost, the distribution (i.e.
incidence) of dialect sounds may beome confused in certain cases
under the influence of RP.   If two vowels, for example, are kept
distinct in the dialect but not in RP, the dialect speaker may use
these two vowel sounds indiscriminately.   Some "erratic" uses may
well be accounted for in this way'.   We noted above some such
'erratic uses' in the case of /ɛɪ/-/e:/, where [ɛɪ] is occasionally

heard in words which generally seem to belong to the /e:/ set,
and also some /ɛɪ/ words occur with [e:].   A very similar situation
was observed with /ɔʊ/ - /o:/: we have given above the words which on
account of their occurrences in my data seem to belong to /ɔʊ/ or to
/o:/, but numerous instances were found where this pattern of incidence was not followed.   [ɔʊ] was observed in odd occurrences of *ago,
although, bloke, both, broken, clothes, coal, coat, close,
comb, don't, float, go, Grosvenor, hello, home, load, local, motor,
Negro, notice, Oakes, only, open, over, Polish, road, rope, smoke,
so, social, though, won't;* none of these are /ɔʊ/ words in traditional dialect, and they are much more frequently heard with [o:] (as
also are *no* and *coke*, which also occurred with [ɔʊ] - but this is
not so unexpected since they do belong to the /ɔʊ/ set in dialect.

Just as we found with (ɛɪ/e:) that [ɛɪ] occurs 'erratically' in
some /e:/ words but that the opposite situation, of the 'stronger'
/e:/ tending to take over some /ɛɪ/ words, seems more common, something similar appears to be happening with (ɔʊ/o:). We have just
noted a fair number of /o:/ words where odd [ɔʊ] pronunciations were
heard. But the opposite situation, i.e. words with *ol* or *ow*
spellings (where [ɔʊ] is most usual) being pronounced with [o:] is
considerably more common, and we shall examine this statistically
here. It should be noted that

a) only pronunciations with [o:] and [ɔʊ] are considered here:
    other variants such as [o·ʊ], [oʊ], [əʊ] are ignored - we are
    examining the incidence of the most 'regional' forms only.

b) the two main groups of /ɔʊ/ words are in some cases examined sep-
    arately, i.e. those with *ol* and those with *ow* in their spellings.

c) findings are expressed in terms of the percentage of [ɔʊ] pro-
    nunciations, i.e. the degree to which the 'expected' incidence,
    that commonest in conversational styles, is maintained.

Figures for the social classes presented a quite irregular picture, and will not be given here; the different age-groups also
appeared to show no clear pattern. But the following table, which
distinguishes between style, town, and subgroup of /ɔʊ/ words, is
worth noting:

	CS		FS		RP		WL	
	ol	ow	ol	ow	ol	ow	ol	ow
Bfd	94	65	87	80	82	53	80	61
Hfx	75	40	76	46	37	13	45	42
Hudd	60	40	40	37	34	22	45	12

128   DIALECT & ACCENT IN INDUSTRIAL WEST YORKSHIRE

It seems to emerge that 'subgroup' may be a significant factor
in whether [ɔʊ] or [oː] is used in certain words.   In the *ol* group,
nearly all of which have /ɔʊ/ in traditional dialect, [ɔʊ] is more
likely to occur than in the *ow* group; this latter contains some
items with /ɔʊ/ in traditional dialect, but also some with /ɔː/.
This fact may seem to offer an explanation - traditional/ɔː/ words
give [oː], and traditional /ɔʊ/ give [ɔʊ]?   However, this is certainly not entirely the case: *know*, for instance, from the traditional /ɔː/ group, was heard with [ɔʊ] on numerous occasions, as
well as with [oː] quite frequently, [ɔ:] occasionally - and of
course with other forms modified in the direction of RP.   Often
[ɔʊ] and [oː] pronunciations were heard from the same speakers[94].
Differences between the towns may also be significant.   My '/ɔʊ/
and /oː/ groups' were set up on the basis of the total incidence in
conversational data - but in fact, only in the Bradford sample was
[ɔʊ] the majority pronunciation in both groups of /ɔʊ/ words; in
Halifax, and even more so in Huddersfield, there is a marked tendency for [oː] to occur in both /ɔʊ/ groups, and particularly in
those spelled with *ow* .   Style may also be important: particularly
in Halifax and Huddersfield there are signs of a tendency for [oː]
to occur in /ɔʊ/ words more frequently in the more careful styles
than in general conversation, which suggests that some speakers may
feel [oː] to be less regionally 'marked' than [ɔʊ]; (we may recall
a similar suggestion in respect of [eː]).

As an aside at this point we may briefly examine one member of
each subgroup of /ɔʊ/ words which my records show to have had a much
stronger tendency than the average to be pronounced with [oː] rather
than [ɔʊ]:

---

94 Various other examples could be quoted of informants varying
between [ɔʊ] and [oː] pronunciations of the same word.
  a) In conversational data, three elderly Huddersfield informants
     actually varied within one sentence: "I used to do a lot of bowl-
     ing [ɔʊ] ...you know, crown green bowling [oː]".
     "...roll 'em [oː], like...you know, roll 'em [ɔʊ]".
     "You get it up in t'Colne Valley [ɔʊ]...Yes, up in t'Colne
     Valley [oː]".
  b) In the reading passage, several informants varied between [ɔʊld]
     and [oːld] in the two instances of *old*, and one or two between
     [fɔʊk] and [foːk] with *folk*.
  c) In the word list, where *snow* and *show* appeared consecutively,
     three informants had [snoː], [ʃɔʊ] (which could possibly fit with
     the historical explanation - traditional dialect being [snoː], [ʃɛʊ]),
     but two had [snɔʊ], [ʃoː] .   Other variations among neighbouring
     words in the list included [koʊt,kəʊld,kloʊðz,koːl], [kɔʊt,kɔʊld,
     kloʊðz,koːl], [ɔʊld,oʊpn,oːn] etc.

- with the *ol* group, *folk* was the exceptional case: the total
  percentage of [ɔʊ] as opposed to [o:] pronunciations by style
  is as follows (CS and FS are totalled, since occurrences of
  folk were not numerous - nor is any other breakdown possible
  for this reason):

	CS	FS	RP	WL
ol words	79	75	56 .	61
folk		75	46	5

- Of the *ow* group, *know* is the odd one - and also by far the commonest, since it occurs so frequently in phrases like 'I don't
  know' and 'you know': figures for [ɔʊ] pronunciation by town
  and style are:

	CS		FS		RP		WL	
	ow	know	ow	know	ow	know	ow	know
Bfd	65	52	80	48	53	63	61	62
Hfx	40	30	46	38	13	17	42	8
Hudd	40	30	37	23	22	27	12	0

Folk shows more than half [o:] forms in the reading passage,
and almost all such in the word list; the figure for conversation
is more 'average' but may not be reliable because examples were
few.   With *know* the picture is complicated but it seems that in
conversation, possibly because of weak forms in 'you know', 'I don't
know whether...', [o:] is more common in this word than in other *ow*
items; but while in the other towns [ɔʊ] pronunciations decrease
to some extent in more careful styles, in Bradford, where [ɔʊ] is
generally commoner in *ow* words, *know* is more likely to be brought
into the /ɔʊ/ group in these styles.

Historical considerations may be relevant in the case of *folk*;
some traditional dialect works (for example, *English Dialect Grammar*)
give [fʊək] alongside [fɔʊk] in this area, so [fo:k] would not be
surprising - while with *know* some explanation may lie in its possible
homophony with *no*.   The latter is given in traditional sources as
[nɔʊ], [nʊə] and [nɔ:] (see Easther, Wright, SED etc.), so both [o:]
and [ɔʊ] forms might be expected.   Unfortunately, neither the traditional accounts nor this study have adequately distinguished the
different uses of *no*: for example, 'No!', 'it's no good' etc. - and
this might have been relevant to which form was most likely.   It
seems that [no:] is by far the commonest overall, and this form may

have 'attracted' that of *know*, with which it is homophonous in RP
and many other dialects.   The percentages of [ɔʊ] pronunciations in
conversational styles were:

	Bfd	Hfx	Hudd
know	50	35	26
no	18	14	10

It is interesting that although *know* was historically not diphthongal
and is so today less frequently than other words spelled with *-ow*,
it is nevertheless more often pronounced with [ɔʊ] than is *no*, for
which there was a historical [ɔʊ] form.

    The discussion up to this point has been concerned with incid-
ence.   It seems to emerge that while most groups of speakers in
our area have both/ɔʊ/ and /o:/, the incidence pattern of these two
phonemes is rather confused, as a result of both historical factors
and the influence of RP.   RP, it seems, is probably responsible for
the facts that the total incidence of /ɔʊ/ plus /o:/ is equivalent
to that of RP/əʊ/;   and that because the two are not distinguished
by speakers of RP or RP-like dialects, the incidence difference between the two is becoming less clear.   There are also indications
that /o:/ is 'gaining ground' over /ɔʊ/ (just as /e:/ seemed to be
over /ɛɪ/).

    But of course we cannot exclude the question of realisation –
as we have artificially done up to this point by concentrating
on the [ɔʊ] and [o:] pronunciations, even though they form the majority in my data.   Realisation as well as incidence is very relevant to inventory: a speaker may become aware that he has a
different sound from RP in *daughter* or *hope* and so make incidence
changes such as /ɔʊ/>/ɔ:/ or /ʊə/>/o:/ respectively, or he may
become aware that his 'o' in [bo:t] "sounds different" from RP [bəʊt],
and so modify his realisation to [o·ᵘ], [oʊ], or [əʊ].   Similarly
he may narrow his diphthongal pronunciation of say *told* from [tɔʊld]
to [toʊld] or even [təʊld].   The possible effect of such realisation changes is obvious: there may be a merger of /ɔʊ/ and/o:/
in [oʊ] or [əʊ].

    Details of the realisation of (əʊ) will be discussed below
(see p. 161).   Here we shall only consider how many informants
made a realisation distinction between /ɔʊ/ and /o:/ words in the
artificial minimal pairs situation.   It should be noted that the
usefulness of this measure is even less than usual in this case,
since we have seen that /ɔʊ/ 'survives' more strongly in *ol* words –

but here no minimal pairs are possible: we are reduced to working
with *ow* -/o:/ contrasts.   There are a few minimal pairs of this
type e.g. *knows/nose* (for some), *rowed/road*, *grown/groan*, *nowt/note*;
unfortunately only the last occurred to me when devising the questionnaire, so I used this and the near-minimal *grow/go*.   But because
nowt is a dialect or 'slang' word, few informants used it naturally
(some laughed, or said they did not say this, or used the form [naʊt]
which also occurs in the North, and so on), and this data cannot be
relied on. With *grow/go* (as with *late/straight* above), possibly
because it was not truly minimal, an unexpectedly small proportion
of informants distinguished the vowels: Figure 9 shows the distribution by social class:

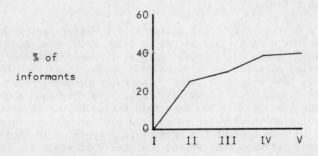

Figure 9: (ɔʊ/o:)- *grow/go* distinguished

No Class I informants made a distinction; 25% did so in Class II,
and there was then a shallow 'rise' towards the lower end of the
social scale. But what is not shown here is the realisation of
the merger forms - which higher on the scale tended to be [oʊ], and
towards the lower end [o:].   There was little difference between
the sexes in whether the vowel segments were distinguished, but not
surprisingly in view of our earlier findings, Bradford informants
(47%) were more likely than those in Halifax (21%) or Huddersfield
(27%) to make the distinction.

My conclusions are that a combination of internal and external
pressures - in other words, structural pressures for symmetry within
the vowel system, and pressures to sound less different from other
dialects ([o:] is found in traditional dialects not far away) and
also of course from RP - have given rise to a new phonemic contrast
within our area.   But continued pressure from outside is affecting
both the incidence and the realisation of these phonemes, and seems

to be making the distinction unstable.   Some of the population, particularly in Halifax and Huddersfield, appear to be strengthening the
position of /o:/ at the expense of /ɔʊ/ (though there is no evidence
from the age-groups that there is any steady movement towards a merger
in /o:/);   the result of this could be that [ɔʊ] will give way to [o:]
entirely, or that it will survive only as an allophone in the environments of following /l/.   Other sections of the population, by
modifying the realisation of both phonemes, are tending to merge
them in [oʊ] or [əʊ].   The question of 'who has what system?', when
some speakers produce forms with [ɔʊ], [o:], [o·ᵘ], [oʊ] etc. alongside each other, is, as in all cases of inventory variables, virtually
impossible to answer except in the 'extreme' cases.

The Variable (ɔə)

      Works on the traditional dialects of our area portray a situa-
tion where the phoneme /ɔ:/ occurs in *blow, crow, mow, slow* etc.
(see above);   *born, ball, bald, order* etc;   *either, neither*;   *half,
calf*;   and so on - and the phoneme /ʊə/ occurs in *go, no, both,
hope, road, loaf* etc. (see above);   *poor, moor, door, floor, more,
sore, pork, sort, board, broad* etc. etc.   We have seen above that
part of the load of /ɔ:/ has been transferred by the majority of the
urban population to /ɔʊ/ (or /o:/), and part of that of /ʊə/ has
split off to form most of the present /o:/ words.   In this section
we are concerned with the remainder of the /ɔ:/ words i.e. *born,
ball*,...*either*...*half* etc. and of the /ʊə/ words i.e. *poor, door,
more, sort*... etc.

      As regards /ɔ:/, the present situation appears to be that items
such as *either, neither, half, calf* etc. have been 'transferred' to
the lexical sets of the phonemes these items have in RP; other words,
where /ɔ:/ occurs in the RP form too, have retained /ɔ:/.   But with
the /ʊə/ set the situation is more complex, probably because the
corresponding RP situation is so too.   Let us examine this latter
in some detail, by referring to a number of major works in chronological order.

      Daniel Jones's *Outline of English Phonetics* shows that many
speakers have a symmetrical system of centring diphthongs: ɪə   ʊə
                                                                 ɛə   ɔə
Of /ɔə/, he says that this diphthong 'may be heard in...words written
with *oar, ore*, and ..*our*;   ..also in the words *door* and *floor*[95].   It
must be noticed on the other hand that many speakers of Received

---

95 Samuels (1972:142) suggests that with *oor* words the selection
of /ʊə/ after labials e.g. *poor, boor, moor* but /ɔə/ after other
sounds e.g. *floor, door* is a not unexpected development.

English...do not use the diphthong /ɔə/ at all, but replace it
always by /ɔ:/'[96]. And of /ʊə/ he says that it is used in two
categories of words: a) most of those spelled with *oor* and *ure*
e.g. *poor*, *sure*, and some with *our* eg *tour*; b) those with *ua*, *ue*,
ewe, followed by a consonant in a stressed syllable e.g. *truant*,
fluent, *jewel*. However, words in category a) nearly all have variants with a diphthong [oə], and many of them also have alternative
forms with /ɔə/ or /ɔ:/.   Jones thus portrays a situation in which
a three-way contrast is possible, say *paw* /ɔ:/ - *pore* /ɔə/ - *poor*
/ʊə/, but where this is reduced to /pɔ:/ - /pʊə/ or even simply to
/pɔ:/ by some speakers, with whom /ɔə/ has disappeared from the
system altogether, and the incidence of /ʊə/ is much reduced - leaving only those words in his group b).

The latest edition of Jones's *English Pronouncing Dictionary*,
as revised by one of his disciples (1967) has reduced [ɔə] to the
status of 'variant of another pronunciation' - mainly /ɔ:/ e.g. *pore*
pɔ: [pɔə]; *pour* ditto; *soar* sɔ: [sɔə]; *sore* ditto; *shore*
ʃɔ: [ʃɔə]; but it may also be one of the variants of /ʊə/ e.g.
poor pʊə [pɔə,pɔ:]; *pure* pjʊə [pjɔə,pjɔ:,pjə:]; *sure* ʃʊə [ʃɔə,ʃɔ:,
ʃə:].

Gimson (1970; and also 1964) includes as one category of words
with /ɔ:/ those spelled with *ore*, *oor*, *oar*, *our*, saying that '/ɔ:/
increasingly replaces earlier [ɔə] forms..., though [ɔə] is retained
both in conservative RP and in many regional dialects... In RP some
[ɔə] forms < /ʊə/ have a form with /ɔ:/ e.g. *sure*...and occasionally
poor'.   He summarises the situation thus: '/ɔə/ having coalesced
with /ɔ:/ for most RP speakers, the pattern of centring diphthongs
is rendered assymetrical, there being only one back glide of this
type opposed to the two front glides.   As a result, the first
element of /ʊə/ can be lowered considerably without risk of confusion.   Thus several words with /ʊə/, which have a pronunciation [ʊə]
for some RP speakers, are given by others a glide [ɔə] e.g. in *poor*,
sure.   This glide [ɔə] may in turn be levelled with the realisation
of /ɔ:/.   Thus *Shaw*, *shore*, *sure*, still pronounced by some /ʃɔ:,ʃɔə,
ʃʊə/, are levelled by many others to /ʃɔ:/ for all three words'[97].

There is thus a contrast in inventory between traditional West
Yorkshire dialects, which have /ɔ:/-/ʊə/, and some forms of RP and

---

96   A young female informant (Class II), a bilingual secretary, told
me that she had shorthand problems at college with words like *door* ;
she wrote two syllables whereas the 'correct' version had only one.

97   Strang (1970:46) also states that a primitive sampling of her
students had shown the /ɔ:/-/ɔə/ contrast to be in decline, and that
potential ambiguities were insufficient to defend the older system.

other dialects which have /ɔ:/-/ɔə/-/ʊə/. But /ɔə/ is disappearing from RP, leaving an /ɔ:/-/ʊə/ situation there too. However
the incidence of /ɔ:/ and /ʊə/ is very different between traditional
West Yorkshire and RP: the latter has /ʊə/ in a very restricted
lexical set e.g. *truant*, *fluent*, etc. whereas in the dialect /ʊə/
carries a considerable load - its lexical set includes many items
which in RP have either /ɔə/, or in less 'conservative' forms, /ɔ:/
(as well as those with /əʊ/ in RP).

My concern in this section is with inventory. We shall return
below to the more complex matter of the realisation of the traditional lexical set of /ʊə/ as [uə],[ʊə],[oə],[ɔə],[ɔ:] etc. (see p. 158),
though it is admitted that this separation, in the interests of
clarity, is artificial.

Deciding who has what inventory on the basis of conversational
data involves the same difficulties as were encountered with all the
other variables examined in this section: the same speaker may
produce examples of the variants [ɔ:], [ɔə],[oə],[ʊə] etc. in the
same lexical set, or even the same word, in the same style.   For
this reason we shall confine ourselves here to the findings of the
minimal pairs word list.   Now it has been seen above that often
this situation produces results which are quite untypical of general conversation; but for two reasons I do not think the results
in this case will be so unreliable.   First, there is no evidence
of any stigma or prestige attaching to either /ɔ:/ or /ɔə/ here -
nor to /ʊə/ except when its incidence is as in the traditional dialect rather than as described by Jones, Gimson and others (see
p.280 below);   Second, the contrasts in question were presented
quite late in the test, by which stage informants had realised,
sometimes with overt surprise, that not all words spelled differently are pronounced differently.

In the minimal sets list I included *Shaw*/*shore*/*sure*, *paw*/*pore*/
pour/*pure*, and *saw*/*sore*/*soar*/*sure*.   I found that, as suggested in
the above sources, there was variation between three phonemes, two
phonemes, and one phoneme.   And this variation was not only within
the total sample, but even within the same informant, i.e. some
speakers made a three-way contrast in one set, but only a two-way
one in another, and so on.

The three-way contrast was generally realised as [ɔ:] - [ɔə] -
[ʊə], though particularly in Halifax and Huddersfield the /ʊə/
phoneme was frequently, except towards the top of the social scale,
realised as [uə] (17 informants pronounced it solely thus, 9 varied

---

She also notes the levelling with these of /ʊə/, whose functional
load is light, and holds this to be a 'development which has considerable importance for linguistic history'.

between [uə] and [ʊə].   Four older informants, low on the social
scale, had a realisation [ɔ:] - [ʊə] - [uə], with [ʊə] in the '/ɔə/
set';   and two middle-aged speakers varied between this and a two-
way [ɔ:] - [ʊə].)   The two-way contrast was usually [ɔ:] - [ʊə]
(with similar [ʊə ~ uə]), though one or two had [ɔ:] - [ɔə].   Those
who had a single phoneme (three informants showed 2 ~ 1;   only one
had just one phoneme in all three sets) realised it as [ɔ:].

The lexical incidence on the various contrasting units was generally
as described in the standard works referred to above (though one
difference I observed in general conversation was that, in addition
to words spelled with *oar*, *ore* and *our*, /ɔə/ occurs with some speakers in those spelled with *or* plus voiceless consonant e.g. *pork*,
sport, *export*, *sort*, *force* etc.⁹⁸).   In the 'minimal sets' list the
three-way contrast was generally:

/ɔ:/	/ɔə/	/ʊə/
Shaw	shore	sure
paw	pore, pour	poor, pure
saw	sore, soar	(sure)

though a few informants had /ɔə/ in *poor*, and on the other hand quite
a number had /ʊə/ in *pour*.   (With the [ɔ:] - [ʊə] - [uə] realisation the incidence was the same, and *poor* varied between [ʊə] and
[uə].)   In a two-way contrast, the /ɔ:/ and /ɔə/ groups generally
merged - but *pour* quite often had /ʊə/, and among older speakers so
too sometimes had *pore*, *shore*, *sore* and/or *soar*.

    To examine whether the size of inventory as revealed by this
test showed signs of relating to any of the usual non-linguistic
factors, I scored informants as follows: those who definitely had
a three-term system scored 3, those varying between three and two
terms 2½, those with only two-way contrasts 2, those varying between two and one 1½, and those with only /ɔ:/ 1.   I then totalled
the scores of the various groups of informants and divided by the
number of informants in that group to produce a group score.   Thus,
for example: in Class III, 11 x 3 = 33, 7 x 2½ = 17½, 9 x 2 = 18,
1 x 1½ = 1½;   total 70, divided by 28 informants: score 2.50.

    The scores for class and sex groups were as follows:

---

98   See Wright (1892): such words are listed with /ʊə/, but others
such as *lord, form* etc. with a voiced consonant following have /ɔə/
(which other authorities would render /ɔ:/).

	I	II	III	IV	V	Total
M	2.00	2.93	2.45	2.48	2.85	2.59
W	-	2.25	2.53	2.57	2.17	2.47
Total	2.00	2.62	2.50	2.52	2.63	

Total scores for the towns were: Bradford 2.41, Halifax 2.57, Huddersfield 2.67.   Details of the age-groups were:

	3	2½	2	1½	1	Av
10		4	7	2	1	2.00
20	4	8	10			2.36
30	4	6	2	1		2.50
40	3	6	3			2.50
50	8	3	1			2.79
60	8	4	2			2.71
70	11	5				2.84
80	3					3.00

Figure 10 gives age-group average scores in graph form:

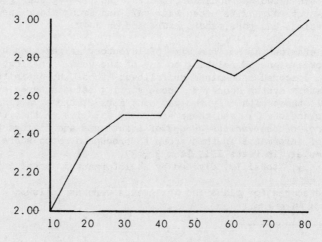

Figure 10: (ɔə) - size of inventory by age

No regular picture seems to emerge from the scores for the different social class or class plus sex groups, which suggests that neither of these factors is particularly important.   With the total

scores for the towns (more detailed breakdowns do not yield a clear
picture), the fact that in Bradford the [ʊə] variant is not common
could be important: in Halifax it is more frequent and in Huddersfield almost 'usual'; it would perhaps not be surprising if with
such a variant the system is spread over more phonetic space and as
a result there is less likelihood of merger.   It seems fairly clear,
however, that the clearest correlate of the size of inventory here
is age: Figure 10 is a remarkably regular graph, suggesting that
the three-way contrast is giving way to a two-way, with signs among
the youngest informants of a further reduction to simple /ɔ:/.

Now in view of the developments taking place in RP this does
not seem surprising: the works cited above indicated that this is
just what is occurring there too.   But we may note first, that from
our age-group scores it seems likely that the development in the area
is some years behind RP, judging by the date those descriptions were
written;   second, and more interesting, that the oldest groups in
our sample, born in or soon after the period described by works on
traditional dialect, have a three-way contrast: /ʊə/-/ɔə/-/ɔ:/,
whereas the traditional descriptions are unanimous in portraying a
two-way /ʊə/-/ɔ:/.

My conclusions are as follows: if the situation as described
in the works on traditional dialect did exist in our towns at an
earlier date, then there has been a change in inventory in this
phonetic area from /ʊə/-/ɔ:/ to /ʊə/-/ɔə/-/ɔ:/, probably under the
influence of other dialects, including RP.   However, the latter are
undergoing a number of changes by which /ɔə/ merges with /ɔ:/, and
/ʊə/ is left with a light load because some of its lexical set is
also undergoing the change [ʊə>ɔə>ɔ:]; and speakers in our urban
area seem to be following this same development.   The change seems
to be with 'time' only: social status and prestige factors do not
appear to be involved.   The end result may well be that in West
Yorkshire the system will be /ʊə/-/ɔ:/, which was what existed before
the relatively brief appearance of /ɔə/.   But there is an excellent
illustration here of a point made during the development of 'structural dialectology': that to consider inventory without incidence
can be very misleading.   The traditional dialect /ʊə/-/ɔ:/ situation
is different from the urban one, in that several items have been
lost from the lexical set of /ɔ:/, but very many others have shifted
from /ʊə/ to /ɔ:/.   The result, in both RP and urban West Yorkshire,
will be that /ɔ:/ has a large lexical set, and /ʊə/ a very small
one: e.g. *truant*, *fluent*, *sewer* etc.[99] .

_____

99 *Sewer* was included in my word lists, and was pronounced with
/ʊə/, even by those informants who had levelled /ʊə/-/ɔə/-/ɔ:/

The diphthongs /aɪ/ and /aʊ/

Though they will not be examined here, something must be said
about these diphthongs since it is clear from a reading of Chapter 5
that in traditional dialects words belonging to their lexical sets
in RP were involved in important differences of inventory and incidence both within our area and between it and RP.

In the traditional descriptions /aʊ/ does not exist: items
with this phoneme in RP follow two main systems within the area,
those of Bradford and Huddersfield - with Halifax apparently lying
somewhere near the isogloss. In Bradford most '/aʊ/ words' belong
to the lexical set of /a:/ e.g. *doubt, house, now, out* etc; the
incidence of /a:/ is thus much greater than that of /ɑ:/ in RP, including also both RP /ɑ:/ words e.g. *cart, harvest*...and others
such as *work N, worst, servant, warm, room* etc. With one or two
words such as *ground, pound* Bradford lies close to an ʊ/a: isogloss,
Wright assigning them to the former, some other authorities to the
latter.   In Huddersfield, most 'aʊ/ words' belong to /ɛə/ e.g.
about, down, ground, house, how, loud, now, out, round etc. etc.
from those in Haigh (1928); the /ɛə/ lexical set is thus much larger
than in RP, including also, besides RP /ɛə/ words like *fair, swear*
etc., many of the other words with /a:/ in the Bradford system e.g.
arm, card, yard, park, room etc.

With /aɪ/ there is a similar geographical difference: Bradford
and Huddersfield have different systems, and Halifax lies near the
isogloss.   In Bradford /aɪ/ occurs in some words which have this
phoneme in RP e.g. *mice, time, write* etc., and also in a few which
do not e.g. *pick* - but the incidence of /aɪ/ is much smaller since
many RP /aɪ/ words have /i:/ in Bradford e.g. *night, light, sight;
tie, die, eye; mild* etc. etc., and some have /ɛɪ/ e.g. *right, fight,*
etc.   In the Huddersfield system these latter two sets of words
are generally the same as in Bradford, but the words which do have
/aɪ/ in Bradford have /ɑ:/ e.g. *dry, fine, find, hide, like, my,
mine, pike, shy, time, while, why, write,* etc: the long vowel inventory is thus different, having an a:/ɑ: contrast in open position,
and so is that of diphthongs since /aɪ/ is absent or at most of
very restricted incidence.

My preliminary investigations in the area suggested that the
traditional works did not represent anything like the situation in
the towns today, and my survey established that in fact /aʊ/ and
/aɪ/ now function very much as in RP.   Thus /aʊ/ has become part
of the vowel system for virtually all speakers, with a lexical set
made up of part of the traditional /a:/ or /ɛə/ sets, depending on
the town.   And the position of /aɪ/ in Bradford has been strengthened by the transfer of part of the lexical sets of /i:/ and /ɛɪ/,

while in Huddersfield /aɪ/ has come into the system partly through
a similar transfer, and partly through a diphthongal pronunciation
of those words formerly in the /ɑ:/ set.   The pronunciation of
'/ɑʊ/ words' with [a:] was uncommon (only 7% in conversational
speech), and with [ɛə] only occurred once or twice.   Pronunciation
of '/aɪ/ words' with [i:] or [ɛɪ] was very rare;   as were [ɑ:] forms
in Huddersfield.   With such small numbers of occurrences there is
no point in attempting to establish any patterns in the variation.

My conclusion is that for virtually all my informants /ɑʊ/ and
/aɪ/ are now fully established members of their vowel inventory,
and that this change within the vowel systems of the area has been
brought about through the influence of RP or at least that of some
system where these diphthongs have RP-like incidence: no other
explanation seems possible for why just some members of the traditional lexical sets of /a:/ or /ɛə/ have 'broken away' to produce
/ɑʊ/ with an incidence as in RP, and similarly why just some items
from /i:/, /ɛɪ/ have gone to /aɪ/, which also now has a lexical set
very much as in RP.

2   Distribution Variables

Here we shall be concerned with differences between the speech
of our area and RP which involve permitted combinations of phonemes.
There appear to be fewer differences of this sort than there are of
the other three aspects of phonological system: inventory, incidence,
and realisation.   I decided to examine as variables just two, but
two which are quite different from each other in several respects:
one concerns vowels and the other consonants;   the former is one of
which many informants are conscious or can be made conscious, while
the latter for very many is below the level of consciousness;   the
former involves stigma, while the latter does not (evidence on the
latter two points will be found in Chapter 7 - my selection of the
two variables was based on my less formal preliminary observations
on such matters).

The Variable (-ow)

We are concerned here with a fairly large set of words with
final unstressed /əʊ/ in RP.   Most of them are disyllabic and
spelled with -ow e.g. *borrow*, *pillow*, *widow* , *window*, *yellow*,
etc;   but a few are trisyllabic and/or spelled with final o e.g.
tomorrow, *piano*, *potato*, *tomato* etc.

According to the traditional dialect descriptions of the area,
the final vowel of such words is /ə/ (usually, but see below).   Thus
the distribution of what corresponds in the West Yorkshire dialects

to RP /əʊ/ is different from the latter in that it does not occur
in unstressed word-final position. Now we have seen above that
there are today two West Yorkshire phonemes corresponding to RP /əʊ,
a long monophthongal /o:/ and a wide diphthongal /ɔʊ/. It emerges
from my survey that in this environment there is variation nowadays
between /ə/ and a full vowel; and that when the latter occurs in a
regional form, it is almost invariably /o:/ (although we saw that
many words spelled with ow have /ɔʊ/) - thus in today's speech it is
diphthongal /ɔʊ/ that is more restricted distributionally.

Two exceptions to the regular picture of non-standard /ə/ corresponding to RP /əʊ/ have to be noted:

i) The /ə/ seems never to occur in a small number of words with
    final unstressed -ow.   One example is the name Barlow, which
    is never [ba:lə]; but this cannot simply be because it is a
    proper name, since say Yarrow can be pronounced [jarə].   A
    possible reason is that the preceding vowel is long, whereas
    in all those disyllabic -ow words which can have /ə/ the pre-
    ceding vowel is short.   But /ə/ is not possible in the word
    elbow either, where the preceding vowel is short.   However,
    here, unlike almost all the others, the first vowel is foll-
    owed by two consonants - so perhaps /o:/ can occur if the
    preceding syllable is 'heavy' (in the sense familiar from
    Latin metre, i.e. it contains either a long vowel or a short
    followed by two consonants[100]): I can think of only one
    example that seems to disprove this hypothesis: window (which
    is frequently [wɪndə] - but here, unlike elbow, the consonants
    are homorganic.

ii) Another non-standard form of final vowel is occasionally heard
    in some of these words: /ɪ/ e.g. borrow is sometimes pronoun-
    ced [bɒrɪ].   I heard only nine examples of this in my survey:
    eight in the reading passage and one in the word list, out of
    a total of over 1000 such words (five each in the RP and the
    WL for over 100 informants).   This form appears to be res-
    tricted both lexically - in that examples were heard in only
    a small subset of those words where /ə/ is possible; and
    regionally - of the eight informants who used it five were
    from Huddersfield and two from Halifax[101]; the other, though
    long resident in Bradford, had spent her formative years much
    nearer to Huddersfield.

100 Abercrombie (1964b) has demonstrated that this type of syllable
has functional identity in English today; and there is evidence
from Old English metre that it has done so throughout the history
of the language.

101 EDGr has [felɪ] fellow for South Lancashire, and several traditionalists (e.g. Ellis) have said Huddersfield and Halifax show

In my statistical treatment of variation I counted both [ə] and
[ɪ] pronunciations as non-standard, and give here the percentage of
these of the total of (-ow) words.   I counted all full-vowel forms,
whether regional [o:] or RP-like [oʊ] and [əʊ], as 'standard' for
the purposes of this variable, since the concern here is with distribution rather than realisation.

The following table shows the percentage of non-standard forms
by class and style:

	CS	FS	RP	WL	MP
I	0	0	0	0	0
II	83	13	8	0	0
III	56	21	10	0	0
IV	85	78	26	10	9
V	87	29	39	15	21

Figure 11 shows the total average scores (excluding minimal pairs)
by class and sex, and Figure 12 (overleaf) those for the age-groups,
with conversational styles separated from the more artificial ones.
Figures for the different towns are not given since no interesting
differences emerge.

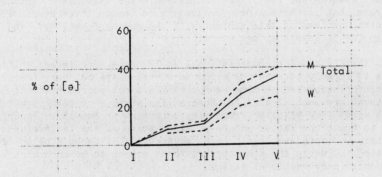

Figure 11: (-ow) - Class and Sex

---

strong similarities with this area.   Note too that Emily Brontë
used this form of *fellow*: see Petyt (1970:43), and Haworth shows
certain similarities to these towns.   SED gives little evidence of
this pronunciation, except for the form [wɪnɪ-ɪn] *winnowing*.

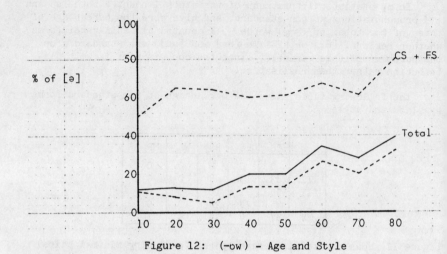

Figure 12:   (-ow) - Age and Style

We shall see in Chapter 7 that there is evidence that [ə] pronunciations are stigmatised in this area, and this being so one
would expect the differences by class, style and sex which show up
here: towards the top of the social scale the castigated variant
is rare, but it becomes progressively more common lower down; all
classes use less of this variant with increasing formality; and
women use it less than men overall.

The figures for conversational styles show some irregularities -
this is largely because the words in question are not very frequent
in conversation and so some scores here are not representative;
patterns are much clearer in those styles where a certain number of
such words were elicited from every informant.   But it is important
not to trust the latter entirely, since where stigma is involved
certain variants are likely to be suppressed: it should be noted
that on the whole the non-standard forms appear to be much more
common in conversational styles.

This variable provided further evidence of the artificiality
of the minimal pairs situation when stigma/prestige is involved.
Only eight informants failed to distinguish between *pillow* and
pillar, and three of these then 'corrected' themselves.   Moreover
a good proportion introduced an 'abnormal' distinction: 20 informants stressed the second syllable of *pillar* to emphasise its difference from *pillow* - which they had in fact pronounced with (əʊ) -
presumably because they were aware of a tendency to say [pɪlə].
(14 of these made this stressed vowel [a:] or [ɑ:], 3 had [ə:],2[a],
and one [ʌ].   One man who did pronounce *pillow* as [pɪlə] invented
a distinction by making *pillar* [pɪlɑ:].

With the age-graph the total scores seem to show some tendency
for the non-standard variant to be on the decline; though those
for conversational styles are less clear (possibly because of the
low numbers of instances), it may be relevant to note that of the
eight informants who failed to make a distinction in the minimal
pairs five were in their sixties or over, and a sixth was in his
fifties.

Conclusions from this section are that the RP-type pronunciation has come to be used alongside that of the traditional dialect,
and there is a fairly classic situation of variation between a
standard variant and a non-standard such as is commonly found where
prestige/stigma attaches to the former/latter; there is some indication from the age-group scores (unlike the otherwise similar
picture with say (h)) that the present situation is not 'stable';
and the minimal pairs situation does not give a reliable picture in
cases such as this.

The Variable (n̄ch)

The lexical set in question here includes all those words spelled with *nch*: e.g. *branch*, *inch*, *pinch*, *lunch*, *wrench* etc. In
Jones's EPD they are transcribed with [ntʃ], but with the [t] in
italics indicating that it may or may not be present. Gimson
(1970:176) states that some people omit the [t] element in the final
group /ntʃ/ (this was not mentioned in the first edition of his book
but other evidence suggests that this is not a recent development[102]).
By contrast with these authorities who take the affricate as basic,
Abercrombie (1964) transcribes such words as ending in /nʃ/.

The RP situation, as implied above and as my own observations
confirm, is that there is variation between /ntʃ/ and /nʃ/ forms -
though if questioned, RP speakers and Southerners generally will
claim to have the affricate. But the traditional dialect descriptions of West Yorkshire, from Ellis and Wright to SED, suggest that
/nʃ/ is universal there, and my own preliminary observations seemed
to find the majority of Northerners consistent in this respect. ·We

---

102 Ekwall (1975:77) says that /tʃ>ʃ/ after /n,l/ is attested from
the 16th Century. (He attributes the fact that this does not
affect *Manchester, Winchester* etc. to the influence of *Chester* —
though the difference in syllable-position seems the more likely
explanation to me: compare *pilchard,* which is never *ᵱɪlʃəd].

may conclude that the phonetactics of Northern English generally do not permit the /n + tʃ/ group, and that this is therefore a distributional difference from RP.

(Gimson also says that /ltʃ/ varies with /lʃ/ in RP, and /ndʒ/ with /nʒ/; in the North words with *lch* such as *filch, mulch, Welch* etc. are usually pronounced with /lʃ/, but /ndʒ/ does occur nowadays in words such as *hinge,revenge* etc. (whereas Wright has /nʒ/ in such) - so the distributional pattern is somewhat skew.)

Since I did hear occasional instances of [ntʃ] in the area, I decided it would be worthwhile to examine a sizeable amount of data relevant to this unusual situation - where in RP [ntʃ] is assumed to be usual but [nʃ] can occur, while in this region [nʃ] is most frequent but [ntʃ] may sometimes be heard - to see whether there is anything systematic about the variation. Unfortunately, this consonant-group is not common - in fact, in the whole of my data no examples occurred in what I took to be casual speech, and only 14 in formal; it is therefore necessary to base the examination on the more artificial data of the reading passage and word list, into each of which I had deliberately written a number of such words. But this probably matters less than it would with most phonological variables since the above descriptions of RP suggest that no prestige/ stigma is involved here; and as will be shown below (p.271), the difference is for many informants below the level of consciousness: quite a number cannot distinguish [ntʃ] and [nʃ] even when their attention is drawn to this.

Since neither variant can be called 'non-standard', scores will be given in terms of the percentage of the one less common in the area: [ntʃ]. Those for class and style were as follows:

	I	II	III	IV	V
RP	46	7	20	11	11
WL	44	10	33	20	26

Breaking these figures down further by sex reveals no clear pattern, but overall women score somewhat higher than men:

	M	W
RP	8	22
WL	17	33

No very clear difference is apparent between the towns, though Huddersfield (24%) scored somewhat higher overall than Halifax (17%) and

Bradford (15%).   Figure 13 gives the total figures by age group.

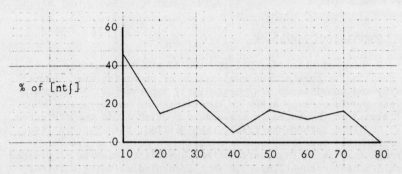

% of [ntʃ]

Figure 13: (nch) - Age

There is no obvious relation between the use of [ntʃ] and
social class: it is true that the Class I score is considerably
higher than the others, but it has been noted that figures for this
group, which contains only three members, should be treated with
caution, especially when at variance with a general trend (or the
lack of one).   And it is interesting in this case to examine the
informants of Class I (all ex-public school) in detail: one of them
used no [ntʃ] forms at all - and he was not the one who had been
to a Yorkshire school and had retained a number of Yorkshire features (he used 35% [ntʃ]), but one who had no trace of a Yorkshire
accent and had been educated at a school in Scotland; the youngest
member of this group used 100% [ntʃ] in the examples recorded.

The table giving figures by style suggests that there may be
some tendency for [ntʃ] to be the more 'careful' variant - and this
might be thought to be supported by the generally higher scores
among women.

Though the graph is not regular, it might be held that Figure
13 shows some slight signs of an increasing use of [ntʃ] variants,
the figures for teenagers being surprisingly high and those for the
80-plus being zero (since class is apparently not significant, it
is not unreasonable to include this group in the reckoning here),
but the trend is by no means as obvious as may be observed with
certain variants definitely on the way 'in' or 'out'.

We may conclude that though a more 'standard RP' [ntʃ] has come
to be used to some extent alongside traditional [nʃ], there is a
situation where apparently no significance attaches to either variant, and though there may be some partial correlation with formality
we have an example as near as anything observed in my survey to

'free variation'[103].

3   Realisation Variables

I referred above (p. 39) to some of the difficulties involved
in handling matters of the realisation of phonemes, where phonetic
acuity and consistency are particularly important.   A particular
caveat should perhaps apply to the scores for the separate towns.
I listened to the tapes in the order in which I did the fieldwork,
i.e. Bradford informants first, then Halifax, then Huddersfield;   if
therefore the town scores show a rise or a fall from Bradford
through Halifax to Huddersfield the possibility must be considered
that I became harsher/laxer in what I counted as being within a
certain part of a phonetic continuum.

It is obviously necessary, in spite of these problems, to give
some attention to matters of realisation, since they are clearly
involved in the questions of 'dialect' and 'accent', and the persistence or modification of regional features, which is my main subject.
I shall therefore examine a number of variables of this type, but
in those cases where I am not confident in my skills as a phonetician I shall present my findings more tentatively and in less detail.

The Variable (t)

We shall be concerned here with the realisation of /t/ as a
glottal stop [ʔ] in *better*, *petrol*, *get out*, *you bet!* etc.etc.

The traditional dialect works on this area make virtually no
mention of the glottal stop[104].   The reason for this could be
either that it is a relatively recent phenomenon or that the traditionalists simply did not distinguish it from [t].   In RP the
glottal stop has various uses (see Gimson, 1970:167):   it may serve
as a syllable boundary-marker in words like *co-operate*, *geometry*

---

103 It has been observed that some RP speakers who pronounce *nch* as
[ntʃ] do not distinguish pairs such as *prince/prints*, pronouncing
both with final [nts].   I found six informants in the reading passage and five in the word list (and two more in general conversation)
who clearly produced forms such as [dants] or [wʊnts]: all of these
produced some instances of the [ntʃ] variant.

104 Only SED has the glottal stop transcribed distinctly from [t],
and only comparatively rarely does it appear there.   It may be noted
that the preglottalisation of medial /tʃ/ in words like *teacher* was
apparently not noticed by SED, though I found it almost universal in
the area.

etc; it may occur between words where some other speakers have
'intrusive r', e.g. *law and order* or a regular 'linking r' e.g.
later on; it may reinforce an initial accented vowel as in *she's
awfully good*. All these are fairly common uses in RP; less common
is the use of [ʔ] to reinforce a final [p,t,k,tʃ] - or even to replace final [p,t,k] when a consonant follows[105]. Clearly this last
usage is different from the others, where the glottal stop is inserted for emphasis or to avoid a glide with 'substandard' connotations:
here the glottal stop actually represents a particular phoneme[106].
In non-standard speech in various parts of Britain this usage is
extended far beyond what is acceptable in RP.

My preliminary observation made it quite clear to me that in
the West Yorkshire towns the use of [ʔ] for /t/ is much commoner
than the traditional descriptions suggest; moreover, it is a feature of which many people are aware and which produces strong
reactions (see Chapter 7); and it does not appear to be equally
common in all environments: its occurrence does not seem to be
possible word-initially except in the word *to* (and its compounds
such as *today* and *tomorrow*) and as the definite article (see p.197):
and even in those environments where it is possible there seem to
be differences of frequency.

To test a hypothesis that there is some gradation of acceptability according to environment, I decided to divide (t) into a
number of 'subvariables'. I ignored the environment V̲#C i.e. at
the end of a word or morpheme and before another word or morpheme
with initial consonant e.g. *that table, get down, at last, football,
outset, nutshell* etc., since on the one hand this seems to occur
fairly commonly in RP, and on the other it is sometimes difficult to
distinguish [t] and [ʔ] here on tape. I distinguished two word-
final environments: V̲#‖ i.e pre-pausal: this I have also heard
in RP, but it seems to be less common than the above; and V̲#V i.e.
before a word beginning with a vowel or (h) e.g. *get off, what is
it?, get home*: this does not seem to occur in RP. I also distinguished two word-medial environments: V̲V e.g. *butter, letter* etc.
and V̲́L i.e. after a stressed vowel and before a liquid or /m/ e.g.
bottle, atlas, petrol, bottom. (Note that before /n/ it is more
widely used, even by some RP speakers e.g. *cotton, button*: the

105 The glottal stop may sometimes represent /k/ as well as /t/ in
such environments in West Yorkshire too: e.g. [laɪʔ ðaʔ]. This
phenomenon is not examined here.

106 Interestingly, Samuels (1972:13) takes this as an example of
the well known 'economy of effort' principle: 'plosion is preserved,
but is performed by the vocal cords themselves, not by tongue or
lips'. This would fit in with the popular criticisms that it is
'lazy' or 'sloppy'.

fact that [t] and [ʔ] are sometimes difficult to distinguish here
may account for the greater acceptability of [ʔ]; before /l/ after
an *un*stressed vowel it is also relatively common in RP e.g.*definitely*
as it is in certain particular items like *Scotland*: these were
ignored). My preliminary impression was that a glottal stop may be
somewhat more frequent in V̌_L than in V_V[107].

Word Internal (t)

(VtV)

Most of the words in question here have intervocalic /t/ e.g.
butter, *letter*, *water*, *daughter*, *Saturday*, *writing* etc., though
wanted, *painting*, *twenty* etc. will also be included.

The following tables show the percentage of [ʔ] by a) class and
style, b) sex, c) town, d) age-group; in the last three only casual
and formal speech scores are shown:

a)

	CS	FS	RP	WL
I	0	0	0	0
II	10	1	0	0
III	11	2	0	0
IV	17	6	1	0
V	12	4	5	0

b)

	M	W
CS	16	8
FS	5	1

c)

	Bfd	Hfx	Hudd
CS	17	10	7
FS	5	2	2

d)

	10	20	30	40	50	60	70	80
CS	35	17	12	15	9	12	8	0
FS	11	6	1	5	2	3	2	0

---

107 In this area the glottal stop also occurs in one 'special' environment: 'Bradford' is commonly pronounced [braʔfəd]. (It is
possible that this is still a case of /t/> [ʔ], following on voicing
assimilation which is common in this area.) Though I did not keep
a systematic record of this I have the impression that it is commoner than with any of my four subvariables: certainly I heard it in
the speech of several 'well-spoken' people who would be most unlikely
to use [ʔ] except as in RP.

The use of [2], especially in this environment, is one of the
most highly stigmatised non-standard features in this area, and provoked much spontaneous comment (see Chapter 7):   it is therefore
perhaps surprising to find that it is a comparatively uncommon phenomenon[108] compared to other stigmatised features such as h-dropping
- though of course the strength of reaction may in some degree be
responsible for this infrequency.

Though as one might expect with such low frequencies there are
certain minor 'irregularities', the class/style table shows broadly
the pattern one might expect with a stigmatised variant: it is
increasingly unlikely towards the upper end of the social scale and
among all classes as formality increases.   Similarly, women show
less use of the castigated form than men.   The figures for the
different towns are interesting here: Bradford appears to be
'central' to the use of [2], which is less frequent with increasing
distance from that town - and this fits in well with the remarks of
a number of informants in the other towns to the effect that [2]
was typical of Bradford (see p.281).   The age-groups scores also
offer support to the incidental remarks[109] of some informants about the
increasing use of [2] among the young (and it is interesting to
note that though there seems to be some class-correlation with [2],
the 80-plus group, though entirely Class V, produced no [2]);   the
'dip' caused by the 30-plus group has been remarked on above (p.108).
Unfortunately the numbers in the age-groups in each town are too
small to provide a clear picture, but there is some indication that
in Huddersfield the glottal stop is almost entirely confined to
those under 30 (increasing 'towards' the teenagers):   among the
older age-groups there are some non-standard pronunciations, but
many of these are with some sort of flap (see below, on (Vt#V)).

The conclusions from this data are that the glottal stop occurs
in such a pattern in relation to class, sex, and style as is commonly

---

108 Contrast the situation in Norwich described by Trudgill (1974a:
95): 'the WC as a whole has almost 100 [2] in CS'

109 In response to the question in Section IV about 'counting out'
rhymes, one young man and his mother (60-plus) together recited "one
potato, two potato...";   it is interesting to observe that though
both were 'broadspoken' he clearly said [pəte:2ə] and she [pəte:tə].
(Note: in this rhyme the word *potato* occurs six times in two lines;
I therefore ignored it in my scores, whether pronounced with [t] or
[2], as this was clearly an artificial situation.)

found with stigmatised variants; that there is a definite indication from the 'apparent time' findings (i.e. the age-groups) as well
as from the 'real time' evidence of the traditional dialect records
(though it must be admitted that this is an *argumentum ex silentio*)
that the use of [ʔ] is on the increase; and that Bradford may be
the 'regional centre' from which this usage is working outwards.

(V́tL)

The corresponding tables to those above for the percentage of
glottal stops in words such as *little*, *bottle*, *petrol*, *bottom* etc.
are as follows (note that in table d) the two conversational styles
are not distinguished, because the small number of instances recorded
would result in an even less clear pattern than there is);

a)

	CS	FS	RP
I	0	3	0
II	15	9	0
III	14	7	2
IV	16	11	7
V	15	24	13

b)

	M	W
CS	22	6
FS	16	4

c)

	Bfd	Hfx	Hudd
CS	18	17	7
FS	15	9	9

d)

	10	20	30	40	50	60	70	80
CS + FS	38	21	0	12	8	3	17	4

The amount of data here was smaller, and so less regularity of
pattern would not be surprising.   But the class, style, and sex
differences are again broadly as one would expect with a stigmatised
variant, and table c) shows again that [ʔ] becomes less common as
geographical distance from Bradford increases.   With the age-groups
the picture is a little less regular, with an unexpectedly high score
in the 70-plus group (the low score among the 30-plus is less unexpected, as it was frequently observed): the small numbers involved
may be responsible for this; but again the highest use of [ʔ] among
the youngest groups is apparent.

Figure 14 (opposite) compares the amount of [ʔ] usage in (VtV)
and V́tL): the latter is consistently greater.   My conclusion is
that though the glottal stop in this environment is still a stigmatised variant, it is either slightly less unacceptable than in
intervocalic position or simply more 'advanced' in its progress.

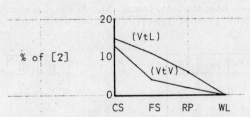

% of [2]

Figure 14:   (t) word-internal - Style

Word Final (t)

(Vt#V)

   We are concerned here with examples such as *get out*, *let off*, *what I mean* etc.   This environment is of course similar to (VtV), but there is a word-division after the /t/.

   In the area I investigated there are in fact two non-standard forms possible in this environment: besides the glottal stop may be heard a sort of 'linking r' (realised by either the usual frictionless continuant or a flap).   Thus *get out* may be realised as [gerau2] as well as [ge2au2] in non-standard speech.   So before turning to the amount of glottal stop usage, let us first see what percentage of non-standard forms have [r] rather than [2].

   Table i) following presents the figures by social class;   ii) by sex;   iii) by town;   and iv) by age-group:

i)

I	II	III	IV	V
94	32	14	24	25

ii)

M	W
26	14

iii)

Bfd	Hfx	Hudd
14	24	45

iv)

10	20	30	40	50	60	70	80
13	13	25	18	21	43	41	64

Note that these figures do not refer to the *amount* of [r] -usage (Class I, for example, does not produce as many such non-standardisms as any other class), but to the proportion of non-standardisms that are [r] rather than [2].

   Turning now to the use of glottal stop variants in this environment, the following are the corresponding tables to those in the above subsections for the percentages of [2], after examples with

[r] have been discounted (Casual and Formal speech are not distinguished except in the first):

a)

	CS	FS	RP
I	0	0	0
II	11	5	2
III	34	22	3
IV	31	19	5
V	28	19	12

b)

M	W
20	15

c)

Bfd	Hfx	Hudd
30	16	11

d)

10	20	30	40	50	60	70	80
36	39	19	20	17	10	9	4

Figures 15 and 16 present comparative graphs for both prevocalic
environments, i.e. (VtV) and (Vt#V), by class and age.

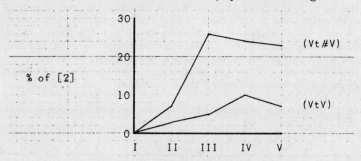

Figure 15:   (t) prevocalic in CS + FS - Class

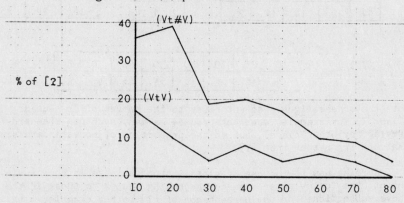

Figure 16:   (t) prevocalic in CS + FS - Age

The figures for the proportion of [r] among non-standard forms seem to indicate that this is the older non-standardism: table iv) shows that among the older informants this accounts for a greater percentage of non-standard pronunciations than among the younger, and table iii) that further away from Bradford it is progressively more common among such non-standardisms as do occur. Table i) shows that such forms account for more of the non-standard forms among the middle than the working classes (in Class I there were 16 [r] and only one [2] among the 342 occurrences of (Vt#V) in conversation.

The second set of tables show that the amount of [2]-usage among the three working classes is about the same in conversation but that they follow the 'expected order' in respect of bringing this non-standard feature 'under control' in the reading passage; and that [2] is much less common among the middle classes.   These facts, and the lower usage among women, are again in line with [2] being a stigmatised feature; and the tables for town and age-group again suggest that the glottal stop is on the increase and is 'moving outward' from Bradford.   The comparative graphs, Figures 15 and 16, show that in each group [2] is more common as a realisation of /t/ in prevocalic position if a word boundary follows /t/.

My conclusions are that though the glottal stop is a stigmatised variant it has advanced further in this environment than word-medially; as in other environments, it is increasing in its frequency from a regional centre in Bradford; and it shows signs of ousting the older non-standard variant [r][110].

(Vt# #)

Comparable tables for the realisation of /t/ as [2] in pre-pausal position are:

a)

	CS	FS	RP	WL
I	19	17	5	1
II	36	25	5	4
III	43	29	11	4
IV	42	32	16	8
V	36	32	10	15

b)

	M	W
CS + FS	35	31

c)

	Bfd	Hfx	Hudd
CS + FS	36	46	29

110   Anecdotal evidence in favour of this is the incidental remark of a 63-year old Class II man during the 'Self Evaluation' experiment: referring to [le2ə] and [pe2rəl] he exclaimed "That's another thing that's bad round here now - dropping t's: they say [gɒ2ə] where I would say [gɒrə] (and, incidentally, nobody can do that like a Yorkshireman!)".

d)

	10	20	30	40	50	60	70	80
CS + FS	64	55	28	25	25	22	22	18

Figures 17 and 18 compare the amount of [2] in my two word-final
environments, by class and age-groups.

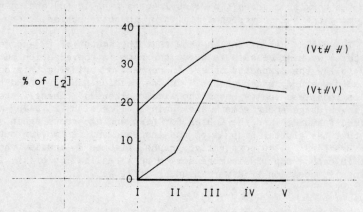

Figure 17:   (t) word-final in CS + FS - Class

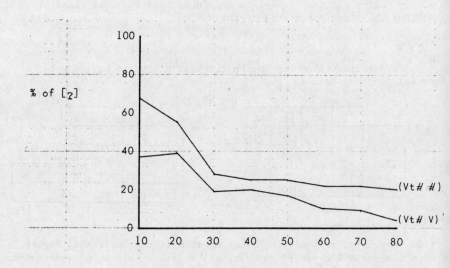

Figure 18:   (t) word-final in CS + FS - Age

Pre-pausal [ʔ] whether at the end of a clause or sentence or because of hesitation) is a phenomenon I have occasionally observed among RP speakers. Presumably therefore it is less unacceptable than the glottal stop in other environments. The facts that the above figures are higher than for the other subvariables examined here, especially in Class I, and that the differences between the sexes and the towns are less marked, seem to be in line with this.

We may conclude that, though not regarded as 'standard', the glottal stop in this environment is less stigmatised; Figure 17 suggests that it is even more sharply on the increase.

My general conclusions about the realisation of /t/ as [ʔ] are first, that it is unusual among the changes I have observed in the speech of the West Yorkshire towns in that it is not bringing the area more close to RP; second, that it is a feature which attracts overt stigmatisation, and varies in frequency between classes, styles and sexes in the way commonly found with such; nevertheless, third, it is increasing in frequency in this area and seems to be spreading outwards from a regional focal area in Bradford; and finally, the increase in the use of [ʔ] appears to be taking place by environments, in the following order:

1   V_#C: word/morpheme-final before consonant. Here it
            occurs even in RP.

2   V_# #: pre-pausal. Occasionally heard even in RP.

3   V_#V: word-final before vowel. Stigmatised but increas-
            ing.

4   V́_L: word-medial before liquid or /m/. Ditto.

5   V_V: intervocalic. Highly stigmatised and least common
            but nevertheless increasing.

The Variable (ɛə)

In our examination of the traditional dialect accounts in Chapter 5 it emerged that in respect of this diphthong there are differences both between different authorities and between different parts of the area. We saw that Wright had a unit /eə/ which most other works 'divided' into /ɛə/ and /eː/; and it appeared that in 'the Huddersfield system' the lexical load of /ɛə/ was greater since it included many words that had /aː/ elsewhere (i.e. '/aʊ/-words' such as *ground*, *south* etc. and some '/aː/ words' such as *park*, *yard* etc.)   My own preliminary observations suggested that in all three towns /ɛə/ and /e:/ are separate phonemes; and that the incidence of /ɛə/ is now very much as in RP - the typically Huddersfield forms have disappeared as far as the majority are concerned, as have /ɛə/ forms of *master*, *rather* etc: these 'dialect forms' have given way to ones with the same phoneme as in RP; on the other hand most people have 'transferred' *there*, *where* from /ɪə/ to /ɛə/, which also brings them into line with RP. However, it appeared that there is some phonetic variation in the realisation of /ɛə/.

Gimson describes /ɛə/ (1970:143) as a glide from around the half-open front position [ɛ] in the direction of /ə/ (whether of the more open or mid type depending on whether the syllable is open or closed); he notes that in both conservative and advanced RP the start-point may be more open, that in 'popular London speech' it may be closer to [e], and that in another form of advanced RP a long pure vowel [ɛ:] may be heard especially in a non-final syllable. In analysing the data of my survey, I felt able to distinguish the following variants occurring in the /ɛə/ lexical set as defined in RP (rather than in traditional dialect, since the great majority of speakers now have RP-like incidence): i) the [ɛə] pronunciation described by Gimson as the basic form; ii) the diphthong with a start-point closer to Cardinal 2 i.e. [eə] such as he said occurred in London speech; iii) a long monophthongal [ɛ:], described by Gimson as 'advanced RP', and occurring in my data even in final syllables; iv) very occasional 'dialectal' forms of *there*, *where* with [ɪə].

Being mainly interested in the extent of monophthongal pronunciation, since it was the variation between [ɛə] and [ɛ:] that had first struck me, I rated these as 1 and 0 respectively, while the less common [eə] and rare [ɪə] were scored as 1½ and 2.   An RP-like speaker should, according to Gimson's description and my method of scoring, receive a score of around 100 - the total score as a percentage of the total number of occurrences of (ɛə); a score lower than this indicates some monophthongal forms and one higher must be due to a number of regional [eə] and/or [ɪə].

Scores by class and sex are given in the following table.   A quite irregular picture emerged when subdividing by style, and there was no significant difference between the towns.   However, the age-groups scores (Figure 19) do look interesting.

	I	II	III	IV	V
M	74	96	79	97	102
W	-	60	76	82	81

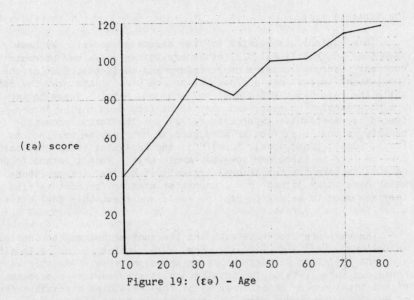

Figure 19: (εə) - Age

There is apparently no clear relation between (εə) and social
class or style, which suggests that no real significance is attached
to one's pronunciation as [εə] or [ε:].   Women do however appear to
use more monophthongal forms than men.   The most important factor
in the realisation of (εə) seems to be age: Figure 18 shows that
there is a marked 'drop' from the 80-plus group to the teenagers,
apparently reflecting a change [eə>εə>ε:].   The scores over 100,
reflecting some [eə] (and possibly [ɪə]) are confined to the over-
70s;   informants in the 50-plus and 60-plus groups have a score
around that we would expect from the above description of RP, i.e.
mostly [εə]; below that age monophthongal pronunciations are increasing and are in fact commoner than Gimson's account would lead
us to expect.   The one 'irregularity' in the graph is caused by the
30-plus group, and this very fact may support the hypothesis that
little social significance attaches to (εə) since it has been seen
that this group in my sample tended to have fewer 'regionally
marked' forms than their neighbours.

My conclusions are that a linguistic change is in progress
from a diphthongal to a long monophthongal realisation of this phoneme; and that this change is simply a function of time rather than
of any social significance attaching to variants (the fact that the
two main varients both occur in RP is presumably relevant here).

The Variable (ʊə)

This variable is related to (ɔə) discussed above. We have seen that in traditional dialects there was an /ɔː/-/ʊə/ phonemic contrast; through changes of inventory and incidence, much of the traditional lexical set of /ʊə/ has become part of the new /o:/ set, while the rest has yielded new /ɔə/ and /ʊə/ sets.   These latter are not 'stable' however, and many items from each may be 'transferred' by particular informants to /ɔː/.   The actual phonetic reality is that a particular word such as *door* may be realised as [dɔː], [dɔə], [doə], [dʊə], [duə][111]; and assigning it as 'basically' /ɔə/ or /ʊə/ is therefore somewhat arbitrary. What I intend to do here is to take the traditional lexical set of /ʊə/ (except those which have today joined /oː/), no matter whether for most people they now seem to belong to /ɔə/ or /ʊə/, and treat this (ʊə) set as a realisational variable.

The variants I operate with and the scores assigned to them are as follows: [ɔː] = 0, [ɔə] = 1, [oə] = 1½, [ʊə] = 2, [uə] = 2½ (if a slight [ᵂ] glide was detectable in any diphthongal form this was ignored e.g. [uᵂə],[ɔᵂə]). The total score is expressed as a percentage of the total number of occurrences of (ʊə), yielding a possible range of 0 - 250: any score over 100 thus indicates at least some [oə] or [ʊə] pronunciations, and so on.

Total scores by class and sex were as follows:

	I	II	III	IV	V
M	43	133	100	122	137
W	-	62	93	111	98

No interesting differences show up between the towns and scores are not given here.   Differences between styles were also not clear-cut, but there were signs of a general increase in more RP-like forms as formality increased.   Total scores by age-group are given in Figure 20 .

---

111 To quote some specific examples: though for a majority *more* belongs to the /ɔə/ set, one 70+ man pronounced it as [mu:ᵂə] in the word list; another said (*shore*) "[ʃoə] - that could be [ʃʊə]"; at least half-a-dozen pronounced words like *door, more, before* etc.with [oə] or [oᵂə] (and the 'dialectal' [fɔʊə] *4* is not uncommon, though the instances I recorded in the survey were all from elderly speakers) and one old gentleman said (*courting*): "[kɔətɪn - jə gɒr ə bɪ2 ə jɔ:kʃə ðɛə. dɪd jə noːʔɪs ɪ2 wə nɪərə kʊətɪn nə kɔətɪn]"

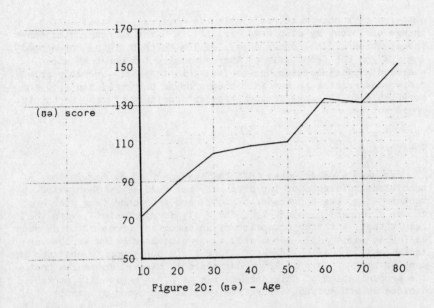

Figure 20: (ʊə) - Age

As regards social class, Class I scores much lower than the rest, averaging only 43, which probably reflects the RP tendency for many /ɔə/ and /ʊə/ words to merge with the /ɒ:/ group.   A score of 0 would indicate that this had occurred everywhere, whereas [43]/250 probably reflects the fact that though words like *poor* may be pronounced with /ɔ:/ in RP, the /ɔ:/-/ʊə/ contrast is still preserved by many (see p.137).   Otherwise, though more regional variants overall were heard in the lowest two classes, there is no clear pattern.   Women do appear to use more RP-like pronunciations than men, but there is no obvious class stratification.

Figure 20 shows that a striking correlate of variation in the realisation of (ʊə) is age: informants in their teens and 20s score lower than 100 on average, which must reflect the increasing tendency to merge /ɔə/ and /ʊə/ sets with /ɔ:/ (see p.136); above the age of 30 the 'average pronunciation' is [ɔə] plus some [ʊə], and in the older groups there is obviously a considerable amount of [oə], [ʊə], and [uə] pronunciation.   Note that this age-factor probably explains why Classes II and III are in 'reverse order' for male informants: Class III contains [4]/11 men under the age of 30, Class II only [1]/7.

My conclusions are that a linguistic change is in progress which is affecting the realisation of what remains of the traditional /ʊə/

set, and this change of realisation is obviously crucial to the
change of inventory discussed earlier; and the increasing monophthongisation of /ɔə/ shows a parallelism to that of the corresponding /ɛə/ on the front axis.   There are slight signs that more
social significance attaches to (ʊə) than to (ɛə); probably this
difference relates to the fact that whereas both [ɛə] and [ɛ:] are
acceptable in RP, some of the 'broader' variants of (ʊə) certainly
would not be.

The Variable (ɑ:)

We have already noted that the load carried by /a:/ in the
traditional dialects of the area has been reduced by changes of inventory (e.g. the appearance of /aʊ/) and incidence (e.g. /a:/>/ə:/
in *world*, *worst*, *servant* etc., /a:/>/ɔ:/ in *warm*, etc.), with the
result that, with the exception of an important group of words such
as *laugh*, *pass*, *path*, *dance* etc. to be discussed below as the variable (ɑ:/æ), the incidence of 'long A' in our towns is now much the
same as that of /ɑ:/ in RP.   But since it was my impression that
the pronunciation of this phoneme was at times regionally marked, I
decided to attempt to measure its realisation among my sample.

According to Gimson (1970:110), the phoneme /ɑ:/ as in *large*,
cart, *father* etc. is in RP generally 'somewhat nearer to Cardinal 5
than to Cardinal 4'; but 'a variety of /ɑ:/ fronted towards Cardinal 4 is heard...in many regional types of English'.   West Yorkshire is one area where fronter variants are commonly heard; but
since there is no front/back phonemic contrast with the open vowels
(though we noted in Chapter 5 that such a contrast did exist in the
traditional dialect of part of the area), a considerable degree of
phonetic variation is possible.

I felt that with my phonetic abilities I could not operate with
more than three admittedly arbitrary and impressionistic divisions:
if the pronunciation heard sounded fairly close to what would be
accepted as RP i.e. [ɑ:˕] to [ɑ:], this counted as 0; if it was an
obviously front [a:], quite close to Cardinal 4, it was scored as 1;
if it was somewhere mid-way between these i.e. [a:˔], closer to
Cardinal 4 than 5, it rated ½.   This is of course very crude, and
the notion of an 'average pronunciation' among a group is even more
dubious than that of an 'average score' when dealing with a two-
value variable, so I present my findings only very tentatively.

Use of non-standard i.e. fronter variants appeared to relate
to some extent to social class, though with the exception of Class
I (who had many more RP-like variants) the groups were not widely

separated. But as regards style, while fronter pronunciations were
commoner in casual speech, otherwise, though there was some slight
decrease in such variants with increasing formality, there was not
a great deal of difference between the styles. These points may
indicate that little significance is felt to attach to the pronunciation of /ɑ:/. However, it appeared that women are more sharply
differentiated by class, with Classes II and III much closer to RP
than the corresponding men, among whom, though the middle classes
show a lower score, the three working classes are in no 'regular'
order; this may indicate that women are more sensitive to the pronunciation of this phoneme than men. With reference to the different towns, the caveat on p. 146 should be noted: it is possible that
at different stages I was more strict about what I counted as say
[a:] rather than [a:ʳ]. But the fact that Huddersfield speakers
(whom I analysed last) generally scored higher than those in Halifax
would suggest that this was not entirely the case. Halifax does
appear to use less front variants than the other two, and the fact
that Huddersfield apparently has more front variants than Halifax
may be partly due to the historical fact that the phonemic contrast
/a:/-/ɑ:/ was commoner in that area.

    My conclusions are that realisations of /ɑ:/ as more front than
in RP do occur in the area, especially among the working classes
in Bradford and Huddersfield, but that little significance is generally attached to these fronter variants, possibly because this
difference from RP is more difficult to pin down than some others;
however, perhaps because they are more aware of the 'harsher' sound
(as some informants expressed it), women tend to use less regional
variants than men and present a clearer pattern of class stratification.

The Variables (eɪ) and (əʊ)

    We discussed earlier the inventory variables (ɛɪ/e:) and (ɔʊ/o:),
and found a considerable degree of parallelism. We noted that these
two phonemic contrasts, which do not exist in RP, show signs of
weakening; obviously important in this process is the realisation
of the phonemes, as a modification in the direction of RP is likely
to bring about mergers. For this reason, and also because, whether
or not the phonemic contrasts are fully maintained, 'the way he
sounds his [eɪ]s and [əʊ]s' are an important part of our main theme
- the persistence or modification of Yorkshire forms - something
must be said about the realisation of these phonemes.

    Most (eɪ) words, as defined by the incidence of /eɪ/ in RP,
belong in West Yorkshire to the /e:/ set. The commonest pronunciation of this is as a long monophthong, somewhere between Cardinal

Vowels 2 and 3, which will be referred to as [e:][112]; sometimes an
'impure diphthong' is heard, i.e. a prolonged first element with
only a very brief glide at the end: [e·ɪ]; the third variant recognised is the true diphthong [eɪ] as most usually heard in RP.
The few words in the /ɛɪ/ set are usually realised with a wide diphthong [ɛɪ]; if this is narrowed to [eɪ] the result is of course
indistinguishable from the RP sound and also from this possible
realisation of /e:/.   The 'new' West Yorkshire phoneme /o:/ accounts for the majority of (əʊ) words.   Its most common realisation
is as a long monophthong somewhere between Cardinal Vowels 6 and 7,
which will be referred to as [o:], though occasionally a more open
variant closer to Cardinal 6, [ɔ:], is heard (mainly, in my data,
in those items where this sound occurred in traditional dialect).
Sometimes one hears an impure diphthong [o·ʊ]; if a true diphthong
is produced it is usually a fairly back one [oʊ], the RP-like [əʊ]
with its centralised start-point is less common.   The /ɔʊ/ phoneme
has as its 'basic' variant a wide diphthong starting close to Cardinal 6, [ɔʊ]; if the diphthong is narrowed to [oʊ] it will of
course be indistinguishable from that variant of /o:/, as it will
also if produced with the centralised start-point as [əʊ]

I attempted, when listening to the tapes, to score every instance of (eɪ) or (əʊ) as one of the above variants; but this was
one of the areas where I felt the least confidence in my ability
to hear and record with accuracy and consistency.   (Was the start-
point of a particular instance really closer to [ɛ] than to [e]?;
was there really a slight glide at the end, i.e. was it [e·ɪ]
rather than [e:]?; and so on.)   I shall not therefore detail my
findings, but simply present my conclusions as general impressions,
which may be checked by a more skilled phonetician.

In almost all sections of the population the percentage of regional pronunciations is high: only in Class I and among women of
Class II do RP-like forms appear to be in a majority.   The classes
are in the 'expected' order, but the three working classes show
little real difference from each other.

Sex does appear to be an important factor: these two variables
seem to be stratifying features for women much more than for men.
Women show a marked but steady decrease in regional variants as
one looks higher on the social scale; and women of Classes II and

---

112   Some writers (e.g. Samuels, 1972:22) have chosen to represent
it by [ɛ:].   I prefer [e:], but I think I occasionally noticed variation within an individual's speech, e.g. *take* [ę:], *neighbour*
[ɛ̧:] - but I could see no pattern, and anyway I have insufficient
evidence or trust in my own ear to draw any conclusions.   It may
be noted that the Standard English realisation of both /eɪ/ and /əʊ/
was monophthongal some 2½ centuries ago (see Strang, 1970:110).

III had many fewer Yorkshire forms than did men of the same groups; with men, the working classes were hardly differentiated, and even though those of Class II produced fewer regional forms, these were still in a majority. These findings suggest that women are more aware of the regional sound of certain variants.

The scores by style showed some decrease in regional variants as one passed from casual speech to the more careful styles, but it was neither sharp nor regular. No pattern was discernible between the age-groups, so any change in progress is taking place by class, rather than simply with time as with (εə) for example. Between the towns there was no marked difference; such as did occur could probably be accounted for in terms of the different class- or sex-composition of the three samples.

My conclusions are that while the incidence of (eɪ) and (əʊ) is now very much as in RP, the realisation of these commonly-occurring variables is one of the most persistent regional features in West Yorkshire. While there are signs that women are more aware than men of these variables, there is comparatively little evidence of social significance attaching to the various pronunciations and consequently no clear sign of a change to more RP-like forms in progress.

The Variables (aɪ) and (aʊ)

The phonemes /aɪ/ and /aʊ/ were briefly discussed above from the viewpoint of inventory and incidence,with the conclusion that the traditional dialect situation in this area has now largely given way to one very like that in RP. But their realisation may still be regional to some extent.

Gimson (1970:130 and 136) says that in RP the glide of /aɪ/ begins near to the C4 position [a] and moves in the direction of [ɪ], whereas that of /aʊ/ usually starts somewhat closer to C5 than C4 and moves towards [ʊ] i.e. they are 'front-closing' and 'back-closing' diphthongs respectively. In West Yorkshire I think the realisation may differ in two ways. The first concerns their start-points: it seems to me that these are often 'reversed' in relation to RP i.e. the sound in *bout* has the fronter start while that in *bite* is towards the back: a more appropriate transcription might then be /ɑɪ/ and /aʊ/. Thus:

RP according to Gimson   aɪ   aʊ↑   W Yks   aʊ   ɑɪ

Unfortunately, I felt that my phonetic acuteness was insufficient
for me to attempt to decide on the start-point of each example of
(aɪ) or (aʊ) in my data, and this should best be left for a later
investigation (possibly by spectrographic analysis of some of my
material).   The second possible difference is in the length of first
elements.   Both these diphthongs may not be 'pure' in the sense
that neither vowel is of greater duration: possibly because of the
influence of traditional dialect where /a:/ occurred, particularly
in the 'Bradford system' (see p. 82) in many of what are now '/aʊ/
words', it seems from my observation that besides the small percentage of [a:] pronunciations that still occur, a sort of 'compromise variant' [a·ʊ] i.e. an impure diphthong with a prolonged first
element is sometimes heard.   And a similar variant of (aɪ) seems to
occur in [ɑ·ɪ];   whether this is also due to the traditional dialect
/ɑ:/ I hesitate to say in view of the facts that on the one hand the
traditional /ɑ:/ phoneme did not occur throughout our area: it was
restricted to the Huddersfield area, with Halifax apparently near
the isogloss (see p. 98), while [ɑ·ɪ] variants are observed throughout;   and on the other hand only part of the modern lexical set of
(aɪ) belonged to /ɑ:/ (or /aɪ/ in the Bradford system):   much of the
rest came from /i:/ e.g. *light*, yet [a·ɪ] variants seem to occur in
these items too.

In scoring these variables according to the 'purity' of the
diphthong, I attempted in each case to employ a three-way division
as implied above: [aʊ] - [a·ʊ] - [a:] and [aɪ] - [ɑ·ɪ] - [ɑ:].
But as is commonly the case in matters of realisation, though the
extremes are sufficiently distinct from each other for one to be in
no doubt whether what is heard is say [aʊ] or [a:], there is considerable room for inconsistency between [aʊ] and [a·ʊ], or [a·ʊ]
and [a:]:   it is not easy for a relatively unskilled phonetician
to decide whether the first element of a diphthong is really lengthened or whether there really is a quick glide towards a close-vowel
position at the end (rarely does it in fact get past half-close, of
course);   I have therefore less confidence in my findings here.

I noted only a small proportion of instances of the monophthongal variants [ɑ:] and [a:], and comparatively few impure diphthongs
(less than 25% even in casual conversation).   Such instances as did
occur seemed to relate to class and style in the way 'expected'
with stigmatised variants, but no clear pattern was observable between the sexes or the age-groups.

There were more examples of the long monophthongal [a:] variant
of (aʊ) than there were of the [ɑ:] variant of (aɪ);   but the percentage of the latter was some 2½ times greater in Huddersfield than
in Bradford, and in Halifax too it was higher than in Bradford -
this we might have expected from the traditional dialect situation.

My conclusions are that the situation with the diphthongs /aɪ/
and /aʊ/ in this area is now very much as in RP in the most important
respects of inventory and incidence, but that the realisation of
these phonemes, in respect of the length of the first element, where
in a minority of occurrences there appears to be some prolongation,
and probably also the start-points, may be among the regional features which persist.

4   Incidence Variables

It has already been seen in passing that very many changes of
incidence have taken place in this area, with the result that local
speech has in this respect come much closer to RP.   But a few widespread differences do remain, and we shall here examine four of
these, all of which present some very interesting points.

The Variable (ɑ:/æ)

This involves one of the best-known and most pervasive differences between the speech of different parts of Britain.   The lexical set involved includes a hundred or so words; in RP and also in
the Southern part of England generally these have the phoneme /ɑ:/,
while in the Northern part they have /æ/.   Since the phonemic inventories of both areas contain both /ɑ:/ and /æ/ (both have the
contrast *cart - cat* for example), this is obviously a matter of
incidence rather than of inventory.

The words where this variation occurs are in the main predictable from the environment of /ɑ:~æ/, and specifically, from the
following phoneme or group.   They are those with a) final /s,f,θ/
e.g. *pass*, *laugh*, *bath*; b) final /st,fs,ft,θs~ðz,θt/ e.g. *past* ,
passed, *laughs, laughed, craft*, *paths*, *bathed* (past tense of the verb
bath): c) final /ns,nʃ~ntʃ,nt,nd/ e.g. *dance, branch*, *plant*,
demand[113].   In West Yorkshire virtually all such words are commonly
pronounced with /æ/, whereas in RP the majority have /ɑ:/[114].   The
RP/Southern situation seems to be less consistent than the Northern
because of two groups of exceptions: first, a number of words which

---

113 *Can't*, which always has /ɑ:/, cannot really be counted as an
exception.

114 RP is in fact the 'innovator': until the 17th Century the
short vowel was standard; then [a>ɑ:/_f,s,θ,r,fC,sC,rC] and somewhat later in the environments with a nasal (see Ekwall, 1975:25);
in our area the lengthening only occurred before [r(C)].   Samuels
(1972:31) points out that 'continual swings in fashions of preference
for /a/ and /ɑ:/ took place in the late 18th and early 19th centuries'.

have the above phonological structure but which nevertheless always
have /æ/ e.g. *gas*, *mass* (but *pass*); *expand* (but *demand*); *cant*,
rant (but *plant*, *grant*); *finance* (but *dance*); and derived forms
e.g. *classic* (but *classy*, *classable*); second, a number where some
RP speakers have /ɑ:/ but others /æ/: usually in non-final syllables
e.g. *masculine*, *plastic*, *elastic*, *drastic*, *lather*, *sample*, *example*,
trans-, but also in (-)*graph*. In West Yorkshire all the above are
traditionally /æ/ words.

Since it was quite obvious from both spontaneous comments and
elicited reactions (see Chapter 7) that this is a feature of which
many are conscious, one might well expect it to constitute a variable like the other major North/South difference: (ʌ)

But in fact with the exception of the word *father*, where (unlike
lather) the /æ/ form is now regarded as 'dialect' and virtually all
speakers have /ɑ:/, and *master*, *plaster* (unlike *faster*) where the
/æ/ form is a minority pronunciation, the actual proportion of /ɑ:/
forms I recorded is too small for this to be treated as a variable
like those examined thus far: the great majority of speakers have
/æ/ consistently.

The /ɑ:/ forms which did occur are accounted for as follows.
First, two informants (both of Class I and educated at public schools
outside Yorkshire) were consistent /ɑ:/ users. Second, several
odd examples turned up, from informants who probably have some sense
of the 'significance' of this form. Seven informants produced just
one such during the interview, all but one of these in the 'artificial' situations of reading passage or word list, where more care was
presumably being taken: they ranged from Class II to Class V (where
three people did this!). Two people produced two such forms,
again in the reading passage or word list: one was a girl who had
been to a private school where some attention was given to 'elocution'
and the other an elderly gentleman of 'lower-white-collar' status
though living on a council estate, who was active in the Catholic
theatre and opera group. Three instances (one in conversation)
were produced by a Class II housewife who said she tried to 'speak
well', and five (two in conversation) by a man in his sixties who
was an experienced public speaker in socialist and atheist circles.
Even in these last cases the /ɑ:/ forms occurred in less than 10%
of the words eligible, and the proportion with the others was still
smaller.

With just three informants did the proportions of the two
variants seem really to justify the term 'variable': they used the
following numbers of /ɑ:/-/æ/:

	CS	FS	RP	WL	MP
Mr. L	1/1	2/0	5/8	3/5	0/1
Miss L	0/2	10/10	10/3	8/3	1/0
Mrs H	-	0/12	7/6	4/3	0/1

Mr L (Class I) had been to public school (but within Yorkshire); he
was a retired mill-owner and magistrate; his performance is interesting in that he used a higher proportion of /ɑ:/ forms in conversation (though admittedly he produced few instances of this variable)
than in the more artificial styles, and in the reading passage he
produced one /ɑ:/ and one /æ/ in the two instances of *laugh* .

Miss L (Class III) was a woman in her seventies, a retired book-
keeper/secretary, whose speech struck one as 'status incongruent' -
probably largely because of her long interest and activity in
recitation and singing with the famous Huddersfield Choral Society.

Mrs H (Class II) was a well-educated housewife in her late thirties,
quite well-to-do and not happy about living in Bradford or the way
people speak there; none of her /ɑ:/ forms occurred in conversation.

    Obviously the amount of /ɑ:/ usage is too low to correlate
meaningfully with any of the usual factors, except that in Class I
two of the three informants were consistent /ɑ:/ users and the
third was Mr L; and that style ties in to a limited extent in that
/ɑ:/ is much more likely to occur in the careful styles.   But even
here a lack of 'pattern' obviously causes some difficulty: in the
minimal pairs list, where informants were shown *gas/grass* only three
people (the two consistent /ɑ:/-users and Miss L) contrasted these
as [gæs] - [grɑ:s]; all the other 103 informants had /æ/ in both.

    My conclusion is that though there is certainly some feeling
that RP /ɑ:/ is a mark of 'superior' speech (in various senses of
that term, see Chapter 7), and people who try to 'improve' their
speech often pick on this as one of the most obvious things they
can change (and most of the informants who produced any /ɑ:/ forms
gave some sign of 'speech consciousness'), yet most speakers cling
to /æ/ here - sometimes belligerently (see p.286).   My impression
is that this is possibly the last Northern feature to be abandoned
if a speaker (perhaps living in the South) *unconsciously* conforms
more and more to an RP-like pronunciation; and many never lose it.
It presents a contrast to the other major North/South difference
(ʌ), and the only explanation that suggests itself is what while the

majority of the English speaking world has the /ʌ/-/ʊ/ contrast and
Northern speakers therefore feel under more pressure to acquire /ʌ/,
with /ɑ:/æ) it is not a matter of inventory, and the Northern form
has a great deal of support from other English-speaking areas.

The Variable (ook)

Words spelled with *oo* generally have a different pronunciation
in the traditional dialects of our area from what is heard in RP:
for example, [muɪn] *moon*, [fuɪt] *foot*, [bluɪd] *blood*. But changes
of incidence have resulted in the great majority of urban speakers
now having the same phoneme as in RP: thus /u:/ in *food*, *moon* etc.,
/ʊ/ in *good*, *foot* etc., and the variable (ʌ) in *flood*, *blood* etc.
But one group of fairly common *oo* words, which includes *book*, *cook*,
hook, *look*, *nook*, *shook*, *took*, *mistook* etc. present a different
picture both in traditional dialect, where unlike the above which
have /ʊɪ/ the pronunciation is with /u:/ or, according to some
authorities (see p. 85), /ɪu/; and in urban speech today, where
though RP has /ʊ/, a form with /u:/ is still quite commonly heard[115].

All the words in the lexical set involved have /k/ following
the vowel in question, but that this is a matter of phonemic incidence rather than distribution is clear from the fact that the
sequence /ʊk/ is quite possible, occurring in *luck*, *muck* etc. for
the majority of speakers. In fact the lexical set involved in
this variable is generally predictable from the spelling *ook*[116].

Superficially, this might appear to be another example of a
situation quite commonly found: a regional pronunciation in variation with an RP-like one.   But when we examine the percentages
of /u:k/ forms in relation to the usual non-linguistic factors we
find that in one respect at least this is a very unusual variable.

The scores by class and style are given in Figure 21, and by
sex and style in Figure 22.   The following table gives scores

---

115 It is not only in West Yorkshire that /u:k/ forms occur; my
impression is that it is even more common (especially among younger
age-groups) in parts of Lancashire.   (One of my informants in her
30s claimed [lu:k] was 'Lancashire' when I offered it in the self-
evaluation section - and then realised that her own father used it.)

116 See Ekwall (1975:11): in the environment /-k/ the change
ME ō >EModE ū later [ʊ] (as in *good, foot*) was arrested in this
region.   Several 16th and 17th century grammars still show a long
vowel for English generally.

by age and style, and the total scores by age-groups are shown in
Figure 23.   No marked differences showed up between the three towns.

	CS	FS	RP	WL	MP
10	0	0	5	10	29
20	7	0	0	2	23
30	0	0	7	10	23
40	4	11	27	45	50
50	19	27	40	29	67
60	26	10	56	64	71
70	12	30	49	57	75
80	57	14	95	100	100

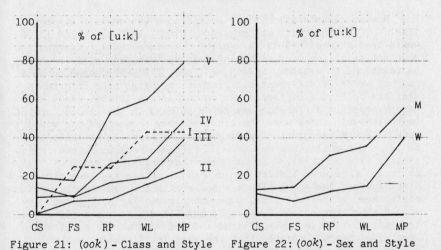

Figure 21: (ook) - Class and Style   Figure 22: (ook) - Sex and Style

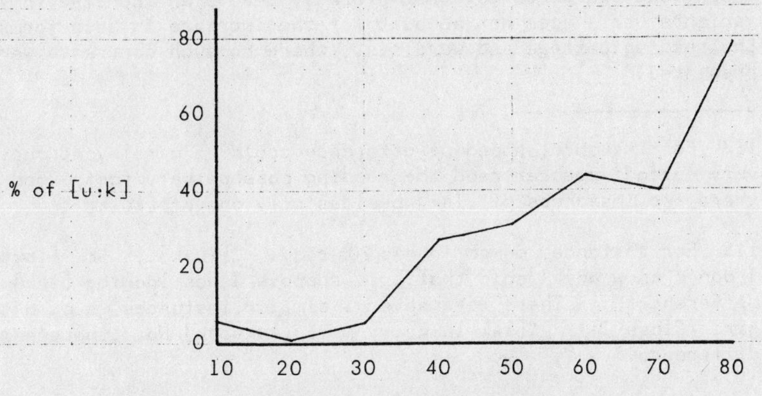

Figure 23:   (ook) - Age

The above scores were all broken down by style, since this is
the most interesting apparent correlate of variation in this case.
The situation most commonly found with the variables examined in
this chapter has been for the regional variant to be most common
in casual speech, and to become less so as formality increases; in
the 'artificial' situations of the reading passage and the word list
informants are much more likely to produce the more RP-like form,
and this is often particularly likely in the minimal pairs situation
But with (ook) this pattern appears to be almost completely reversed
In conversation, little difference showed up between casual and
formal speech (though a larger amount of data on this not very
commonly-occurring variable might show up some tendencies[117]), but
as the situation was made more formal and artificial, the regional
variant became more and more *frequent*.

Now as regards the minimal pairs, some explanation suggests
itself.   The informant was presented with *luck/look*, which in RP
would be distinguished as /ʌ/-/ʊ/.   But since the ʌ/ʊ distinction
does not exist for many of my informants, this pair will for them
be identical in everyday speech, as [lʊk].   However, when shown a
pair of words of different spelling and meaning, many informants
will try to find a difference in pronunciation if they can - and
here a possible difference was ready to hand in the [lu:k] form of
look with which they were familiar, so they pronounced the word
thus[118] although in normal circumstances they might be unlikely to do
so.   But while this may account for some responses, and incidentally fits in nicely with the fact that only in Class I was there
no 'rise' from word list to minimal pairs (these speakers already
distinguished *luck/look* with ʌ/ʊ and so did not need to 'create' a
difference), there are still some unexplained facts.   First, why
should some speakers of Classes II and III who did have [ʌ] in *luck*
also say [lu:k] i.e. they created a double difference (quality and
length)?   Second, granted that the very artificial situation of
seeing the two words together probably led to an increase in /u:k/
variants, this does not account for the increase in such forms in
the reading passage and word list, where no such contrasts were
presented.

_____

117 For instance, speed of utterance could be a relevant factor: one
very 'broad' speaker read the reading passage very fast - and produce
there two instances of [lʊk] besides only one of [lu:k].

118 For instance, a man in his 20s read: "[lu:k]... No, [lʊk]...
I don't know why I said that... I suppose I was looking [lʊk] for
differences".   There were several similar instances, e.g. a teenage
girl (Class II): "[lʌk-lu:k]... No...[lʊk-lʊk] No...there's *some*
difference!"

Turning to the difference between the sexes, the situation is more familiar: figures for regional pronunciations among women are consistently lower than those for men (this holds for all social classes); but both sexes show the unexpected increase in /u:k/ variants as formality increases.

Something like the familiar pattern also holds among the social classes - at least as far as Classes II - V are concerned, with more non-standard variants heard lower down the social scale. But we may note that the classes become increasingly differentiated in the more formal styles: contrast say (h); and that the figures for Class I cut right across the otherwise almost 'regular' class pattern.

There are of course only three informants in this class group, and such a sample could easily be biased; let us examine it further to see whether this is the explanation. First, all three are men, and it has already emerged that men use /u:k/ forms more than women; but surely the difference between the sexes is not great enough for this to be the whole explanation. Second, two came from Huddersfield, and one from Halifax; overall Huddersfield had a slightly greater frequency of /u:k/ than the other two towns, but these differences are probably too small to be significant, and certainly cannot explain away the 'irregularity' of Class I here. Third, perhaps age might be important - closer examination reveals that all the /u:k/ forms in Class I came from the same man (in the word list and minimal pairs he had /u:k/ in all the words in question, which accounts for the 33% Class I score), and he was in his seventies.

Figure 23 does indeed seem to show that age is an important factor: below the age of 40 use of the /u:k/ variant is rare, but then it rises fairly steeply (though the figures for the 80-plus group are of course probably artificially high, since all three informants are of Class V and class has already been seen to be an important factor). When the total figures are broken down by style (see the above table), it is clear that the younger groups use very few /u:k/ forms in normal conversation or even when reading: only in the most artificial situations do they 'recall' them.

My conclusions are as follows: most obviously, a linguistic change towards an RP-like incidence is in progress, with time the most important factor, though class and sex play a less important part; this change is well advanced, with /ʊk/ virtually universal among the under-40s in everyday speech, and even the older groups showing a large proportion of such forms[119]; but the evidence from

---

119 The older groups sometimes show both variants literally

the different style figures suggests that there is no strong feeling of 'inferiority' about the regional variant - indeed there is
some sign that especially lower down the social scale it is felt to
be 'correct'. Finally, as a point of methodological interest, it
has been seen from two such cases that a group of just three informants may give an unrepresentative score where it is biased in respect of some factor that turns out to be significant.

The Variable (eɪC)

This is a variable involving phonemic incidence in a small set
of lexical items: monosyllabic verbs ending in RP/eɪk/ which are
'strong' i.e. they form their past tense by vowel change - by (*ook*)
take,*shake* or (əʊ): *break*, *wake*. Weak verbs of the same phonological shape (*bake, brake, cake, fake, flake, rake, stake* etc.),
and nouns (*cake, hake, flake* etc.,see below) do not form part of the
lexical set in question, but *make* does belong with the 'strong'
group in this respect, though its past tense formation is neither
by vowel change as in the rest, nor by simple suffixation, as with
the weak group. The past tense *made* may also belong to the set,
which accounts for its being labelled (eɪC) rather than (eɪk); so
too may the past participles *taken* and *shaken*, and the noun from
one of the verbs in question: *a break*.

The traditional dialect accounts give forms such as [mak,tak,
ʃak], [brek] in Bradford but [brɛɪk] in Huddersfield, [me:d~mɛəd],
[wakn~wɒkn]. In urban speech today such forms are very rare;
what one usually hears is either a form of the /e:/ phoneme[120] (which
presumably represents the local version of the RP phoneme) or a
pronunciation with /e/. We are concerned here with the variation
in the set as defined above between a long vowel (some form of the
(eɪ) variable) and the short /e/; scores are given in the form of
the percentage of /e/ variants.

The following tables present the scores by a) class and style,

---

alongside each other: for example, a woman in her late 60s said "We
read these [buːks,lʊk]", and a man in his 70s "it didn't [luːk]...,
it [lʊkt]...". It is true that *looked* may not be an example of
(*ook*), since it was shortened many centuries before *look* in the
Standard language; but though a short vowel was commoner among my
sample than in the present tense, I certainly recorded instances
of [luːkt], [kuːkt] etc.

120 With *break*, /ɛɪ/ may occur in Huddersfield.

b) class and sex, and c) age-group; the latter two are for conversation (CS plus FS) only.   Totals (CS plus FS) by town: Bfd 40%,
Hfx 22%, Hudd 33%.

a)   b)

	CS	FS	RP	WL	CS + FS
I	0	0	0	0	0
II	22	13	0	0	16
III	29	13	0	0	29
IV	58	21	2	2	40
V	51	41	0	1	45

	M	W
I	0	–
II	22	5
III	33	27
IV	44	34
V	37	72

  e)

10	20	30	40	50	60	70	80
22	39	18	23	25	41	39	38

     Examples of this variable are not very frequent, so some
'irregularities' might be expected; but in general we find that
table a) shows the relation between the /e/ variant and class and
style that is now familiar with a feature which attracts some stigma;
this is especially obvious in the style figures where the non-
standard incidence is seen hardly ever to occur in the 'careful'
situations.   With sex, the picture is again familiar - women using
less of the non-standard variant than men - except in Class V; but
since only 13 instances of (eɪC) occurred among women of this group
the score is probably not representative.

     No explanation for the less common use of the /e/ variant in
Halifax suggests itself; we have seen with a number of variables
that my Halifax sample was closer to the RP standard.

     The age-group scores contain two points of interest: the 30-
plus group uses the smallest percentage of non-standard variants yet
again; and the figures for the over-60s are comparatively high.
Yet the traditional dialect works seem to suggest that this is a
relatively new non-standard variant: the older works show little
evidence of it, while SED gives it alongside the more traditional
forms.   My findings seem to suggest that /e/ forms were probably
'taking over' from an earlier date than the traditionalists admit.

     Where has this /e/ form come from?   From my findings I have
concluded that a number of changes are in progress and most of these
are in the direction of RP - but here is a new non-standard form
replacing an older one.   Two possible explanations seem possible:
the /e/ forms are recorded in other parts of the North and Midlands
in EDGr - perhaps they have spread at the expense of [mak,tak] etc;
on the other hand it has been suggested that certain 'midway' forms

may develop as a result of the pressure of RP on local dialects
(see Viereck, 1966); could [mek] be midway between [mak] and [meɪk],
with a change in quality but not in length?   Perhaps both factors
are involved - they do not appear to be mutually exclusive.

My conclusions are that there has, for whatever reason, been a
change from the traditional dialect phoneme incidence in this area,
which has brought items from a number of sources into a new lexical
set with a relatively new non-standard variant[121]; this variant
shows the by now familiar signs of being the subject of conscious
or unconscious stigma, and is of low frequency especially among the
middle classes; and were it not for the high score in the 20-plus
group, the age-group scores might point to its becoming less common.

(It was my impression after listening to all my material that
made is less commonly said with /e/ than the other members of the
set, and that if it had been excluded the frequency of /ek/ might
well have proved higher than the above scores for /eC/ suggest.
Since detailed records were not kept this is a hypothesis for future
testing rather than a conclusion).

The Variable (ing)

Variation between /ɪŋ/ and /ɪn/ in participles and gerunds
formed the subject of one of the earliest attempts to correlate linguistic variation with non-linguistic factors by means of a 'quantitative' study (Fisher, 1958), and has also been examined in other
studies, such as those of Labov and Trudgill.   That this is a matter
of incidence rather than of inventory or distribution is obvious
from the occurrence of contrasts such as *sing* - *sin* etc.   This
variation occurs over much of the English-speaking world, and has
done so for centuries[122].   Nowadays /ɪŋ/ and /ɪn/ are standard and
non-standard respectively, the use of the latter as a prestige form
in British English having virtually disappeared.   Traditional dialect descriptions of West Yorkshire suggest that /ɪn/ was universal.

In British English at least this variation is not confined to
participles and gerunds: it occurs with other cases of unstressed
-ing such as *shilling*, *morning*, *during*, *something* etc.   Trudgill

---

121 This new set is strictly defined: one can [mek ɪm tek ɪt], or
(tek ə brek], but one cannot *[bek ə kek].

122 Vachek (1964) in an article discussing the phonemic status of
[ŋ], says that [ŋ~ɪn] has occurred since Early ModE or even Late ME
in the North.

does not make it clear whether he included such under his (ng) variable.   I decided that since variation in these words does occur in
West Yorkshire I would include them; however, because my preliminary observations seemed to indicate that /ɪn/ might not be so frequent here, I subdivided (ing) into two subvariables scored separately: a) Participles and Gerunds, where -*ing* is a separable
element and 'ing-less' forms like *go, walk, run* etc. occur; b)
others, where 'ing-less' forms like **dur-, even-, shill-, someth-*
are impossible.   The two subvariables will hereafter be referred to
as (ing) and (thing); scores will be in terms of percentages of /ɪn/.

(ing)

     Scores by class and style are given in Figure 24.   Table a) sub-
divides this by sex, and table b) gives the total scores (except MP)
by age-group.   No real differences show up between the towns,
though Huddersfield scored somewhat higher overall than the other two.

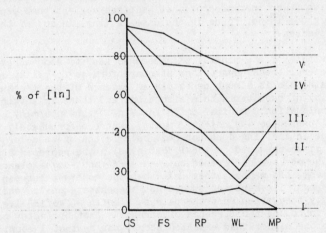

Figure 24: (ing) - Class and Style

a)

	CS		FS		RP		WL		MP	
	M	W	M	W	M	W	M	W	M	W
I	16	–	12	–	8	–	11	–	0	–
II	75	35	57	18	41	21	21	6	43	17
III	90	89	50	57	36	45	14	24	55	41
IV	95	95	75	78	69	78	51	47	59	67
V	95	98	91	94	83	79	73	69	77	67

b)

10	20	30	40	50	60	70	80
63	65	56	62	59	68	79	(99)

The relation between the amount of /ɪn/ and class and style is such as would suggest that this is a stigmatised form: Classes I to V have progressively more /ɪn/ variants and all groups show fewer such forms with increasing formality.   This fits in with the reactions to be examined in Chapter 7, and the opinion several times expressed that "dropping g is lazy"[123].   But two points do not fit so neatly with this: firstly /ɪn/ forms are extremely common in conversation (in casual speech even Class II has more /ɪn/ than /ɪŋ/, and in formal they are still very frequent), and even in the reading passage Classes IV and V have over three-quarters such variants; in these respects (ing) presents a very different picture from say (h).   Secondly, the scores by sex show that the usual pattern of women using fewer instances of a stigmatised variant than men of the same group is not found in the case of (ing) in any of the three working classes.

As with (ʌ), the minimal pairs scores seem to show a reversal of the general trend towards the standard form as formality increases - but again this is almost certainly an example of the frequent unreliability of results in this situation, and there is a fairly simple explanation: minimal pairs for /ɪn-ɪŋ/ are not many, and the example I presented was *coffin/coughing*, where unfortunately the difference in spelling does not rest only in the presence or absence of *g*, which would be ideal, but also in the representation of /ɒf/.   The obvious difference between *-off-* and *-ough-* clearly distracted many informants: they felt that the contrast between the two words must lie here and so did not concentrate on the ending. Accordingly they often read the pair as ['kɒfɪn - "kɒfin] i.e. they tried to introduce a difference of stress!   Another factor contributing to the higher than expected scores may be that I counted as failure to distinguish a few cases where the informant *did* perceive

---

123 Note that West Yorkshire is not in that part of Northern England where a pronunciation actually with /g/ is common e.g. [wɔːkɪŋg] - though seven informants did produce one or more examples of [ɪŋg]: six of these were women, and all examples occurred in the word list or minimal pairs, so one is tempted to put this down to extreme carefulness.   However the facts that all but one came from Huddersfield, and that the two with most instances had grown up South of the town make one wonder whether there could be some regional factor involved.

that the contrast lay in the ending, but read them the wrong way
round; and also two informants who pronounced both as [kɒfɪŋ].

The age-group scores show no steady trend. We may note that
yet again the lowest scores come in the 30-plus group, and there is
some upward swing over the age of 50, which might possibly indicate
an increase in /ɪŋ/ usage early this century.

(-thing)

The following table gives the scores by class and style, with
the comparable figures for (ing) in brackets. Figure 25 contrasts
(ing) and (-thing) in the total scores (excluding minimal pairs) by
class, and Figure 26 subdivides (-thing) scores by class and sex.
There is very little difference between the towns in respect of
(-thing), or between the age-groups (if the class-biased 80-plus
group is excluded); these scores are not given here.

	CS		FS		RP		WL		Totals	
I	17	(16)	4	(12)	0	(8)	0	(11)	5	(11)
II	28	(59)	11	(41)	0	(32)	0	(14)	11	(40)
III	35	(89)	15	(54)	4	(41)	0	(20)	17	(59)
IV	32	(95)	22	(76)	2	(74)	5	(49)	19	(78)
V	47	(96)	22	(92)	2	(81)	0	(72)	23	(89)
Total	35	(89)	17	(63)	2	(59)	0	(40)		

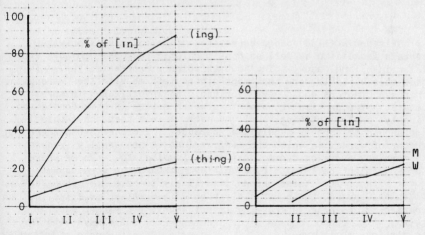

Figure 25: (ing) and (thing) - Class   Figure 26: (thing) - Sex

(-thing) shows the same relation to class and style as does (ing),
in the sense that non-standard forms are progressively less common
towards the upper end of the social scale and are less common among
all social groups as formality increases; but the scores for
(-thing) are in every case very much lower than those for (ing),
and in the reading passage and word list the /ɪn/ variant hardly
ever occurs; and whereas with (ing) there was no real difference
between the sexes over much of the social scale, with (-thing) women
score lower than men in every class.   The facts seem to suggest
that /ɪn/ with words of the (-thing) group is a more 'unacceptable'
variant than in Participles and Gerunds.

My conclusions about /ɪŋ~ɪn/ variation are these: if the
traditional descriptions are accurate in claiming /ɪn/ to have been
virtually universal, then there has certainly been some change in
the direction of RP; but /ɪn/ continues to occur, though as a non-
standard variant (the prestige usage seems to have disappeared), and
it is extremely common and does not present such clear evidence of
being a stigmatised feature as does h-dropping, for example.   My
hypothesis about the different frequency of /ɪn/ between Participles
and Gerunds and other types of unstressed -*ing* was correct: /ɪn/
forms are much less common in the latter - whether this is because
of historical factors (e.g. /ɪn/ is spreading from Participle/
Gerunds to other -*ing* forms and has not yet become so common there)
is a possibility worth considering.   This section has also given
further reason for treating the findings of minimal pairs tests
with great caution.

Fischer's (1958) paper correlated /ɪŋ/-/ɪn/ variation with
certain linguistic as well as non-linguistic factors.   My own division into (ing) and (-thing) subvariables was of this type.   In
fact this variable more than most others left me with the impression
that such factors could very profitably be investigated in more
detail.   Two particular points are worth noting in this connection.
Firstly, after listening to all my data, I felt that the (-thing)
set should be further subdivided, because it includes two different
groups of words, in which the /ɪn/ variant is not equally frequent:
1) *morning*, *evening*, *during*, *shilling*, *Reading* etc. - forms where
the -*ing* might be felt to be a unit even though the word cannot
occur without it; these seemed less likely to have /ɪn/ than Par-
ticiples/Gerunds, but more likely than 2) *something*, *anything*,
everything, *nothing*, where -*ing* is not a unit but rather part of
thing, which can of course occur independently but always with /ŋ/
to distinguish it from *thin*[124].   Secondly, I kept a note of instances

124 The [-θɪŋk] form found in certain parts of Britain in -*thing*
compounds was heard from only one informant.

of word-medial -ing-, mainly occurring in proper names like *Birmingham*, *Buckingham*, *Sunningdale*, *Bridlington* etc. Only 79 examples occurred, but even here there were signs of a similar relation between /ɪŋ~ɪn/ variation and class and style to those seen above. But more interesting is the impression that the likelihood of /ɪn/ varies according to 1) phonological factors: /ɪn/ is most likely if /t/ or /d/ follows, as in *Bridlington*, *Washington*, *Sunningdale*, i.e. there is assimilation in place of articulation - whereas it is less likely before /əm/ as in *Manningham*, *Birmingham* and virtually impossible if these are pronounced with (h), and 2) individual items: even in the last group referred to /ɪn/ seems more likely in *Buckingham* than in *Birmingham*.

I emphasise that these are only hypotheses for future research rather than conclusions.

OTHER VARIABLES

I have discussed above the main phonological variables which were examined in order to investigate some of the most important changes that appear to have occurred or to be still taking place in the speech of West Yorkshire. They have affected the phonological system in inventory, distribution, realisation, and incidence. Now we turn to a number of other features which were common enough in the speech of my informants to be examined as variables; these too are part of the picture of the persistence or modification of regional features.

1   Contracted Negatives

We shall be concerned here with a matter of phonology, but one which does not exactly fit into any of the above categories, though it is perhaps closest to 'incidence variables'.

The lexical set with which we shall be concerned is detailed below: briefly, it is the contracted forms of the negatived copula, auxiliaries and modals. Forms like *wasn't*, *hadn't*, *can't* etc. are of course quite common in Standard English; in most cases a contracted form of *not* [nt] has been added to the preceding verb form e.g. [ɪznt, hævnt] etc. The few exceptions are mostly where the final consonant of the verb has been dropped (perhaps, in some cases, for phonotactic reasons), and the vowel has changed, usually in both length and quality e.g. [ʃæl nɒt]>[ʃɑːnt],[kæn nɒt]>[kɑːnt] [wɪl nɒt]>[wəʊnt] and sometimes [æm nɒt]>[ɑːnt]. (When used in declarative sentences, e.g. [aɪ ɑːnt duːɪŋ ɪt], this form, though not uncommon among working-class speakers, is frequently castigated as substandard, [aɪm nɒt] being regarded as 'correct'; but in

interrogatives [ɑ:nt aɪ] is more commonly accepted, probably because
[æm aɪ nɒt] seems over-formal).   In [du: nɒt]>[dəʊnt] the vowel
change is only in quality, and there is of course no loss of consonant[125].

Though there is surprisingly little trace of such forms in the
traditional dialect accounts of the area[126], in West Yorkshire today
non-standard forms produced by a further contraction are common.
For the description of this phenomenon it is useful to divide the
contracted forms of Standard English into two groups, since a) these
differ in terms of the phonological shape of both the standard and
the non-standard forms; b) while one of these groups is subject to
secondary contraction over a wide area of Britain, according to my
own informal observations, the other is contracted only in a much
smaller region, including West Yorkshire.

1   The first group has the phonological shape /XVCnt/ (where X = C
or Ø), and contains the following:

isn't	doesn't	mustn't
wasn't	didn't	needn't
haven't	couldn't	mightn't
hasn't	wouldn't	oughtn't
hadn't	shouldn't	(usedn't)

The form *usedn't* is bracketed here because observations suggest
that it is relatively uncommon in colloquial English today; certainly it is very rarely heard in the area I am concerned with.   A
form such as 'I didn't use to do that' is much more likely than 'I
usedn't to do that'; the former is subject to secondary contraction
(affecting *didn't*), the latter, being much more formal, is not.

The form *oughtn't* is sometimes similarly replaced by *didn't
ought*, but my observations suggest that this is not so commonly the
case: I have noticed many instances of *oughtn't* in the colloquial
speech of the area, and this form *is* subject to secondary contraction (as also is *didn't* in *didn't ought*).

---

125 [du:nt] would of course be odd phonologically, since /u:nt/ does
not occur in English. *Won't* is probably to be explained partly in
terms of ME *wol*, an alternative to *wil*, and *don't* may be modelled on
this.   For further discussion see Strang (1970:151).

126 Perhaps because of the artificiality of the single-word response
style, SED seems only to have noticed *wasn't* [wɒnt] (in various localities), *hasn't* [ɛnt] (at Y26), and *you haven't* [jamt] (at Y31).
Earlier sources do not seem to refer to them at all, though they have
a number of interesting negative forms e.g. [amət] *am not*, [wɪlnt ~
wɪənt] *will not* etc. in Wright (1892) - none of which I heard.

2   The second group has the phonological shape /X$\bar{\text{V}}$nt/ (where X = C or ∅), and contains:

aren't	won't	daren't
weren't	shan't	(mayn't)
don't	can't	

The form *mayn't* is bracketed because observations suggest that in the 'permission' sense it is hardly ever heard in the area (even in uncontracted form), *can't* being used instead; in the 'possibility' sense it sometimes occurs in tags e.g. 'it may be so, mayn't it?', in which cases it is probably never contracted[127].

The secondary contraction follows the same basic pattern in both groups: the first member of the final consonant group is dropped.   This could be expressed in terms of the following rule:

$$\text{C} > ∅ \ / \text{V}\_\_\_\text{C}_1^2$$

where the deleted C may be /n/.   (The symbolization C_1^2 indicates that there may be (at most) two or (at least) one consonant following that which is deleted in this secondary contraction).

Because the phonological shapes of the two groups differ, so also do the effects of this rule:

i)   in the first group it is the final consonant of the verb which is deleted.   Thus: /XVCnt/ > /XVnt/

   Note that there is no change in the vowel; this is then a difference from the primary (Standard English) contraction as it affects say [ʃæl nɒt] or [wɪl nɒt], where the final consonant is also lost: there the change is /XV$_1$Cnt/ > /X$\bar{\text{V}}_2$nt i.e. the vowel is lengthened and changes in quality also.

ii)   in the second group the consonant affected is the /n/ of the negative.   Thus: /X$\bar{\text{V}}$nt/ > /X$\bar{\text{V}}$t/

   Note that though the phonological shape /X$\bar{\text{V}}$nt/ also occurs in English words not produced by the primary contraction of

---

127 There is evidence that *mayn't* is becoming uncommon in English generally: Palmer (1974:21) says simply 'There is no negative form *mayn't*.   We have only *may not*'; and Quirk and Greenbaum (1973:37) say that *'mayn't* is restricted to British English, where it is rare'.

'verb + not' e.g. *count* (this is not the case with the
/XVCnt/ shape), the secondary contraction is lexically restricted to words derived by the primary contraction: thus
[ka:nt] > [ka:t] but not [kaʊnt] > *[kaʊt].

The actual forms will now be examined in more detail.   Since
this is a feature only of non-standard English, non-standard forms
will be referred to: using RP forms as examples would be totally
artificial since secondary contraction would never apply with say
[hædnt] or [dəʊnt] - whereas they are quite likely with [adn2].

1   /XVCnt/

isn't	[ɪznt] > [ɪnt]	oughtn't	[ɔ:tnt] > [ɔ:nt]
wasn't	[wɒznt] > [wɒnt]	needn't	[ni:dnt] > [ni:nt]
doesn't	[dʊznt] > [dʊnt]	mightn't	[maɪtnt] > [maɪnt]
didn't	[dɪdnt] > [dɪnt]	mustn't	[mʊsnt] (>[mʊnt])
couldn't	[kʊdnt] > [kʊnt]	hasn't	[aznt]	> [ant]
shouldn't	[ʃʊdnt] > [ʃʊnt]	hadn't	[adnt]	> [ant]
wouldn't	[wʊdnt] > [wʊnt]	haven't	[avnt] > (see below)

The final consonant has been written throughout as [t], though especially in the forms which have undergone secondary contraction [2] is
common, though less so in prevocalic than in preconsonantal environments.

Examples

[ɪt ɪnt i:zɪ tə du: ða2]   [jɔ:nt tə se: ða2]
It isn't easy to do that   You oughtn't to say that

[wɒnt ɪt ə pɪtɪ]   [jə ni:nt ansə, ðen]
Wasn't it a pity?   You needn't answer, then

[ɪ dʊn2 laɪk du:ɪn ða2]   [a maɪnt ə bi:n e:bl tə stɒp]
He doesn't like doing that   I mightn't have been able to stop

[a dɪn2 wɒnt tə kʊm]
I didn't want to come   (see below, on *mustn't*)

[kʊn2 jə du:ᵂ ɪ2]   [i: an2 dʊn ðat, az ɪ]
Couldn't you do it?   He hasn't done that, has he?

[jə ʃʊnt ə sed ða2]   [i: an2 dʊn ðat, ad ɪ]
You shouldn't have said that   He hadn't done that, had he?

[a wʊn2 laɪk tə bi: ə:]
I wouldn't like to be her   (see below, on *haven't*)

While an example such as that given here for *couldn't* is not unusual,
the contracted form is sometimes avoided because of homophonic taboo
resulting from the fact that the /ʌ/-/ʊ/ contrast is absent from the
phonemic inventory of the majority of speakers in this area;   schoolboys of a certain age sometimes perform the contraction in the phrase
you couldn't with obvious delight!

The form [mʊnt] is bracketed because it is uncommon.   It can
be heard: e.g. [ɪ2 mʊs bɪ ðaʔ, mʊnt ɪʔ], where it obviously is the
contracted negative of *must*.   But one must be careful to distinguish such instances from those where it is the negative of the
'dialect' modal *mun* e.g. [ɪ mʊn duː^w ɪ2, mʊnt ɪ]; *mun* is of Norse
origin, and according to Wright (1892:151), it was in traditional
dialect used for 'a necessity dependent on the will of a person', as
distinct from ' a logical or natural necessity' for which *must* was
employed.   In the area today *mun* has virtually disappeared, and the
majority of speakers simply do not contract *mustn't* any further:
it is thus an exception to the rule; whether the fact that it has
usually already 'lost' a final consonant (i.e. it is [mʊs] rather
than [mʊst] except prevocalically) has anything to do with this is
not clear.

Contractions of *hasn't* and *hadn't* produce the homophonous [ant].
One would have expected *haven't* to yield the same result, and this
can occasionally be heard in other parts of Britain; but in this
area *haven't* is kept distinct from the other two in a way which
suggests that the contraction rule may not be quite as simple as
that given above.   In all the words in this group except *haven't*
the C of /XVCnt/ is alveolar and thus homorganic with the following,
but in *haven't* it is labiodental - and here the contracted form is
[amt~am2] or occasionally [aɱ2].   So perhaps something like the
following applies:

1 / XVCnɒt/ > / XVCnt   'Primary Contraction'

2 /n/ assimilates in place to /C/   (Applies vacuously except
                                     with *haven't*)

3 /C/> ∅   'Secondary Contraction'

4 [ŋ] > [m]   (Applies only to *haven't*;
                               caused by loss of condition-
                               ing environment through 3.
                               It should be noted that it is
                               only the nasal which assimi-
                               lates: final [t] does not
                               change place of articulation
                               - witness prevocalic [amta]
                               haven't I, never *[ampa];
                               (even *haven't we* is [am2 wɪ]

rather than *[ampwɪ] as might
have seemed phonetically plausible; also [am2jə] *haven't you*,
[am2ðə] *haven't they* etc.).

Contracted forms other than those listed here can sometimes be heard.
In interrogatives a 'tertiary contraction' may yield [ɪnɪ2] *isn't
it*, [wɒnɪ2] *wasn't it*, [dʊnɪ2] *doesn't it*, [anɪ] *hasn't he* etc., with
the /t/ of the negative now deleted. I have observed such examples
from working-class speakers; they are included in the statistical
treatment below with the secondary contractions since this process
has also occurred. Higher up the social scale /t/ is also occasionally omitted, in forms like [dʌznɪt], [ɪznɪt], [wʊdnɪt], which
I have heard as high as Class I; but since the secondary contraction has not operated, these forms were ignored in my scoring for
this variable.

     The amount of /XVCnt/ secondary contraction in each class and
style is shown in Figure 27, and Figure 28 shows the total of CS/FS/
RP scores by age-group.   No pattern is apparent when scores are broken down by sex, and all three towns showed much the same percentage
of contracted forms: these figures are not presented here.

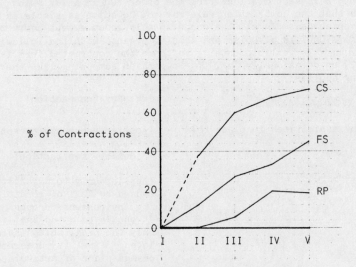

Figure 27: (XVCnt) - Style and Class

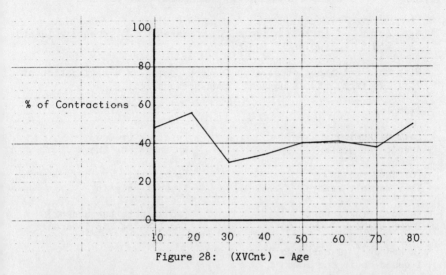

Figure 28:   (XVCnt) - Age

It is obvious that secondary contractions relate to style in
the way one has come to expect with features consciously or unconsciously felt to be substandard: no-one produced such forms in the
word list; they are found only in connected speech, and more frequently as formality decreases.   The social classes are also in the
'expected' order, with the working classes producing a considerable
proportion of contracted forms in conversation.   (It may be noted,
as a matter of methodological interest, that the score for casual
speech in Class I almost certainly owes its 'irregularity' to the
small amount of data: there were only eleven instances of (XVCnt),
since this small group of informants produced little casual speech;
if the next instance had been contracted the score would have been
'regularised'!)

The age-graph shows the greatest amount of contraction among
the two youngest groups, but there is no overall trend such as
usually shows up with a variable currently involved in linguistic
change.   (This is not entirely due to the fact that yet again the
30-plus group showed the lowest percentage of non-standard forms).

Some if not all of these contracted forms occur in other parts
of Britain; the precise regional distribution is not known to me,
but I have observed them as far South as London.

2   /XV̄nt/

aren't	[a:nt] > [a:t]	shan't	[ʃa:nt] > [ʃa:t]
weren't	[wə:nt] > [wə:t]	can't	[ka:nt] > [ka:t]

don't   [do:nt] > [do:t]   daren't   [dɛənt] > [dɛət]
won't   [wo:nt] > [wo:t]

With this set the glottal stop is very common as a realization of
/t/; in fact, [t] is unusual, even prevocalically.

Examples:

[a:ʔ jə kʊmɪn]   [wɪ ʃa:ʔ bɪ ðɛə]
Aren't you coming?   We shan't be there

[ðɪ wə:ʔ redɪ]   [a ka:ʔ elp ɪʔ]
They weren't ready   I can't help it

[a do:ʔ θɪŋk a wɒnt tə]   [ad laɪk tə bʊr a dɛəʔ]
I don't think I want to   I'd like to but I daren't

[a kʊd du:ᵂ ɪʔ bʊr a wo:ʔ]
I could do it but I won't

A special contracted form of *don't know* [dʊno: ~ dʌnəʊ] etc. was
observed in all social classes. It was ignored for 'scoring' purposes.

    The forms of *dare not* vary within the area. While [dɛənt] and
[dɛət] are heard in most parts, in some parts (I have insufficient
data, but I suspect from observation and from remarks of informants
that it is mainly in Bradford) there may occur what looks like a very
irregular form [dɛədnt] e.g. [ad laɪk tə du:ᵂ ɪʔ bʊr a dɛədnt], where
a consonant appears to have been added rather than one deleted. Now
in fact this [dɛədnt] is homophonous with the contracted form of the
past *dared not*. Nelson Francis (1968), discussing the negatived
past and present forms of modal *dare* shown up by the Survey of
English Dialects, says that there is an 'exceedingly complex and
confused situation...*dare* is in a very unstable state morphologically
which is perhaps partly a consequence of its position on the periphery of the modal system'. Formerly there was a contrast in English
generally between strong *dare* - *durst* (modal) and weak *dare* - *dared*
(full verb), but the *durst* form has now disappeared from Standard
English and also from some dialects, with *dared* taking over, and many
speakers do not distinguish present and past in the modal anyway.
Nelson Francis shows that for over 50 per cent of SED informants the
past and present forms are homonymous, and in just under half of
these it is the past form which has been extended to the present.
Now in Yorkshire the levelled form is most commonly the present (and
I have observed *daren't* used as past by speakers from the area of my
survey e.g. [a dɪdnʔ du:ᵂ ɪt - a dɛənt]), but at SED locality Y22 on
the outskirts of Bradford, the past form [da:dnt] was recorded in
present tense usage; this form, under the phonetic influence of the
standard language yields the [dɛədnt] familiar today.

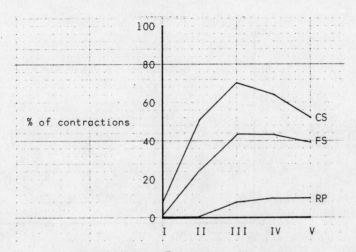

Figure 29 : (XV̄nt) - Style and Class

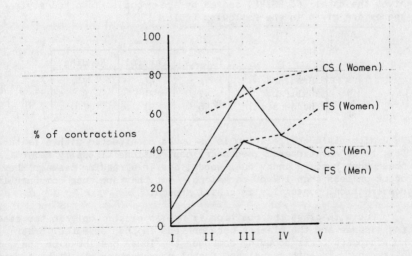

Figure 30: (XV̄nt) - Sex, Style and Class

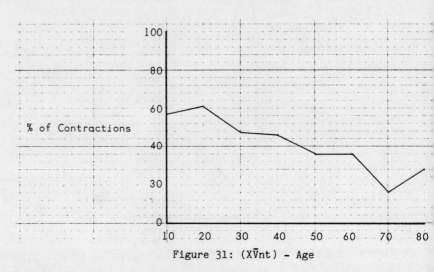

Figure 31: (XV̄nt) - Age

Figure 29 shows the percentage of secondary contraction in /XV̄nt/
words and Figure 30 breaks this down further by sex.   Figure 31
gives the total (CS/FS/RP) scores by age-group.   Town and style
scores are given in the following table:

	Casual	Careful	Reading
Bradford	76	46	7
Halifax	47	33	8
Huddersfield	46	31	9

With style the relation is as would be expected with a feature
felt to be substandard: secondary contractions virtually never
occur when reading individual words, and in a reading passage they
occur on less than 10% of occasions; but they are much commoner in
conversation, especially in casual speech.

But with class the position is not so clear: only in the reading passage are the classes more or less in the 'expected' order -
non-standard forms becoming commoner the lower one looks on the
hierarchy; in both casual and formal conversation the highest score
are in Class III, followed by Classes IV, V and II in that order
(Class I scoring low in any style).   Yet when the figures are subdivided by sex it appears that this order applies only to men, where
as women are more 'regularly' stratified in respect of this feature
(Also, women score at least as high as men overall, which is unusual
with a stigmatised feature).

The age-group figures are of particular interest, both because
they show that (ignoring the class-biased 80-plus group) there is
a steady increase in the use of secondary contractions from the 70s
to the 20s (this increase occurs with both sexes, but the fairly
small amounts of data for some groups make the graph not quite so
regular); and also because they help to answer our questions about
the order of classes among men and thus serve as a methodological
caveat: use of contracted forms is highest among the 10-plus and
20-plus groups and lowest over the age of 60; the percentage of
male informants in Classes III to V in these age-groups was as follows:

	III	IV	V
10+/20+	55	40	15
60 and over	18	27	61

These figures surely go some way towards explaining the unexpected
positions of men of Classes III - V in respect of (XV̄nt), and serve
as a warning against over-hasty conclusions about upper working class
men spearheading a linguistic change.

The scores for the different towns show that (XV̄nt) contractions are commoner in Bradford than in the other two. In my observation this type of secondary contraction is much more regionally
restricted than that of (XVCnt); it could be that Bradford is quite
close to its centre.

My conclusions are that though neither type of secondary contraction occurs in RP, contractions in the (XVCnt) group of words
show certain relations which suggest they are regarded as substandard, but they are probably fairly 'stable' from a historical point
of view; whereas those in the (XV̄nt) group, though also showing
signs of being regarded as substandard and though being more typical
of this area than the other set, nevertheless seem to be on the
increase with time and (as with the other change 'away from' RP, the
glottal stop) Bradford is probably leading the way. Also we
have noted two methodological points, both warning that care is
needed in interpreting results - when the amount of data is small and
when the sample is of such a size that the informants in any one
sub-group may not be representative in respect of all factors.

2   Grammatical Variables

Grammatical features pose for a study of this type at least

two problems, which are not so apparent with phonological features.
Firstly, they cannot easily be elicited; generally, one must just
wait for them to turn up in the course of conversation, and certainly
they cannot be measured through the use of reading passages since
usually one simply reads what is there, whatever grammatical variant
has been written[128].   Secondly, they may occur very infrequently:
most phonological variables will turn up quite commonly (and those
which do not can be elicited by a reading passage and/or word list),
but there is no guarantee that a certain grammatical feature will
figure at all in an interview - and too few instances may occur to
provide reliable data for a particular sub-group of informants.

    For these and other reasons I have not attempted to handle most
of the non-standard grammatical features recorded in my survey within
the same 'variable' framework as has been used for phonological
features: they will be described in section 2) of the present chapter.   But here I have tried to deal with just a few such features,
which involve only very small and fairly frequent constructions.

The Variable (our)

    The First Person Plural possessive pronoun in Standard English
is *our* in all environments; but in West Yorkshire other forms may
be heard in unstressed positions.   The traditional dialect accounts
of the area are agreed in giving [a:(r)] as the stressed form of *our*;
in unstressed positions Wright (1892) gives [wə(r)], but Easther
(1883) has *us*, which EDGr (s 411) gives as a Northern and Midland
counties form, and SED records at all points in our area.

    My own observations suggested that nowadays [wə(r)] is very
rare, but that *us* not uncommonly occurs for the unstressed *our* e.g.
'we all take us cars to work nowadays'.   However, my experience in
school is that this is a highly castigated feature.

---

128 For example, I wrote into my reading passage the phrase *three
foot six inches*, which quite a number of my informants would probably
not normally say - but only two (both women) 'amended' it to *three
feet*...and even in these cases the explanation could be that the type-
script was unclear (*o* and *e* can look very similar).

    Wolfram (1969:204) solemnly speculates about the apparently sur-
prising (to him) fact that non-standard variants of his grammatical
variables virtually never occurred in his reading passage.   Surely
it would have been more surprising if they had, since this would involve substituting completely different forms - and this must be the
explanation rather than there being 'more conscious awareness of
socially diagnostic variants in grammar' (though this of course there
may be also).

I kept a record of all instances of unstressed (our) in conversation, scoring them under the two variants *our* and *us*, whatever
their actual phonetic form (the form *us* is itself involved in two
phonological variables: the vowel is (ʌ), and the consonant may be
/s/ as in RP, or /z/: see p. 205 .   These variables are to some
extent interdependent (i.e. there are 'implicational relations' between them): it would be extremely unlikely for a speaker to use
us for (our) but have /ʌ/ and/or /s/ here e.g. *[ʌs ko:ts] is most
unlikely, whereas [ʊz ko:ts] would be quite usual).

The percentages of *us* by class and style were as follows:

	I	II	III	IV	V
CS	0	0	31	57	40
FS	0	0	23	35	33
CS + FS	0	0	26	43	36

The overall scores by sex were: Men 35, Women 22; and by towns:
Bfd 18 Hfx 23, Hudds 49.   The age-graph is quite irregular (possibly
because there were not enough examples in each of the relatively
small groups).

The figures by class, style, and sex do fit in with this being
a stigmatised variant: it does not occur among middle-class speakers,
it is more likely in casual conversation, and commoner among men than
women.   The 'reversed' positions of Classes IV and V may be due to
inadequate data on the latter, smaller group.

The differences between the towns is interesting: we saw above
that Wright did not give *us* for his locality on the outskirts of
Bradford, whereas Easther did give it for Huddersfield.   Possibly
this usage is more recently established in Bradford, which could
account for the lower score there than in Huddersfield.

My conclusions are that *us* is a grammatical variant under pressure from Standard English: it is restricted to the working classes
and is a minority phenomenon there.

The Variable (Measure)

Whereas the above non-standard grammatical feature is one that
is relatively restricted in its regional distribution, this one is -
like such phonological features as constitute variables like (h) and

(ing) - of more widespread occurrence in England.   It concerns
phrases of measure such as 'two years', 'three tons' etc.   Although
in Middle English 'measure-, weight-, time-, and price-words were
largely uninflected in the plural' (Ekwall, 1975:92), this situation
does not generally persist in Standard English today.   With the
exception of certain expressions of weight: *just over twelve stone*
(possible), *twelve stone four* (probable), and compounds like *four-
year-old, seven-pound jar* etc., phrases of measure follow the normal
rules of number concord: *one mile/two miles, one year/two years,
one ton/two tons, one gallon/two gallons, one shilling/two shillings*
etc.

But in non-standard grammar one frequently hears forms with no
plural marker: thus, 'he worked there for twenty year', 'it's
fourteen mile', 'it cost me three shilling'; and it may be noted
that besides numerals some other quantifiers may behave in the same
way: 'a few week', 'a couple of year back', etc.   It appears. however that the situation is not quite straightforward: the plural
marker can be omitted only with certain measure-nouns; with others
it seems to be obligatory: I have never heard, for example, anything
like *'they'll blast off in ten second'.   Here is a list of the
commonest measure nouns at the time of my survey, with an asterisk
beside those which, from my observations and my native-speaker
intuitions, seem *not* to occur without the plural marker in phrases
with numerals:

Distance:	inch, foot, (?*)yard, mile
Area:	acre
Time:	*second, *minute, *hour, *day, week, month, year
Weight:	ounce, pound, stone, hundredweight, ton
Liquid:	gill, pint, quart, gallon
Money:	*penny, shilling, pound

When scoring those measure-phrases that occurred in conversation
during my survey, I excluded all those asterisked here, where the
singular seems impossible, and also those like *ten stone two* and
ten-year-old where Standard English could have the singular.   There
remain then examples where Standard English would definitely have a
plural form but where non-standard speech may have either singular
or plural.

Figure 32 (opposite) shows the percentage of singular forms by
class and style.   The overall scores by sex are: Men 29, Women 27;
and by town: Bfd 25, Hfx 24, Hudd 36.   Those by age-group are:

10	20	30	40	50	60	70	80
25	26	5	22	37	43	26	(50)

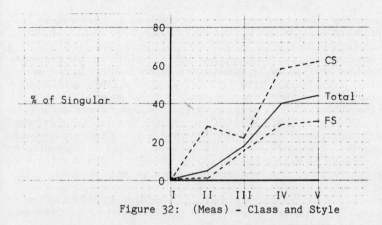

Figure 32:   (Meas) - Class and Style

The class and style figures are such as might indicate that
this is felt to be a substandard feature, though the number of instances recorded is probably too small for every figure to be
reliable (thus the CS figure in Class II seems irregular, and the
'total' score is more realistic).   Huddersfield again shows the
highest proportion of non-standard forms, but no geographical explanation seems likely in this case.   The age-graph is again
irregular, but we may note that the 30-plus group scores lowest
again; and were it not for the lower figure in the 70-plus group
(which may of course be unreliable) there would be some suggestion
of a decline of this usage among the younger half of the population.

My conclusion is that this is a feature which has now, under
the pressure of Standard English, come to be felt as substandard and
is largely confined to the working classes; it may possibly be
declining in frequency.

The Variable (was)

Our concern here is with a very common grammatical item: *was*
as both copula and auxiliary.   In Standard English,except for the
'conditional' uses, *was* and *were* are in complementary distribution -
was occurring after *I*, *he*, *she*, *it* and singular noun phrases, *were*
elsewhere.   In the traditional dialects of our area, Wright (1892)
gives '[wɒ(r)] or [wə(r)]' throughout the paradigm;   this represents
two differences from the standard language: the absence of [z] in
was and the possibility of 'intrusive r' to match the 'linking r' in
were;   and the use of the two forms in the same rather than complementary environments.   The picture given by SED for some sixty years
later is of [wə(r)] throughout the paradigm: this would seem to
represent the disappearance of [wɒ(r)] and a simplification of the

paradigm in that now one form occurs throughout, as compared to the
two of Standard English.

My own observations suggest that while [wə(r)] in environments
where Standard English would have *was* is quite common e.g. [a wə
dʒʊs kʊmɪn] 'I was just coming' (cf [wɪ wə dʒʊs kʊmɪn], with homophonous [wə]); [ɪ wə gʊd] 'he was good' (cf [ðɪ wə gʊd]), nevertheless the SED picture is inaccurate for the urban areas in two
respects. Firstly, [wɒz ~ wəz] as in Standard English is also commonly used; and secondly, the form [wɒ(r)] is still to be observed.
But its distribution does not generally appear to be as suggested by
Wright: rather, it most commonly occurs where Standard English would
have *was* i.e. after *I*, *he*, *she*, *it* and singular noun phrases.

Perhaps SED failed to record [wɒ(r)] because of deficiencies of
its methods.   It appears to present a picture, where the difference
from the Standard language is

St Eng: was ['wɒz ~ wəz]/Sg Pron and NP
         were ['wə:(r) ~ wə(r)]/elsewhere

                           Dialect: were [ˈwə:(r) ~ wə(r)]

The two variants of *was* and *were* in Standard English are 'strong'
and 'weak' i.e. they occur in stressed and unstressed environments
respectively.   Though SED does not give instances of [wə:(r)] I
have occasionally observed this form where stressed [wɒz] would be
standard: e.g. [i:'wə:] 'he was', which would support the SED picture of the generalisation of *were*.   However, it is my impression
that, though the picture is confused by the variation between standard and non-standard, the more usual system among urban speakers is

Standard: was ['wɒz ~ wəz]/Sg Pron and NP
           were ['wə:(r) ~ wə(r)]/elsewhere

                 Non-Standard: was ['wɒ(r) ~ wə(r)] /Ditto
                                were ['wə:(r) ~ wə(r)] / "

In other words, the main difference between the two systems could be
seen simply as the absence of [z] from forms of *was* in non-standard,
and the possibility of intrusive *r*; an incidental result of this is
that [wə(r)] occurs as a weak form of both [wɒ(r)] and [wə:(r)].

Examples of weak [wə(r)] for *was* and *were* were given above;
recorded examples of strong [wɒ(r)] are: (stressed) [i:,ɪ 'wɒ fʊnɪ]
'ee, he was funny'; (sentence-final) [ɪ wə bɪgə nər aɪ wɒ] 'he was
bigger than I was'; (both) [nɒn əv əz ˈwɒ] 'none of us was'; (pre-
pause, stressed) [ðə bju:tɪ əv ɪ? 'wɒ...] 'the beauty of it was...';
intrusive r is seen in [ɪ? 'wɒr ə bʊgə].

In what follows, scores are given in terms of the percentage of non-standard forms (i.e. [wə(r)] and the less common [wɒ(r)] together) among occurrences of (was).

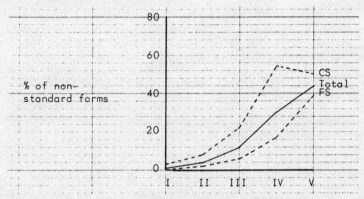

Figure 33: (was) - Class and Style

Figure 33 gives the scores by class and style in conversational speech (only one informant produced any non-standard variants in the reading passage). Subdividing the class scores by sex gives the following table:

	I	II	III	IV	V
M	1	4	18	39	48
W	-	2	8	29	33
Total	1	3	12	34	44

The overall scores in the three towns were: Bfd 26, Hfx 16, Hudd 34. Those by age:

10	20	30	40	50	60	70	80
32	24	13	15	16	35	31	(52)

It is apparent that the non-standard forms are a minority feature in any group, and that the relations between their frequency and the non-linguistic factors of class, style, and sex are such as are commonly found with variants felt to be sub-standard. Only in the two lowest classes is there a fair proportion of such forms. As with several other non-standard grammatical features, Huddersfield scores highest among the towns. The age-graph does not appear to indicate any steady trend; the lowest scores are among the middle

aged, where possibly there is a greater consciousness of the importance of speech for 'getting on'.

My conclusions about (was) are that while it probably is still
for many speakers a feature which helps to signal that they come from
our area, it has come under considerable pressure from Standard
English.   The result is, firstly, that [wɒz ~ wəz] is now much more
common than the regional [wɒ(r) ~ wə(r)], which is now largely restricted to the working classes;   and secondly, that the distribution
of variants of *was* and *were*, even in their non-standard forms,
is now very much in line with that of Standard English rather than
that given in traditional dialect works.

The Variable (the)[129]

This variable concerns the morphological shape of another very
common grammatical item, the definite article.

Yorkshire dialect prose and poetry represents the article by
t' and/or *th'* (denoting a shortened form such as was widespread in
Britain some centuries ago[130], but which has now in Standard English
given way entirely to [ðə ~ ðɪ]);   but the precise phonetic interpretation of this is not clear.   Traditional dialect works on our
area do not present a clear picture: for Bradford, Ellis (1889) and
Wright (1892) give [t] throughout;   for Halifax, Ellis has mostly
[θ] but some [t];   for Huddersfield, Ellis has [θ], but Easther (1883)
says there is variation between [t] and [θ], and Haigh (1928) says
the two are used 'indifferently before consonants' but before vowels
[θ] is usual.   SED shows [t] before consonants at all SW Yorks localities, and variation with [ʔ] in a smaller region within this,
while before vowels [θ] or [tθ] is given for Y21, Y29, Y30 and [t]
elsewhere;   and before initial [t], [tʔ] is usual, with occasional
[ʔ];   however, in SED's 'incidental material' the area of glottal
forms is greatly extended, with the Pennines apparently the focal
area, and since this material is probably the closest SED came to
casual speech it is perhaps reasonable to conclude that [ʔ] is shown
to be on the increase.

---

129   Recent studies of the definite article in dialect include
Jones (1952) and Barry (1972).

130   Ekwall (1975:94): 'the vowel was often lost in ME and EModE...
this shortened form was later abandoned'.   Strang (1970:137): 'The
definite article was commonly elided before vowels in both literary
and colloquial style' (referring to 1570-1770).

My own interpretation of the traditional evidence, (aided by observations of rural dialect) is that an isogloss crossed the area of my study: on one side of it, an area which included Bradford, the article was always [t]; on the other, including Huddersfield and at least part of Halifax, it was generally [θ~tθ] before vowels and [t] before consonants (though there is some evidence, in earlier works and SED, for some fricative forms before consonants). But comparison of earlier and later traditional accounts suggests that the 'fricative' area became smaller, and that the glottal stop was becoming more frequent.

My examination of the urban areas today showed that:

a) by far the commonest shortened form of the article is [ʔ]; this occurs before both consonants and vowels, and assimilations may take place 'across it' e.g. [ðɪ wʊŋ ʔ kʊp las jɪə] 'they won the cup last year'.

b) the fricative forms are very rare: I only recorded 3 instances of [tθ] and one of [θ], (all in Huddersfield), and four of [ð][131] (3 Hfx, 1 Hudd). All these occurred prevocalically.

c) the commonest form after the glottal stop was [t], of which I recorded 12 instances in pre-consonantal position and 30 in pre-vocalic (this represents only a tiny fraction of the number of [ʔ]); the great majority were from informants aged over 70, which seems to support the view that this was the earlier form which has now given way to [ʔ][132].

d) before dental consonants the article may be represented simply by a lengthening of that consonant: [ɒn tɒp əv ɪʔ] 'on top of it', but [ɒn t:ɒp ə ʔ wɔːdroːb] 'on the top of the wardrobe'.

e) all these non-standard forms together represent only a small percentage of the total number of instances of (the); like other uses of the glottal stop, this form of the article tends to be

---

131 This included one instance of [ðʊðə] 'the other', which even in those dialects with fricative forms is more usually [tʊðə]. It should be noted that the [t] in this form is of a different origin from the rest, being the result of 'wrong division' or 'metanalysis' (see Strang: 1970:137) of *that other* - and this form is of much wider distribution in regional dialects than the [t] form of the definite article.

132 One informant I would describe as a 'dialect speaker' had 160 [ʔ] and only 3 [t] pre-consonantally, but 14 [ʔ] and 15 [t] prevocalically.

regarded as 'sloppy' or 'lazy', or as 'missing words out' (see
Chapter 7), and probably at least partly as a result of this the
Standard English forms now account for the great majority of
instances overall[133].

In view of this last point, rather than giving percentages of
non-standard *variants* as usual, we shall examine this variable in a
different way: in terms of the numbers of *informants* using non-
standard forms.

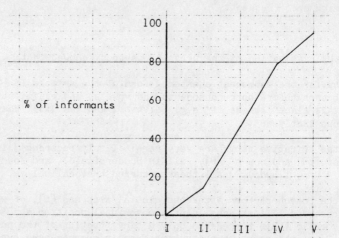

Figure 34: (the) - any non-standard forms, by Class

Figure 34 shows the percentage of informants in each social
class who produced *any* non-standard variants.   Breaking these figures down by style produces an irregular graph because of the often
small numbers of occurrences, but that there is some relation between
the occurrences of these forms with style is shown by the following
figures:

106 informants: 67 produced some such forms, in one style or
                                                        another;
                61 did so in casual style;

_____

133 Many people have standard and non-standard variants side by side:
thus, (actual survey example) [ðə nju:z ə 2 wə:ld].   Barry (1972)
discussing the SED material, says the occurrences of [ðə] in West
Yorkshire, particularly in those parts near to the 'edge' of the [t]
area, suggests a general invasion of this area by RP forms, especially in the industrial parts.   My findings confirm that this has
progressed a good way.

49 did so in formal;
4 did so in the reading passage[134].

The following tables are of percentage of informants using any shortened forms by a) sex and class, b) town, and c) age-group:

a)

	I	II	III	IV	V
M	0	14	64	77	92
W	-	17	35	81	100

b)

Bfd	Hfx	Hudd
69	54	65

c)

10	20	30	40	50	60	70	80
71	55	46	67	67	71	63	(100)

These figures are of course very crude, but they seem to indicate that though these regional variants occur in a minority of
instances of (the), their usage at all bears some relation to class
and style such as is frequently found with stigmatised forms: the
classes are in the 'expected' order, with these variants largely
confined to the working classes, and they are most likely to occur
in the most spontaneous styles. Except in Class III, where women
show signs of aiming at the middle-class standard while men seem to
go along with the working class, there is not much difference between the sexes. The age-group figures do not seem to show that
these forms are being forgotten (note that yet again the 30-plus
group scores lowest).

Let us try to make these figures a little less crude by introducing some indication of the numbers of such forms produced, and also
subdividing this by environment. Figure 35 (overleaf) shows the percentage of informants in each class who produced more than 10% non-
standard forms, and those with more than 50%, in preconsonantal and
prevocalic positions. Figures by other non-linguistic factors are not
given here: they do not show any substantial difference from the above
in the relative 'order' of sexes, towns, or age-groups.

It is obvious that even the 10% cut-off reduces the figures
substantially, while that of 50% shows that the regional variants of
(the) are a minority phenomenon in any group, and only in the lowest
classes is there a fair amount of such forms. The phonological
environment does not appear to be an important factor.

134 Only two of these produced a significant proportion of shortened
forms, and even one of the 'broadest' informants had three [ðə] alongside two [ʔ] in the same sentence.

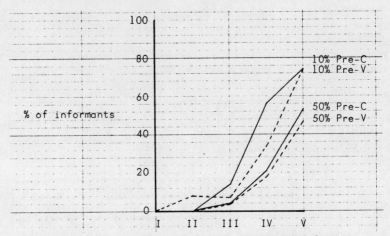

Figure 35: (the) - amount of non-standard forms,
              by Class and Environment

My conclusions are that standard English [ðə] has taken over
from shortened variants as the most usual form of the definite article
in this area, leaving the latter as a mainly working-class feature;
nevertheless a substantial proportion of the population do use the
shortened variants from time to time, and since these are a typical
feature of the area they probably act as an important signal of a
speaker's provenance; finally there has been among the shortened
variants a considerable expansion of [ʔ] at the expense of [t] and
the more localised [θ ~ tθ].

The Variable (that)

We are concerned here mainly with the word *that* as it functions
as a conjunction and a relative pronoun in many varieties of English
(the homographous *that* as demonstrative is excluded from what follows)

In Standard English with RP the only form is [ðət].   In the
traditional dialect accounts of West Yorkshire too, this form appears
but alongside it most give [ət], which looks like a reduced form.
However Wright points out (1892:91) that historically this is a separate form of Norse origin, and so, strictly, [ðət ~ət] is grammatical rather than phonological variation.   Somewhat surprisingly,
most sources do not mention another possibility of grammatical variation: *as* [əz], which is also used as conjunction and relative, is
fairly widespread in the North.

My own observations were that all three forms occurred, and so
I kept a note of them when listening to my tapes.   I found that
[ðət] occurred 1250 times altogether in conversational styles, while
the non-standard [ət] and [əz] were heard 234 and 21 times respectively.   It is interesting to find that certain patterns in relation to non-linguistic factors show up even with such a relatively
small number of examples.

Counting [ðət] as 0, [ət] as 1, and the few occurrences of [əz]
(since these are more clearly grammatically non-standard than [ət])
as 2, and expressing the total scores as a percentage of the number
of occurrences of (that), the following results show up in terms of
a) class, b) sex, c) town, and d) age-group:

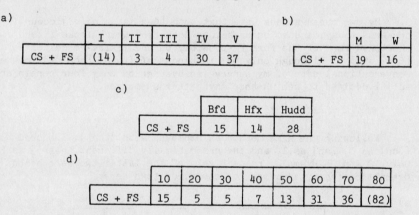

a)

	I	II	III	IV	V
CS + FS	(14)	3	4	30	37

b)

	M	W
CS + FS	19	16

c)

	Bfd	Hfx	Hudd
CS + FS	15	14	28

d)

	10	20	30	40	50	60	70	80
CS + FS	15	5	5	7	13	31	36	(82)

Instances were too few to yield a regular picture when subdivided by style, but there were considerably more non-standard forms
in casual than formal conversation, and only one instance of [ət]
and none of [əz] occurred in the reading passage, although two
examples of (that) had been read by all 106 informants.   As regards
class, Classes IV and V are clearly separated from the rest: Class I
is of course too small to be representative and its 'unexpectedly'
high score is due to the interference of the apparently significant
age factor: 9 out of 11 instances of [ət] in Class I came from the
informant in his 70s.   The age-group table shows that the non-standard forms are commonest among the elderly, and the figures for the
towns show that yet again Huddersfield scores highest on a feature
of non-standard grammar.

My conclusions are that pressure from Standard English has led
to non-standard forms accounting for only one-sixth of the occurrences

of (that), and that these are now largely confined to the lower end
of the social scale and to the elderly; but even with such small
numbers of examples of one particular item, there are clear signs of
patterns similar to those seen with much more frequently-occurring
variables.

The Variable (than)

The form introducing the 'basis of comparison' in Standard
English with RP is [ðən].   Virtually all the traditional dialect
accounts of our area give the grammatically different [nə(r)]: thus,
[ɪ wə be2ə nər 'ɪm] 'he was better than him'.   This form, *nor* is
attested in English literature and clearly was an older standard
form (it also occurs in the full form [nɔ:(r)] in certain dialects).

My own observations were that both [ðən] and [nə(r)] occur in
the area today, and so on occasions does [ən] which looks like a
shortened form of the former (possibly on the 'false' model of
[ðət~ət].   Although only 427 instances of (than) occurred in the
conversational data of my survey (an average of only four per informant) I decided to see whether any patterns emerged.

Following the same method as employed with (that), I scored
[ðən] as 0, [ən] as 1, and the grammatically different [nə(r)] as 2.
Only 10 and 28 examples respectively of the latter two were heard.
Overall scores by a) class, b) style, c) town were:

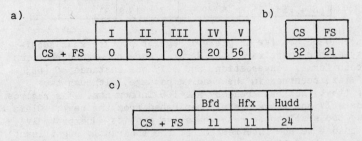

a)

	I	II	III	IV	V
CS + FS	0	5	0	20	56

b)

CS	FS
32	21

c)

	Bfd	Hfx	Hudd
CS + FS	11	11	24

With regard to style we may also note that in the reading passage
only one informant (Class IV, M, 60) rendered the one example of
(than) occurring there as [ən] and only one (Class IV, M, 70) substituted [nə].   As regards sex, only two women produced any non-
standard forms, as compared to 13 men.   The examples are too few to
produce a reliable age-graph, but we may note that the 50s and over
produced scores over 30, and the two youngest groups scored 0.

Even with so few instances of non-standard forms, traces of familiar patterns remain: they are more common in casual speech, among
the two lowest classes, among male speakers, among the elderly, and
in Huddersfield, which has scored highest on most features of non-
standard grammar.

My conclusions are that yet again there are clear signs of the
Standard English forms driving out those of the traditional dialects;
but the few instances of the latter which do occur follow the usual
patterns.

3   Phonological variation in some individual 'grammatical words'

The final few examples of variation I shall examine concern a
handful of common 'grammatical' (as opposed to 'lexical') words,
which show phonological variation in their form.   It could of course
be held that some of the items treated in the last section were of
this type - but I think that with all of them there was also the
possibility of grammatical variation of some sort.   Three pronouns
and two other common 'function words' will be examined, to see whether phonological variation here follows the patterns which by now
have become familiar.

The Variable (I)

The RP form of the First Person Singular pronoun is [aɪ], and
I have found that if asked to pronounce the word in isolation nearly
everyone will give this; but in normal conversation other forms do
occur.   In the traditional accounts of our area we find the forms
[a], [ɒ], [ɔ:], and [ɑ:]; the clearest picture of their local distribution is in SED, where [ɒ~ɔ:] is at Y21 i.e. furthest West,
[ɑ:] at those localities around Huddersfield, and [a] in the Bradford area mainly, but sometimes as a weak form elsewhere.

My own initial impression was that the last of these, [a], was
now quite common throughout the area (as indeed it seems to be in
other parts of Britain too[135]).   However, it would not normally
occur in certain types of environment: for example, though it is
usual preconsonantally [a wɪʃ a kʊd bʊr av gɒt tə go:], it is unlikely prevocalically [aɪ ɔ:lwe:z du: ðat], or when stressed [i: kn
du:ʷ ɪ2 be2 nər 'aɪ kan] 'He can do it better than I can'; we may

---

135 I have observed it in both North and South - but though widespread it does not appear to be universal.

note also examples such as ['aɪ 'kaːnt 'duː "ðat], and 'who does it?
- ['aɪ duː], but [a duː laɪk tə biː bɪsaɪd ðə siːsaɪd] etc.   Nevertheless, in spite of these restrictions the [a] variant occurs in a
very considerable proportion of the instances of this pronoun.

        I scored informants according to their use of [aɪ] and [a] in
those environments where the latter is possible.   The percentage of
[a] by style and class is given in Figure 36.   The scores by sex
were almost identical in each class, and there was no marked difference between the towns or the age-groups.

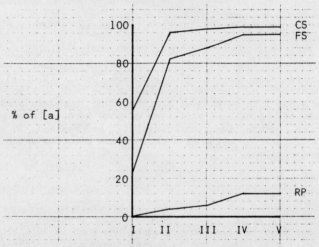

Figure 36:   (I) - Class and Style

        Though there is an obvious difference between reading and
conversational styles, with [aɪ] usual in the former and [a] in the
latter, there is no real indication that this non-standard variant
has any substandard connotations;   except in Class I, which approx-
imates to the RP norm, it occurs on over 90% of occasions in conversation, and no remarks by informants (such as those discussed in
Chapter 7) suggested that this is a feature of which informants are
at all conscious.

        My conclusion is that one of the traditional non-standard forms,
that found mainly in Bradford, has now become usual throughout the
area, and, possibly because it is quite widespread in Britain generally, it carries no significance as far as the majority are concerned.

The Variable (they)

The RP form of this pronoun is [ðeɪ]; the traditional dialect
accounts of our area show [ðe:~ðeɪ] as strong form and [ðɪ~ðə]
weak.

My impression is that [ðɪ] can be heard quite widely in Britain
(though it is not given as RP in the standard works) whereas [ðə]
is more regionally restricted. I therefore decided to check whether this more localised form showed any sign of being 'felt' to be
such, by examining the percentage of weak forms which were [ðɪ] or
[ðə].

I found the patterns not so regular as with many variables,
though [ðə] was clearly more common in casual than in formal style,
and whereas in conversation generally the overall scores for Classes
III - V were all in the 40-50% range, Class I showed no [ðə] and
Class II only 24%.   The other non-linguistic factors of sex, town,
or age presented no clear picture.

My conclusion is that while this non-standard feature may serve
as a 'localising' and stratifying feature to some extent, it is not
generally perceived as having much significance.

The Variable (us)

The RP form of this pronoun is [ʌs].   All traditional accounts
agree that the West Yorkshire form is [ʊz], a pronunciation which
is also commonly heard in other parts of the North.

The vowel is of course involved in the (ʌ) variable discussed
earlier; the consonant I have heard commented upon (both by my
schoolteachers and in the opinions of my informants reported in
Chapter 7), so I decided to examine the amounts of [s] and [z] pronunciation.

In fact however the number of [s] pronunciations in my data is
so small that we could probably say that this is not a variable for
the great majority of speakers, [z] being virtually categorical;
only 21 [s] forms were recorded (less than 5% of the total instances
of this pronoun) and even some of these are probably due to a tendency in this area, not investigated in this work, for final voiced
consonants to be devoiced by assimilation to an initial voiceless
consonant in the following word.   Such a number is of course too
small for any meaningful correlations with non-linguistic factors to
show up.

My conclusion is that with this pronoun, as with the two preceding, virtually no social significance attaches to a common nonstandard variant which presumably helps to signal a person's regional origin.

The Variable (with)

The RP form of this preposition is [wɪð] (or occasionally [wɪθ] before voiceless initial consonant). Most traditional dialect descriptions of West Yorkshire state that the local form is [wɪ].

Since I had heard both [wɪð] and [wɪ] commonly used in the area I decided to examine how far the dialectal form had given way to the standard one. In what follows, scores represent the percentage of instances of (with) which were pronounced [wɪ].

Scores by class and style for my whole sample were:

	I	II	III	IV	V
CS	8	13	12	35	35
FS	3	9	6	13	26
CS + FS	4	10	8	23	30

The style difference is 'continued' by the reading passage scores; three instances of (with) occurred in the passage, but only three informants produced any [wɪ] forms (and only one, who might be called a 'dialect speaker', used this in all three cases).

The number of examples was too few to yield regular graphs when broken down by age-group and sex, but [wɪ] was less common overall among women, and most common among the over-60s.

After listening to all the Bradford tapes, I formed the hypothesis that [wɪ] was now less common before an initial vowel than before a consonant[136], and so I scored my Halifax and Huddersfield informants separately according to these environments: Figure 37 shows the scores by class and environment.

---

136 A subsequent more detailed examination of the most recent traditional-type data, that of SED, showed that [wɪ] had been found to be virtually universal in this area before a consonant, but that prevocalically there was variation between [wɪð] and [wɪ].

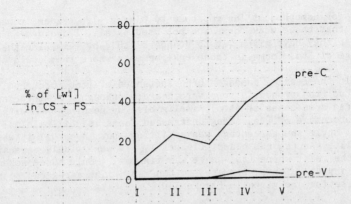

Figure 37: (with) - Class and Environment
[Huddersfield and Halifax only]

Even with relatively few occurrences, indications emerge from the scores by class, style, and sex that [wɪ] is now felt to be sub-standard, and the age scores suggest that it is an 'older' form. The 'unexpected' position of Class II in the table and Figure 37 is largely due to the fact that in a small group with relatively few examples one elderly, talkative, informant, whose speech struck one as 'unusual' in a person of his background, and who just happened to produce a good number of instances of (with), can have an undue effect.   Figure 37 indicates that my hypothesis regarding environ-ment was correct.

My conclusion is that the [wɪ] form is yielding to standard [wɪð].   The former has virtually disappeared in pre-vocalic environ-ments where it is more 'obvious';   it presents signs of the patterns of usage familiar with stigmatised variants;   and it is largely confined to Classes IV and V.

The Variable (too)

The RP form of this word is always [tu:].   In the traditional dialects of our area this pronunciation is used when *too* means 'also', and when *too* as an adverb of degree modifying an adjective or adverb is stressed: thus, [ɪts nɒt 'tu: bad].   But when the latter is unstressed, weak forms may occur: preconsonantally, [tə] e.g. [ðats tə bɪg], ['i: wə tə gʊd fə 2 θəːd dɪvɪʒn] 'he was too good for the Third Division';   prevocalically [tə~t] e.g. [2ʊvn wə tˢ ɒt] 'the oven was too hot', [ɪ gɒt tɔʊld tə pleː fə 2 dʒuːnɪəz] 'he got too old to play for the juniors' (actual example, at first misunderstood

by me for homophonous 'he got told to play...'). Since it was clear
to me that these weak forms are not used by all, I decided to see
how far they have given way to standard [tu:] by examining the percentage of [tə] forms in those environments where they could occur.

In the reading passage three instances of (too) occurred, but
only two [tə] pronunciations were heard; (though some informants
rendered some cases of (too) 'ineligible' by reading them with stress
the percentage of [tə] among unstressed forms is still minimal). In
formal style the percentage was still low, but in casual it was 20%
overall. As regards class, Classes IV - V were widely separated
from the rest, where [tə]-usage was minimal. Only three women produced any [tə] forms, compared to ten men. The age-group scores in
conversation are given in Figure 38.

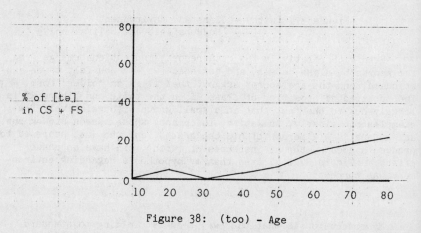

Figure 38: (too) - Age

Obviously [tə] forms are very few nowadays, but signs of the
usual 'substandard patterns' in respect of style, class, and sex
remain, and the age-graph seems to indicate a gradual disappearance
of these forms.

My conclusion is that the 'dialectal' [tə] variant has largely
given way to the RP form, such non-standard pronunciations as still
occur being mainly confined to the elderly and to Classes IV - V.

* * * * * * *

A general conclusion about the variables examined in this last
section is that even with single items, and with very few examples

(with (too) only 177 instances occurred in conversational data: i.e.
less than 2 per informant) signs of correlation with non-linguistic
factors emerge: there is obviously very little 'free' variation.

Some general conclusions about variation

On the basis of the above examination of thirty or so variables
of different sorts, it is possible to draw a few tentative conclusions about variation in West Yorkshire, and its relation to non-
linguistic factors.

In the case of virtually all the variables we have looked at,
it has emerged that there is variation between a form such as the
traditional dialect descriptions imply was once generally employed
in the area and a form that would pass for RP (or Standard English,
in those cases where grammar rather than pronunciation is in question); in a number of cases there are also 'intermediate' forms.
There are only a few exceptions to this: for example, (ɑ:/æ) and
(us) where the regional variant is almost universal, and the inter-
related variables (ɔʊ/o:) and (əʊ) where the regional form is not
given in most of the traditional sources.   (The fact that major
changes in incidence have also affected the traditional picture has
of course to be recognised also, even before this regional/standard
variation in the 'surviving' set is considered.)

Presumably many informants are in some way aware of there being
a difference between the form often employed locally and that accepted as 'standard' English.   But how far the latter comes to take
over from the former seems to depend on whether 'non-standard' is in
some way interpreted as 'substandard'.   More detailed evidence on
this question will be examined in Chapter 7, but for the moment let
us just accept what my own experience as a native of the area suggests: that in some cases the local variant may be stigmatised (e.g.
h-dropping), while in others the 'standard' form may be prestigious
(e.g. the use of [ʌ]) - though it is important to note that there is
no mutual implication between these situations: the fact that one
variant is stigmatised does not necessarily imply that another is
prestigious, or vice versa.   If either of these situations holds,
we usually see what we may call the 'classic' pattern of relation
between linguistic variation and non-linguistic factors - the pattern seen commonly in earlier works such as those of Labov and
Trudgill: the proportion of standard forms increases from Class V
to Class I, and in all classes as the style becomes more formal;
also, women generally use a higher proportion of standard forms than
men.

While this is the general pattern, there are differences possible within it: for example, with (h), where there is overt stigmatising of the regional h-dropping, the graph is very 'spread out'

i.e. people differ widely in terms of h-usage in casual style and
there is marked 'movement' among all classes towards using [h] as
style becomes more formal; with (ʌ) on the other hand, where
regional [ʊ] attracts little overt stigma and it is more of a case
of [ʌ] having some (not necessarily conscious) prestige in certain
sections of the population, the graph shows less apparent differentiation between classes, less marked changes between styles, and
generally a much lower proportion of standard variants employed.

Where there is no definite feeling of prestige or stigma, patterns of variation are less clear: for instance, with (ɑ:/æ) the
use of [ɑ:] is only spasmodic, and with (nch) there is little more
than 'free variation' between [ntʃ] and [nʃ].

The fact that there is any variation between a regional and a
standard form could be taken as implying that some change has affected the situation as portrayed in the traditional descriptions.
With some variables this change seems to be simply a function of
time: for example, the age-graphs for (ɛə) and (ɔə) seem to show
that newer variants are becoming commoner, but that social factors
have little part in this process.   With others, however, prestige
or stigma must be involved, and are related to the 'route' by which
a change is proceeding through the population: some changes may
start with middle-class women, then pass to their menfolk, then to
upper-working class women, and so on; others start and are trans-
mitted by different groups.

Let us look at some of our general findings in respect of particular non-linguistic factors:

Class. We may note that we have *not* found support for two 'important'
claims made in previous works within this model.   On the one hand,
like Trudgill, we have not seen evidence of the 'hypercorrection'
made much of by Labov: he used the term in an idiosyncratic sense,
referring to the way the Lower Middle Class showed even more stylistic variation than the Upper Middle Class in respect of some variables - to the extent that their use of the 'better' variants in
the most formal styles 'passed' that of the higher class; this was
held to be because of their anxiety to 'get on', and was claimed to
be an important factor in linguistic change (see Labov, 1966b).   On
the other hand, we have not found that the Middle Class /Working
Class difference is as important a break in the social class continuum as Trudgill held (see 1974a:62 etc.).   There certainly are some
variables where the classes are 'grouped' in their performance as
say I and II vs III-V, or I--II---III-IV-V: for example (our), (the),
(eɪ), (əʊ); but there are others where the clearest break was between Class I (MMC) and the rest: thus (ɑ:/æ), (I), (ɔʊ/o:), (ʊə)

etc; and in quite a number Class III, which is the 'boundary'
class (some of its members strike one as or claim to be Middle Class,
others Working Class - but no clear objective line can be drawn),
goes along with Classes I - II in contrast to the 'definitely'
Working Classes IV - V: this situation occurs with (was), (than),
(that), (Meas), (with), (too) etc. - i.e. many of the features that
one might reasonably label 'dialect' (see Chapter 8).

I think it is possible that the claims of Labov and Trudgill
could result either from 'freak' results of the particular sample
employed; or from the way the social class continuum was divided
into social class groups: there is bound to be something arbitrary
about this process, so it should not then be treated as if it has
produced something that really exists.

Style. We have referred above to the 'classic' pattern by which
non-standard variants are most common in Casual Style, and progressively less so in Formal Style, Reading Passage, Word List, and
Minimal Sets. This was observed in a number of variables. In addition, the following points of interest have emerged.

First: in the case of most of those items involving a 'dialectal'
variant (in the sense of the term 'dialect' which I shall be propos-
ing), for example (was), (the),(than), (that), (with) etc., the pattern was generally CS > FS > Ø i.e. the non-standard variants occur
only in conversation: they are not heard when material is read (when
it would sometimes be a case of substituting a different form or
construction for that written down).

Second: with some variables there was little or no evidence of variation with style in any regular pattern e.g. (ɛə), (eɪ), (ɑ:), (ʊə).
This would seem to run counter to Trudgill's claim, that stylistic
variation is to be be expected with variables either a) undergoing
change, or b) subject to overt corrective pressures, or c) involved
in surface phonological contrasts, or d) markedly different from
prestige accent equivalents (1974a:103): at least one of these
situations seems to hold with all the variables where I found little
or no stylistic variation.

Third: with the minimal pairs situation, however, there is good
reason to agree with Trudgill's conclusion that this highly artificial style might produce results which have to be interpreted with
great caution: some people may produce a phonological contrast here
which they would be most unlikely to have in 'normal' conditions -
shifting their pronunciation either in a 'standard' direction:(h),or
just the opposite:(ook).

Fourth: the variable (ook) produced a 'reverse' style pattern such
as does not appear to have been reported in previous works of this
type.

Sex: We have already noted the finding that women often use fewer
non-standard variants than men in cases where some prestige or stigma
is involved - thus confirming Trudgill's results, for which his suggested explanation (1974a:94) is that women are more status-conscious
and therefore more aware of the social significance of linguistic
variation, because a) their position in society is less secure and
generally subordinate to that of men, and b) men are more likely to
be judged by what they do, women by what they appear.   In addition,
my results show women approaching closer than men to the 'standard'
form in the case of variables like (ɑ:), (ɛə), (ʊə),(eɪ), (əʊ):
with these realisation variables I found little style variation and
less clear differentiation of classes, which would seem to suggest
that generally no strong social significance attaches to the variants - so perhaps women score lower than men in these cases simply
because they think it 'sounds nicer'.

Age.   Besides those cases where the age-graph shows a fairly steady
trend either away from a non-standard variant (as is the case with
(ook) or (-ow), for example), or towards one (as with the glottal
stop), which strongly suggests that a linguistic change is in progress, a number of points seem to recur in my age-group scores.

First: with quite a number of variables the 30-plus group used the
lowest percentage of non-standard forms (and with (h) we saw that
when the figures are further broken down this 'dip' was repeated in
the different classes, thus removing the possibility that this was
simply a result of the class-composition of this age-group in my
sample).   There were also a number of cases where the other middle-
aged groups, 40-plus and 50-plus, also scored relatively low.

Second: in several cases the highest percentages of non-standard
forms (excluding here variables such as (t) where there is evidence
that such are generally on the increase) occurred among the two
youngest age-groups: 10-plus and 20-plus.

Third: in quite a number, the older age-groups (60-plus, 70-plus,
80-plus) recorded a higher-than-average percentage of non-standard
forms - excluding those cases where a steady trend through the
age-groups suggests that these are dying out, as with (ook), for
instance.

      Now, taking these facts together - and in some cases they do
occur in combination - I would suggest that they may relate to general attitudes to speech at different stages in one's life.   Though
quite young children do sometimes notice regional or social differences, and people in their teens and twenties are certainly aware of
them, it may not be until well into the twenties that many of them
start to 'do something about it'.   In the thirties a person is
likely to be most ambitious about 'getting on', an attitude persist-

ing through middle age, when social consciousness is greatest - so
the use of non-standard variants is lowest in these groups.   In old
age speech may seem less important, and several writers have suggested that there can be some regression to childhood patterns (see
Wright, 1905: vii; Moulton, 1972:217, for example).

Thus a graph for age-groups such as Figure 39:

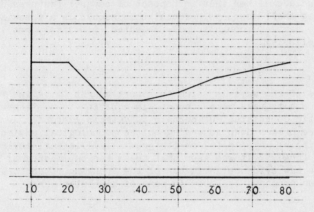

Figure 39

may perhaps reflect a fairly stable situation of standard/non-
standard variation, and have nothing to do with linguistic change.
(On the other hand, of course, it is possible that the 'drop' to
the 30-plus group could be a change in progress which will affect
the youngest groups as they become more aware of the social significance of the different variants they hear.)

Town.   Apart from a number of differences between the towns that
are probably of the traditional 'isogloss' type (for instance,
traces of [ɑ:] in '/aɪ/ words' seen mainly in Huddersfield; final
/ɪ/ in some (-ow) words in the same area; differences in the incidence of /ɛɪ/; etc.), a number of points emerged.

First: Bradford showed the highest percentage of non-standard variants of (t) and (XV̄nt); in both cases these variants appear to be
on the increase, and it may be that Bradford is leading the way
among the wool towns.

Second: Halifax showed the lowest percentage of several non-standard variants, whereas Huddersfield on the other hand scored highest
overall on several, particularly the more 'dialectal' ones such as

(our), (was), (the), (than), (that) etc.   It is true that Halifax
had the highest average social class rating of the three towns (see
p. 58), and that Huddersfield had the highest proportion of Class V
informants (among whom grammatically non-standard forms are commonest);   these facts go some way towards explaining these differences,
but it was found with (eɪ) and (əʊ) that Halifax used the fewest
non-standard variants *in each class.*   This being so, presumably we
must conclude either that in respect of several features Halifax is
less 'regional' nowadays, or that this result is a freakish one and
that the sample, though soundly selected, was simply not large enough
to be reliable.

    One of the ways in which this work sought to refine Trudgill's
methods was to take some account, in addition to the above non-
linguistic correlates, of certain *linguistic factors:* some lexical
sets were broken down according to the phonological environment of
the variable, as with (t),or its grammatical/lexical environment,
as with (ing).   It was seen that these can be important: in other
words we saw evidence in favour of the 'ranking of constraints' on
variation proposed by Labov in some of his later work.

2   OTHER NON-STANDARD FEATURES

    The variables examined above are not of course the only features
of the speech of West Yorkshire towns which are relevant to my main
theme, which is the persistence or modification of aspects of the
traditional dialects of the area.   The features examined within the
'variable' framework were a selection chosen for the reasons given
(see p.101), bearing in mind the criteria suggested by Labov.   In
this section I shall examine a large number of other non-standard
features which turned up during my investigation and are also clearly
relevant to my theme, but which cannot be treated in the same way.

    It should be emphasised at the outset that many of these fea-
tures cannot be regarded as 'typical' of West Yorkshire - in other
words their use is not restricted to this part of the country.   All
of them are well established in the area; a few are 'localised', in
that they are rarely heard outside it, but many are more widely
used in the North of England, and some are probably just 'general
non-standard English'.   But I do not think this means that they are
not part of traditional West Yorkshire speech; after all, probably
the great majority of the features of any variety are not restricted
to that area (for example the absence of /ʌ/ from the phoneme inven-

tory and the use of short /æ/ in a large set of words where RP has
long /ɑ:/, are not specifically 'Yorkshire' features; but they are
certainly part of the traditional speech of the county and help to
'give away' a Yorkshireman). A non-standard variety comprises a
number of features which have various regional distributions - it
may be only the total combination of these which is typical of the
particular area.

In the reading passage and the word list I included a considerable number of items for which a 'dialectal' pronunciation is given
in the traditional descriptions. These styles do not of course
represent the everyday usage of my informants, but from the examination of variables it has become clear that many phonological non-
standardisms do 'survive' in them, and so this material can be assumed to give some indication of the common pronunciations of these
items.

Now of course grammatical and lexical features could not be
tackled in this way, for people will read a passage with the constructions and vocabulary 'as supplied'. But within each interview, since hardly any could be described as quite 'dead', there
occurred a greater or lesser amount of what SED called *incidental
material*: amplifications of answers to questions, volunteered information, general conversation, and so on. This yielded much
interesting data of various sorts, and of a more 'genuine' nature,
since it was not specifically elicited. Besides providing further
phonological material, this was my main source of grammatical and
lexical data. But it is not as suitable for statistical treatment
as the (mainly phonological) variables examined above: it is not
possible to be so certain about the extent of use of a particular
grammatical form or construction, or a particular lexical item,
because they are not of such frequent occurrence as phonological
features. Therefore there is no guarantee that a speaker will
produce a certain feature during the interview, even if he has it
in his repertoire; and even if he does, with this limited amount
of data it is possible that the amount of usage may not be representative of his general habits.

All I shall do here then is to say that, from the limited
amount of material available, such and such appear to be non-standard
features occurring in the area, and they seem to be heard more commonly among such and such types of informants.

a) PHONOLOGICAL FEATURES

i)   Inventory Features

The phoneme /ʍ./

While it might seem odd to treat this as a 'non-standard feature', it was more characteristic of Northern than Southern speech
(see Strang 1970:45)[137] .   However, there is no trace of this phoneme in the traditional dialect descriptions of our area.   Gimson
(1970:217) points out that while it has phonemic status among some
speakers (possible contrasts include *which/witch, whine/wine* etc.),
it has declined rapidly in RP, especially among male speakers.

In conversational speech I noted very few instances, and even
in the reading passage there were less than a dozen; but in the
word list 65 examples were heard (out of a possible 500 plus), which
suggest that though /ʍ/ cannot be counted as part of the phonemic
inventory of this area since it virtually never occurs in connected
speech, it is seen by some speakers as part of a standard to be
aimed at.   These speakers were spread fairly evenly between sex
and age groups, but Classes II and III (with 54% and 36% of informants producing at least one example) came a good deal higher than
Classes IV and V (16% and 21%), and all four informants using [ʍ]
consistently in the Word List belonged to Classes I - III ; so it
would seem to be seen as a 'Middle Class' feature.

The phoneme /ə:/

We noted in our discussion of the traditional dialect descriptions that they differed over whether this phoneme occurs in this
area (see p. 81 etc.).   It will be seen from the list below that
one or two speakers seemed not to have it, pronouncing words like
*bird, burnt, church, first, hurt, learn, shirt, turn, weren't,
word, worse, work, world* with [ə]. *Work* and *first* were produced
thus by at least a dozen speakers, the rest only a few times each.
Users were predominantly male, over 60, and of classes IV - V.

ii) Distribution Features

Dental +/l/~Velar +/ḷ/

Substitution of /kl,gl/ for /tl,dl/ in words such as *bottle,
middle* is often heard in the speech of young children, and it is
usually bred out of them by effort or ridicule.   Though the environment, usually word-final, is one where contrast is not common
(*tittle/tickle, diddle/Diggle* etc. are hardly likely to cause confusion!), nevertheless, the substitution is regarded as substandard.
In word-initial position no contrast is possible, since according

---

137 Strang says that while /w/-/ʍ/ characterised *Northern* speech at
all periods, it has largely been absent from Southern English since
the Norman conquest, but the authority of the written form led to
its reintroduction to some extent.   She goes on to say she found it
declining year by year among her students.

to RP phonotactics /tl,dl/ cannot occur; so, as Gimson points out[138]
(1970:166), 'a substitution may occasionally be heard both in RP
and in other forms of English'; it is of course an example of reg-
ressive assimilation.

The traditional dialect descriptions give /tl,dl/ for /kl,gl/
as normal in this area, and I have certainly heard it in various environments: thus, [dlas] *glass*, [saɪtl] *cycle,etc.* But the number of
examples noticed in my survey data was not high (though it must be
admitted that it can be difficult to detect), and so the following
conclusions can only be tentative. More examples seem to occur of
/dl/ than of /tl/ nowadays - definite instances of the latter in
clean, *close* etc. came from persons aged 70 or over; both are
commoner among men (12 informants) than women (7); they are commoner in the lower classes: 10% of informants in Classes II - III
produced at least one, 14% in IV - V; and the following age-group
figures for percentages of informants suggest that they are dying
out:

10	20	30	40	50	60	70	80
7	5	0	0	25	50	31	67

/Close vowel + l/

The traditional descriptions of the area give diphthongal forms
for *fool*, *school* etc. [fʊɪl], [skʊɪl], but with *field*, *wheel*, *meal*
etc. there are both [i:] and [ɪə] forms to be found. In the area
today the RP-like /u:l/ and /i:l/ are common, but alongside are /uəl/
and /iəl/, as in [skuəl], [wiəl] etc; such forms are often heard
from children and are frequently castigated.

I noted only half-a-dozen examples of /uəl/, but many more of
/iəl/; 66 of the 106 informants produced at least one of the latter
in the reading passage or word list. There is little to suggest
that such forms carry any social connotations, being evenly spread
over the sexes, age-groups, and classes (even an RP speaker produced
some). It is however interesting to note that frequency varied
according to the particular item involved: virtually everybody who
used [iə] at all did so in *field*; about 60% of these did so also

138 I have heard it on TV even from eminent politicians - though
only very rarely. Strang (private communication) believes that the
distinction between dental and velar plus /l/ is usually undetectable
to RP speakers, even after a measure of ear-training.

in *wheel*;   about 25% in *meal*;   and almost as many in *steel*.

/'er/ ~ /'ər/

Before /r/ in a stressed syllable in words like *America*, *berry*, *bury*, *clerical*, *derelict(ion)*, *Eric*, *ferry*, *Jeremy*, *merit*, *perish*, *sherry*, *terrace*, *terrible*, *terror*, *Terry*, *therapy*, *very* etc. the traditional descriptions show the vowel /ə/ in the area including Bradford, whereas Huddersfield usually has the more RP-like /e/ and Halifax is around the isogloss.   This constitutes an important distributional difference from RP, where /ə/ cannot occur in stressed syllables.

I noted several instances of /'ər/ in conversation, but it was with *very* in the word list that some clear indications of the extent of this usage emerged: 10 informants definitely pronounced this word as [vərɪ] and all but one (from Halifax) were Bradfordians; it was predominantly a working-class form, being about four times as common in Classes IV - V as in Classes I - III.

/sju:/ ~ /su:/

The traditional dialect forms of words like *suit*, *sewer*, *superior*, in this area begin with [sju:] (and it may be noted that in EPD these pronunciations (historically older, see Ekwall, 1975:34 are given as still the more usual in RP).   But in the towns today a pronunciation with [su:] is much more common.

Only 18 of my informants used [sju:] in these words in the reading passage or word list.   13 of these were over 60, and only one was under 40;   37% of informants in Class V used such pronunciations, Class IV being next highest with 16%.   It would seem then that /sju:/ is giving way to /su:/, and that the former (surprisingly in view of the RP situation) shows a pattern of use more characteristic of substandard features.

(*True* and *blue* have the same historical sound and also have /ju:/ in traditional dialect - but in RP /ju:/ is no longer acceptable here, and in the West Yorkshire towns such forms are very rare today).

/-ŋ-/ ~ /-ŋg-/

Traditional dialect works give [fɪŋə] for *finger* etc. for Bradford;   but SED has [fɪŋgə] for the localities around Huddersfield. The form without /g/ would seem to be disappearing: only three old men, Classes IV - V, used the form [fɪŋə] in the word list;   surprisingly, in view of the SED picture, one was from Huddersfield (the other two were Bradfordians).   Other odd examples in incidental material included [ɪŋlɪʃ], [jʊŋə], [laŋwɪdʒ].

/ɔʊd/ ~ /ɔʊld/

Forms of *old, cold, shoulder* etc. without /l/ are commonly
given in traditional works on this area.   Only a handful of examples occurred in my data - with no discernible pattern of use (except that they all occurred with informants who would popularly be
described as 'broad' - though there are obvious risks of circularity
here!).

Final and pre-consonantal /r/

Though the traditional accounts show an r-pronouncing area ex-
tending into Yorkshire, usually somewhat to the West of our towns[139],
it is perhaps more likely that most of the seven informants who
produced varying quantities of /r/ in the reading passage or word
list, usually after centring diphthongs, did so because they were
trying to speak as clearly as possible.   Only two, whose remarks
showed them to be fairly 'speech conscious' produced examples during conversation.

iii) Realisation Features

The glottal stop

The glottal stop has been seen to be a non-standard feature
which is unusual in that, firstly it is not one 'surviving' from
traditional dialect but a relatively new one, and secondly, it is
on the increase.   This refers to its use to realise /t/ in various
environments (see p.146) including its use as definite article (see
p.196).   There remain a number of other uses which can be heard in
this area, some of which *do* appear in the traditional accounts.

a) [ʔ] = morpheme-initial/t/

This was heard mainly in *to:* 19 informants produced at least
one example of [ʔə]; 2 of them also used [ɪnʔə] *into*; one said
[wɒnʔə] *want to*; and several had [aʔə] *have to* e.g. [alaʔəgo:] *I
will have to go*; [ʔəde:] *today* and [ʔəmɒrə] *tomorrow* also occurred.
The only morpheme-initial [ʔ] not involving *to* which I noted was in
two instances of [sʊmʔaɪmz] *sometimes*, both from teenagers.

Of the 19 informants producing [ʔ] 13 were from Bradford, 4
from Halifax, and 2 from Huddersfield, which is added evidence to

---

139 Ellis writes final and pre-consonantal /r/ almost universally in
Huddersfield and Halifax and occasionally in Bradford; and Haigh says
/r/ is 'rarely dropped'; but the more reliable Wright clearly has
/r/ only in linking positions, and SED has no /r/ around Bradford and
only some in the Huddersfield area.

our earlier conclusions about local distribution within the area.
The relations with other factors were also much the same: the percentage of speakers in each class using [2] was I 0, II 8, III 14,
IV 16, V 37; only 2 of the 19 were women; and 13 of the 19 were in
the lower half of the age-range.

b) [2] 'reinforcing' /t/ in numerals

In certain numerals [2] may occur before initial /t/ of the
final morpheme; SED found such forms in traditional dialects through
out our area.   They seem to fall into two groups:

1) 13,14 [θə2tiːn] [fɒ2tiːn]; 30,40 [θə2tɪ], [fɒ2tɪ].   In these
cases [2] seems as it were to 'replace' the vowel length of the more
RP-like forms.   Less than a dozen instances occurred in my data
(though I have observed such forms not infrequently), almost all
from speakers of Classes IV - V, mainly men and over 60.   It could
be that these 'older' uses of [2] are not among those on the increase.

2) 18,80 [ɛɪ2tiːn], [ɛɪ2tɪ].   In these cases [2] seems as it were
to represent the first of the 'etymological' two /t/s.   These forms
were more common, and occurred from Classes II - V, and all age-
groups and both sexes - which suggests that they are not felt to be
as 'substandard' as the above.

c) [2] as Indefinite Article

In this case, exceptionally, [2] does not seem to have any
relation to /t/. We noted the quite common use of [2] as definite
article, replacing the traditional [t]; it appears that in prevocalic position [2] may sometimes be used instead of [ən]: e.g.
[jə wəkt 2aːd deː] 'you worked a hard day'; [fə 2ɒlɪdɪ] 'for a
holiday'; [2ʊndrəd n wʊn] 'a hundred and one'; [ðats 2ʊdəsfiːld
wəːd] 'that's a Huddersfield word'; [ɪt əd biːn ʊp 2ʊndrəd jɪəz]
'it had been up a hundred years'.   It may be relevant to note that
all these examples recorded involved h-dropping.

Though by no means as frequent as the definite article usage
(I only heard such forms from half-a-dozen speakers during the
interview), this is not very uncommon.   It was mainly heard from
men of Classes IV - V; some were my oldest informants, which suggest this is not a recent development.

iv) Incidence features

I shall discuss first a few cases of non-standard incidence
that were used by quite a number of my informants; then those occurr
ing just once or twice will be given in list form.

'Either' and 'Neither'

All the traditional dialect descriptions give the forms
[ɔ:ðə(r)] and [nɔ:ðə(r)] for this area, but only one such instance
occurred;   the great majority of town-dwellers use [(n)aɪðə(r)], as
is usual in RP, or [(n)i:ðə(r)], which is given in EPD as less
common but still acceptable[140]

The latter occurred less frequently: 38 informants (i.e. 36%
of the sample) used [i:ðə] in the reading passage or [ni:ðə] in the
word list, and only 24 of these had both.   No real differences
between the towns, sexes, or age-groups showed up, but the percentage of informants in each class using [(n)i:ðə(r)] was I 0, II 0,
III 32, IV 47, V 47.

Clearly, the traditional dialect form has given way to those
used more widely in English, but the forms with /i:/ now seem to be
used mainly by the working classes.

Love

Traditional sources have [lʊv] in Bradford but [lɒv] in Huddersfield and to some extent in Halifax too.   I found a total of 21
informants using either [lɒvɪŋ] in the reading passage or [lɒv] in
the word list (12 of them both),   2 of these were from Halifax and
the other 19 from Huddersfield;   five examples also turned up in
conversation;   no other factors than town seemed important, roughly
equal proportions of the sex, age, and class groups using this pronunciation.   This appears to be a case where a traditional form has
survived to some extent: perhaps the widespread use of /ɒ/ in other
(ʌ) words is related to this: see p.117.

Final /ɪ/ ~ /ə/ in names

Traditional dialects had /ə/ rather than /ɪ/ at the end of the
names of days of the week and of towns such as *Shipley*, *Ilkley*,
Otley, *Wibsey*, *Keighley* etc;   SED shows that Huddersfield was on
the edge of the area where this pronunciation was common.   I noted
only one or two incidental examples such as [sʊndə], but with names
of towns a total of 21 speakers used such forms in either the reading passage or the word list (and more examples occurred in the
incidental material).   They were somewhat more common in Classes
IV - V, in Bradford, and among the older informants.   This looks
then like a form which could be on the way out.

---

140 One informant retailed the old Yorkshire joke about someone
asking of a Yorkshireman 'Which is correct, [i:ðə] or [aɪðə]?'
After some thought he replied, 'Well, [ɔ:ðə] 'll do'.

Other examples of non-standard incidence

Apart from those included in various of the above categories,
a considerable number of non-standard forms occurred only once or
twice; these are listed below, with the number of informants producing them in the reading passage, word list, or incidental material.

*   indicates that the form was used by Mr. F, a Bradford man in his
       70s, Class IV, who could most clearly be classed as a 'dialect-
       speaker', according to the definition I shall propose for
       'dialect': see Chapter 8.

ǂ   indicates that it was used by Mr. W, a Huddersfield man in his
       early 60s, Class V, the next most 'dialectal' speaker.

ø   indicates that it was used only by speakers over 65 years old
       (this symbol will not appear if only Mr. F used the form, but
       it may appear as well as ǂ).

Unless any comment to the contrary is appended, these forms can be
found in the traditional dialect works (and many were referred to
in Chapter 5 or in earlier parts of this chapter: only in a few
cases will cross-reference be made).   A dash in the appropriate
column indicates that this item was not included in the word list or
reading passage.

Item	Pronunciation	WL	RP	IM	Comments
again	əgɪən	1*		1*	Nearly all informants had [ageɪn ~ əge:n] rather than
against	əgɪənst ~ əgɪn	-	-	1*	the 'first' EPD form [əgen]
almost	ɔ:məst	-	1*		
"	ɔ:lməst	-	1ø		
all right	ɔ:raɪt	-	-	Common	
any	ɒnɪ	1*	1*	2*ø	
beast	bɪəst	-	-	1*	
beat	bɪət	1*	-	1*	
before	əfoə	-	-	7*ǂø	The first element of the diphthong sounded closer to [o] than to the [ʊə] given in traditional works.

Item	Pronunciation	WL	RP	IM	Comments
bird	bəd	1*	1*		
blue	blju:	2ø	1ø		
boot	boɪt	1*			Again the first element sounded closer to [o] than to 'traditional' [ʊ]
	bʊt	6			
borrow	bɒrɪ		3	1≠	see (-ow). All were from Huddersfield.
both	boəθ	1*		1*	
bright	bri:t	1*			
broken	brɒkn	2*≠	2*ø		
came	kem	-	2*ø		Not in traditional accounts, which give [kʊm ~ kʊmd ~ kɒm ~ kam]
chimney	tʃɪmlɪ	-	-	1*	
church	tʃətʃ	2*≠	2*≠		
clean	tlɪən	2*ø	1*		
cloak	tloək	1*	-		
closed	tloəzd ~ tlɔɪzd	1*	1*		
clothes	tɫoəz	1*	1*		EPD gives an 'old fashioned'
"	klo:z	1	7		pronunciation without [ð].
coal	kɔɪl	2*≠	1*	2*≠	
coat	kɔɪt	1*	1*		
daughter	dɔʊtə	1*			
dead	dɪəd	2*ø	1*		
deaf	dɪəf	2*≠	1≠		
death	dɪəθ	-	-	1*	
decent	dɪəsənt		1*		
Derby	də:bɪ	-	-	1ø	

Item	Pronunciation	WL	RP	IM	Comments
deserve	dɪzaːv		1*		
die	diː			1*	
don't	doənt	2*⌀	-		
eat	ɛɪt	1*	1*		
eye	iːʲ	1*	-		Only the plural form was included in the RP; in dialect this would have the form [iːn].
father	faðə	5*⟋	2*⟋	5*⟋	
feet	fɪt	1*			
-field	-fɪld	-	-	2⌀	e.g. 'Huddersfield'
fight	fɛɪt	1*			
find	fɪnd	2*⌀			
first	fəst	2*⌀	1*		
fool	foɪl	1*			
foot	foɪt	2*⟋	1*		
for	fɒ	-	-	3	e.g. [wɒt fɒ] 'why?'
fortnight	fɔːʔnɪt	-	-	1⌀	
game	geəm	-	-	1*	
garden	gaːdɪn	2*⌀	-		
go	goə		1*		
good	goɪd	1*			
green	grɪən	-	-	1*	Traditional [griːn]. Analogy of other [ɪə~iː] forms? see p.217.
ground	grɛənd	1⟋			
half	ɔːf	1*			
hang	eŋ	1*			

Item	Pronunciation	WL	RP	IM	Comments
have	ɛv ~ e	1*		2*≁	
head	ɪəd	2*≁			
hold	ɒld	1			
hole	ɔɪl	1*	5*≁ ∅		
horse	ɒs	1*	1*	1*	
I	ɒ			1∅	Huddersfield speaker
late	lat		1*		
learn	lɪən	1*			
"	lən		1≁		
length	lɪŋθ	-	-	1∅	
light	li:t	2*≁			
like	lɑ:k	1≁			see p.98, and *sky*, *time* below
make	mak	1*	1*		see (eɪC).
never	nɪvə	1*		2∅	
night	ni:t	1*	1≁	1*	
noon	noɪn	1*	1*		
not	nʊt	1*			
only	o:nɪ	-	1	2	
open	ɒpm	2*≁	1*	1*	
over	ɒvə	-	2*≁	8	Adv [ɔ:l ɒvə], Prep [ɔ:l ɒvə 2 ple:s]
parcel	pa:sɪl	-	-	1*	
rather	re:ðə	-	-	1*	
reason	rɪəsən		1≁		
right	rɛɪt	1≁	-	1*	

Item	Pronunciation	WL	RP	IM	Comments
rind	rɪnd	10ø	5ø		The WL figure could be artificially high: several informants seemed not to recognise the form in isolation and perhaps just read phonetically.
road	roəd	2*≠	-		
rubbish	rʊbɪdʒ	-	2		
Saturday	sa2dɪ	-	-	3	
school	skoɪl	2*≠		1*	
sea	sɪə	-	-	1*	
seat	sɪət	-	-	1*	
shirt	ʃət	-	1*		
since	sɪn	-	-	1*	
sky	skɑ:	1≠			
slovenly	slɒvənlɪ	-	-	1	Huddersfield: cf.*love?*
so and so	so ən soə	-	-	1ø	
sour	saə		1*		
squeak	skwɪək	1*	1*		
swear	swɪə	1*	1*		
take	tak	1*			This speaker switched to [tek] in the RP.
tea	tɪə	1*		2*	
teach	tɛɪtʃ	-	-	1ø	
there	ðɪə	1*			
these	ðɪəz	-	-	1*	
thought	θɔʊt	3*≠ø			
time	tɑ:m	1≠			

Item	Pronunciation	WL	RP	IM	Comments
tongue	tɒŋ	–	–	1	Halifax speaker
tooth	toɪθ	2*↲	1*		
true	trju:	1ø			
tumble	tʊml		1↲		
war	wa:	–	–	1↲	
warm	wa:m	–	3*↲ø	1↲	
water	wɒtə	2*ø	1*		See Ekwall (1975:40): both
	watə	1↲			these forms are more 'genuine' historically than [wɔ:tə].
weak	wɪək	1*			
well	wi:l	1*			
weren't	wənt	1ø	1*		
"	wɔ:nt		1		
where	wɪə	1*			
word	wəd	1*			
work	wək	1*	2*ø		
world	wəld	2*↲	2*↲		
worse	wəs	1*	1 ↲		
year	jə:	–	–	14	12 Huddersfield, 2 Halifax
yeast	jɪst ~ jest	–	–	1*	
yesterday	jəstədɪ	3*		6	

The reading passage and word list thus succeeded in eliciting a number of the relatively few 'dialect' forms that survive. But it is worth noting that the majority were heard from just one out of 106 speakers, and even he did not use them consistently: several which occurred in the word list were not used in the more fluent reading passage or general conversation (in a sense then his stylistic shifts were the reverse of the usual, i.e. he produced *more*

non-standard forms in the more careful styles: he was proud of his
Yorkshire speech and perhaps 'recalled' more in these situations
than in normal conversation).   Only a small minority of speakers
produced any 'dialect' forms during general conversation; but this
may of course be due in part to the fact that the items where these
might have occurred just happened not to turn up.

v) Stress Features

Some polysyllabic words can occasionally be heard with stress
placed otherwise than in RP.   The only ones recorded in the interviews, each once only and from working-class speakers, were *inter-*
ésting, *indústry*, *educáte*.

Not all of these words can be checked in the traditional dialect records, but it is interesting to note that Wright has [edɪkéət].

vi) Features of Connected Speech

a) Weak Forms

In the West Riding the list of common words which may have
a reduced form when occurring in unstressed positions in connected
speech is greater than in RP (see Gimson 1970:264-5), and includes
besides the main batch of 'grammatical words' - pronouns, conjunc-
tions, auxiliaries etc., a few common 'lexical words'.   Those noted
in my data (excluding *that*, *than*, *with*, *too* etc. which were examined
as variables) included:

Item	Reduced Form	Examples	Comments
Auxiliaries			
have	ə	[a kʊd ə dʊn ɪ2̃]	Common
have to	atə ~ a2a	[al atə dʊ ðat]	"
may	mə	[spɪnɪn jə mə kɔ:l ɪt]	Very rare: only 1 example, from oldest informant.
shall	s, sl	[as bɪ 75 təmɒrə]	Rare: 2 instances from old informants.
should	səd	[a səd θɪŋk]	
Prepositions			
by	bɪ	[bɪ tre:d], [bi naʊ]	7 informants

Item	Reduced Form	Examples	Comments
in	ɪ	[ɪ 2 sku:l],[ɪ 2 mɪl], [ɪ bra2fəd]	17 informants: 10 Hudds, 16 in Classes IV-V.
of	ə	[ə lo:d ə rubɪʃ]	Common
on	ɒ	[ɒ 2 duə]	One example, Mr. W≠. Not in traditional records - analogy with *in?*

Verbs

do	dʊ ~ də	[jə ka:2 də ða2]	Common (Gimson gives these, but only for *do* as Auxiliary)
give	gɪ	[gɪ əz ə spaɪs] 'give me a sweet'	Quite common, but only 2 examples in data.
go	gʊ	[a ka:2 gʊ tə 2 matʃ]	Common
going to	gʊnə	[am gʊnə traɪ]	Common
have	a	[a l a t a 2 lampɒn] 'I will have to have the lamp on'	Not rare, but only 1 example, recorded from oldest speaker.
know	nə	[a do:2 nə weðə...]	Common
say	se	[a wʊn2 se ðət...]	" cf RP [sez]?

Adjectives

no	nə	[ðats nə gʊd]	15 informants, most over 60, Classes IV-V

Adverb

always	ɔ(:)lɪs/z ɔ(:)ləs/z	[aɪ ɔ:ləz du:]	12 informants: 8 over 80

Except for those marked 'common', these forms were largely restricted to Classes IV-V,and usually to men; they can be found in traditional dialect works.

b) Elision and Liaison

Apart from instances of forms like [sʊmdɪ] *somebody*, [spo:z]
suppose, [naɪpns] *ninepence*, which do not seem to me to be particularly typical of this area, the main cases of elision I recorded
involved words with weak forms of the phonological shape /Cə/:

to	Infinitive	[a laɪk tɪə jə tɔːk]	*I like to hear you talk;*
	Marker:	[a wɒntɪd t^ə ask]	*I wanted to ask.*
	Preposition:	[am go:ɪn t^ə alɪfaks]	*I'm going to Halifax*
		(about a dozen informants)	
you	Pronoun:	[jɪə ðat ə lɒt]	*you hear that a lot,*
		[ja2 tə du:^w ɪ2]	*you had to do it* (Few, elderly).
so	Adverb:	[a do:2 kʊm s^ə ɒftən]	*I don't come so often*

Liaison by means of /t>r/, as in [a kʊd bʊr a wo:2] *I could
but I won't,* has been noted in connection with (t) see p.151;
'intrusive r' is occasionally used in places where it would not occur
in near-standard English:

[kʊd jər av tu:^w əv əm] *could you have two of them?*

Again the forms noted under this category occurred mainly with
members of Classes IV-V.

b) GRAMMATICAL FEATURES

In this section and the next we shall be dealing almost exclusively with features observed in general conversation with my informants.   In a reading passage the material, whether standard or not,
is most likely to be produced 'as given', and very few of my informants made any changes of construction.   Unless otherwise stated it
can be taken that all the features described below were heard predominantly from speakers of Classes IV and V, and more commonly
among men than women, and that they are familiar from traditional
dialect accounts;   (however, since these are often very thin on
matters of syntax, such points are sometimes difficult to confirm).
In some cases I have added a comment on their apparent frequency,
which is based on my own native-speaker experience of the area.   As
I noted earlier, many of these features are not specifically 'Yorkshirisms', but they are aspects of the total picture of non-standard
speech in the area.

i) Morphology

Nouns

Two elderly Huddersfield informants each produced one instance of the older plural form *childer* [tʃɪldə], and another had [tʃɪlən~ tʃɪldən], the latter looking as if it could be a blend of *childer* and *children*. (A single example of 'regularised' [haʊsɪz] was probably a slip.)

Pronouns

Certain phonetic differences in the forms of some personal pronouns have been examined above as variables.

Morphological differences from the standard language mainly involve reflexives, where there are 'regularisations' of the para- digm by bringing *himself* and *themselves* into line with *myself*, *yourself*, *yourselves*, *herself*, *ourselves* where the first morpheme is a possessive pronoun: 8 informants produced [(h)ɪzself~(h)ɪsːelf] and 4 each [ðəselvz] and [ðəself]. In this last the 'redundant' double marking of plurality is removed, as in *yourself*(pl) and *ourself* which I have also heard in the area). The only other non- standard forms occurring were [aselvz] *ourselves*, with [aʊə>a:>a] and [ʊzsen] which shows three non-standard features: *us* for *our* (which could have *us* used as possessive (see above) or be modelled on *himself* with objective pronoun); *-sen* for *-self* (which can occur throughout the paradigm); singular for plural (as above; [-senz] is also possible in the area)[141].

Verbs

Several non-standard past tense forms occurred:

1) a few common verbs have the same form used for past as for present: e.g. *Jack come up* for *came* (21 informants, including one example in the Reading Passage); *give* (7); *run* (4); *send* (1)[142].

---

141 These non-standard reflexives all have respectable histories: Strang (1970:198) says genitive forms in reflexives were common in ME, and that in *Canterbury Tales* the MSS are equally divided between *usself* and *ourself*. Traditional dialect works show [sel], [sen], [seln] in this area; the second is most common in recent times - and I used it as a child with my peers.

142 Strang (1970:148) and Ekwall (1975:107) show that these uses of *come* and *run* were quite common in earlier ModE.

2)   One or two verbs have weak past forms where Standard English
     has strong: e.g. *telled* (4 informants), *heared* (1 example
     each in Reading Passage and Incidental Material).

3)   on the other hand, *swoll* for *swelled* (1), and *tret* for *treated*
     (1) show strong for weak forms.

4)   a different strong form from Standard English occurred in one
     example of [rit] *wrote* (which I cannot find in the traditional
     dialect descriptions).

5)   phonological rather than morphological differences occurred in
     [gev] *gave* and [kem] *came* (several examples); [θɔʊt, brɔʊt, ɔʊt]
     thought, brought, ought (2 or 3 each); [tiːd] *tied* and [brɒk]
     broke (1 each).

There were also a number of non-standard past participles:
most were instances of a reduction in the number of 'principle
parts' from 3 to 2, e.g. *take/took/taken* > *take/took* (on the anal-
ogy of *spin/spun, lose/lost* etc.): thus *took* (taken), *broke*
(broken), *spoke* (spoken), *wrote* (written), *hid* (hidden), *bit* (bitten)
forgot (forgotten), *wore* (worn), *wed* (wedded)[143];

More interesting perhaps are *give* (given) e.g. *I've never give
much thought, you've give up,* which could represent a reduction of
principle parts from three to one, since *give* also serves for *gave*
(see above); and *tret* (treated), which serves as a participle as
well as a preterite (see above) and is an instance of 'strong for
weak'.

Most of the above occurred only once or twice, and were more
common among the elderly.

Prepositions/Adverbs

The form *afore* (before) occurred several times (a similar formation, *atween,* can also be heard, but less commonly: it did not
occur in my data).

ii) Syntax

The Noun Phrase

The use of a phrase such as *me and Tommy* for *Tommy and I* as

---

143 See Ekwall (1975:99): 'in ModE the preterite and past participle have frequently influenced each other...the form of the preterite
often occurs with the function of the participle'.

subject is heavily castigated in the schools, but is nevertheless quite common and several examples occurred in my data.

Less common now is the use of *on* for *of* in phrases like *all on us*, *three on 'em* etc. of which only two or three instances occurred. I have suggested (see Petyt 1970:37) that the distribution of this use of *on* is restricted to environments involving personal pronouns with initial vowel or semivowel (note the impossibility of **the bottom on the cupboard*).

Two non-standard uses of demonstrative pronouns/adjectives are not uncommon: *this here* for *this* was heard from seven informants, mostly elderly (*that there* is also used, but no examples occurred in my data); and *them* for *those* occurred with 18 informants. The range of environments represented was quite wide: *all them years*; *in them days*; *they were difficult, were them*; *all them little childer*; *no time for them that wasn't clever*; and even *them are my honest contentions!*

The use of *us* for the indirect object *me* is common in this area: e.g. *give us a sweet.*

In the adjective phrase a few double comparatives occurred (e.g. *more broader*, *more posher*) and also one double superlative (*the most rottenest jobs*). In place of the intensifiers *very* or *so* occur not infrequently *right* (e.g. *I'm right fast for band = I'm very short of string*) and *that* (e.g. *my father's been that busy*): each was used by about half-a-dozen informants during the interviews [144]. One example occurred of what looks like a blend of two adjectival constructions: *I'm not used to pronounce 'em.*

The Verb Phrase

The use of past for present participles with verbs of 'posture'. as in *he was sat/stood/laid there* is quite common; in my material *sat* occurred in such contexts with 8 informants (including 2 women of Class III), and *stood* with 5.

The use of past participle for perfect tense is less common now: EDGr s441 says it is restricted to strong verbs, and I record-ed it only with *been* (e.g. *I never really been keen; where you been?*), heard from 7 speakers; *seen* (*you maybe seen that*), *done*

---

144 Such forms all occurred earlier in ModE generally: see Ekwall (1975:94) and Strang (1970:138) on double comparatives and super-latives, and Strang (1970:138) on *right*; the latter is of course still used in *Rt.Rev.* and *Rt.Hon.* etc; (in this area it is also frequently used as an adjective meaning 'proper, confirmed' e.g. *a right devil, a right Conservative.*

(we done a lot of...), got (you got to be careful :   it may be noted
that have got is only perfect from a morphological, not a semantic,
viewpoint), from one informant each.

Another type of 'omission of auxiliary' is much more common in
phrases like What you going to do?, but this could perhaps be considered a case of elision.

The use of adjective for adverb is not unusual, and the following examples occurred: dressed shabby, speaks /talks nice, I wouldn't
use them ordinary, talked lovely, speaks more polite, I don't speak
bad, time passes quick, talk clear, doing very fair, put in separate
words spelt different and mean different.

Deserving of somewhat more discussion in this section is a
phenomenon by which non-standard speech appears to have an 'extra
auxiliary', in that we find [d əv ~ d ə] corresponding to Standard
English had.

This construction was heard from over 20 informants during my
survey.   They were of all ages and from Classes II - V; moreover
I have observed it to be widespread both in this area and in British
English generally - I have even noticed it on radio and TV in apparently scripted material, which means that either the writers have
written this construction (and I do not recall having seen it
written, except in say Dickens) or that the actors have unconsciously
substituted it for what was written: in either case it is an indication that it is a fairly common phenomenon.   It is to be observed
in the following constructions:

a)   most commonly, in the protasis of conditional sentences:
thus,in the form [d əv], if she'd've read it..., if I'd've had to...;
and as [d ə] If you'd [ə] put that..., if you'd [ə] been living
then...   Note that in such cases the protasis verb phrase may thus
be made parallel to that of the apodosis: if I'd [ə] jumped, I'd
[ə] been killed; if she'd've asked me, I'd've told her; if you'd [ə]
gone in the mill, you wouldn't've understood (the [ə...əv] here seems
to be less common).   This parallelism may also occur in the following use:

b)   in temporal clauses: by t'time you'd [ə] gone, you'd [ə] been
......

c)   in optative clauses there is no parallel clause: in these
cases only [d ə] occurred in my material: I wish I'd [ə] stayed,
I wish I'd never [ə] done it.

Now I have heard within the area (though not during my survey),
examples such as if somebody would have explained it to me... - and

similar examples have occurred on radio and TV: e.g. *If our lads*
would have scored..... (football manager); *If I wouldn't have been*
able to do that.......... (young film actress, interview); *If*
women would have had the pluck... (elderly Northern woman).   These
suggest that the full form of the usual [d əv ~d ə] is *would have*,
whereas Standard English has *had*.   Of course [(ə)d] can be a weak
form of either *would* or *had*, so which is it to be interpreted as in
this construction?

     In support of *would* are the following points: a) examples
such as the above, though not frequent in the area; b) since the
full form of the apodosis in conditional examples is *would*, perhaps
the parallel form is so too; c) this construction also occurs in
American English,and American linguists have told me in discussion
that *would* is the full form there.

     Against this, and in favour of *had* can be set the evidence of
such full forms as did occur in my survey, in a) Emphatic forms:
(conditionals) *if I* ['ad əv] *been*..., *if I* ['had əv] *done it*...,
if it ['ad ə] *been*..., *if I* ['ad ə] *been waiting*; (optatives -
again only [ə] occurred for *have*) *he wished he* ['ad ə] *done, I wish*
I ['ad ə] *done*; b) Negative forms: only conditional occurred in
my data (again with [əv ~ ə]): *If we* ['hadnt əv] *come here*..., *if*
if you ['adn't əv] *saved* ..., *if I* ['adnt ə] *gone* ..., *if I* ['ant ə]
done... [145] .

     From the above evidence it would appear that in our area *had*
have rather than *would have* is usually 'felt' to be the full form
nowadays.   A clue to the probable historical development is seen
in Strang(1970:101) where she says of the expression *you'd better*...
that the [d] was originally *would* but by 'false expansion' of this
ambiguous weak form the full form is now *you had better*...;
probably something similar occurred in the construction discussed
here.

The Prepositional Phrase

     As an adverbial phrase of time, the preposition *of* plus Indef.
Art. plus Noun (part of day, or day of week) as in *of a morning/*
afternoon/evening night, of a Monday, is a not uncommon construction,
though only a few examples occurred in my data.   There were a
similar number with *on* instead of *of*: *he comes on a night/morning*
(of course, with days of the week *on* is Standard English); whether
there is any connection with the above use of *on* for standard *of* is
unclear.

---

145 Note that the reduction of *have* to [ə] only seems to occur along
with h-dropping in *had* i.e. there is an 'implicational relation' between the two.

The use of *over* in meaning 'about/because of' e.g. *I'm going to tell (the teacher) over you*; *I get told off over it* is not unusual though only the odd example turned up.

The word *while* serves as a preposition meaning 'until' for many speakers: e.g. *I'm stopping while Monday*; though it may be pronounced [waɪl], it is more often reduced to [wel] (whereas most of the traditional sources give [wɒl]).

Conjunctions

The above use of *while* as a preposition may have developed out of that as a conjunction, again in the non-standard sense of 'until'. e.g. *wait while I get there*; *you couldn't go full-time while you were thirteen*; here again the pronunciation [wel] is commoner than the full form.   An unusual construction, heard only once was ... *while when I gave up* ('until I retired').   (Note: the use of *while* as a noun meaning 'period' e.g. *a long while ago* is also quite common; in *I haven't been down of a long while* we also see *of = for*, a somewhat different use of *of* in adverb phrases of time from that referred to above).

Features of the Clause

Existential Subject

I noted one clear example of *there used to be* ... where the first word was pronounced [ðɪ], which is in fact a weak form of *they*; though this was the only instance in my interview data I have heard others[146].   The form usually occurring in such contexts is [ðə], which in this area is ambiguously a weak form of either *there* or *they* (see p.205); perhaps because of this there has been confusion leading to the use of [ðɪ], which is unambiguously *they*.

Indirect Object

Two non-standard constructions were recorded: *I didn't show it Harry*, where Standard English would have either *to* or reversal of the last two words; and *open me t'door*, where *for me* at the end would be standard.   Though these only occurred once in my data, they are not very unusual in the area.

Concord

a) $NP_{pl} + VP_{sg}$ 33 informants produced one or more examples each

---

146 They are also to be observed in attempts to portray dialect in written form: see Petyt (1970:39), for example.

(all but three of them, who were older people of Class III, belonged
to Classes IV - V). Most involved the verb *be*, either as auxiliary:
I wondered why you was doing it[147], *we was married, they wasn't
paid, some on 'em is wed, some is and some isn't, the men isn't
losing it* etc; or as main verb: *this house and that was one, we
was at Leeds, these mills was busy, where t'vehicles is, Yorkshire
puddings is different, these people's better* , and so on. Other
auxiliary verbs did occur but less commonly: *three or four has
shut, the other two has been built on, the children doesn't play
marbles now, the old ways gets stamped out*, etc.

Particularly interesting is a construction, occurring in my
data only from one old man, in which the main verb or auxiliary was
plural, but the tag was singular: *they've got too big, has the
unions; people speak very fair, does a lot of them; they're very
similar to us, is Halifax (sc.folk?)*.

Only a few examples of this irregular concord occurred with
main verbs: e.g. *some of 'em talks all right*.

Examples involving existential *there* were quite common, but I
think they fall into two subgroups. On the one hand examples such
as *there isn't many Pakistanis here, ...whether there is any
societies, there was grammar schools, there isn't the jobs* etc,
seem to be treated as definitely substandard (judging from the sorts
of speakers who employ them). On the other hand are examples like
*there isn't a lot of coloureds, there's a few banks, there is a few
thousand,* etc, where a singular verb is much more widely accepted
with *a lot of, a few, plenty of*. *There's a lot of/a few/plenty
of people coming* is acceptable, provided that the verb is not uncontracted: thus, **there isn't a lot* but *there's not a lot*.

b)   *NP_{sg} + were*   Examples such as *it weren't his car, not like
it were, where I were* present an interesting problem. We saw above
(p. 193 sq.) that corresponding to Standard English [wɒz]/[wəz] as
strong/weak, the usual non-standard forms in this area are [wɒ]/[wə];
now [wə] is also the Standard English weak form of *were*, and it may
be that in these examples we see a 'new' non-standard strong form
created by a back-formation from [wə], replacing [wɒ].

c)   *Pron_{1}st_{sg} + V_{3}rd_{sg}*   Though only one example occurred in
my data (*I jumps on*), this construction is not uncommon in narrative,
especially amongst garrulous women! e.g. [a sez tʊ ər,a sez...ðen a
gʊz ɪntə ʔ taʊn ən a si:z...]

---

147 *You was* to one person was common in the 16-18th Centuries: see
Ekwall (1975:118), and Strang (1970:140) who describes it as a device,
unfortunately abolished by purists, for restoring the distinction of
number lost when the thou/you contrast disappeared.

Double Negatives

This feature is heavily castigated in certain sections of the population (see p.249) and especially in the schools, but it is still quite common, particularly in Classes IV - V.   Examples recorded included *I was never scared of nobody, you don't think nothing about it, he couldn't get a job nowhere, you wouldn't never think that...* etc;   those with *no* as the second negative seemed particularly common: *I never went there no more* [no:~nə], *I never had no trouble with..., that weren't no good, there's nothing no funnier than...,* and so on.

Half-a-dozen informants produced examples which might be called 'quasi double negatives' i.e. where the second is not a 'full' negative: for instance, *they never hardly come here, there's nothing only pubs, my mother never spoke only good English, you don't hear very little of that now, I don't understand it very little, I don't think that's used very little.*   In such cases it is the main or 'first' negative which seems redundant.

Relative Clauses

Two non-standard relatives (apart from those discussed on p.200) were heard.   Firstly, *what* with either human or non-human nouns: *letters what you don't sound, the yarn what it's spun, those what stay, it's me what..., other people what I've heard, we what was up here*:   8 informants (including 3 in Class III) produced examples including these.   Secondly, a 'zero relative': *I've a sister lives there; I'd a brother came over from Australia, and he...; there's a man lives up here talks very broad; we have a coach comes down, he's very good.*   All these four examples which occurred involved human nouns.

Purpose Clauses

The purpose construction seen in *I'll have to go and do the shopping, I must just go and get a pencil* etc. was observed quite commonly from informants of all types.   Less commonly, only one example occurring in my data, this may be reduced by the 'omission' of *and*: *I have to go pick a car up.*

Comparative Clauses

Two instances were recorded of a construction in which a (superfluous) *what* is inserted into a comparative clause: *...as good as what they were, ...sooner than what the old ones did.*

Tags

Several of the examples quoted in this chapter involve a tag construction not recognised as Standard English in works such as Quirk and Greenbaum (1973:429). Besides the tag statement which they quote, consisting of 'NP plus operator' (i.e. auxiliary/modal), as *'He likes a drink now and then, Jim does'*, which is common in our area, there frequently occurs the reverse: *'He likes a drink now and then, does Jim'*, *'He's all right, is John'*, *'He's got his head screwed on, has Dave'*, etc. Though not recognised as standard today, this has a respectable history in English literature.

c) VOCABULARY

Being a native of an area, and familiar with most of the everyday words, I have some difficulty in knowing whether certain items are Standard English, but the following, which turned up in my survey, are almost certainly regionally restricted, even if not strictly 'Yorkshirisms'. All of them can be found in traditional dialect descriptions of the area.

Nouns

[sʊmət] *something*, [ɔʊt] *anything*, [nɔʊt] *nothing* are in common use, though mainly in Classes IV - V, in spite of being castigated in the schools. Each was recorded a good number of times; (one informant actually substituted [ɔʊt] in the Reading Passage). *Nowt* is usually pronounced [nɔʊt] though [naʊt] was also heard ([aʊt] for [ɔʊt] is less common).

Other local nouns, each occurring only once or twice, were *tenter* (as in *furnace-tenter*), and distinctive uses of forms heard also in Standard English: *band* 'string', and *speak/spake* 'expression' e.g. *a Yorkshire speak*.

Adjectives

Flayed [fle:d] 'frightened' was the only non-standard adjective recorded.

Verbs

Brus 'burst', *gan* 'go', *pawse* 'kick' occurred only once, from Mr. F (the most 'dialectal' speaker). *Laik* [le:k] 'play', though not uncommon, occurred only twice. *Give up/give over* 'stop' e.g.

it never gave over, *give up roaring* [gɪv ʊp rʊərɪn] 'stop crying' -
with *roar* also used in a localised sense - are quite common and occurred several times. *Learn* in the meaning 'teach' is highly stigmatised but quite frequently heard; four informants used it during
the interviews. One instance occurred of *belong* meaning 'own':
the lady 'at belongs it.

Adverbs

The phrase *and all* [ən ɔ:l] is in common use, especially sen-
tence-finally, in the sense of 'also': for example, *What you, and
all?* 'Et tu, Brute?'.

Only two examples occurred of *any road* 'anyway' (note also
you'll never manage it that road, though not heard in the survey),
though this usage is not uncommon.

Aye for 'yes' occurred a number of times; *Nay* is not uncommon,
but is most commonly employed as a sign of surprise or disapproval
rather than meaning 'No'.

Prepositions

Only two informants produced examples of *through*, in the weak
form [θrə] meaning 'from': thus, [θrə bra2fəd].

*   *   *   *   *   *

What general conclusions can be drawn from this examination of
the non-standard features which turned up in my survey of a random
sample of speakers from the three main 'wool towns'?

First: the popular view of 'dialect' usually concentrates on
          vocabulary (and one recalls the large numbers of 'glossar-
          ies' produced by traditional dialectology); however, it
          is quite obvious that very few vocabulary items which are
          'regionally-specific' are in common use, and certainly the
          vast majority of my sample could not be readily identified
          as Yorkshiremen on lexical evidence: they use 99% of words
          which would be accepted as Standard English. Lexical
          items are not then the most persistent West Yorkshire fea-
          tures.

Second: there are a fair number of non-standard *grammatical* forms
          and constructions, some of them specific to this area, which
          have persisted, and no doubt these play their part in help-
          ing to identify some speakers. But though my description
          of these was not so 'statistical' as with the variables

discussed earlier, it does appear firstly, that they are
for the most part of low frequency (and this applies particularly to the definitely 'regional' features); and
secondly, that they are largely confined to Classes IV - V:
speakers of higher social status generally use Standard
English grammar. Now of course Classes IV - V account for
60% of my sample, and so quite a large proportion of the
urban population probably do use *some* such non-standard
features; but the traditional descriptions suggest that
previously there were many more of them, and it therefore
seems likely that Standard English is gradually ousting
non-standard grammar, working 'down' the social scale.

Third: the *phonological* variables examined showed that it is features such as these which are the most persistent aspects
of regional speech, even quite high on the social scale.
However, there are various differences between types of
phonological features in this respect: this question will
be discussed in more detail later (see Chapter 8), but for
the present it may be noted that very many changes of
'incidence' have taken place as far as the majority of
speakers are concerned. The small numbers using such forms
as are listed on pp. 222-7 show that most people now have
something much closer to what may be described as 'Standard
English incidence'.

Of course I would not claim that I have discussed all
the persistent features of West Yorkshire phonology, or
even the most important ones. Some features call for
greater phonetic acuity than I possess: for example, the
'openness' of /æ/, the 'front-backness' of the start-points
of /aʊ/ and /aɪ/, the devoicing of consonants by assimilation to a following voiceless one, and the intonation patterns: (on all of these my recorded material can be used in
the future either for spectrographic and other mechanical
investigation, or by more gifted phoneticians). And one
probably crucial feature, the 'West Yorkshire tone of voice',
variously described as 'harsh', 'loud' etc. (see below),
must await the further development of techniques for handling 'articulatory settings' (see Honikman, 1964; Lever,
1968; Trudgill, 1974a:185).

CHAPTER SEVEN

THE PRESENT SITUATION: EVALUATION

The changes which appear to have occurred or to be taking place
at present in the speech of the West Yorkshire towns, and also the
social differentiation in speech which Chapter 6 has shown up, must
surely result in some measure from the fact that speakers somehow
perceive different variants and also 'evaluate' them.   An examination of speakers' opinions about and reactions to various features
of speech is therefore very relevant to a study such as this, and
will form the subject of this chapter.

Three methods were employed in order to investigate speakers'
evaluation of the speech of the area.   First, in order to draw out
the conscious feelings of informants on such matters, I asked direct questions such as 'What do you think about the way people speak
around here?', 'Is there anything in particular you dislike about
it?', and so on.   But feelings about speech might well not be so
'close to the surface'; and since some informants, particularly the
less intelligent, may have difficulty in putting their feelings into
words, I also adopted from Labov two experiments which aimed to
elicit both conscious and subconscious reactions, particularly to
phonological variables.

Informants were asked first to perform 'self-evaluations' in
respect of certain features: in other words, they were asked to say
which of two or more possible pronunciations they thought that they
themselves used.   The aim here was to discover what standard they
saw themselves as aiming at - since they might well claim to say
what they felt they 'ought' to say or would like to say, rather than
what they actually said.   Also, since they were invited to say
whether they considered another of the pronunciations to be better
or more correct than the one they used, this might be another way of
eliciting some conscious feelings, particularly of 'linguistic insecurity'.

As a later task, informants were asked to make judgements about
the social status of a number of speakers, after hearing tape-

recordings of samples of their speech.   This 'subjective evaluation' experiment aimed to discover not only how much agreement there
was about a particular speaker, but also how consistent were the
judgements about the same speaker who produced several utterances
containing examples of different non-standard features.   In this
way I hoped to obtain evaluations of these features.

1   OPINIONS AND ATTITUDES

A section of the interview was devoted to questions which sought
to elicit informants' opinions about speech, particularly their own
speech and that of West Yorkshire in general.

The questions were in some cases 'open':   in other words they
did not encourage a Yes/No response;   and even those which did permit this were often expanded on, sometimes at my prompting.   The
answers therefore did not always fit into a small set of definite
categories, as would have been the case if it had been considered
appropriate to ask such questions as could be answered Yes/No/Don't
know, or by means of a numerical scale.   But interpretation in
terms of some such categories for statistical purposes was not found
to be difficult, or to leave much room for doubt.

The first question was a deliberately general one and did permit a Yes/No reply: this ensured that virtually nobody was stumped
for some sort of answer.

*Do you think that the way a person speaks is important for getting
on?*[148]

There was a range of responses, but apart from just two cases
of 'don't know' they could all be assigned to the following categories:

        Yes! ("Definitely", "No doubt about it", etc.)
        Yes
        Possibly ("Maybe", "Sometimes", "Could be", "In some jobs",etc.)
        No? ("Not really", "Not much, these days", "Don't *think* so",
          etc.)
        No

---

148 Several informants were specific about what they understood by
'getting on': for example, they said that at interviews for certain
jobs, or in doing them, a Yorkshire accent might be a detriment. One
young man, of grammar school background but quite 'broad', said that
since becoming a manager he was more speech-conscious.

In order to measure the degree of positive/negative opinion on this
question, we have to decide where to divide this scale.   I think
there are two possibilities: either, to count the first three above
as 'Yes' and the last two as 'No';   or, to discount the middle group,
on the ground that they were not sure either way.

   Taking the Yes!/Yes/Possibly groups as positive, we find that
over 90% overall feel that the way one speaks is or can be important for getting on in life.   There is little difference between
the various social class, sex or age groups.   If the 'Possibly'
category is excluded and we consider only those responding more
clearly on either side, a more interesting picture emerges.   The
following table shows the degree of positive response by class and
sex:

	I	II	III	IV	V
M	(0)	43	42	27	67
W	-	50	50	67	71
Total	(0)	46	46	46	68

The age-group graph is irregular, but one notable point is the fact
that the 30-plus group showed markedly the highest percentage of
'Yes' responses.   No regular differences between the towns show up.

   The small Class I (in fact, those who speak 'best') did not
seem to consider speech very important - whereas the 'lowest' class,
which was seen in Chapter 6 to use the most non-standard forms, were
most definite about the fact that it is important;   the three intermediate groups scored much alike overall.   Women seemed to set more
store by speech than men, and this was especially so in the large
working-class group, Class IV.

   The conclusions seem to be that on the one hand there are signs
that some of those groups which were seen in Chapter 6 to come
closer to Standard English/RP are also those who openly believe
speech to be important: for example, women, and the 30-plus age-
group.   On the other hand, the most non-standard group, Class V,
seem to be most aware of the importance of speech, whereas the 'best
spoken' have perhaps had less reason to bother about this.

   The next question was more specifically about the speech of
this area:

What do you think about the way people speak in this town or in West Yorkshire generally - do you like it?[149].

Again the responses can reasonably be classified in terms of a small set of categories: Yes/Neutral/No/No!   The last two can be taken as 'Negative'[150] and the first as 'Positive'.

'Neutral' accounts for a large proportion of responses: $^{45}/106$. Replies were such as "It doesn't bother me", "I don't mind one way or the other" etc.   Distribution of the more definite feeling by class and sex was as follows:

	I	II	III	IV	V
Pos %	(33)	23	25	31	47
Neg %	(33)	54	39	17	6

	M	W
Pos %	36	26
Neg %	21	30

Figures for the age-groups show no regularity, but it is noteworthy that the 30-plus group showed the highest proportion of 'negative' responses, which outbalanced the 'positive' in this group.   A somewhat higher proportion of Bradford informants were 'negative' than in the other two towns.

In the first table we see that (if we ignore the small group of Class I speakers whose numbers are too small for percentages to be reliable) Yorkshire speech seems less 'popular' the higher one looks on the social scale.   In the second, women are seen to be more negative than men, and to be negative rather than positive overall.

It seems reasonable to conclude that the responses to this question are broadly in line with the performance data examined in Chapter 6:   those groups using fewer non-standard variants (women, 30-plus, and 'higher' classes) show more 'negative' feelings about West Yorkshire speech.

---

149   Apart from saying whether they liked or disliked West Yorkshire speech, about a dozen informants said that it was not as broad now as it had been - and about half of these distinguished between 'true' Yorkshire dialect and the 'sloppy speech' of today.   One woman bemoaned the fact that "Yorkshire speech is going out", and said "But it's plainer!   Some of these refined TV speakers...I can't tell what they say!"

150   I included with the 'Negative' reactions a few who said they were sometimes embarrassed when they heard broad speech, whether from public figures or from their own family.

The next two questions attempted to get informants to be specific about non-standard features common in the area.

*Is there anything in particular you don't like about West Yorkshire
speech?*

We shall examine the features picked on a little later (after
the next question).   Here we shall just consider how many informants were able to focus on particular points.

The first of the following tables compares the percentage in
each social class who gave a negative response to the preceding
question with those who mentioned some specific dislike (we should
note, however, that it must not be assumed that the same informants
were involved: several who liked West Yorkshire speech in general
nevertheless said that certain things irritated them: for instance
the increasing use of [2] which they regarded as 'sloppy' rather
than as 'real Yorkshire').   The second table divides the latter by
sex:

	I	II	III	IV	V
Neg. to Q 2	(33)	54	39	17	6
Spec.dislikes	(33)	46	46	23	0

	I	II	III	IV	V
M	(33)	43	27	14	0
W	–	50	59	50	0

Among the age-groups, the 30-plus had easily the highest proportion
(46%) mentioning specific dislikes, with the other middle-aged groups
(40-plus and 50-plus) coming next.   Among the towns, a higher proportion of Bradford informants mentioned specific dislikes.

It is perhaps not surprising that those low on the social scale
should be less able to pick on particular points, since education
and intelligence are probably important factors in this.   The facts
that women in general and certain age-groups in particular were more
specific about their dislikes is in line with our findings in respect of their performance.

The conclusions seem to be that for the most part the response
to this question fits in with our general picture up to this point;
but especially among women there are quite a number who object to
particular features of the speech of this area while not disliking
it in general.

The next question tried to elicit the same sort of information
in another way.

Have you ever corrected your child (or, for those who were not
parents, 'Do you remember, as a child, being corrected by your parents or teacher') *saying "Now, then - you don't say that; talk
properly"? What sort of things were you/they getting at?*[151]

18 of the 105 could not say one way or the other; the percentages who answered 'Yes' in each class and sex group were as follows:

	I	II	III	IV	V
M	(33)	50	50	71	33
W	-	100	69	53	50
Total	(33)	75	62	61	38

No pattern emerged among the age-groups.   Among the towns, Halifax
informants claimed to do the most correcting, Huddersfield the least.

With one irregularity, the above table appears to show a
greater concern with 'correctness' higher on the social scale; but
this is largely confined to women, men showing less clear differentiation and a generally lower proportion of correcters.   These
findings are not out of line with our general conclusions up to
this point.

What sort of features were mentioned in connection with these
last two questions - which aspects of the speech of this area pro-
voke overt dislike or criticism?

A number of features were referred to as 'lazy' or 'sloppy'
speech, most of them matters of phonology.   'Missing out words'
generally referred to the use of glottal stop for the definite
article, as volunteered examples made clear: this feature was mentioned by 7 informants.   Related to this in some informants' minds
was 'cutting words' (for example [2ə] for *to*, [kɒs] *because*, [wɒnə]
want to - each mentioned by one informant); this label, or
'missing letters out' also referred to the use of glottal stop for

_____

151 One woman said that her mother used to 'threaten her with
elocution' if she 'talked broad'!   Several other informants talked
about elocution lessons, which seem to be regarded in this area
mainly as a means of 'correcting' Yorkshire speech.

/t/ (14 informants)[152], [-ɪn] for *-ing* (2), h-dropping (12); 6 informants could give no specific examples. One woman (a schoolteacher who said she felt she ought to improve her English and get
rid of her Yorkshire accent 'for the sake of the children') referred hypercorrectly to 'missing *r*' Sometimes included under the
above labels but sometimes just illustrated was substitution of /r/
for pre-postclitic /t/, as in [ʃʊrʊp], [gerɒf] etc. (4 informants).
The secondary contractions [am2 wɪ], [ɪn2 ɪ2], and [ɪnɪ2] were each
mentioned once.

Several other phonological non-standardisms were referred to:
/ə/ for final unstressed *-ow* in [jelə] etc; /ə/ instead of /e/
before /r/ in words such as *very*, *terrible* etc; the diphthongis-
ation of /i:/ to [i:ə] and /u:/ to [u:ə] before /l/ in *field*,
school etc; and regional forms of individual words: [ʊz] *us* , [jə]
you, [grab ɒd] *get hold*, [watə] *water*. Apart from this last,
picked on by 3, the other points were mentioned by one informant
each.   Two informants said they disliked local speech because it
was 'flat'.

A few grammatical points were each mentioned by one informant:
'double negatives', *you was*, *us* as possessive. The tags *you know*
and ...*like* were referred to by three and two respectively.

Non-standard vocabulary was picked on by several: [sʊmət], [ɔʊt],
[nɔʊt] by six; [wɒt fɒ] *why* (1); *Yeah* (2); [fɪʃɔɪl] *fish shop* (1);
one simply said 'slang words'.

The next few questions concentrated on the informant's feelings
about his own speech.

*What do you think about the way you speak yourself - have you always
been quite happy about it?*

A number of replies to this question were somewhat guarded;
it could be that even at this stage in the interview some informants were still suspicious about my motives, and half expected me
to try to sell them elocution lessons.   It is possible that some
people professed themselves content with their speech for this
reason.

Quite a few informants answered in general terms as well as
saying they were or were not happy about their manner of speaking,

---

152 One ot two informants each from Halifax and Huddersfield said
the glottal stop was not really typical of their town, or at least
was only to be heard among the young (see p.155).

and some of the comments are interesting.   For example, a considerable number said they did not think they had   much of an accent -
and several of these would be judged to be among the broadest!
Others said, more realistically, that most people regard their own
way of speaking as normal, and think it is other people who have an
accent; and two demanded "Who is to say which is the correct form
of English - Queen's or any other?"   Two young men volunteered the
opinion that whatever the efforts of one's family, one's speech is
most likely to be influenced by one's peer-group: schoolfellows,
friends, work-mates etc.   One middle-aged man made the perceptive
remark that one does not worry about one's speech in the teens -
it is somewhat later in life that one becomes aware of differences
(see p.212).   Two people said: "You don't want to talk la-di-da",
and one of them went on to tell of an acquaintance who did so and
who consequently 'had no mates'.   Several had had the common experience of hearing their voices on a tape-recorder and disliking
them; one woman added as an afterthought, "But I must like it, I
suppose, or I'd try to change it".

More specific responses to the last part of the question can be
classified as Yes/No? ("Well...not really, you know..."etc) No/
Neutral, this last category including 18.   Grouping 'No?' and 'No'
together, the following tables show percentages with positive/
negative feelings about their speech, by class; sex and class;
age-group.

	I	II	III	IV	V
Yes	(100)	31	39	44	63
No		54	47	37	16

		II	III	IV	V
Yes	M	29	45	50	77
	W	33	35	38	33
No	M	57	46	23	0
	W	50	47	52	50

	10	20	30	40	50	60	70	80
Yes	57	55	31	33	33	43	63	(67)
No	29	18	61	67	50	43	12	(33)

The first table shows that (apart from Class I, the figure for
which, if reliable, indicates that they are quite self-confident
about their speech, as one might expect with a group of ex-public
schoolboys) there is an increasing amount of 'linguistic insecurity'
the higher one looks on the social scale.

The second table indicates that this is mainly the pattern for
men; women show pretty well the same feelings about their speech
whatever their class, and in all classes more women are unhappy

than happy about it; (with men, this is only clearly the case in
Class II, and in Classes IV - V men are predominantly content with
the way they speak).   The final table shows that it is in middle
age that one is most sensitive about one's speech.

We may conclude that informants' answers to this direct question seem to fit in well with their actual performance as measured on
the variables examined in Chapter 6: towards the top of the social
scale, among women more than men, and particularly in middle age,
there is a greater tendency to strive towards 'standard' forms.

Have you ever tried to change the way you speak?

It was in many cases necessary to make clear that I was referring here to *deliberate* attempts to change one's speech *perman-
ently:* a considerable number of informants said that they often
found themselves speaking either more broadly when angry, or more
carefully when answering the telephone or in certain company.   In
other words they were aware of the different 'styles' or levels of
formality that virtually anybody employs and which I treated in
Chapter 6 as one dimension of variation[153].   Quite a few also spoke
of the way they adapted to other people's regional accents: when
working in Scotland or with a bunch of Scotsmen, they had picked up
something of a Scots accent, for example.

Only 18 informants said they had tried to change their way of
speaking - and several of these were not very definite: "Well...
Yes...I suppose I must have, really..."   A number of them said
they had changed because they were outside Yorkshire for longish
periods; of these, one elderly man said "I shouldn't be speaking
like this as a Yorkshireman - it isn't natural".   On the other
hand a younger women who said she found herself "slipping back more
and more into Yorkshire" since returning to the area, had tried to
'correct' this because "You never know when you might need to speak
correct".   With only 18 involved it is not to be expected that clear
relations with other factors will show up, but more women than men
were among this number, and it contained no-one from Class V.

---

153 Two women who had worked as telephonists mentioned having had
to be particularly careful at that time.   Two of the most interesting replies were from an ex-mayor of Halifax, a broad-spoken boss
who said he would vary in style for three main situations: a council
debate, public speaking, and in private; and an old man who could
be described as a 'dialect speaker' (Mr. F, p.222) who said that when
speaking in church services he would use 'English, not Yorkshire'!

Other points about the 18 who claimed to have changed their speech are worth mentioning. 6 of them (two in Class III, and four in Class IV) would probably strike a hearer as speaking 'better' than he would have expected from the average member of their social group; this was a much higher proportion of 'incongruent' speech than in the sample as a whole. 3 of them were 'upwardly mobile': in other words, their present social status was different from what it would have been in childhood (when it would be that of their fathers) or earlier in adult life[154]. Several of them could be described as 'speech conscious', in that they made quite perceptive remarks about speech. Two of these had long been involved in public speaking or performance: one man in his 60s was a well-known socialist and atheist in Bradford, and a woman in her 70s had been for many years a member of the great Huddersfield Choral Society, and had also done recitations and elocution.

In conclusion we may say that the small number who have tried to change might be taken to indicate that definitely negative feelings about Yorkshire speech cannot be very widespread; and that certain 'types' are well represented among this small number.

Has anybody ever made fun of the way you speak?

My own experience suggests that it is not uncommon for good-natured fun to be poked at Yorkshire speech; I was therefore a little surprised that only 30 informants admitted that they had been mocked for the way they spoke. The low figure could indicate that people are not sufficiently sensitive to remember such incidents - or that they are too sensitive to admit it (some replies were of the type "They'd better not"); on the other hand the 'most RP' speaker said it would never occur to him to make fun of a Yorkshire accent.

The 30 who said they had been laughed at were fairly equally divided between the sexes; there were too few to show a clear pattern among the classes, but the highest figure was in Class II (54%); this was the highest group to retain a fair number of regionalisms, and also perhaps the one most likely to have wider social contacts and a greater sensitivity about their accent.

Most of those who had had this experience could not say that anything specific had caused the amusement, but one man was still mystified after 30 years about why his army comrades should have thought his pronunciation of *cocoa* [ko:ko:] was unusual, let alone hilarious.

---

154 It is worth noting also that a building society clerk said that he now tended to speak better than he used to when in a manual job.

Has anybody ever said to you "I know where you come from" when they heard you speak?   .....Were they right?

This is obviously a common experience for Yorkshiremen, since the immediate reply to the question was "Oh, Yes!".   88 of my informants said this had happened to them at some time.

Only 18 of my sample said they had not had this experience, and 5 of these were not sure about it.   The number is too few to be related regularly to social characteristics, but not unexpectedly, 2 of the 3 Class I speakers (both RP) had not had this happen.   Of the remainder, 4 were teenagers who may well have this experience within a few years, and 7 were over 60:   it may not have happened to them because they had not been geographically mobile, or perhaps they had just forgotten.

In response to the supplementary question, most people said they had been identified simply as coming from 'Yorkshire';   only a few said they had been placed much more precisely.   Some said that one is often assigned just to 'the North' - and sometimes even to Lancashire!

The obvious conclusion is that most Yorkshiremen are not ashamed to admit that their speech 'gives them away' - but nowadays they may only be identifiable as coming from a region rather than from a particular town.

To those who replied 'Yes' to the preceding question, I then asked:

Now what do you think gave them the clue? (To all:)   *What sort of things do you think give a Yorkshire person away?*

Several informants were quite unable to say what might have given them away, and were clearly baffled about it;   some others answered in terms so wide as to be useless (for example, two said simply 'the pronunciation' and could go no further, and another just "we talk broader");   but a good proportion were able to suggest some particular feature.

Nearly 30 thought that an important clue lay in features of intonation or 'tone of voice' (it is not always easy to decide which of these labels is more appropriate to a particular response).   'Intonation' is probably indicated by the following: 'pitch' (1), 'low pitch' (1), 'flat' (3), 'monotonous' (1), 'boring' (1), and 'intonation' (1);   'tone' (3) could be taken in either sense;   so could 'delicate inflectional differences' (1), 'heavy' (1), and

'broken' (1);   more probably referring to tone of voice are 'hard'
(2), 'coarse' (2), 'loud' (1)[155], 'sharp' (1), 'curt' (1), and perhaps 'down to earth' (1), 'blunt' (1), 'slow' (6).

A considerable number referred to Yorkshire vowel qualities.
There were general responses such as 'vowels' (1), 'broad vowels'
(4). 'deep vowels' (1), 'exaggerated vowels' (1), 'full vowels' (1),
'wide vowels' (1), 'flat vowels' (1), and, rather different, 'chopp-
ing vowels' (1), and 'economising on vowels' (1).   More interesting are remarks referring to particular vowels: first, the two well-
known Northern diagnostic features: /ʊ/ corresponding to Southern
/ʌ/ (13 responses of various sorts[156]), and /æ/ corresponding to
Southern /ɑ:/ in certain words (9, plus 2 who said 'short A'/'broad
A' and seemed to be referring to the same phenomenon: this feature
drew a certain amount of unfavourable comment and was often regarded
as 'talking posh' or 'la-di-da'); more perceptive were two remarks
about the local realisations of /æ/ and /ɑ:/: "flat A in *cat* (the
South is more like [ɛ]", referring obviously to local [a] compared
to RP [æ]; and "flattened A in *cart* [ka:t]", perhaps referring to
local [a:] for RP [ɑ:]: the monophthong corresponding to RP [eɪ]
was mentioned by one informant, and [o:] corresponding to [əʊ] by 3;
the diphthong [ɔə] where many have [ɔ:], [u:k] for RP [ʊk] in (ook)
words, and [u:əl] for [u:l] in words like *school* were each mentioned
once.

A smaller number of informants referred to consonantal features:
3 mentioned h-dropping; 2 illustrated the glottal stop, and 2 more
talked of 'missing out of /t/'; one mentioned [ɪn] for [ɪŋ], and
[an] for [and]; one said simply 'missing letters' and 11 spoke of
'shortening words' - some of these doubtless meant the specific
points mentioned here, but one illustrated by [wɪ] for [wɪð].

What might be termed 'fluency features' were 'missing words' (1)
and more specific references to the reduction of the definite article (3); 3 spoke of 'running words together', and one of 'slurr-
ing'.

There were (perhaps realistically) few references to particular
words or expressions: 4 informants mentioned *thee*/*thou* forms;

---

155 This informant held the theory (which I had heard before and
which may not be as fanciful as it sounds at first) that people in
the area speak loudly because of the difficulty of being heard over
the noise of textile machinery.

156 The Cockney wife of one informant intervened to tell of the
confusion caused when she first asked a grocer in Halifax for [batə],
which was intended as *butter* but understood as *batter*. She was
told that Yorkshire people made their own.

2 spoke of [sʊmət/ɔʊt/nɔʊt]; 3 of the use of *Aye* for *Yes*, and one
of *Nay*; and one each mentioned *Ee*, [jə] *you*, [mɪ] *my* (these latter
two are not particularly typical of Yorkshire, of course), [wɪə]
where, [θə2tɪ, fɒ2tɪ] *30*, *40*, and the local pronunciation [bra2fəd].

Obviously most of the features I had decided to investigate
within the 'variable' framework - as well as many others I recognised as potentially diagnostic but felt I either could not handle
at all (for example, 'tone of voice': see p.241) or should not
attempt to deal with as variables but simply note (as in the last
part of Chapter 6) - were identified by informants in response
either to this question or to the third or fourth questions of this
section. This was valuable confirmation of my preliminary choice,
and guidance in adding to this.

The next question aimed to uncover any sensitivity Yorkshire
people might feel about their regional speech:

Do you think that people down South like the way we talk here?

Only 6 informants replied 'Yes' (and even this number included
one who was doubtful and one who appended the remark 'for a laugh');
7 thought Southerners felt fairly neutral about the matter, and
one thought they found it amusing; 28 were 'don't knows' of various
descriptions (ranging from "I really don't know" to the more bell-
igerent [a do:2 gɪv ə bʊgə]).

The remaining 64 informants, almost two-thirds of the sample,
believed that Southerners do not like the way Yorkshire people speak,
and quite a number of these said they probably dislike it heartily.
The percentage replying 'No' in each social class was:

I	II	III	IV	V
(67)	85	75	49	47

A somewhat higher overall proportion of women than men replied 'No'.

Leaving aside the small Class I, it appears that the feeling
that Southerners dislike Yorkshire speech becomes stronger towards
the upper end of the social scale. It is interesting to note the
feeling (which I have often come across, and which was voiced by 5
of these informants) that people in the South 'talk correct' or 'are
elocuted'[157].

---

157 One Class V informant added that a Southerner would say [ʃagə]
for *sugar*.

From these responses we may conclude that many Yorkshiremen
feel that their speech is not viewed favourably by outsiders, and
that this sensitivity is stronger among those groups who appear from
Chapter 6 to try to avoid non-standard forms and to use more neutral
ones.

The final question in this section of the interview was asked
because some people claim that there still are differences between
the speech of the various towns of this area (one informant, in general conversation, said he could hear differences even between parts
of Bradford).   I hoped to discover how widespread this feeling was,
and whether people could back it with specific points.

*Do you think that people here in Bfd/Hfx/Hudd speak any differently
from the way they do in (the other two)? (If 'Yes', In what sort of ways?)*

The replies in the different towns to the first part of the
question were as follows:

	Yes	No	dk	Yes%
Bfd	31	7	8	67
Hfx	17	9	2	61
Hudd	17	13	2	53
Total	65	29	12	61

There were no real differences between sex, class, or age-groups in
respect of these opinions.   There is some evidence that Halifax and
Huddersfield speakers think they are more similar to each other than
they are to Bradford (thus agreeing with some traditional dialectologists):   one Halifax informant said he thought Bradford was different but not Huddersfield, and four from Huddersfield said Bradford
was different but not Halifax (all these have been included under
'Yes').

Though the above table indicates that a majority think there
are differences in speech between these major wool towns, relatively few informants could say in what respects they differ[158].   The
following were the only suggestions offered.

In Bradford it was alleged that:

---

158 Two different male informants told me of going to Rugby League
matches and thinking of the opposing supporters "Well, we're all
Yorkshire...but they sound different, somehow..."

a) in Halifax, the definite article takes the form [θ]; *tongue*
    is pronounced [tɒŋ]; *school* is [sku:əl]; and speech is gen-
    erally 'broader' and 'nearer Lancashire'.

b) in Huddersfield, *love* is pronounced [lʊv]; and speech gener-
    ally is 'less clipped' or 'broader' or 'very coarse'.

c) both Halifax and Huddersfield use [θ] as definite article; they
    differ in 'tone' and 'vocabulary', and are 'broader'.

All these opinions, except the last (heard three times) were expressed only once.

In Halifax it was claimed that:

a) in Bradford, *-ation* is pronounced [ɛɪʃn] rather than [e:ʃn];
    dare not is turned to *daredn't*; and generally speech differs
    in 'vowels' and 'intonation'.

b) in Huddersfield, speech is either 'broader', or 'nicer', or
    'politer'!

c) both Bradford and Huddersfield say [tɒŋ] for *tongue*; they use
    more intervocalic glottal stops; their speech is 'broader and
    worse'; and they have 'some different words'.

This last opinion was voiced by two informants; all the others by
only one.

In Huddersfield it was said that:

a) Bradford people have more intervocalic [ʔ]; words like *very*,
    terrible have [ə] rather than [e]; and pronunciation is 'clipped'
    or 'rounder'!

b) in Halifax, *tongue* is [tɒŋ]; *cover* is [kʊvə] instead of [kɒvə].

c) both Bradford and Halifax have a different form of the definite
    article and use some different words.

Only the points about glottal stops and [tɒŋ] had as many as two
proponents.

    We may conclude that the feeling persists that differences
exist between the towns, but that most informants are hard put to
suggest in what ways. While some suggestions were quite perceptive,
many were vague, or based on traditional dialect features (for example, [θ] as Article), or just plain contradictory (the alleged
distribution of [tɒŋ], which regrettably had not been written into

the word list and reading passage; and the 'clipped' or 'rounder'
pronunciation). It may be noted that in the experiment described
in the last section of this chapter all the tape-recorded speakers
except one (a 'regionally-neutral' RP speaker) were from Bradford -
but no Halifax or Huddersfield informant remarked on this.

During this section of the interview, a subject which arose in
spontaneous comments by at least 15 informants was *the relation
between education and speech.*

Five said that 'broadness' had connotations of a lack of education; one man said, "I don't like to hear my younger son talk
broad - he's supposed to be educated". Several felt that education
got rid of many local features: one man (Class V) thought his sons
were broader than him at present, but that education would change
this; a schoolgirl (Class II), who seemed resentful about her
speech being corrected, said she supposed the teachers did it so
that their pupils would be able to get better jobs. A number
thought that education was levelling out regional differences (several others put this down to the influence of radio and TV). Two
informants who had attended secondary modern schools believed it
was at grammar schools that children learned to speak more correctly;
another, apparently thinking along the same lines, said to me, "I
can tell you're a Yorkshire lad. I'm surprised - I thought you
might have had elocution to get rid of it".

My own experience, however, is more reflected in what was said
by an informant still at public school: that schools (and this is
almost certainly more true of state schools) do not deliberately
eradicate regional speech (except such features as are considered to
be 'incorrect' - for example, the use of *us* for *our*, double negatives etc.); it is simply modified spontaneously if contacts are
made with those not so broad. I am sure that the experience of
one woman whose daughter had been to a 'semi-grammar' school ("they
talked lovely there") is not a usual one: "They had a mistress
there who told the PTA that none of them could speak properly; she
used to say [pɑːs ðə batə; pɑːs ðə dʒɑːm]" (sic!)[159] .

As a general conclusion from this section, we may observe that
the overtly expressed opinions of a group often show an interesting

---

159 Though there is some predictability about the distribution of
'long A' (see p.165), unlike that of /ʌ/, it does cause some difficulties even for some of the better educated: a man of Class II said he
tried to 'speak well' but did not "go in for saying things like
[mɑːθs]"!

relation to their speech performance as described in Chapter 6. For example, those groups which show greater sensitivity or more negative feelings about regional speech also tend to use fewer non-standard variants. Also, specific points mentioned by informants offered some confirmation of my choice of features worth examining in detail; and some interesting possibilities for further investigation are suggested: for example, the 'ambivalence' that appears to exist about regional speech.

2   SELF-EVALUATION

In this section of the interview I adopted an experiment previously used by Labov (1966a:455sq) and Trudgill(1972:184sq). Informants are shown a number of words in their normal spelling; each word is then pronounced in two or more possible ways, and informants are asked to indicate which of these pronunciations they normally use. The aim of such an experiment is to see what standard the informant sees himself as aiming at - and also to see whether this corresponds to what he actually does say. Labov and Trudgill found numerous cases of 'inaccurate responses': in other words, the form the informant says he uses is *not* the one he usually employs, during the interview at least[160]. The term *over-reporting* has been used to describe a situation where an informant claims to use a form which other evidence suggests is the more prestigious one, and where the informant does not in fact appear to use this form. This phenomenon has been interpreted as revealing some sort of *linguistic insecurity* - a (probably subconscious) feeling that one's own usage is not correct. Conversely, Trudgill claimed to have found evidence of *under-reporting*: in these cases informants claimed to use non-standard forms, whereas their actual usage appeared to be closer to the standard. Trudgill used this evidence to argue that non-standard speech may enjoy among certain sections of the population a 'covert prestige' - a connotation of masculinity and toughness, for example.

Both Labov and Trudgill asked informants to respond to the

---

160 Quite a number of informants made remarks such as "It's rather unfortunate...I've said some of these before and...it might come out different on the tape"; "I've probably contradicted myself..."; "Of course, I'm saying what I use on my best behaviour..."; "These are what I try and say...it might be different as I'm talking to you"; "There's one or two that you might say different if you weren't thinking about it..."; and one husband present said to his wife, "I think you were cheating on some of them".

alternative pronunciations by marking on paper the number corresponding to the pronunciation they thought they used: for instance,
if a word was read in three ways, they had to circle the number '2'
if they used the second pronunciation. A little later informants
were asked to do something similar: they heard two possible pronunciations of a number of words, and had to tick the one they normally
used *and* circle the one they considered correct. If these did not
correspond, this was taken to indicate a conscious feeling of linguistic insecurity.

My own experiment differed in a number of small ways from those
of Labov and Trudgill. First, I tried to combine their two separate tests for self-evaluation and linguistic insecurity. I had
just one set of words, and asked informants to identify which of the
pronunciations they used and also to say whether they considered
another to be more correct. In fact I found very few informants
who said they thought another variant was better, unless I specifically prompted them, usually because they giggled on identifying
their own version). Whether this would have been more common if I
had followed Labov's method more closely, and especially if I had
asked informants to respond in writing, is impossible to say[161].

A second difference in the form of the experiment was that I
did not ask informants to write their responses, though I did show
a card with the word in question written on it, so that there was
no doubt about the item referred to. I simply asked informants to
identify pronunciations by saying 'the first', 'the second', and
so on[162]. I suggested above that the results might have been rather
different if informants had had to mark a card twice; on the other
hand, I believe that a number, particularly the older ones, would

---

161 There were odd pieces of evidence of a general insecurity from
just one or two informants (e.g. one young man remarked that this
section had made him realise how badly he spoke; and a woman in her
30s who was insecure socially (bitterly resenting her drop in living-
standards since divorce) insisted that her pronunciation was not
correct, even though in many cases she did not use a non-standard
form; etc.) - but just as many examples of informants demanding
"But who's to say which is correct?", or clearly regarding 'the way
we say it' as correct.

162 Quite a few informants, who did identify pronunciations thus,
employed the regional form of the definite article e.g.[ʔfəːst ∼ ʔfəst]
[ʔsekənd], [ʔlast]. Though I counted these when deciding whether an
informant used any non-standard variants of (the), I did not do so
when counting how many he used, since these were outside normal contexts and could have led to an artificially high score.

have found this more difficult and tiring.   There might well have
been some who would have given up or marked the card randomly. so
the results could have been more misleading.

A number of problems arose, in the administering and interpreting of the experiment.   First, though I asked informants to refer
to a pronunciation as say 'the first' rather than repeat it, quite
a number did respond by repeating.   In some cases, the reason for
this may have been that they were unsure, and so left me to decide
from an example;   often I then checked, by saying 'the second?' etc.,
to see whether they then accepted this.   But this was probably not
the usual reason, since this would mean that quite a large proportion were incapable of properly distinguishing the various pronunciations;   in most cases it is more likely that they simply found
this easier than identifying by number, for it was obvious from their
reactions that they could differentiate.   In a few cases the explanation seemed to be that I had not imitated the non-standard pronunciation quite accurately!

I do not think that an informant's repeating rather than identifying by number need invalidate his response: after all, he had
just been exposed to various pronunciations and if he had wanted
to 'conceal' his normal pronunciation and claim another he could
still have done so.   Moreover, one or two older informants seemed
to make mistakes when identifying by number, as could be seen in
some cases where they repeated as well as giving a number.

The second problem concerned those items (a minority) where I
offered three possible pronunciations.   In these cases I got a
number of 'unexpected' responses.   I think it probable that some
informants found difficulties in giving the right label where there
was more than binary choice, and the result was that they said for
example 'Number 1' when what they meant was 'Not that last one,
certainly';   the fact that some repeated a form and then gave its
wrong label probably supports this.   It is therefore probably best
in such experiments to present not more than two alternatives, or
somehow to use a succession of binary choices.   (Labov offered *four*
possibilities with some items, and one must wonder whether this led
to some inaccuracies.)

A third problem concerns deciding what qualifies as 'inaccurate
responses'.   Labov, when dealing with (r), decided that if a subject
claimed to be an r-user but actually in formal style pronounced /r/
in less than 30% of the environments where it might occur, then he
was over-reporting.   Trudgill differed on two points: he used casual rather than formal style, since he considered this more closely
approximated to everyday speech;   and he decided that the 30%

dividing line was too lenient and that 50% was more reasonable.   I
decided to take the total of casual and formal speech as my usual
basis of comparison, partly because of the difficulties discussed
earlier of distinguishing these consistently, and partly because they
both represent normal conversation.   A speaker will vary within
this style-range in his everyday speech, depending on the subject-
matter, the addressee, etc;   it is therefore reasonable to give informants the benefit of the doubt in this way.   (In fact only a
small minority would have been differently rated had I relied solely
on the casual speech scores rather than the total of conversational
speech.)   As regards the admittedly arbitrary point at which one
decides whether a person is over-reporting, I think that a different
line may be appropriate with different features: for many, 50% is
reasonable, but for others I decided to draw the line higher or
lower than this.

    The features examined in this experiment were mainly a subset
of those investigated in the first section of Chapter 6.   They were
items concerning inventory, (h) and (Λ);   inventory and realisation,
(εI/e:), ($\mathcrm{u}$/o:),(uə);   realisation, (α:) and (t);   distribution,
(nch) and (-ow);   and incidence (α:/æ), (ing), and (ook).   In all
these a considerable proportion of the population use a non-standard
variant.   I also offered a few items where the majority in fact use
an RP-like form, and the other alternative was a 'dialect' pronunciation or a 'fashionable' or 'advanced RP' one: I hoped to gain
some evidence of the attitudes of the population to 'broad Yorkshire'
and to see how far they are influenced by more recent prestige forms.
My findings will be presented in terms of, first, the pronunciations
informants said they used;   second, the apparent accuracy or otherwise of these responses;   and finally any comments about 'correctness'.

The Variable (h)

    We saw in Chapter 6 that variation in (h) relates to class,
style, and sex in such a way as to suggest that h-dropping, though
common, is stigmatised and regarded as substandard or incorrect.
We shall now see whether the self-evaluation of informants tends to
support this conclusion.

    The two words *hand* and *hot* were each read to informants with
and without initial [h].   (They were not read successively: where-
ever two items involved the same variable they were presented several items apart.)

    The responses were as follows.   The percentages of [h] forms which members of class and sex groups said they used were:

	I	II	III	IV	V
M	(100)	86	82	77	58
W	-	92	94	88	75
Total	(100)	88	89	83	63

No clear pattern emerged with age, though it may be noted that the 30-plus group had the highest percentage who said they pronounced [h]. (Age and town will hereafter in this section only be referred to if some interesting pattern showed up. Figures for Class I and the 80-plus age-group are given in brackets, to indicate that these groups were very small, and therefore the figures may not be reliable).

As regards the accuracy of these self-evaluations, we noted above (p.109) that individual performance scores ranged from 0 - 100%; let us adopt 50% as a dividing line: if a person, in conversational speech, uses less than 50% of [h] in contexts where RP would expect it, he will be regarded as over-reporting if he says he pronounces [h] in *hand* and *hot*. (With about a dozen informants who claimed [h] in only one of these, we shall regard them as over-reporting if their actual score was less than 25%. A similar policy is adopted with any variable where two items were presented for self-evaluation.)

Percentages of informants who over-reported [h] were:

I	II	III	IV	V
(1)	8	44	72	68

It may be noted that the apparently impossible figure of 68 under Class V here (where the earlier table had only 63) is due to the fact that the two tables do not measure in exactly the same terms: The first refers to the percentage of [h] forms reported, the second to whether the individual informants were generally inaccurate. Thus, with two informants and two relevant items, if A said he used [h] in both and B only in one, this would amount to a 75% reporting of [h], while if neither actually used substantial amounts of [h] a figure of 100% over-reporting would result. (This complication only arises where more than one example of a given variable was included.) No clear differences showed up between the sexes or the age-groups, though we may note that the 30-plus group showed the least over-reporting.

Since only a small proportion of informants 'admitted' to
h-dropping, it is not surprising that there was little evidence of
them saying they used one form but regarded the other as more
correct - betraying the 'manifest insecurity' spoken of by Labov.

As regards self-evaluations, the proportions of informants who
say they pronounce [h] relates to social class and sex in the way
one might expect from their actual performance; but the 'exaggerations' increase as we move down the social scale: in the working
classes a high proportion say they use [h] whereas they did not do
so in the majority of instances.   Probably, as Labov put it (1966a:
455), there was 'no conscious deceit involved': informants were
simply reporting what they felt they were saying or would like to
say - they 'perceived their own speech in terms of the norms at which
they were aiming rather than the sound actually produced'.

My conclusion is that for the great majority of the population
the RP-like form is now seen as the standard of correctness to be
aimed at, even by those who use regional forms to a large extent;
these findings therefore support those in Chapter 6.

The Variable (ʌ)

In Chapter 6 we saw that, granted the difficulty over when it is
appropriate to say that an individual does or does not 'have' a
certain phoneme, the existence of /ʌ/ - /ʊ/ as opposed to simply /ʊ/
varies with class, style and sex in such a way as to suggest that
the two-vowel situation is seen as 'better', but that there is a
difference from the situation with (h), in that instead of an 'even
spread' of group scores it is only at the top end of the social scale
that [ʌ] is fairly commonly used.

In the self-evaluation test the words *cut* and *come* were the
items primarily intended to investigate the /ʌ/ - /ʊ/ situation (but
see also the note below about *butcher* and *government*);   each was
read with [ʌ] and [ʊ].

Findings were as follows.   The percentages of [ʌ] reported by
each sex and class group were:

	I	II	III	IV	V
M	(100)	0	27	17	12
W	-	75	37	35	8
Total	(100)	35	31	26	11

The accuracy of self-evaluation was assessed as with (h): a
50% dividing line (25% in exceptional cases) was applied to the
total of each informant's conversational speech.   Table i) below
shows over-reporting as so assessed, while table ii) shows under-
reporting (i.e. the informant says he uses [ʊ] but in fact uses
more than 50% (25% exceptionally) of [ʌ]):

i)

	I	II	III	IV	V
M	(0)	0	18	23	15
W	-	17	29	38	17
Total	(0)	8	25	30	16

ii)

	I	II	III	IV	V
M	(.0)	57	0	5	0
W	-	0	24	10	0
Total	(0)	31	14	7	0

Comments by informants that they used one form but regarded the
other as more correct were all in terms of saying they used [ʊ] but
regarded RP-like [ʌ] as better: they were:

	I	II	III	IV	V
M	(0)	57	36	9	15
W	-	0	24	15	25
Total	(0)	31	29	12	18

With regard to percentages of reports of [ʌ], with one exception
the picture is not unexpected in the light of the findings earlier:
only in Class I and with Class II women do a majority say they have
[ʌ]; women make considerably higher reports overall than men; and
the classes in general are in the 'expected' order.   The exceptional
case is that of men in Class II, none of whom say they use [ʌ].

When we turn to inaccurate reporting, we have a very different
picture from that seen above with (h) in that, first, no clear trends
show up (except, perhaps, that women in each class over-reported more
than men), and second, we have in addition to the phenomenon of over-
reporting also that of under-reporting.   Labov appears not to have
found this a serious problem, but Trudgill did come upon the phenomenon in Norwich, and in (1972) offered a theory to explain it: he
held that whereas the standard language enjoys considerable prestige,
especially among women, there is a 'covert prestige' attached to
working-class regional speech; this has desirable connotations of
masculinity and toughness (see also Labov, 1966a:495), and male
speakers therefore tend to claim to use features typical of such
speech to a greater extent than they actually do.   By this reasoning one would presumably account for the above figures for under-

reporting of [ʌ] by saying that at the bottom of the social scale
it does not occur because there is very little use of [ʌ] anyway,
but that in Class II there is a fair amount since there is more use
of [ʌ] but a subconscious feeling that [ʊ], though less 'correct',
is more rugged, tough, friendly, or whatever.

But I believe such an argument would be difficult to uphold
here, for two reasons. First, though the total class figures show
progressively more under-reporting from Class V to Class II, when
broken down by sex it appears that only in Class II do men do a
significant amount of under-reporting, whereas with women under-
reporting occurs in Classes III and IV which are the ones which also
show the greatest amount of *over*-reporting! Second, the third set
of figures, which are taken as revealing 'insecurity' about one's
usage, show that with men of Class II the figure is exactly the
same as that for under-reporting: surely it is hardly reasonable to
maintain that the one reflects insecurity and the other the covert
prestige of the non-standard form.

A quite different explanation seems more probable to me: that
under-reporting is simply another manifestation of linguistic insecurity.   Men in Class II are more aware of the ʌ/ʊ distinction than
in any of the lower classes - some indeed use /ʌ/ on most occasions -
but as the occurrence of /ʌ/ is so difficult to predict, and lapses
and hypercorrections with this feature are among the commonest ways
in which a Northerner gives himself away, they are not confident
in their use of it and so admit that it is quite likely that they
have /ʊ/ in the words in question (their reactions and comments
during other sections of the interview also gave this impression).
A similar explanation is possible in the case of women in Classes
III and IV: they are conscious of the distinction and sometimes try
to make it, but they are more diffident about their ability to do
so correctly and so more reluctant to claim to be able to than are
those in Class II.   (We may note that they also show a similar
amount of 'insecurity', as the last table shows.)

My conclusions are that since reports of using the RP-like form
are considerably lower than in respect of (h), probably a majority
do not regard the standard at which they are aiming as containing a
phoneme /ʌ/[163]; also, there is a good deal of uncertainty and

_____

163 The reaction of informants when I read the words in question
are interesting: several laughed, and quite a few commented that
[ʌ] pronunciations were 'Southern', 'posh', 'affected', or even
'incorrect' (some of these remarks were spontaneous; others I
elicited when the informants showed some reaction to the contrast).

insecurity about this feature among various groups in the population, which manifests itself in various ways.   These findings are not out of line with those reported in Chapter 6.

Appendix to (ʌ)

Though *cut* and *come* were the main items included and examined from the point of view of self-evaluation in respect of (ʌ), I also presented two more words relevant to this, with somewhat different aims in mind:

1) *butcher:* this is a word frequently subject to hypercorrection in respect of /ʌ/-/ʊ/ (see p.116), and I included it in order to have more evidence about the 'uncertainty.' over /ʌ/.

2) *government:* in the month preceding the survey I had noticed a number of BBC reporters pronouncing this word as [gɒvnmənt]; I included this pronunciation along with those with [ʌ] and [ʊ] in order to see whether this minority fad or fashion in an authoritative source might have produced any response, either in terms of informants saying they used this pronunciation or of their believing it to be correct.

With *butcher*, the contrast [bʊ2tʃə] - [bʌ2tʃə] was greeted by laughter from a number of informants - but this was not always be-, cause they realised it was a trick question.   The following tables show, first, the percentages claiming to use the hypercorrect [bʌ2tʃə], and second, those commenting that it was correct (since I had not kept a specific record of this word in conversation it cannot be considered in terms of over/under reporting):

	I	II	III	IV	V
M	(0)	0	18	9	0
W	-	33	15	21	0
Total	(0)	15	16	15	0

	I	II	III	IV	V
M	(0)	21	18	9	0
W	-	0	18	5	0
Total	(0)	12	18	5	0

The patterns are somewhat haphazard, but it does seem that there is more evidence here for our above conclusion about insecurity and uncertainty in respect of /ʌ/.

By contrast with such reactions, one elderly gentleman who in fact used a higher proportion of [ʌ] than the average for Class IV seemed not to hear the difference clearly.

With *government*, no informant said he used [gɒvnmənt] or believed it to be correct (the only comment, from a member of Class I,
being that this form was 'ultra-South' and 'going beyond good English), so there is no evidence that a short-lived minority fashion
had any effect on the great majority.   But the results with this
word are of interest from a methodological point of view: I read
the three pronunciations [gʌvnmənt], [gʊvnmənt] [gɒvnmənt] in that
order, and found that reports of using the [ʌ] form were markedly
higher in all groups within the population than with *cut* and *come*.
Since a few informants responded "[gʊvnmənt] - the first", I think
that many who simply said 'the first' really meant 'Not that last
one, at least': i.e. that this was an example of the difficulties
involved in offering more than a binary choice.

The Variable (-ow)

We concluded in Chapter 6 that this variable shows the relations to class, style and sex that suggest that [ə] is a stigmatised
pronunciation, and that the age-group scores give some indication
that it may be on the decrease before the more RP-like [əʊ ~ oʊ ~ oː].
In the self-evaluation experiment I offered [ə] and [əʊ] pronunciations of *window* and *fellow*.

It soon appeared that the acceptability of non-standard [ə] is
not equal in these two items, and that it has more definitely substandard connotations in *window* than in *fellow*.

Reports of using the [əʊ] variant were as follows: whereas 52
informants held that they pronounced both words with [əʊ] and 22
said they had [ə] in both, 20 said they used [wɪndəʊ] but [felə] and
3 said they used the latter in addition to [feləʊ] and [wɪndəʊ] -
while only 6 said they had [wɪndə] but [feləʊ][164]. The percentages
of informants reporting [wɪndəʊ] and [feləʊ] are shown in tables i)
and ii) respectively:

i)

	I	II	III	IV	V
M	(100)	100	73	52	46
W	-	83	88	81	67
Total	(100)	92	82	66	53

ii)

	I	II	III	IV	V
M	(83)	100	27	36	62
W	-	83	60	67	33
Total	(83)	92	47	51	53

---

164 The other three informants reported: both [ə] + [wɪndəʊ]; both
[ə] + [feləʊ]; both [ə] and both [əʊ].

With the age-groups, the figures for both words combined were:

10	20	30	40	50	60	70	80
59	52	65	63	79	71	70	(83)

The accuracy of these self-evaluations is not easy to assess.
In the first place, since detailed records had not been made, it was
not possible to treat the two words individually; I could only
employ the individual's overall score on (-ow). In the second, this
is not a frequently-occurring variable, and in over a third of the
interviews it did not occur at all in conversation; I decided therefore to use the reading passage performance also. In the third, it
is difficult to decide on reasonable 'pass-marks': I eventually
decided that with those informants producing any examples of (-ow) in
conversation I would adopt a 75% cut-off if the informant said he used
only [əʊ], and 50% if he admitted to [felə]; in the reading passage,
since this is a style where informants are more careful about their
speech, it is fair to set the mark higher - and so if he said he used
only [əʊ] but in fact produced one or more [ə], he counted as over-
reporting; while if he admitted to [felə] he counted as over-reporting if his (-ow) score was less than 80% - the 20% allowing for the
example of *fellow* in the reading passage to be pronounced [felə].
Finally, since there appeared to be some under-reporting I attempted
to measure this too; in conversation, over 25% [əʊ]-usage counted
as under-reporting if in his self-evaluation an informant said he
used [ə] in both words, and over 50% if he had admitted to [felə];
in the reading passage, any score over zero counted as under-reporting if an informant claimed to use only [ə] and over 80% if he said
he used [felə].

The following tables show over-reporting, as assessed by conversational and reading passage data respectively:

	I	II	III	IV	V
M	(0)	20	22	50	64
W	-	50	33	50	33
Total	(0)	29	27	50	53

	I	II	III	IV	V
M	(0)	43	0	27	46
W	-	0	24	48	33
Total	(0)	23	14	37	42

Figures for age-groups are rather irregular, but there are signs of
more over-reporting among the older groups.

These tables present corresponding figures for under-reporting:

	I	II	III	IV	V
M	(0)	0	44	8	9
W	-	0	17	0	33
Total	(0)	0	33	5	18

	I	II	III	IV	V
M	(0)	0	45	41	31
W	-	17	24	14	28
Total	(0)	8	32	28	30

With (-ow) more than with most variables informants who said
they used the non-standard variant stated that in fact they believed
the other ([əʊ]) to be more correct. The figures for the two items
were as follows:

window	I	II	III	IV	V
M	(0)	0	36	41	46
W	-	17	12	18	33
Total	(0)	8	21	30	42

fellow	I	II	III	IV	V
M	(0)	0	73	41	31
W	-	17	40	33	50
Total	(0)	8	53	37	37

The percentages of reports of [wɪndəʊ] relate fairly regularly
to social class, and appear to indicate that the majority see this
as the standard of correctness to be aimed at.   Women generally
show higher claims than men; the one irregularity, Class II, is
accounted for by a schoolgirl who had said she resented any attempts
to change her Yorkshire speech and claimed to use more non-standard
forms than in fact she did.   The figures in the last table above
are fairly regular (the 17% among Class II women is caused by the
girl just referred to), and also seem to point to [wɪndə].

With *fellow* the picture is by no means as clear: table ii)
shows that more women than men seem to regard [feləʊ] as correct
(the Class II women's score being accounted for by our schoolgirl),
but there is no clear class relation among the male informants. (The
Class I figure is produced by one informant who said he could use
both [feləʊ] and [felə].)   However, the last table ('insecurity')
shows a clearer class-relation with women, and also appears to indicate that all informants who admit to saying [felə] yet feel that
[feləʊ] is more correct (compare the figures with those of table ii:
those for Classes II and III total 100.).

The tables for over-reporting are also not 'tidy', but in general they show an increasing tendency to exaggerate one's use of
[əʊ] towards the lower end of the social scale, which again may be
taken to indicate a growing feeling among the working classes that
the traditional regional pronunciation is incorrect.   This may
also account for the scores for the age-groups in respect of claiming

to use [əʊ]: rather surprisingly, in view of our findings (see
p.143) that [ə] variants seem to be decreasing with the younger
groups, the self-evaluations show them in fact claiming fewer [əʊ]
variants; the only explanation that suggests itself is that the
older groups are becoming more conscious of the substandard status
of their usual variant (note also the fact that they show more signs
of over-reporting) while the younger, though using more [əʊ],
are less concerned about the prestige or stigma involved.

The figures for under-reporting are however a complicating
factor. They are somewhat 'erratic' - which could mean that the
methods adopted for assessing this phenomenon are inadequate; on
the other hand males of Class III seem particularly inclined to
exaggerate their use of non-standard [ə]. Some might wish to take
this as evidence of the covert prestige of working-class variants
as proposed by Trudgill, but if Labov's interpretation of data such
as are given in the last table as 'manifest insecurity' is correct,
it might seem to clash with this view. On the other hand, of
course, these figures could be taken as indicative not of insecurity
but of the attitude 'I know what they say it ought to be - but *I* do
so-and-so'.

In conclusion we have to admit that in respect of (-ow) this
experiment has not provided very clear evidence. Except for suggesting that [felə] is not regarded as substandard to the same extent
as [wɪndə], possibly because the former has at times been acceptable
in 'upper-class' speech, and giving a general indication that the
more RP-like variant is now regarded as their standard by most informants, many of the figures are unclear. This is particularly so in
the case of those relating to the accuracy or otherwise of self-
evaluations, and possibly my methods of assessing this are inadequate.

The Variable (-nch)

We concluded above (p.145) that the situation with this distribution variable is the closest to 'free variation' that was encountered. In the self-evaluation experiment the words *bench* and *inch*
were each offered with [ntʃ] and [nʃ] pronunciations; these items
were chosen because they do not involve any other variables, as
would say *branch* or *lunch*.

This variable was soon found to involve a problem that was
uncommon in this experiment: some informants could not distinguish
between the two pronunciations. This fact emerged in several different ways:

- the informant actually said "Those two are the same" or "I can't tell the difference"; in such cases it is quite definite that the informant is unable to distinguish the variants.

- the informant hesitated, requested a repetition, or responded in a tone of voice which suggested that he was just guessing; in these cases it seems likely that he could not really hear the difference.

- the informant reported saying [bentʃ] but [ɪnʃ]. This could indicate that he varies between [ntʃ] and [nʃ] (as I assumed to be the case with similar situations in respect of (h), (ʌ) etc., where there was no other evidence that the informant was incapable of distinguishing); but since I read the alternatives in the order [bentʃ/benʃ] but [ɪnʃ/ɪntʃ], it could be that he was following the policy 'if in doubt, say "the first" '. The fact that 19 claimed [bentʃ] but [ɪnʃ] and only 8 [benʃ] but [ɪntʃ] might seem to support this.

The percentages of informants in the first group just referred to, and in the first and second groups combined, were:

	I	II	III	IV	V
M	(0)	0	9	14	23
W	–	0	0	14	0
Total	(0)	0	4	14	16

	I	II	III	IV	V
M	(0)	0	36	27	38
W	–	33	24	19	33
Total	(0)	15	29	23	37

Of the ten informants in the first group, who openly admitted that they could not hear a difference, nine were referring to *inch* and one to *bench*; but I decided that their responses should be treated as unreliable and so ignored them both. Those in the other two groups were however given the benefit of the doubt and their responses are included in what follows.

The following table shows the percentage of reports of using [ntʃ], by class and sex:

	I	II	III	IV	V
M	(83)	14	50	18	20
W	–	25	44	19	42
Total	(83)	19	46	19	28

By age-group the distribution of reports was as follows:

10	20	30	40	50	60	70	80
54	40	33	18	30	12	23	(0)

As regards the accuracy of such self-evaluations, it is in this
case virtually impossible to base our comparisons on conversational
speech: (nch) is of such comparatively infrequent occurrence that
no examples at all were heard in the casual or formal styles of over
half the informants, and it is therefore necessary to include the
performance in reading passage and word list. (Of course, if there
is little social significance involved with this variable, the using
of such more artificial styles is not very important, because there
is likely to be less stylistic variation than with variables involving prestige or stigma.) Also, since even RP speakers may vary
between [ntʃ] and [nʃ], it seems reasonable to set the 'pass-mark'
fairly low, so over- and under-reporting are reckoned as follows:
if an informant claimed [ntʃ] in both words, then he was counted as
over-reporting only if his total [ntʃ] score was less than 25%,
while if he claimed [ntʃ] in only one word less than 10% actual use
of [ntʃ] counted as over-reporting: similarly over 10% or over 25%
[ntʃ] counted as under-reporting if he claimed [nʃ] in both or only
one of the words. Percentages of informants over-reporting and
under-reporting were:

'over'	I	II	III	IV	V
M	(33)	14	50	0	20
W	-	17	12	6	17
Total	(33)	15	26	3	19

'under'	I	II	III	IV	V
M	(0)	0	10	21	0
W	-	0	29	17	17
Total	(0)	0	22	19	6

Only a handful of informants stated that they used one variant
but believed the other to be better or more correct - and not all of
these were 'in the same direction'.

Reports of using the [ntʃ] pronunciation seem to be fairly
randomly distributed among the social class groups. This is possibly due to the following factors: the inability to distinguish and
resultant 'guessing' (note particularly the high claims to [ntʃ] by
some groups and the 'probable inability' of these same groups as
shown in the tables above; and the fact that informants may hear the
difference but attach no social significance to it). The age-groups
scores do show a somewhat clearer pattern, with the youngest groups

apparently displaying a greater tendency to regard [ntʃ] as correct; there was some sign of this in Figure 13, but the trends are not definite.

Figures for over- and under-reporting also look pretty random, and the few informants who volunteered the information that they considered the other variant more correct do nothing to produce a clearer picture.

It seems reasonable to conclude that our earlier feeling that this is a case of virtually free variation, with no stigma and hardly any prestige involved, has received support from this experiment; and there are clear signs that many people are not even able to perceive the difference between the variants.

The Variable (eɪ)

We have seen earlier that this phonetic area involves questions of both inventory and realisation, and that though signs of change exist in both, this remains one of the main 'give-aways' for people of this region.   In the self-evaluation experiment I investigated informants' reports of using RP-like [eɪ] as opposed to regional [e:] or [ɛɪ]:   their attention was thus focussed primarily on realisation.

I offered the word *late* with the alternative pronunciations [leɪt] and [le:t], *straight* with [strɛɪt], [streɪt], and also [stre:t], since it had been seen that there were signs of the /ɛɪ/-/e:/ contrast breaking down in favour of the latter (see p.124). It will be best to examine the two words separately, since the ɛɪ/eɪ difference may be less easily perceived and therefore seen as of less significance than e:/eɪ, and with *straight* , the possible loss of /ɛɪ/ in favour of /e:/ should be considered.

The following percentages of informants in the class and sex groups reported using the RP-like [eɪ] pronunciation:

late   *straight*

M	(67)	36	27	26	8
W		67	53	36	20
Total	(67)	50	43	31	11

M	(33)	33	0	14	0
W	-	40	29	10	17
Total	(33)	36	19	12	5

Figures for accuracy of reporting produced few clear patterns, and will not be given in detail.

There were very few responses indicating that an informant considered as more correct a variant other than the one he reported: 8 informants said this of [[leɪt] and 2 of [streɪt].

In the case of *late* the reports of [eɪ] relate to class (informants lower on the social scale are progressively less likely to report this) and sex (women are a good deal more likely than men to report [eɪ]), in a way one would have expected from earlier findings. But note that reports are generally at a low level (even one Class I informant reported [e:]), which suggests that this feature of realisation is not considered particularly important from a 'correctness' viewpoint.   But in proportion to the numbers making such reports, the amount of over-reporting is quite high: except for women of Class II, most informants who reported [leɪt] were over-reporting;   for this minority then, [eɪ] is seen as a standard to be aimed at, and this must also be the case with the 8 who said they considered this to be correct though they used [le:t].

With *straight* the situation is more complex: not only were reports of [eɪ] lower throughout, but also there are obvious 'irregularities' between the various groups, and we even find two of the three Class I informants saying they used [strɛɪt].   Several factors are probably responsible here.   First, a number of informants (3 men, 2 women) said that they could not distinguish between the narrower and wider diphthongal pronunciations (compared to only 2 who said [leɪt]/[le:t] sounded alike):   these were of course ignored when the above figures were being worked out, but it is possible that arbitrary responses by others who did not actually admit to an inability to perceive the distinction may have affected the scores.   Second, the pronunciations were read in the order [strɛɪt], [streɪt], [stre:t].   The last is least likely (see p.123) and it is possible that informants responding 'the first' may simply have meant 'not the last, at any rate'.   Finally, we noted earlier that the wider diphthongal form does seem to be left unmodified by some informants who have changed their obviously regional [e:] to [eɪ] (see p.121)

What seems to remain is the fact that the difference between regional [ɛɪ] and RP-like [eɪ] attracts less attention than between [e:] and [eɪ].   Support for this seems to come from the facts that 23 informants reported [leɪt] but [strɛɪt] (and only 8 reported [streɪt] but [le:t]);   and only 2 informants felt [streɪt] to be more correct than the form they used.   However, the fact that a substantial proportion of those reporting [streɪt] were over-reporting may indicate that a minority do feel the difference has some social significance.

Of the 85 informants who said they used a regional variant of *straight*, 12 said they had the unetymological [stre:t].   Though many of these were inaccurate according to my records of what they

actually said, this may be some more evidence that the lexically
very limited /ɛɪ/ phoneme is giving way to the commoner /e:/;   i.e.
there is a growing tendency to have only one phoneme in this phonetic area (like RP), and the merger form may be either [eɪ] (as in
RP) or regional [e:].

My conclusions are that [ɛɪ], though there are signs of the
phonemic distinction weakening further, shows less sign of being
perceived as something 'not correct' than does [e:];   and only a
minority perceive the RP-like [eɪ] realisation of either /e:/ or
/ɛɪ/ as being the standard of correctness.   These findings are in
line with those reported in Chapter 6.   (We have also found further
evidence for saying that presenting informants with more than a
binary choice can lead to problems.)

The Variable (əʊ)

We saw in Chapter 6 that this is another area where both inventory and realisation are involved (see pp.124 and 161), and that
it too probably serves as one of the main signals that a speaker
comes from West Yorkshire.   In this experiment I investigated informants' self-evaluations as using non-regional [əʊ] as opposed to
regional [ɔʊ] or [o:].

Because it appears that the ɔʊ/o: distinction has become somewhat confused, I offered informants the choice of [əʊ],[ɔʊ] and [o:]
in each of the following:

boat, a traditional /ʊə/ word, where [o:] would be expected today;
       (and [ɔʊ] would be unusual);

no, where both /ʊə/ and /ɔʊ/ forms occur in traditional dialects,
       though [o:]</ʊə/ is now commoner;

old, a traditional /ɔʊ/ word, but quite often pronounced with [o:]
       nowadays, especially in the Southern part of the area.

This particular three-way choice I now feel had disadvantages, of
two main types.   First, the problem outlined above arising whenever
there is more than binary choice.   Second, and perhaps more serious,
the fact that (because I realised it would cause difficulties to
present four possibilities), I did not include an [oʊ] pronunciation,
which many folk do use.   This [oʊ] has a starting point as near to

[ɔʊ] as to [əʊ], and this is quite possibly the reason (rather than
confusion of traditional incidence) why a number of informants reported saying [bɔʊt] or [nɔʊ]: they rejected the most common monophthongal [o:], yet [əʊ] seemed a little too 'posh', and so they
went for [ɔʊ]. This line of reasoning is supported by the fact that
such reports of [ɔʊ] were more common with those groups of informants who in fact used more [oʊ] variants (see the first table below).
It might just possibly be argued that similar (though opposite)
reasoning could be applied in the case of claims to use [o:] in *old*:
i.e. that [ɔʊ] sounds too extreme, [əʊ] too refined, but [o:] has
at least the same start-point as [oʊ].   But, as the second table
shows, there is not the same class distribution here, and it is just
as likely that most such reports reflect the fact that [o:] tends to
be a 'merger' form for both /ɔʊ/ and /o:/[165].

[bɔʊt]   [o:ld]

I	II	III	IV	V
(0)	46	23	23	11

I	II	III	IV	V
(0)	30	32	30	26

The following percentage reports of [əʊ]-like variants were made:

		I	II	III	IV	V
No, boat	(100)	40	28	21	6
old	(100)	31	29	15	22

		I	II	III	IV	V
M	(100)	27	15	18	8
W	-	49	37	20	18
Total	(100)	37	28	19	11

     Because of the complications of the various factors involved,
including the faults in the design of the experiment just referred
to, no attempt is made to assess over- or under-reporting in this
case.

     There were only 22 remarks (out of 318 items) to the effect
that [əʊ] is more correct though the informant said that he actually
used one of the other variants.

---

165 The fact that five informants said they thought [bɔʊt] was the
correct form and only one said this of [o:ld] perhaps supports the
arguments of this paragraph.

We may conclude that though this section has brought out several
of the methodological problems in experiments of this type, the findings are broadly in line with those of Chapter 6:   there is some
confusion apparent in the realisations of the traditional /ɔʊ/ and
/o:/ sets;   only a minority of speakers see RP-like variants as the
standard to be aimed at (with the result that this variable 'gives
away' many speakers);   and this minority is spread over class and
sex groups in the way we have come to expect with prestige features.

The Variable (ʊə)

As we saw in Chapter 6, /ʊə/ involves questions of both inventory and realisation.   Considering only inventory here: traditional
West Yorkshire dialect had an /ɔ:/-/ʊə/ contrast, whereas the lexical set of the latter was in RP divided between /ɔə/ and /ʊə/, and
there was thus a three phoneme situation /ɔ:/-/ɔə/-/ʊə/.   Both systems appear to be undergoing change at present: in RP, /ɔə/ words
are tending to join the /ɔ:/ set, and some /ʊə/ words are taking
part in an /ʊə/>/ɔə/>/ɔ:/ development.   In urban West Yorkshire,
the situation is probably just a little 'behind' that of RP: while
some speakers retain the older system, /ɔə/ has developed in many
people's speech, where it is largely distributed as in RP;   but the
same changes as in RP are to be observed among some younger speakers.
But there is little sign of any of the variants in current use involving prestige - or stigma (except possibly for the use of /ʊə/
in some words which in RP would have /ɔ:/ ~ /ɔə/).

In the self-evaluation test I offered *pour* and *sore*, each with
the three variant pronunciations [ɔ:], [ɔə], and [ʊə].   Traditional
dialect would have [ʊə] in each, whereas commonly in urban speech
today [ɔə] occurs, and [ɔ:] is also possible in both words;   [ʊə]
also occurs quite frequently in *pour*, but in *sore* it would be less
likely.   RP could have [ɔə], or in more advanced forms [ɔ:], in both
words;   but not [ʊə].   Since [ɔ:] is the most modern and regionally
neutral variant I shall assess informants' self-evaluations in relation to this.

It should be noted that this variable provides additional evidence about the problems inherent in offering a three-way choice.
I offered the alternants in the orders [pɔ:] - [pɔə] - [pʊə] but
[sɔə] - [sɔ:] - [sʊə];   if by responding 'the first' the informant
really just meant 'Not that last (broad) one' he would claim [pɔ:]
but [sɔə], an unlikely pair.   In fact this combination did occur
14 times as opposed to only 5 cases of the pair which would involve
the informant's being more specific, [pɔə] but [sɔ:].

The following table shows the percentages of [ɔ:] pronunciations
reported in the class and sex groups:

	I	II	III	IV	V
M	(67)	14	34	25	17
W	-	45	35	24	35
Total	(67)	28	35	24	22

It is also interesting to note the following age-group pattern:

10	20	30	40	50	60	70	80
43	52	21	33	19	9	9	(0)

With regard to the other pronunciations reported (i.e. those which were not [ɔː]),these were not randomly or equally distributed between [ɔə] and [ʊə]. The following tables show what percentage of diph-thongal reports were of the 'regionally marked' [ʊə] form:

	I	II	III	IV	V
M	(0)	8	21	36	70
W	-	0	0	30	15
Total	(0)	5	8	33	57

10	20	30	40	50	60	70	80
30	4	0	25	12	50	48	(67)

It may be noted that the figures for Class III here are accounted for entirely by [pʊə]: it was noted above that [ʊə] appears to be more acceptable in this word than in *sore*. 23 informants said they used [pʊə], 18 [sʊə].

Accuracy of reporting was assessed basically by the '50% in conversation' method: taking the percentage of [ɔː] in an inform-ant's use of (ʊə) words in casual and formal styles, if this came to less than 50% he was regarded as over-reporting if he had claimed to use [ɔː] in both *sore* and *pour*; if he claimed [ɔː] in only one, 25% was used as pass-mark. Under-reporting was measured by corr-esponding methods. (Of course these actual words were employed in the 'minimal sets' section: see p.134. I did consider using that performance data for assessing accuracy of claims here, but conver-sational speech seemed a more reasonable basis, and results were not found to be very different anyway.) The following percentages of informants over- and under-reported according to these criteria:

	I	II	III	IV	V
Over-reporting	(0)	8	11	23	21
Under-reporting	(0)	23	18	14	16

More detailed figures by sex, age etc. are no more 'regular' than
these.

No informants stated that they considered a variant other than
the one they used to be more correct.

None of the data on [ɔ:] ~ [ɔə] shows a completely regular trend.
there is no obvious relation between social class and regarding [ɔ:]
as 'correct' for example.   All we can see are certain tendencies,
such as that, in general, a higher proportion of women than men report using [ɔ:]; and the younger age-groups are most likely to report [ɔ:].   On the other hand, [ʊə] shows clear signs of being not
so readily acceptable: there is the difference between social
classes and sexes commonly found in such cases (and the 30-plus
group rejected it entirely).   There are indications too of it being
the older form: it is most commonly acknowledged among the oldest
groups (though there is an unexplained high figure among teenagers).
The figures for over- and under-reporting of [ɔ:] show little pattern, which seems to be in line with the general impression emerging
that the use of [ɔ:] as opposed to [ɔə] is not a matter involving
much prestige or stigma: only a minority in any group say they use
[ɔ:].

We may conclude that the suggestions emerging from this experiment - that the ɔ:/ɔə difference is of little social significance
though it shows some relation to age, but that the use of [ʊə] does
show signs of being regarded as substandard, and of being obsolescent - are broadly in accord both with our findings in Chapter 6, and
with the fact that both [ɔ:] and [ɔə] in these words are perfectly
acceptable in RP, but [ʊə] is not.   The standard of RP seems to have
become the standard for the majority in our area.

The Variable (t)

The use of the glottal stop was seen in Chapter 6 to be a very
interesting variable: it is a highly castigated feature (and shows
signs of the relations to non-linguistic factors common with such),
but it is apparently increasing in frequency - with time and by

environment, and possibly from a regional centre of Bradford.   In
the self-evaluation experiment informants were offered [t] and [2]
pronunciations of *letter* and *petrol* , examples involving different
work-internal environments (the word final environments were not
examined).

Before presenting the findings it is both relevant and interesting to note some of the spontaneous reactions of informants when the
contrast was presented: quite a number laughed before saying they
used the standard form; a few made remarks such as, "I'm not as bad
as that!", "I mean, that's just ignorant", "I can't stand that
knocking off t's" etc; several said something like "That's what the
kids are saying"; some Halifax and Huddersfield informants claimed
it was typical of Bradford rather than of their towns, while several
Bradford people said "that's bad round here".   Such responses fit
in with our more objective findings referred to above.

Even more than with (h) (see above), the great majority claimed
to use the [t] form; most reported it in both words, though a few
said they had [t] in one word but [2] in the other, and several said
they had [t] in both but might also use [2];   only a small number
admitted to [2] in both.   Percentages of reports of using [t] were:

	I	II	III	IV	V
M	(100)	100	89	82	78
W	-	75	100	95	83
Total	(100)	88	96	88	80

Bfd	Hfx	Hudd
87	88	93

(VtV)	(VtL)
91	87

10	20	30	40	50	60	70	80
64	89	100	88	98	98	91	(100)

In assessing the accuracy of these self-evaluations, (t) is of
sufficient frequency in both environments for conversational performance to be used as a basis.   But it was seen in Chapter 6 that
even those groups which might seem to use [2] most commonly in fact
have [t] in a high proportion of cases; a 50% cut-off is therefore
probably not reasonable and say 80% would be better.   If a speaker
uses [2] on more than 20% of occasions he will probably be regarded
as a [2] user; so if an informant says he uses [t] but his score

is less than 80% he will be considered as over-reporting (and under-
reporting will be correspondingly assessed).   Even with such a high
'pass-mark' over-reporting is not common:

	I	II	III	IV	V
(VtV)	(0)	8	0	21	5
(VtL)	(0)	15	18	21	11

No clear differences showed up between the sexes.   Under-reporting
is very rare, but it does account for the irregularity in the [t]-
reports table produced by Class II women: the two informants in
question were both being 'over-honest' in reporting [ʔ] when in fact
they used it on less than 20% of occasions.   Both types of inaccurate reporting occurred most commonly among the 10-plus and 20-plus
age-groups (where we found [ʔ] to be most common: see p.152).

    In every case where an informant admitted to using [ʔ], except
two cases of [leʔə] and three of [peʔrəl], he also said that he
considered the [t] form to be more correct; this is the highest
amount of 'manifest insecurity' observed in this experiment.

    Reports of using [t] rather than [ʔ] seem to fit with our con-
clusions in Chapter 6: they are at a very high level, which is in
accord with the stigmatised nature of [ʔ]; they relate to social
class and sex as one would expect in such a situation (the one 'irregularity' has already been referred to); there are slight signs of
the differences between towns and environments we observed in actual
performance; and only the teenage group showed some readiness to
regard [ʔ] as acceptable, though the 20-plus group were lower in
their [t]-reports than most (and we may note the 100% claims of the
30-plus group, which often scored 'highest' on performance).   With
regard to the inaccuracy of reporting, there is some indication of
the fact that though [ʔ] is commoner pre-liquid it is 'denied' just
as strongly as intervocalically; and the facts that there is little
over-reporting even when the 'pass-mark' is so high (contrast say
(h) where a large amount showed up even with a 50% mark), and that
informants almost always admitted that [ʔ] was 'wrong', are further
evidence of the stigmatised nature of [ʔ] and its relative infrequency.   Both types of inaccuracy being commonest in the two youngest age-groups, where [ʔ] is also most frequent, may indicate that
they are most aware of and uncertain about this phenomenon.

    We may conclude that self-evaluations are largely in accord
with our previous findings on [ʔ]. which is an almost unique feature

in that it is on the increase in spite of its being involved in a
change which is not in the direction of RP, and also a highly castigated usage.

The Variable (ɑ:)

This was examined in Chapter 6 as a matter of realisation:
traditional West Yorkshire dialect had a fairly front vowel [a:] as
compared to fairly back RP [ɑ:], and we noted that somewhat fronter
variants than RP are still common and do not appear to be a matter
of much social significance.   In the self-evaluation experiment I
offered the words *cart* and *father* with a fairly extreme contrast
between [a:] and [ɑ:] to ensure that the difference was clearly perceived (i.e. [a:] was probably fronter than that used by most speakers, and [ɑ:] may have been backer than with some RP speakers).
But I was also interested in reactions to a not uncommon traditional
form of *father*, involving a difference of incidence: [faðə];   this
was offered as the third possible pronunciation of that word.

Reports of using backer variants (i.e. [ɑ:]) were made in the
following percentages:

	I	II	III	IV	V		Bfd	Hfx	Hudd
M	(83)	54	30	31	23		38	64	48
W	-	83	75	57	25				
Total	(83)	67	57	44	24				

The age-group figures are quite irregular, but it might be
noted that the 30-plus group showed the highest percentage of [ɑ:]
reports.

Informants saying they used the [faðə] pronunciation of *father*
are included in the above only in respect of *cart*.   Eight informants
(including only one female - the 'rebel' schoolgirl referred to
earlier) said this was their pronunciation;   a further five men said
they used it occasionally.   All the men involved were from the
working classes: III: 3, IV: 5, V: 4.

Accuracy of these self-evaluations was assessed as follows:
occurrences of (ɑ:) had been classified as [a:], [a:ᵻ], and in fact
the midway form (which I did not offer in this experiment) was most
frequent overall.   I therefore took the instances of [a:] and [ɑ:]
as percentages of an informant's total number of (ɑ:), and only

counted him as over-reporting if he reported [ɑ:] in both words but
in fact [a:] was commoner than [ɑ:] in his conversational speech AND
made up at least 25% of total occurrences, or if he reported [ɑ:]
in one word but [a:] made up more than 50% of occurrences.

Figures for over-reporting so measured indicate that there is
only a small amount, confined to the working classes: III 14% of
informants, IV 12%, V 16%.   With such small figures no patterns
for sex or age show up, but it may be noted that though Halifax
showed the highest percentage of [ɑ:] reports, there was the lowest
percentage of informants over-reporting. (It must however be admitted that the over-reporting of [ɑ:] might look very different if
the half-front [a:⊦] had been included in the calculations.)   Under-
reporting hardly occurred.

No informants volunteered opinions that the other long vowel
pronunciation was more correct than that which they had just said
they used.   But of the 13 who said they used [faðə], 8 said that
they considered a long vowel form to be more correct[166]; it is
interesting that 6 of these indicated [fa:ðə], though of course
since the three variants had been read in the order [fa:ðə, fɑ:ðə,
faðə] some of these could be due to the 'the first' = 'not the last'
problem referred to several times.

Reports of using [ɑ:] variants do show a relation to social
class which suggests that towards the upper end of the scale there
is a stronger tendency to regard this pronunciation as the standard
to be aimed at, and also a relation to sex which shows that this is
much more marked among women than men (with the latter, the working
classes largely have an [a:] standard).   There is also a difference
between towns, with Halifax more than the other two regarding [a:]
as standard.   All these findings fit in with those of Chapter 6;
and the fact that there is little over-reporting and no feeling that
another form is 'better' - if this can be interpreted as an indication that the a:/ɑ: difference is not perceived as having much social
significance - may also fit in with the finding there that there is
little stylistic variation.

The very few informants who said they used the form [faðə], and
the feelings of many of those who did that this is not correct, seem
to indicate that as far as incidence goes the RP-like pronunciation
has largely ousted the traditional dialect one as the standard form
of this word.

---

166 One elderly woman remarked that she dared not use [faðə] as it
would imply disrespect.   Incidentally, Ekwall (1975:26) says that [a] in
father and *rather* would be more regular historically, and that the
long vowel is of disputed origin.

The Variable (ɑː/æ)

We have seen (p.166) that incidence of a long or short vowel
in words such as *class*, *laugh*, *dance* etc., which is one of the most
readily recognisable features distinguishing most Northern (short)
from Southern and RP speech (long), can hardly be described as a
linguistic 'variable' in West Yorkshire since there is little variation, the short vowel being almost universal.   In the self-
evaluation experiment I offered the two words *bath* and *grass* with
RP-like [ɑː] and Northern [a] pronunciations.

Informants saying they used the [ɑː] pronunciation were too few
to tabulate in the normal way.   Two of the three members of Class I
(both RP speakers) predictably said they used this form, and one
woman in Class II (Mrs H, see p.167) and a man in Class III, who
would both probably be regarded as 'well-spoken', said they used
'something in between' my two (probably extreme) renderings.   More
surprising was the fact that three young men, one in Class III and
the others in Class IV, claimed to use the [ɑː] forms: I suspect
that at least one of these was throughout this section giving what
he considered correct rather than what he actually used, and another,
when I queried one of his responses, pronounced [baθ].   Perhaps
most surprising was the fact that none of the three informants whose
performance *did* show variation (see p.167) definitely claimed to be
[ɑː] pronouncers.

Over-reporting obviously is too minor a phenomenon to tabulate,
but it was definitely the case with all informants referred to in
the above paragraph, except those in Class I.

In many cases I specifically elicited comments about the correctness or otherwise of the long vowel variant (with other items I
generally left informants to volunteer such opinions), and the responses are interesting and relevant.   22 informants did say this
was more correct, 14 of them women, but there is no pattern over
the class groups: there were 3 in Class II (23%), but one of the
two men here qualified his statement by saying "Well...more refined",
and the other added "Perhaps"; of the 9 in Class III (32%) one
woman added "But it's really a [baθ]!", and another "It sounds better
but I would feel silly", and another "But not if it sounds unnatural": of the 6 in Class IV (14%) one said "Well, it gives a better
image", and another "But they'd laugh at me"; and of the 4 in Class
V one was dubious and another added "But it's swanky".

In addition to these rather negative remarks by those saying
that [bɑːθ] was more correct, there were a considerable number who
definitely held that it was not: a lot of informants (especially

in Class II) positively said that they did not prefer the long-vowel
form or that they really detested it or even that it was incorrect[167];
over half-a-dozen said "There is no R in [baθ]" and a lot held [ɑ:]
forms to be simply 'Southern', 'posh', or 'affected'.

        I think it is reasonable to conclude that our findings in
Chapter 6 are largely supported by the evidence of the self-evaluation experiment: with this variable the RP form has had little
effect on the population at large, who follow what perhaps may be
called the 'Northern standard' in this respect.

The Variable (ing)

        We saw above that [ɪŋ] varies with [ɪn] in relation to class
and style, in such a way that suggests that [ɪŋ] is seen as the
'better' variant; but that [ɪn] is very common in everyday conversation, where even informants of Class II averaged around 50% non-
standard variants.   We also examined the different frequency of
[ɪn] in participles and gerunds on the one hand and words which do
not have 'ing-less' forms on the other; this hypothesis was only
formulated during the survey, and so the two items included in the
self-evaluation experiment were not chosen with it in mind: rather,
I picked a fairly neutral participle/gerund, *rocking*, and a form
which could be participle/gerund but is more likely perhaps as a
colloquial adjective, *smashing*.

        This variable, though it is very much more common than (nch),
and though the ŋ/n difference is phonemic in *thing*/*thin* etc., was
found to involve something that was otherwise only encountered
with (nch): some informants were unable to distinguish between the
alternative pronunciations.   In fact this phenomenon was much commoner with (ing) than with (nch)[168];   the following percentages of

---

167 [ɑ:] forms had provoked some spontaneous comments from informants earlier in the interview - one or two showing that they saw it
as a prestige form but others stressing that they did *not* regard it
as correct and would never use it.   An elderly man (Class IV) remarked about [grɑ:s], "You hear that on the wireless - but then,*they*
say [ɒnvǝlo:p] though it has an E, but you don't say [ɒlɪfǝnt]!"

168 Mr W (see p.222), who, though perhaps describable as a 'dialect
speaker', had shown himself to be very acute in perceiving a number
of distinctions and regional differences, was quite unable to hear
[ɪn] from [ɪŋ].   This may not be uncommon in Britain generally:

informants in the class and sex groups said they were unable to
hear a difference between [ɪŋ] and [ɪn] (some people said this with
both words, some with only one - but the latter were treated as
incapable of distinguishing and their responses were ignored):

	I	II	III	IV	V
M	(0)	0	27	27	54
W	-	0	12	43	50
Total	(0)	0	18	35	53

Corresponding figures for the age-groups were:

10	20	30	40	50	60	70	80
21	18	33	33	42	43	13	(67)

    Discounting those informants included in the above, the follow-
ing percentages of reports were of using the standard [ɪŋ] variant:

	I	II	III	IV	V
M	(100)	64	65	47	40
W	-	83	74	44	14
Total	(100)	73	71	46	32

10	20	30	40	50	60	70	80
50	53	67	69	64	63	39	(50)

21 informants said they used [ɪŋ] in only one of the two items: 18
said they had [smaʃɪn] but [rɒkɪŋ], and only 3 [smaʃɪŋ] but [rɒkɪn].
Also, two said they used [ɪŋ] in both words but also [ɪn] in one of
them.

    Accuracy of these self-evaluations was assessed by the '50% in
conversation' standard (or 25% if only one [ɪŋ] was claimed). Under-

---

for instance, several well-known broadcasters, including the sports-
men Sir Alf Ramsey and Jim Laker who had obviously modified their
speech considerably in various respects, invariably used [ɪn] even in
slow and formal delivery.

reporting was virtually non-existent, while over-reporting was distributed among the following percentages of informants (excluding
those unable to distinguish).

	I	II	III	IV	V
M	(0)	14	63	41	50
W	-	17	53	42	33
Total	(0)	15	57	41	44

Figures for the age-groups, which after excluding those unable to
distinguish are sometimes very small, are quite irregular.

With (ing) more than with most variables examined, some inform-
ants reporting [ɪn] said they considered [ɪŋ] to be more correct.
There were 27 such statements, 17 of them made in respect of *rocking*.
With such a number it is hardly reasonable to examine percentages of
each subgroup, but there was a similar proportion in each of Classes
II-V and there do seem to be signs of a pattern among the age-groups:

10	20	30	40	50	60	70	80
36	26	22	6	14	6	7	(0)

The relatively high proportions incapable of distinguishing
[ɪŋ] and [ɪn] would seem to suggest that in certain sections of the
population, particularly Classes IV - V and some of the older age-
groups (the figure for the 70-plus group is a surprising 'irregularity'), the difference cannot be seen as having much significance.
Among those who can distinguish the variants, Classes IV - V contain
a majority who seem to regard [ɪn] as their standard, though figures
for over-reporting indicate that a minority do feel that [ɪŋ] is
definitely better;   Class III would seem to show particular sensitivity about the correctness of [ɪŋ].   The middle classes are fairly
accurate in their assessment of themselves as having [ɪŋ] as their
standard.   There do not seem to be consistent differences between
the sexes in respect of this variable (as also appeared to be the
case in Chapter 6).   Among the age-groups, though the middle-aged
groups show the highest reports of using [ɪŋ], there are signs that
towards the younger end of the age-scale there is more conscious
feeling that [ɪŋ] is 'better' than the traditional [ɪn].

We may conclude that these findings are largely in line with

those of Chapter 6:   (ing) is certainly not seen as a matter of as
much prestige/stigma as say (h), but there are signs that the RP-like
[ɪŋ] is taking over as the form seen as the standard to be aimed at -
though many in the working-classes still treat traditional [ɪn] as
their standard.   We have also found some support for one of the findings of Fischer (1958): the particular lexical item involved can be
significant in the frequency of [ɪŋ] or [ɪn] - we have seen signs
that the latter is more acceptable in a colloquial item like *smashing*
than in a neutral one.

The Variable (ook)

This was seen in Chapter 6 to be an incidence variable with some
interesting characteristics: though there are clear signs that [uːk]
forms are giving way to [ʊk], partly via the class system but also
very clearly with time (i.e. age-groups), there is a strange situation of [uːk] being more common in the more formal styles - a phenomenon usually indicating that a variant is felt to be more 'correct'.

Two of the commonest (ook) words, *book* and *look*, were offered
in the self-evaluation experiment with the alternative [uːk] and [ʊk]
pronunciations.

62 informants said they used [ʊk] forms of both words;   13 said they
had [uːk] in both;   31 in effect reported varying in some way between
the two (16 said they had [buːk] but [lʊk];   10 [luːk] but [bʊk];
2 said they had [ʊk] in both but also [luːk];   2 said they used [uːk]
in both and also.[lʊk];   and one [uːk] in both but also [bʊk]).   The
following tables show the percentage of [ʊk] forms reported.

	I	II	III	IV	V
M	(83)	86	82	73	58
W	-	100	91	60	58
Total	(83)	92	88	66	58

10	20	30	40	50	60	70	80
86	100	92	63	75	64	41	(33)

The following table shows the percentage of informants reporting
only [ʊk] forms:

	I	II	III	IV	V
M	(67)	86	73	55	38
W	-	100	88	33	50
Total	(67)	92	82	44	42

In assessing the accuracy of these self-evaluations, there are
two difficulties. First, (ook) is not sufficiently common for
conversational data to be used as a basis of comparison in many cases
I therefore took the total of all styles except minimal pairs (though
we noted some increase of [u:k] in more formal styles, the results
produced were rarely different from what would have been obtained
from conversational speech where this could be used[169]).   Second,
since [u:k] is readily admitted to by quite a number of informants
and does not appear to attract much stigma, a 50% cut-off did not
produce any interesting results. I therefore decided to treat
reports as 100% (both [ʊk]), 66% (both [ʊk] plus one [u:k]), 50%
(one each),33% (both [u:k] plus one [ʊk]), and 0% (both [u:k]) -
though I admit that this is very debateable - and to assess over-
and under-reporting in terms of actual usage being more than 10%
different; in fact most inaccuracies were considerably greater.

The percentages of informants thus assessed as over-reporting,
and under-reporting were:

'over'	I	II	III	IV	V
M	(33)	14	9	23	46
W	-	17	18	10	0
Total	(33)	15	11	16	26

'under'	I	II	III	IV	V
M	(0)	14	27	27	38
W	-	0	29	43	33
Total	(0)	8	28	35	37

Figures for the age-groups are fairly random, but it may be noted
that most under-reporting came from the oldest groups.

Of the few informants who commented on'correctness', 3 said
[lʊk] was more correct than [lu:k] which they used, and 4 made similar remarks about [bʊk].   But 6 remarked that they thought the
[u:k] pronunciation was more correct (one man commenting that [lʊk]
was L-U-C-K!).

---

169 One unusual example was an informant who used 100% [ʊk] in his
few conversational examples but only 19% overall - which since he
claimed one [u:k] and one [ʊk] would be under-reporting and over-
reporting respectively!

The percentage of [ʊk] reported would seem to indicate that it
is taking over from [u:k] as the form regarded as the standard to
aim at, and that this is generally proceeding by class (i.e. from
the top) and age (i.e. [ʊk] becoming the only form as time passes) -
though each table contains some 'irregularities'. But a much lower
percentage of informants in Classes IV - V than in the higher groups
reported using it exclusively, which might suggest that the feelings
about which is correct are less definite there. The figures for
inaccuracy of reporting are not clear in their import, but it is
interesting to observe that there is more under-reporting than over-
reporting, and that the former increases towards the lower end of
the social scale. It would seem reasonable to conclude that feelings about 'correctness' are not so clear-cut and that in the working-classes there are signs that [u:k] is still to a considerable
extent felt to be the standard. Overt remarks about correctness
reinforce this reasoning.

I think we may conclude that this experiment backs up our earlier findings: RP-like [ʊk] is taking over from traditional [u:k]
as the standard, and this is proceeding by age and social groups;
but there is still, especially in the working-classes, considerable
ambivalence about [u:k] - the evaluation data here being in line
with the unusual stylistic variation noted in Chapter 6.

Other items included in the self-evaluation experiment

The items discussed above all exemplified variables examined in
Chapter 6. In every case a substantial proportion of the population
appeared to use a non-standard variant, and I was concerned to investigate how far claims to use the standard variant indicated that
this RP-like form was regarded as the one to be aimed at.

I now turn to a small number of other items where the great
majority of the population appeared from my preliminary observations to use an RP-like pronunciation, but where they might be expected to be familiar with a non-standard form which was either a
traditional dialect form (as with the [faðə] pronunciation of *father*
already referred to), or a 'fashionable' form, in some cases classed
by the standard texts as say 'Advanced RP' (the [gɒvnmənt] pronunciation included above might have been so classed had it survived).
I hoped to see how many would report using the dialectal forms and
what the general reaction to them would be, and also whether any
would be so 'speech-conscious' as to claim to use the 'hyper-RP'
pronunciations.

To examine dialectal forms, I offered *there* with [ðɪə]

alongside the now usual [ðɛə]; *loud* with [la:d] beside [laʊd]: and *time* with [tɑ:m] alongside [taɪm].

With *there*, several informants responded with laughter and remarks such as "Nay, I'm not as bad as that!"   About half-a-dozen said [ðɪə] was 'broad Yorkshire'.   However a few did say they used this form;   all belonged to Classes IV - V: Mr F (see p.222) and another man in his 70s and one i n his 60s, of Class IV;   and Mr W (ibid) and, surprisingly, one man in his 20s and another in his teens, of Class V.   The only female to claim to use this form was the 'rebel' schoolgirl referred to several times, who said she said this at home.   The last three here did seem to report a number of non-standard forms they seemed unlikely to use, and this may be through misunderstanding the instructions;   the others quite poss- ibly do use [ðɪə] at times.   All but two of those saying they used [ðɪə] said that [ðɛə] was more correct.

With *loud*, only two men reported saying [la:d].   The [a:] variant of (aʊ) is in fact commoner than [ðɪə] and [tɑ:m] etc., but in isolation and in a possibly ambiguous form it is not surprising that it was 'denied'.   Both men said they considered [laʊd] more correct.

With *time*, two informants, a man of Class V and a woman of Class IV, both in their 50s and from Halifax, said they could not hear the difference, and there were two others who said 'Number 2' ([tɑ:m]) in a tone of voice which suggested that this was the case with them also.   Only two informants quite definitely said they used [tɑ:m]: both were from Huddersfield (we saw in Chapter 5 that /ɑ:/ for /aɪ/ was a feature of traditional dialect in this town and possibly in Halifax).   Of these a man in his 50s (Class III) said he only used it sometimes, and Mr W (Class V) said he used it but regarded [taɪm] as more correct[170].

To examine 'hyper-RP' forms, I offered *off* as [ɔ:f] and [ɒf]; *solve* as [sǝʊlv] and [sɒlv]; *tower* as [taǝ], [taʊǝ], and [tɑ:]; and *fire* as [faɪǝ], [fɑǝ], and [fɑ:].

The [ɒf] pronunciation of *off* is commonest in RP nowadays, the older [ɔ:f] being given in EPD as the second (bracketed) form. When confronted with these alternatives none of my informants

---

170 Several informants who 'repeated' their pronunciation rather than identifying by label produced an 'impure diphthong' i.e. [tɑ·ɪm] (see p.164), but clearly the long-vowel form is hardly ever regarded as normal nowadays.

reported the latter[171].   Five made comments about it: one RP
speaker said it was "ultra-South, going beyond good English"; one
Class II woman said it was "a bit Southern", while another said
"I hate that!"; a Class IV woman who gave many indications of linguistic insecurity, said she was not sure which was really correct,
while an elderly man of the same class, though his speech was more
'standard' than the average for that group, castigated it as "one
of the Southern exaggerations".

   In recent years a number of verbs terminating in -*olve*, such as
solve, *involve*, *resolve* etc., had developed a pronunciation in [əʊ]
alongside the more usual [ɒ].   When these alternatives were presented in *solve* not one informant claimed to use the [əʊ] form.
There were two spontaneous comments: a Class II woman said "I can't
stand that - it's a fashion at present", while another woman of
Class III, who had once had elocution lessons and was rather self-
conscious in careful speech, said she thought [səʊlv] was correct.

   The triphthongs /aʊə/ and /aɪə/ can be pronounced as an /ɑə/
diphthong in RP or even further 'reduced' to /ɑ:/.   I offered all
three with *tower* and *fire*, and so allowed the problems of multiple
choice to come in (see above): it seems likely to me that at least
some of the two who claimed to say [taə], the two who claimed [tɑ:],
and the two who claimed [faə] did so by confusing the order in which
they had been heard.   Even if this was not the case they are only
a very small minority.   Several comments were made: two informants
said they thought [taə] the correct form though they did not use it,
and three felt the same about [faə] (the teenage member of Class I,
an RP speaker, opted for both these); only one thought [fɑ:] was
correct and no-one said this about [tɑ:] - this last was labelled
by Mr W as "very collar-and-tie".

   We may conclude that there is little evidence of there being
sufficient 'speech-consciousness' or linguistic insecurity among the
population of our area for them to seize on what seem to be the most
fashionable or refined forms of certain words.

Some general conclusions

   My findings relating to what pronunciations informants 'think'
they use largely confirm my earlier conclusions about what they
actually do use.   With one or two exceptions, the differences between the class and sex groups (and in some cases between the age-

---

171 In fact one man in Class V did so, but he was semi-literate and
the fact that he then repeated the word as [hɔ:f] makes me think he
was probably mistaking it for *half*, the traditional dialect form of
this being [ɔ:f].

groups and towns) which show up in informants' self-evaluations
reflect similar differences between the groups in performance.
Moreover, not only are such relations between groups confirmed, so
also in many cases are differences in the frequency of variants: for
example, (h) and (ʌ) show similar relations between class and sex
groups in respect of using and reporting the use of RP-like variants,
but they differ considerably in the extent to which the different
groups use or report these: except in Class I there is much more
usage and reporting of [h] than there is with [ʌ].

Also, my findings confirm what the earlier findings suggest
about a shift in 'standards' of correctness within the area.   In
respect of most of the items examined it is clear that there has been
some shift from the 'traditional norm' towards that of RP.   In the
case of say (h) and (-ow) (and also some individual items like
father, *there* etc.) this has affected the majority of speakers; with
(ʌ), and with realisation features like (ɑ:), (eɪ), (əʊ), as yet only
a minority seem to be aiming at an RP-like standard;   while with
(ing) and (ook) the two norms seem to be about in balance at present.
Two notable exceptions are (ɑ:/æ), where a 'Northern standard' is
strongly entrenched, and (t) where there are signs of a shift among
a minority away from the RP-like traditional norm towards one which
is at present highly stigmatised.

One aspect of experiments of this sort which leaves me with
considerable doubts is the treatment of 'inaccuracy of self-evaluation'.   This seems in several cases to leave much room for debate
both about the measurement of this phenomenon (as has been seen,
where to draw the line that divides the accurate from the over/under-
reporter is a matter which is largely arbitrary and depends on the
'feel' of the investigator), and about its interpretation (for instance does under-reporting, as Trudgill suggests, really indicate
the 'covert prestige' of a non-standard form?   The only examples
I found seem better interpreted as further evidence of uncertainty
and perhaps insecurity).

3   SUBJECTIVE EVALUATION

The Washington study by Putnam and O'Herne (1955) was one of
the first to employ an experiment in which subjects were played tape-
recordings of various speakers about whom they were asked to perform
certain judgements.   Twelve negro speakers from different 'positions
on the prestige continuum' retold in their own words an Aesop fable
that had just been narrated to them, and a total of 70 'judges'
rated them for social status.   This 'free narrative' method did of
course obviate the disadvantage of the less literate being more
likely to betray themselves than if they had been asked to read a
passage, but of course it was even more likely that the better

educated would show up through their sentence-construction, grammar,
vocabulary, memory for detail, and so on.   So the result that the
judges' assessments were largely in accord with objective status is
perhaps not so remarkable.   Another criticism of the experiment
could be that the judges were predominantly white women, and all of
them were of high educational status (postgraduate students and
teachers);   such people might well be more capable than average of
assessing speakers in this way.

Labov (1966a) also included a tape-recording experiment in his
New York survey.   However, a major difference from the above was
that he was concerned not so much with the 'general impression' of
a speaker's status, such as Putnam and O'Herne's method produced,
but rather sought to get at the subconscious reactions hearers may
have to particular variants (as opposed to their more conscious
responses elicited by the other two evaluation methods - direct
questioning and the self-evaluation experiment).   Labov made a
selection from his exploratory interviews of five women reading a
passage consisting of five paragraphs: the first was a 'zero section', supposedly containing none of his main variables[172], then came
a paragraph with a concentration of words containing (oh), then one
with (eh), then (r), and finally (th) and (dh).   The five speakers
were selected not for their social characteristics but for their
contrasting uses of these variables.   The readings of the 'zero'
passage by all five were recorded, and these were played first to
subjects, in order to get their reactions to the five speakers on
a neutral section: these would serve as a reference-point from
which 'up'- or 'down-grading' might occur according to their performance on the variables.   This zero section is necessary in order to
cancel out the effects of voice quality - a subject might rate a
particular voice at a certain level for no apparent reason (or for
what he considers very good reasons);   so this section provides the
starting-point, whatever it might be, for future ratings of the same
voice.

The rating was produced by giving the subject a list of seven
hierarchically-graded occupations and asking him to imagine himself
as a personnel officer: which of these jobs did he think the speaker
was capable of holding, speaking as he did?[173]   (Most subjects agreed
that the job-hierarchy given was correct as far as 'speech qualifi-

---

172 Though as far as I can see it does include instances of (r),
(eh), and (oh).

173 The subjective evaluation test employed in Labov's later work
(Labov et al., 1968) was somewhat more sophisticated in that besides
'job suitability' there were other seven-point scales for 'toughness',
'friendship', and 'self-knowledge', and subjects were also asked to
identify the speaker's racial background.

cations' were concerned; if they had reservations about this, they
were asked to treat the scale simply as a set of points running from
perfect to terrible speech.)   After the zero-section, Labov included
two or more readings of each of the other paragraphs, each with a
different treatment of the concentrated variable, and informants
rated these in the same way.   The way a subject rated one of these
paragraphs was then compared not so much with the way others rated
it, nor with the way he rated another version of the same paragraph,
but rather with the way he had rated the same speaker on the zero
section.   In other words, the actual rating was unimportant in
itself; what mattered was whether it was higher, equal, or lower
than the point of reference.   Thus for example, one informant might
rate a certain reading as '3' and another as '6', but if their ratings of the same speaker on the zero section had been '2' and '5'
respectively they would both count as having a 'negative' reaction
to the variants employed by the speaker.   Such a negative reaction
might be supposed to indicate a stigmatised variant, while a 'positive' reaction could show that it was a prestige one.   Labov attempted to correlate such reactions with the customary non-linguistic
factors such as class, sex, age, ethnic group, and so on - with some
interesting results: for instance, he found cases where a group
which used a high degree of some stigmatised variant showed the
highest negative response to it; the correlations, or the lack of
them, were found to vary according to whether or not the variable
was involved in linguistic change; and more generally, this experiment could be taken as providing confirmation of the findings with
regard to performance - for instance, if there was a high degree of
positive response to a variant which the figures for class and style
differences had suggested was a prestige one.

Labov had a few informants who did not take this 'test', and
also three 'who can best be described as "dialect deaf".   With the
best will in the world they could not hear any significant differences between the speakers.... A few other informants showed tendencies in this direction....' (1966a:413).

I have described Labov's subjective evaluation experiment in
some detail, because I attempted to devise one along very similar
lines.   Trudgill had not employed this evaluation technique in
Norwich, so it seemed not to have been tried with British data.   My
experiment and its findings will be described below; but I should
state at the outset that I have a number of serious doubts about
this Labov-type approach.

The first and most serious problem concerns 'extraneous variables'.   Labov says he aimed to expose subjects to particular values
of variables 'with all other variables held constant'.   This is

just not possible.   Labov was investigating only five main variables, but even so it was found to be impossible not to draw in some
of the others when writing a paragraph concentrating on one of them:
thus, in the (oh)-concentrated section he had one instance of (eh)
which he admitted must contribute to the effect;   and his (eh) section shows two instances of (oh);   and so on.   Now of course there
are other important variables in New York, in addition to Labov's
five main ones: indeed, he refers elsewhere in his book to some of
'a great many other variables'.   So, inevitably, examples of these
must have been included in paragraphs purporting to test reactions
to one of his five main variables;   and their effect is difficult
to assess.   I was probably more aware of this problem because I
examined many more than five variables, and I found it quite impossible to exclude all but the one specifically under concentration.
And of course it is not often that performance on these extraneous
variables can be considered to be 'held constant'.   It may however
be countered that if a particular variable is very concentrated in
a passage then this is most likely to be the one responsible for a
subject's positive or negative reactions.   This is quite possibly
so in many instances, but with a variable which produces no strong
reactions, it is also possible that just one occurrence of a highly-
stigmatised or prestigious extraneous feature may be responsible for
such swings of evaluation as do occur: an example of this will be
seen below, when considering the (nch) variable.

A second problem concerns 'speaker recognition'.   With the
paragraphs concentrating on particular variables, Labov saw to it
that his five speakers appeared in different orders, and that not
all of them read any one paragraph;   thus, Labov believed, a subject 'would not be able to know exactly how he had rated the same
speaker in a previous utterance'.   I believe that this is true only
to a certain extent: I had quite a number of informants who quite
plainly recognised the same speaker (some of them remarked on this),
and though their ratings sometimes did change, in other cases they
were obviously rating the same speaker consistently: they had decided that he sounded like a shop-steward say, and so they kept
putting him on whatever rank they considered appropriate to a shop-
steward;   only an extremely strong reaction to some feature would
shift such ratings.

My third serious doubt concerns the interpretation of informants' reactions.   A change in the rating of a speaker by a subject,
from say '3' on the zero-section to '1' or '5' in response to particular variants, may reasonably be interpreted as 'positive' or
'negative' reaction respectively;   but what of those cases where
there is no change in rating?   These could in most cases be taken
to mean that the subject is more or less indifferent to the variant
in question.   However Labov, reasoning that with a speaker rated
quite low to start with there is little room for downgrading, decided
to take both 'equal' and lower together as indicating negative

response in the case of (oh).   Now while this may be justifiable
for the speaker rated low to start with, it is questionable whether
it should also be done with two others, as Labov did.   These two
were not so low to start with; and it is interesting to note that
if he had applied this 'equal = negative' to the fourth speaker reading this paragraph, it would have produced a very negative reaction
to what are supposedly 'better' variants - but this he did not do,
since this speaker started higher.   With (eh) too he counted cases
of 'equal' rating as negative reactions; whereas with (r), where
he played two samples of the same speaker (one with consistent[r]
and the other with [r ~ ∅]), rating the latter as 'equal' to the
former was taken along with rating consistent [r] higher as indicating an 'r-positive' response, and only rating [r ~ ∅] as higher is
'negative'.   Labov's reasoning seems rather tortuous on this point,
but it may be sound.   However I am not convinced that it is justifiable to take 'equal' as equivalent to either 'lower' or 'higher'
except in a very few cases; I found that where there was a definitely positive or negative reaction, this did show up in more
'higher' or 'lower' ratings overall (in both Labov's and my own
experiments), even where the speaker had generally been rated high
or low to start with.

     In my experiment, I was interested both in general reactions
to different speakers (like Putnam and O'Herne), and in more specific responses to particular variants (like Labov).   My procedure
was closer to that of the latter in that all my speakers read the
same set passage, rather than speaking freely.

     I began by suggesting to informants that perhaps we judge
people in some way by their speech, and that different standards of
speech are thought necessary to different occupations.   I handed
them a card with a list of five jobs: a) BBC Newsreader; b) Personnel Officer (I expanded verbally to the effect that I meant one
in a large company, where he would be dealing with top people as
well as everyone else); c) Teacher (in an ordinary local school);
d) Shopkeeper (of a local shop); e) Labourer.   Most informants
agreed that this was the right hierarchical order[174].   I then said
I had on tape about two dozen sentences spoken by different men.
I emphasised that they were reading, so that their judgements should
not be affected by the content - though I do not think this was
entirely successful.   I said that there were more than five senten-

_____

174 The few reservations concerned the relative order of b) and c).
If informants were still doubtful after I had amplified on what sort
of members of these professions I meant, I asked them simply to
treat a) - e) as labels for a grading of speech (see Labov, 1966a,
and Labov et al. 1968).

ces,and that the speakers came from a range of jobs - not those on
the card - so it was not a matter of matching one to one. After
each sentence they should say which of jobs a) to e) they thought
the speaker was fitted for, speaking as he did.

Several informants were not very happy about this experiment,
feeling that it was a bad thing to judge people in this way; nevertheless 93 of the 106 informants completed this test. Of the 13
'failures', 2 did not attempt this section because of lack of time,
whereas the remaining 11 started but were so obviously at sea that
it was abandoned. These, presumably similar to those labelled
'dialect deaf' by Labov, were predominantly towards the lower end
of the social scale and in the upper age range;   several more members of these groups, though they completed the test, made a number
of 'strange' evaluations which suggested that they were hardly capable of performing the judgements requested (and these subjects
account for some of the unexpected scores below). However, the
majority clearly could perceive differences between the various
speakers, and were able to rate them accordingly.

In the calculation of 'positive' or 'negative' response I
decided that to follow Labov in including the 'equal' evaluations
(rating a particular sentence with a concentration of a variable
at the same level as the 'zero' sentence read by the same speaker)
either with the 'lower' or with the 'higher' in particular cases
would give a distorted picture of the proportion of informants reacting either positively or negatively. Thus, whereas for Labov,
figures such as

Higher	Equal	Lower		
18	34	30	=	78% negative response to (oh)
and 15	19	50	=	82% " " " "

I experimented with several other methods of calculation in order
to find what seemed intuitively to be the most reasonable result[175].
Finally I decided on the 'common sense' solution of simply taking
the number of 'lower' (as percentage of the total) as indicating
the degree of negative response, and so on. Thus:

2	6	14	=	64% negative (^{14}/22)
2	2	11	=	73%
0	2	1	=	33%, and so forth.

175 Other possibilities examined were, for instance, a) negative =
'lower minus higher as percentage of total' e.g. 2 6 14 = (14 - 2)/
22 = 55%; 4 2 10 = 38% etc: the results seem intuitively to be
too low; b) negative = 'lower minus higher as percentage of changed
opinions' e.g. 2 6 14 = (14 - 2)/16 = 75%; 4 2 10 = 43% etc; this
is worse, the first seeming too high, and the second too low.

Admittedly, this method gives no special weight to those who react
'positively' when the general movement is negative: they are essentially lumped along with the 'equal'.   But I do not feel this is
too unreasonable, since when examined in detail these often turn out
to be informants who generally performed erratically and gave other
indications that they were just guessing.

Having carried out this experiment, I feel that it had certain
defects which I would seek to remedy were I to repeat it.   Firstly,
the use of 'occupational labels' for the five grades I employed was
intended to assist informants; in the event I think it would have
been better simply to use letters or numbers referring to a scale of
'good speech' (though this would be measuring a different sort of
reaction, of course).   Some informants, in spite of my explanations,
seemed to think they were required to guess which of these jobs the
speaker actually had; others became confused because they thought
of some workmen they had known who spoke better than some 'bosses',
or some teacher 'who sounded just like that'; and so on.

Secondly, like Labov, I used just five speakers; all were
males of my acquaintance, recorded while I was trying out my survey
questionnaire.   Though they were of a fairly representative range
in terms of occupation, education, and income groups, and though
they used differing variants of the variables, which was supposedly
the most important thing, yet they seemed to be too easily recognisable.   This may not be too important - strong reactions to certain
variables can still show up - but I noticed a tendency among some
informants to grade consistently at a certain level a voice which
they recognised.   Possibly the most serious aspect of this was that
one speaker stood out from the rest, firstly, because the others
were all more or less of an age, whereas he was a good deal younger;
and secondly because the others had a more 'regional' general voice
quality, whereas his was fairly neutral (he was more or less an RP
speaker).   The consequences of this will become clear below.

Thirdly, the attempt to produce a passage composed of paragraphs which contained concentrations of ten different variables
resulted in a rather unlikely and artificial dialogue, which may
have had an effect both on the naturalness of the speech used, and
on the responses of my informants.

Since it was obviously impossible to examine more than a few
variables in this experiment, I chose the following: the inventory
variables (h) and (ʌ), the distribution variables (-ow) and (-nch),
the realisation variables (ɑ:), (əʊ) and (-t), and the incidence

variables (ook), (ɑ:/æ), and (ing). The passage used was not one
that figures in the interview (more of the sample would probably have
noticed the concentration of variables had they seen the passage in
writing). It was as follows:

a) While I was in the street today, I listened to a conversation
    between two men. Obviously, they were on a job of crime, but
    began to fall out. The first said:

b) "We can do the French teacher's place easy. We stand on that
    bench outside the ventilator that's fifteen inches across; I'll
    wrench it off, and we can climb in and pinch the pictures. It'll
    be a cinch!"

c) His friend said: "The cook might be in. I took a quick look
    yesterday, and I'm not sure. An apron was on the hook, and a
    recipe book was there on the table".

d) The first laughed. "It was a plant! The crafty devil likes
    his brass. That's a trick from France to lead us down the
    path. You can't ask me to pass over a chance like this; we've
    got to grasp it, and fast!"

e) "Well, that fellow will be worse than the widow you tried to
    follow last week. And she soon had you out of the window, you
    yellow fool!"

f) "Get off! But a lot of good you were, for that matter. You
    set off like a petrol bomb. A kid could do better. I've got
    a fine mate!"

g) "And you used half an hour to start that parked car we nicked -
    I can't see a quicker way to be marched off to the Yard by the
    long arm of the law!"

h) "If that bloke will hold my coat, I'll let you know what's
    what, you old idiot. I'll go for you, and throw you through
    that open door into the cold store".

i) "Come on, then, and I'll rub your face in the muck in that
    puddle. I'll chuck you under a bus, you stupid lump - unless
    you run away first". And he jumped on the other one.

j) Then a policeman came dashing towards them, puffing and panting.
    Sweat was streaming down, and he was shouting and calling for
    assistance. The men stopped fighting and ran.

k) "Who heard them?" he said. He had a hope! How many people

have time to help the police?   However, I had seen them, and
heard them, and could tell him that the bigger man was Harry
Holmes.

The five speakers, and the general reactions to them

Speaker 1 had spent his life in Bradford, except for several
spells of a year or so working elsewhere.   He had attended a grammar school, and had a job of moderate responsibility: head of the
show-card printing department at Bradford's best department store.
His income was fairly low; he lived in a private terrace-house with
medium standards of comfort.   By the method of social class grading
adopted for my survey he would be Class IV. He was about 60.

Speaker 2 was a native of the North Midlands, but had also
lived some years in the South and was virtually an RP speaker.   He
was an Oxford graduate, and had worked as a University lecturer and
in a responsible position with the British Council.   His income,
since he was only in his early 30s, was not yet high, but he lived
in a private detached house with good standards, and would be rated
as Class I.

Speaker 3 had lived and worked within a few miles of Bradford
all his life.   He had been to grammar school and he was a skilled
fitter, who had held jobs of moderate supervisory responsibility
in the textile trade before starting up a small business employing
a number of workers (mainly women) and dealing with balling and
packing wool.   He had a fairly good income and lived in a private
terrace-house with medium standards of comfort.   He would be scored
as Class III.   He was about 60.

Speaker 4 grew up about seven miles from Bradford, and attended Leeds University on a scholarship (he held the degrees of BSc
and MEd).   He had taught in several places in the North, lastly
Huddersfield, before taking over a fair-sized factory in which his
father had risen to the top.   He was one of the 'top people' in
the village community where he had grown up and to which he had
returned to live and work.   He had a high income and lived in a
large private detached house with good standards of comfort.   His
social class score would place him in Class I.   He was in his late
60s.

Speaker 5 had always lived and worked in or near Bradford.
He had had only elementary education, but was a skilled sheet metal
worker.   His income was fairly low, but he lived in a private semi
with medium standards of comfort.   He would be scored as Class IV,
and was in his mid-60s.

The above are the 'social characteristics' of the five speakers
whose voices were heard at various times during the experiment. But
of course the informants knew nothing at all of this, and judged
them solely according to their 'linguistic characteristics'.   So
we must outline these briefly - both in general terms and in their
performance on the 'zero' sentence (a), the reactions to which we
shall be examining in this section.   It should be noted that the
'zero' sentence, though not containing any examples of the ten variables concentrated in the following sentences, does contain the
following features, which we have also seen to be variables in this
area: two or three instances of (eɪ), one each of (aɪ), (aʊ), (they),
and two of (I).

Speaker 1 had some obvious regionalisms in his speech, but in
the zero sentence the only points that seem likely to have been
possible 'clues' (apart from his general voice-quality, which does
not strike me as so markedly Yorkshire as many others) were his
[e·ɪ] in *day*, [e:] in *conversation* and less noticeably in *they*, and
[ɑ·ɪ] in *crime*.

Speaker 2 had an 'educated' and regionally neutral voice quality, and his pronunciation throughout would almost certainly qual-
ify as RP.   More informants remarked that they recognised his
voice recurring than with any of the others, and several made comments such as 'from the South'; 'a definitely Southern accent';
'college' or 'talks educated'; 'has authority'.

Speaker 3 read the passage very clearly and 'deliberately', and
this fact seems to have impressed some informants, particularly
lower on the social scale: they graded him fairly highly, with
comments such as 'carefully spoken', 'precise and punctuated'.   On
the other hand his obviously Yorkshire voice-quality was remarked
on: 'broad but well spoken' - and some (particularly higher on
the scale) thought he was trying to speak better than he normally
would: '(e) or (d) trying to speak properly', 'shopkeeper putting
it on'.   Several thought they recognised his voice: two each as
Vic Feather and Hugh Scanlon (prominent Trade Union figures at that
time), and one as 'that chap who does "The Countryside in Autumn"'.
In the zero section his [e:] in *conversation*, *day*, and *they* was
marked.

Speaker 4, 'in spite of' his social standing, habitually speaks
a sort of 'semi-dialect'.   It is possible that he has always done
so; on the other hand it seems quite likely that he would have
modified his speech during his years as a teacher but returned to
'village-type' later.   He was described by one informant as having
'a natural Yorkshire voice', and was thought by another to be 'a
Yorkshire actor I've seen on TV'. another made the interesting
remark that 'it's difficult to say what they are when they're quite

old'.   He read the whole passage very naturally, though perhaps
'dramatically' in parts;   in the zero sentence he used [e:] in *day*
and *they*, and [ɛɪ] in *conversation*[176].

Speaker 5's speech (except when speaking in church) seems a
very natural working-class Yorkshire, and he was described by informants as 'a local lad', 'just Yorkshire - could be a lot of jobs'
and so on.   He read the whole passage naturally, and in the zero
sentence had [a] for one *I*, [e:] in *day* and *they*, [ɛɪ] in *conversation*, and [ɑ·ɪ] in *crime*.

The numbers of informants grouping Speakers 1 - 5 in the various
'occupational slots' (a) - (e) according to their performance in the
zero sentence was as follows:

occ. slot	a	b	c	d	e	Average (a = 5 etc.)	Men	Women
speaker								
1		10	29	39	12	2.41	2.49	2.31
2	21	40	29			3.91	3.94	3.86
3	3	2	9	39	40	1.81	1.76	1.86
4		1	6	41	44	1.61	1.53	1.71
5		3	6	36	46	1.63	1.76	1.48

(Note that the total number of judgements in respect of a speaker is
not always 93 (the number of informants taking part in the experiment) since there were usually one or two 'don't knows'.)

This table gives the ratings of all informants;   when they are
subdivided according to the various factors that have been found in
earlier chapters to relate to either judgements or performances -
sex, class, age, town - few differences are seen.   Probably the
most interesting picture to emerge is that seen in Figure 40, which
shows the average judgements of the five speakers by members of the
different social classes.   (Class I is of course too small to
yield reliable results, but it is interesting to note that, except
in one case where the elderly member had some doubts, their judgements 'fit' with those of the larger classes.)

---

176 He also seemed to substitute an 'r-like' sound for [l] in
fall out - a feature I have noticed in a few Bradfordians.

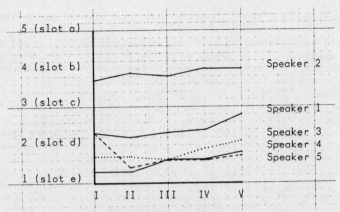

Figure 40:   Average judgements - by Class

The following conclusions seem possible.   First, the table
for the total judgements on each speaker shows obvious 'clusterings';
there is a considerable degree of consistency in the way subjects
rate a certain speaker according to his 'voice' and general pronunciation (that it was in terms of these rather than the few more
regional features noted that judgements were made seems likely in
view of the fact that Speaker 1 was rated higher than Speakers 3 - 4,
though he did produce a number of regional variants).

Second, there is, as Figure 40 shows, also a remarkable consistency of judgement between members of different social classes.
But it may be noted that Class III (the 'borderline' group in many
ways between the 'definitely middle' and 'definitely working' classes)
lumped together as 'definitely working' the three informants with a
markedly Yorkshire tone of voice, while there was some tendency
among Classes IV and V to judge these (and also Speaker 1, who was
'Yorkshire but less so') more generously.

Third, these judgements of a person's probable status, formed
on the basis of his speech in the absence of all other clues, may
be wildly at odds with his actual status.   While those of Speakers
1 and 2 are reasonably 'correct', those of 3 and 4 are well out -
indeed those of Speaker 4 (Class I) place him on almost exactly the
same level as Speaker 5 (Class IV); and in fact both of these speakers are rated low even in terms of the latter's actual status. Speech
is then employed as a clue- but it is an 'unreliable' one.

Fourth, as noted above, the noticeably 'Yorkshire' voices were
ranked low, and the RP one was rated high.   This could be taken as
indicating some subconscious 'uneasiness' among Yorkshire people:

Appendix D shows that generally they feel pride in being 'Yorkshire', and the earlier sections of this chapter seem to indicate that in general they profess to like the local form of English and to feel some antagonism or at least indifference for RP - yet they make the judgements shown here.   The uneasiness felt by those who realised they were doing this appeared in incidental remarks such as the following: 'Accent is the main thing, I'm ashamed to say'; 'I'm finding this very difficult...just because they're talking broad, I'm putting them as labourers...I mean to say...you could get a personnel officer talking broad...and not all labourers talk broad ...'; 'I bet they'd say I was a labourer'; 'One sounded South, so I decided not to give him a better job just because of that - but then I found I did give him b) or c), while all the rest were d) or e)'.   Several other informants revealed their unease by remarks suggesting that perhaps the speakers were really 'better' but were 'putting it on': 'You could be fooling me...'; 'Are any of them taking people off?'; 'Are they really people that are educated but speaking dialect?'

Reactions to concentrations of variables

The Variable (h)

Three of the five speakers were heard reading sentence k), which contained 13 possible examples of the variable (h).   Speaker 3 had [h] in the words *who*, *hope*, *help*, *had* and *Harry*, and [ø] in the remainder; he also had regional variants in the two words containing the extraneous variable (əʊ), but his form of (aɪ) was not markedly regional.   Speaker 2 pronounced [h] in all cases, and his variants of other variables were RP.   Speaker 5 only had three [h]: in *hope*, *help* and *heard*; however he reduced the words *had* and *him* to weak forms where [h] would not be expected; he also had local variants in the two (əʊ) words.

Reactions to the three speakers, as compared to the zero sentence were:

Speaker	Higher	Equal	Lower	(h)
3	25	38	29	$^5/15$ = [h]
2	38	39	16	All [h]
5	21	38	32	$^3/13$ = [h]

Response to speaker 3 was predominantly neutral, 41% of informants
rating him 'equal', and only slightly more than half of the remainder marking 'lower'.   He was of course ranked quite low to start
with, so some of the 'equal' could have been negative reactions.
As one incidental remark observed "he pronounced some [h] and missed
some": this was from a Class V speaker, and indicates that his (h)-
performance was clearly noticeable.   The 'higher'/'lower' responses
show an interesting relation to social class (leaving out the too
small Class I), and to sex:

	II	III	IV	V	M	W
higher	15%	14	39	40	31%	22
lower	45	36	33	7	33	29

Figures for the age-groups from 30-plus upwards are quite erratic,
but the two youngest groups show a more clearly negative response:
20-plus 27 higher/45 lower;   10-plus 17/50.

Response to Speaker 2 was 41% 'higher' and 42% 'equal', which
probably indicates a positive reaction to his performance on (h),
since in view of his high initial ranking some of the 'equal' may
well be so interpreted.   Percentage figures for 'higher'/'lower'
ratings by class and sex were:

	II	III	IV	V	M	W
higher	62	46	32	40	39	43
lower	0	14	21	27	24	14

With Speaker 5 responses are almost certainly indicative of a
negative reaction: though 42% rated his performance 'equal' with
that on the zero section , some of these are probably negative, since
their initial rating was low and the majority of the remainder scored
him 'lower'.   In this case no pattern at all is discernible in the
class or sex figures for 'higher'/'lower'.   Several informants
remarked on this speaker's h-dropping.

The following conclusions seem possible.   First, there is
evidence, from the reactions to Speaker 2, of a generally 'positive'
response to the consistent use of [h], and from those to Speaker 5
and to a lesser extent to Speaker 3, of a 'negative' response to
h-dropping.   Second, the negative reactions to Speaker 3 and the
positive reactions to Speaker 2 fall from a high point in Class II,
whereas the opposite reactions start low and rise toward the lower

end of the scale.   This would seem to indicate a greater awareness of [h] as a prestige form among the Middle Class, becoming less
lower on the class hierarchy.   Third, women show a greater degree
of positive over negative response to [h] and negative over positive
response to [ø] than do men.

These findings generally confirm those reported in Chapter 6
and Chapter 7 ii , which suggest that RP-like [h]-use is taking over
as 'standard" from the traditional [ø], there being a greater degree
of [h]-use with higher position on the social hierarchy, and among
all classes with increasing carefulness of style, and the great
majority of informants claiming to pronounce [h] whether they do so
or not.

The Variable (ʌ)

Sentence i) was read by three speakers: it contained 13 possible instances of (ʌ).   Speaker 1 had in about half the words in
question something that was phonetically neither definitely [ʌ] nor
definitely [ʊ], but in *chuck*, *muck*, *puddle*, *but*, *run*, *other*, *one*
he clearly used [ʊ];   on the extraneous variable (eɪ) he used variants not markedly regional.   Speaker 2 read in a consistently RP
manner.   Speaker 3 clearly had [ʊ] in all (ʌ) words, and also used
[e:] in *away* and *face*, and pronounced *stupid* as [stu:pɪd].

Reactions as compared to the zero sentence were:

Speaker	Higher	Equal	Lower	(ʌ)
1	16	22	54	inconsistent
2	28	38	27	All [ʌ]
3	18	33	42	All [ʊ]

The response to Speaker 1 was clearly predominantly negative, as
was also that to Speaker 3.   The probable reason for the latter
seeming at first sight to produce less negative reaction in spite
of his greater use of markedly regional variants is that he was
rated lower than the former on the zero section and therefore a
higher proportion of those rating 'equal' could really be negative
because they could get no lower.   The relation of this negative
response to social class is not clear:

	II	III	IV	V	M	W
1 - 'lower'	54	56	59	73	57	61
3 - 'lower'	54	50	35	47	43	48

A clear pattern is lacking; a possible explanation for the greater
negative response in Classes IV - V to Speaker 1 over Speaker 3
could be that he spoke first - and at various times during this experiment incidental remarks by members of these classes suggested
that their judgements were influenced by the content: the zero
sentence was neutral, this one was threatening and coarse, and
Class V had earlier rated this speaker higher than the other classes;
but by the time Speaker 3 was heard it was obvious that he was just
repeating a set passage.   The figures for sex show women to be
slightly more 'ʊ-negative' than men.

Response to Speaker 2 was almost exactly equal overall, though
the fact of his high initial rating could mean that some of the
'equal' were reacting positively - though we saw with (h) that a
definitely positive response will show up.   No clear patterns are
apparent in the responses of the classes; but surprisingly men
(35%) showed more positive reaction than women (24%).   Incidental
remarks (such as "He must be higher - he said [mək] instead of
[mʊk]") indicate that some informants were consciously responding
to this speaker's (ʌ)-performance.

My conclusions are, first, that it appears that it is more the
case that regional [ʊ] has negative prestige than that RP-like [ʌ]
is positively prestigious.   Second the fact that more women react
negatively to [ʊ] could indicate a greater awareness of the 'substandard' nature of this on their part.   (No explanation is obvious
for the more ʌ-positive response by men).   Third, the comparison
between responses to (ʌ) and (h) reinforces earlier findings: the
use of [h] is a more obviously 'stratifying' feature than that of [ʌ],
which is a minority phenomenon, though still showing a relation to
social class; claims on the self-evaluation experiment also indicate that [h] is more of a prestige feature than is [ʌ].

The Variable (nch)

We have noted earlier that this is a variable which is unusual
in certain respects; the results of the subjective evaluation experiment on this point are no less unusual.

Two speakers read sentence b), which contained six instances

of (nch): Speaker 1 consistently used the [nʃ] variant, whereas
Speaker 2 produced some clear instances of [ntʃ] (*bench*, *cinch*),
some which I found difficult to decide on (*French*, *wrench*, *pinch*),
and one (*inch*) which seemed clearly [nʃ].   This latter is, in my
experience, a not uncommon situation with an RP speaker.

Reactions as compared to the immediately preceding zero sentence were:

Speaker	Higher	Equal	Lower	(nch)
1	8	34	49	All [nʃ]
2	16	31	46	[ntʃ] ~ [nʃ]

Obviously, negative responses predominate in *both* cases.   But in
view of our earlier findings, that (nch) comes closest of all the
variables examined in detail to being a case of 'free variation',
and that a considerable number of informants were unable to distinguish the two variants, and that among those who could there
was no clear evidence of any social significance attaching to
either variant, it seems extraordinary that these results should
betoken a strong negative response both to consistent [nʃ] usage
and to inconsistent or indefinite [ntʃ].   But what other explanation can there be?

The fact that this was the second sentence heard could be
important.   The zero section was 'neutral' in content, while this
sentence portrayed a thief planning a job.   Even later in the experiment there were several reactions such as "He's speaking well,
but I don't think a newsreader/teacher would say that" - in other
words the informant was being influenced by the content in spite of
its being obvious (and my telling him) that the speakers were reading a set passage.   This reaction would presumably be more likely
earlier in the experiment, and could be some explanation for the
downgrading of both speakers in this sentence, and particularly that
of Speaker 2, who had been rated high on the zero section.

The percentage of negative response by class and sex was:

	II	III	IV	V	M	W
1 'lower'	69	63	42	47	49	60
2 'lower'	46	50	56	40	57	40

The pattern of reaction to Speaker 2 is unclear - as might be expected perhaps if the negative response was not to any definite feature.   But that to Speaker 1, with a marked difference between
Classes II and III and Classes IV and V, and with women more negative than men, suggests that something of social significance *is*
involved.

Important here could be the extraneous variables in this sentence.   Speaker 2 had RP-like forms throughout, but Speaker 1,
though his (eɪ)s,(I) etc. were not markedly regional in this case,
pronounced *climb* with an [ɑ·ɪ] variant and used a glottal stop in
it'll.   We have seen other evidence that the latter is a highly
castigated variant, and the fact that I actually heard a few informants shudder or catch their breath at this point reinforces my
feeling that the very negative response to Speaker 1's reading of
this sentence was probably directed primarily to the glottal stop
rather than his performance on (nch), which has been seen to pro-
voke little such reaction when investigated in other ways.

My conclusions are, that though at first sight indicative of
a negative response to the [nʃ] variant and even to inconsistent
[ntʃ], further examination of the facts, particularly in relation
to previous findings in respect of (nch), suggests that this is
not the case.   Content and extraneous variables may be as important as some concentrated variables in producing reaction among subjects, and this should be borne in mind when designing experiments
of this type.

The Variable (-ow)

Three speakers read sentence e), which contained five instances
of this variable: Speaker 1 used the [ə] variant throughout (and,
as far as the several extraneous variables were concerned, used the
Northern [a] in *last*); Speaker 3 had [ə] in three words but [o·ʊ]
in *window* and *widow* (he also dropped [h] in *had*, and used a markedly
regional pronunciation of *last*); Speaker 2 used RP throughout.

Reactions in comparison to the zero sentence gradings were:

Speaker	Higher	Equal	Lower	(-ow)
1	7	30	53	All [ə]
3	29	37	25	2/5 [o·ʊ]
2	31	44	25	All [əʊ]

Response to Speaker 1 was obviously largely negative, with 59% of
informants downgrading him; and the fact that his performance on
(-ow) was the most obviously non-standard feature of this passage
makes it seem likely that it was his [ə] variants which were being
thus castigated. The relation of this negative reaction to class
and sex is seen in the following percentage figures:

	II	III	IV	V
M	33	73	53	60
W	83	65	57	50
Total	58	68	55	57

It will be seen that women present a more regularly-stratified pattern of negative response than men, whose reactions appear somewhat
erratic.

Though response to Speaker 3 was predominantly neutral, with
41% grading him 'equal' to the zero sentence, the figures for those
rating him 'higher' and 'lower' are interesting:

	II	III	IV	V	M	W
3 'higher'	15	30	42	33	32	32
3 'lower'	31	26	27	27	24	32

While negative reactions are fairly evenly distributed among the
social classes, there is a greater tendency to 'upgrade' this speaker
lower down the scale. If we examine the graph for class-responses
to this speaker on the zero sentence (Figure 40), it appears that
his rating 'rises' from Classes II - III to IV and V: it is then
possible that there was in fact more negative response in Classes
II - III than appears here - since they had rated him low initially
this would appear as 'equal'. Two informants spontaneously remarked
on this speaker's use of (əʊ) in *window*: it is therefore possible
that the lower classes were 'rewarding' him for such of these variants as he did employ. Between the sexes, as with the previous
speaker, women showed more negative reaction overall than did men.

With Speaker 2, using [əʊ] variants consistently, reaction is
also mainly neutral (44% rating him equal), though 'higher' ratings
(31%) slightly outweigh 'lower' (25%), and since this speaker was
rated high to start with it is possible that response is more positive than appears. Figures for higher/lower show no obvious correlations:

	II	III	IV	V	M	W
2 'higher'	38	25	35	20	29	33
2 'lower'	23	21	18	53	24	26

My conclusions are as follows.   The clearly negative response to
Speaker 1 seems to indicate that the [ə] variant is a stigmatised
form, thus confirming the findings reported earlier.   It is possible that the pattern of response to the inconsistent (əʊ) of
Speaker 3 points the same way.   However, though the [ə] variant is
stigmatised, there is no definite evidence that the RP-like variant
is a prestige one, since reaction to the consistent use of it was
largely neutral (contrast this with reaction to the 'long A' below);
it seems simply to have taken over from the traditional form as the
'standard of correctness'.

The Variable (-t-)

Earlier findings have indicated that the use of a [2] variant
of /t/ is a highly stigmatised feature;   it is perhaps not surprising therefore to report that none of the five speakers used in the
subjective evaluation experiment produced a single example of [2] in
the sentence where /t/ in appropriate environments was concentrated
(though I know that one at least used a fair amount of [2] in
everyday speech).   However, it is possible to use the recordings
to examine reaction to the older non-standard variant of word-final
prevocalic /t/:   [r] (see p.151).

Three speakers read sentence f), which contained five instances of (Vt#V), as well as two (VtV) and one (VtL).   Speaker 5 produced one [r] variant, in *but a*;   Speaker 4 had two, in *get off* and
got a;   and Speaker 1 had none

Responses to these three speakers were as follows:

Speaker	Higher	Equal	Lower	(t)
5	7	50	34	1 [r]
4	6	43	43	2 [r]
1	23	35	34	All [t]

Speaker 5 was ranked low to start with, so although the majority of informants rated his performance here equal to that on the
zero passage, 37% marked him lower as compared to only 8% higher,
which suggests that probably many of the 'equal' could be interpreted as negative reactions too (since they were unable to mark him
lower than they had done initially).

The same sort of reasoning may be applied in the case of Speaker
4, who was rated equal lowest with Speaker 5 on the zero sentence;
in his case the actual 'movements' of opinion are also more markedly
negative.

With these two speakers it might appear reasonable to assume
that the negative reactions recorded are in response to the non-
standard variants of /t/, the greater such response coming to the
speaker who used more such variants.   But it should be noted
firstly, that the patterns of class and sex difference in such negative response are unclear:

	II	III	IV	V	M	W
5 'lower'	38	25	38	47	45	29
4 'lower'	38	50	45	47	45	49

and secondly, that Speaker 1, who used no such variants, also attracted a slightly negative response on this sentence: 37% marking
him lower than on the zero sentence (25% higher, 38% equal).

The explanation could lie in the extraneous variables involved
in this sentence, the most important being (eɪ) in the final word
mate. All three informants read this with the local variant [e:],
and as the last word of the sentence this could have affected the
judgements of hearers. It must then be admitted that the negative
response recorded with all three speakers may have been due to their
performance on this (eɪ) variable rather than that on (t), particularly since, in spite of there being numerous instances of the
latter, very few non-standard variants were heard.

However, for two reasons I do not think it likely that this is
entirely the case. First, although Speaker 1 was rated much higher
than Speakers 4 and 5 initially, the overall negative response to
his version of this sentence was considerably less, in spite of there
being less scope for negative response to the initially low-rated
Speakers 4 and 5 (and 25% rated him higher than on the zero section).
Second, several informants visibly and audibly reacted, especially
to Speaker 4, on hearing the [r] variant long before the word *mate*
was reached.

My conclusions are, first, that it has not been possible to measure subjective reaction to the glottal stop in this sentence, presumably because it was 'repressed' through being a stigmatised form, as earlier findings indicated (but we may note the 'accidental' [ʔ] under (nch) above).   Second, that there is some evidence to suggest that the older non-standard variant [r] is also stigmatised.   And finally, the problem of 'extraneous variables' in this type of experiment has been emphasised.

The Variable (ɑ:)

Two speakers read sentence g), which contained eight examples of the (ɑ:) variable.   Speaker 3 consistently used markedly front variants, close to [a:]; it may also be relevant that, as far as extraneous variables are concerned, he dropped [h] in *half* and used [e·ᶦ] in *way*.   Speaker 2 employed much backer variants of (ɑ:) and his speech throughout this sentence could pass for RP.

Responses to these readings in comparison to the zero sentence were:

Speaker	Higher	Equal	Lower	(ɑ:)
3	31	37	23	All [a:]
2	43	38	11	All [ɑ:]

Reaction to Speaker 3 was predominantly neutral, with 41% marking his performance equal to that on the zero sentence.   The following percentages in class or sex groups registered changes of rating:

	II	III	IV	V	M	W
Higher	23	29	42	43	40	27
Lower	15	29	27	21	16	37

Among the social classes, no clear pattern shows up in the negative reactions, but positive response increases down the scale.   The sexes are noticeably different, men being markedly more positive, women negative.

Reaction to Speaker 2, who used backer variants, was clearly positive, with 47% marking him higher than on the zero section - and

of course the positive response could really be higher than this,
since he was rated high initially and some of the 'equal' could be
so interpreted.   Class and sex distribution of positive response
was:

	II	III	IV	V	M	W
Higher	31	52	53	40	41	54

(If 'Equal' were included with 'Higher' the figures would be: II 92,
III 93, IV 85, V 80; M 81,W 93).

My conclusions are as follows.   We saw in Chapter 6 some evidence of a relation between frontness of /ɑ:/ and social class -
the greater proportions of [a:/a:⊦] coming towards the lower end of
the scale, and also that women tend to use fewer front variants
than men.   Chapter 7 ii showed that informants' self-evaluations
in this respect followed a similar pattern, and that they were generally accurate: there was little evidence of such over-reporting
of [ɑ:] as would suggest that [a:] had negative prestige or [ɑ:] much
positive prestige.   Response to Speaker 3 on the present experiment tends to confirm that [a:] is not particularly stigmatised,
though women do show some tendency to reject it.   The rise in positive response down the social scale to this speaker may confirm
that [a:] variants are increasingly readily acceptable in these
classes.   However, the noticeably positive response to Speaker 2
seems to suggest that, though [a:] may not be stigmatised there is
some prestige attaching to [ɑ:], more particularly among women.
In this respect our previous findings are not entirely supported.

The Variable (əʊ)

We have seen that in this phonetic area there are differences
between the speech of West Yorkshire and RP in both inventory and
realisation.   Here we examine informants' unconscious reactions to
a concentration of words with RP/əʊ/, but it is not possible to say
with certainty whether non-standard pronunciations are judged because of both of these factors or only because of their 'sound'.

Three speakers read sentence h), which contained 3 '/ɔʊ/ words
hold, old, cold; 4 '/o:/ words': *bloke, coat, go, open*, and 2 words
of the 'ow' set which historically are /ɔ:/ rather than /ɔʊ/ but
which today may be heard with either /o:/ or /ɔʊ/: *know , throw*.
Speaker 5 pronounced the sentence with 5 [ɔʊ] and 4 [o:]; he also

had regional variants for the extraneous variable (ʊə) in *door* [doə],
and *store* [stʊə].   Speaker 3 read with the same variants, but since
he read throughout the passage with great care and clarity, the regional pronunciation was more clearly perceptible in each case.
Speaker 2 read the sentence with an RP pronunciation.

Responses as compared to the zero sentence were as follows:

Speaker	Higher	Equal	Lower	(əʊ)
5	6	36	48	5 [ɔʊ], 4 [o:]
3	19	38	35	"
2	29	33	30	All [əʊ]

The response to Speaker 5 shows that, even when a speaker has been
rated low to begin with, a definitely negative reaction will show
up: 53% marked him down on this sentence, and since some of the
'equal' could be negative responses in view of his low start, it
certainly looks as if the concentration of regional forms of (əʊ)
has produced a decided reaction.

But in view of this the response to Speaker 3 is somewhat surprising: the largest number (42%) marked him 'equal' and only 38%
'lower' (compared to 40% and 53% with Speaker 5); even counting
'equal' and 'lower' together (this speaker too was ranked quite low
initially) would not produce as great a negative reaction as with
Speaker 5 - and yet the regional variants were even more clearly
marked.   The percentage figures for class and sex do not show any
obvious explanation:

	II	III	IV	V	M	W
5 'lower'	46	39	58	67	65	39
3 'lower'	62	32	33	47	34	43

One can speculate about particular details: for example it is possible that the sex figures for Speaker 3 show that women are more
negative about regional variants, but that because they rated Speaker 5 low to start with this cannot show up (though it would if
'equal' and 'lower' were totalled M: 4-13-32/W: 2-23-16); or that
Class V shows unexpectedly high negative response either because
they 'condemn' what they themselves are particularly 'guilty' of
(one of Labov's conclusions from his experiment), or because their
initial rating of this speaker was higher and so left more room for

lowering.   But I suspect this would be clutching at straws to preserve the notion that this experiment *only* measures response to the
particular concentrated variable.   This is of course unlikely, and
it could well be that here the lower negative response to Speaker 3,
in spite of his most obvious regionalism, is due to some such factor
as his greater clarity as compared to Speaker 5:   this was remarked
on spontaneously from time to time, and surely comparison with rec-
ently-heard readings must sometimes affect judgements - though this
has largely been ignored in the interpretation of this experiment.

Response to Speaker 2 appears to have been almost entirely
neutral, with more or less equal numbers marking his performance
'higher/equal/lower' as compared to his initial ranking.   No clear
patterns of positive or negative response emerge from the more detailed figures for class and sex.

Few conclusions can be drawn here.   Reaction to the regional
variants of Speakers 5 and 3 on the one hand, and the RP pronunciation of Speaker 2 on the other, suggest that it is the former which
attracts negative response rather than the latter which is particularly prestigious.   But earlier findings concerning performance
and conscious judgement of variants (where it was seen that though
there is some class stratification, particularly between the middle
and working classes, use of regional variants is high and is readily owned to be so) did *not* suggest the degree of 'negative prestige' in respect of regional forms of (əʊ) that these subconscious
reactions appear to indicate.   However, comparison between the
responses to Speakers 5 and 3 reduce the level of confidence we can
have in experiments of this sort as measuring response only to particular variants.

The Variable (ɑ:/æ)

Two speakers read sentence d) which contained 11 examples of
(ɑ:/æ):   Speaker 3 read all the words in question with a form of
/æ/:[a], and also had regional variants of a number of extraneous
variables - [a:] in *can't*, [o:] in *over*, [ʊz] for *us*, and [ɪz] for
his (his careful reading style meant that weak forms of these last
two would not be expected);   Speaker 2 had the RP [ɑ:] in all the
(ɑ:/æ) words, and RP variants in all other cases too.

Responses in comparison to the zero sentence were:

Speaker	Higher	Equal	Lower	(ɑ:/æ)
3	33	37	23	All [a]
2	42	30	19	All [ɑ:]

Reaction to Speaker 3 was largely neutral, with 40% rating his performance 'equal'; of the remainder, more marked him up than down, so there is no sign of the [a] pronunciation being stigmatised in any way.   Class and sex percentages were:

	II	III	IV	V	M	W
3 'higher'	23	36	35	47	39	31
3 'lower'	23	16	24	33	22	29

Earlier findings suggest that the short-vowel pronunciation is so much of a 'standard' in this area that it would perhaps not even be noticed.   It is possible therefore that what is being measured here is response to Speaker 3 in general (who was here being heard for the first time since the zero section) by comparison with the last few voices heard - and it may be that the more positive response among the working classes and men in particular is due to his clear manly voice (which was remarked on several times).

With Speaker 2 we find that, in spite of the overtly hostile reactions expressed by some informants to the 'long A' (see p.286), there is a predominantly positive response with 46% marking him 'higher'; and probably some of the 'equal' could be so interpreted since he was ranked so high to start with.   This response was fairly general throughout the population, and only slightly more marked among women:

	II	III	IV	V	M	W
2 'higher'	42	43	44	50	45	48

It appears then that there is quite a degree of subconscious 'respect' for a speaker using the /ɑ:/ form.

But certainly not all the response to this feature was subconscious: more informants made spontaneous comments on hearing this particular reading than with any other, though not all made such specific remarks as "One of these here [bɑ:θ] chaps".   There are interesting signs of some correlation with social class in these

comments: informants in Classes I and II sounded generally unimpressed
- five of them said that he sounded artificial or affected or 'trying to be better than he was'; a sixth commented "I suppose he
could be a personnel officer, but *I* wouldn't like to work with him
or for him"; those in Class III were more neutral - only three
commented, remarking on his 'Southern' or 'long A' pronunciation;
those in Classes IV and V were the most impressed - eight of them
said something to the effect that he was 'college', 'collar and tie',
or 'top notch', and four of these specifically mentioned his 'Long A'
as the reason for this.

We may conclude that the regional short-vowel pronunciation
provokes no reaction: it is accepted as normal (this confirms our
findings with regard to performance and self-evaluation). However, the RP-like 'long A' is a prestige pronunciation, and in this
respect our findings are somewhat contrary to those reported earlier.
And yet again there is some suggestion, in the response to Speaker 3,
that this sort of experiment does not just measure reaction to the
concentrated variable.

The Variable (ook)

Three speakers read sentence c) which contained five instances
of (ook). Speaker 5 had [u:k] throughout; Speaker 1 had [ʊk] in
hook but [u:k] in the other four words. Also, both these speakers
had [e:] variants in the two words *apron* and *table* with the extraneous variable (eɪ). Speaker 2 read the sentence in an RP manner
throughout.

Responses in comparison to the zero ratings were:

Speaker	Higher	Equal	Lower	(ook)
5	13	42	34	All [u:k]
1	22	28	42	1 [ʊk], 4 [u:k]
2	39	32	22	All [ʊk]

Reaction to Speaker 5 was 47% 'equal'; but the 38% 'lower' makes it
likely that this chould be interpreted as a predominantly negative
response since this speaker had been rated low to start with and the
'equal' could in many cases get no lower. This seems the more
likely when we see the response to Speaker 1: even though he used

one fewer [u:k], his initial rating left more room for a negative
reaction to show up in a 'lower' grading. The class and sex distribution of negative response in percentage figures were:

	II	III	IV	V	M	W
5 'lower'	23	32	47	31	49	26
1 'lower'	54	57	38	40	47	45

With Speaker 5 Classes III - V had somewhat more scope for downgrading than II, and men more than women, so the figures for Speaker 1
are probably a clearer indication of reactions, all groups having
rated this speaker initially at such a level as gave room for reg-
istering a negative response. Here we see that such a reaction to
the [u:k] variant is more common in Classes II - III, but that
there is little difference between the sexes.

Response to Speaker 2 was markedly positive, with 42% uprating
him over his performance on the zero sentence - in spite of his
high initial rating which could mean that some of the 'equal' can
be taken to indicate positive response also.   There is no clear
pattern in the distribution of this favourable response over the
social classes, but it is more marked among women than men:

	II	III	IV	V	M	W
2 'higher'	38	36	53	33	37	48

Reference to age groups has hardly been made in this section,
since rarely had any trend shown up in my trial graphs; but since
(ook) seemed to have definite relations to age as far as performance
was concerned, it might be useful to examine this factor in relation to the apparently negative response to [u:k] and positive one
to [ʊk]:

	10	20	30	40	50	60	70
1 'lower'	58	57	54	27	44	50	15
2 'higher'	42	36	25	36	56	52	54

Though there are obvious irregularities in each case, there seems to
be generally more negative feeling about [u:k] in the below-40 groups,
and perhaps more 'respect' for [ʊk] in the 50s and over (though it
should be noted that the highest initial ratings were by the 10-plus
and 30-plus groups so they had less room for positive response).

The (ook) variable presented an unusual picture in terms of both performance and self-evaluation, perhaps because it is definitely involved in linguistic change at present. And generally, the '[u:k]-negative' relations to social class showing up in this experiment confirm our earlier picture - RP-like [ʊk] is more likely to be accepted as 'correct' towards the top of the social scale. '[u:k]-negative' response among the younger half of the population also tends to confirm our previous findings that [ʊk] is the commoner form there; the fact that they may show less '[ʊk]-positive' reaction than the older groups may simply be due to its being 'normal' and therefore neutral as far as they are concerned.

The Variable (ing)

Three speakers read sentence j) which contained 7 instances of (ing):   Speaker 3 used the [ɪŋ] variant in every case, whereas Speaker 1 had [ɪŋ] only in *dashing*, and Speaker 5 had [ɪn] in every instance.   In addition all three used Yorkshire variants of extraneous variables: [e:] in *came*, [ʊ] in *puffing*, [ø] in *He*; to an extent then, other variables were 'held constant' in this case - though Speaker 5 also had [ʔ] in *shouting*.

Responses in comparison to the zero section were:

Speaker	Higher	Equal	Lower	(ing)
3	53	19	20	All [ɪŋ]
1	23	22	48	1 [ɪŋ], 4 [ɪn]
5	16	33	40	All [ɪn]

Reaction to Speaker 3 was more positive than anything so far encountered, with 58% uprating him for his performance on this sentence. The distribution of this response by class and sex was as follows:

	II	III	IV	V	M	W
3 'higher'	46	54	61	73	65	49

Though women had rated this speaker somewhat higher on the zero section and might be less likely to upgrade, the proportion of men doing so is noticeably higher than that of women.   The numbers doing so in the different classes rises from II to V, in spite of the initial ratings by IV and V showing a continuous rise from that by III, so the upgrading is particularly marked.

The reactions to Speakers 1 and 5 were both negative; that to
the former appears more so, but in fact in the latter case many of
the 'equal' are probably to be interpreted as 'lower' since Speaker
5 was rated so low to begin with (this applies particularly to
women, who had less scope to mark this speaker lower).   Class and
sex percentages were:

	II	III	IV	V	M	W
1 'lower'	54	46	53	60	51	52
5 'lower'	23	39	52	50	51	38

Even allowing for differences in initial gradings by the class groups,
there is some indication that '[ɪn]-negative' response increases towards the lower end of the social scale.

'[ɪŋ]-positive' and '[ɪn]-negative' responses increase as we
look down the social scale; earlier findings show a similar increase in the *use* (and acknowledgement) of the non-standard [ɪn]
variant.   We may conclude then that this seems to be an example of
a phenomenon observed by Labov in his similar experiment: that
certain groups tend to 'penalise' what they are themselves 'guilty'
of, and to 'reward' the alternative.   Our earlier findings showed
that the use of the [ɪn] variant is common throughout the population,
and in a sense can hardly be described as 'non-standard'; yet the
reactions noted here, together with the fact that a number remarked
both incidentally during this experiment and at various other stages
in the interviews on 'g-dropping', suggest that there is more awareness of 'right'/'wrong' with this than with many other variables.
It is interesting to recall that we found in the self-evaluation experiment that quite a number of informants (the proportion also
increasing towards the lower end of the social scale) appeared to
be incapable of distinguishing the [ɪŋ] and [ɪn] variants when they
were consciously drawn to their attention; the present experiment
might be taken to suggest that subconsciously they do have some
awareness of the difference, and regard RP-like [ɪŋ] as more correct
than the traditional [ɪn].

*   *   *   *   *   *

At the end of the experiment I asked informants the question
"Now, what do you think you were judging by?"

The majority could only answer in the most general terms: for

example 'by their pronunciation' ('the way they said their words',
'their accent', 'an impression of their education' etc.), or 'by
the tone of voice', which could mean the same thing.   Others were
just slightly more specific, mentioning 'clarity' (10) (and here we
may probably include 'preciseness' (5) and 'laziness' (2));   'speed'
(including 'briskness', 'slowness', etc.) (11); 'confidence' ('authority', 'ease', 'nervousness', 'difficulty' etc.) (9);   'fluency'
('the way they put their words/sentences together') (3);   'naturalness' (4);   'culturedness' ('sounds educated/ignorant' etc.) (8);
'expression' and 'phrasing' (6);   'pitch' (including 'flatness')(3);
and 'broadness' (including 'bluntness' and restricted senses of
'accent') (8).   Of course, this grouping of the more detailed
actual remarks is somewhat arbitrary.

Only a relatively small number referred to specific features:
'h-dropping' (14);   'g-dropping' etc., i.e. [ɪn] (3);   'missing out
t', i.e. [ʔ] (2);   3 referred to 'vowels' in general, and only 4 to
the 'long A' and 1 to [ʊ] for [ʌ] in particular.

Clearly the majority make such judgements about speech without
conscious awareness of any of the detailed features they use as
criteria.

*   *   *   *   *   *

At this point, it is appropriate to draw a number of more general conclusions about the subjective evaluation experiment.   With
regard to the results obtained, some confirmation has been provided
for our earlier findings about certain variants: for example, that
the use of [h] is prestigious and h-dropping is stigmatised - to
varying degrees among different groups in the community;   that certain regional variants may attract some stigma (such as the [ɔʊ/oː]
variants of (əʊ);   the [ə] variant of (-ow);   the glottal stop;   etc.)
without the corresponding non-regional forms being prestigious;
that certain regional variants attract little stigma (for example,
the /æ/ variant of (ɑː/æ);   the [aː] variant of (ɑː));   that age is
important in the case of (ook) which is currently involved in change;
and so on.   On the other hand, there have been certain indications
of prestige or stigma attaching to particular variants that had *not*
shown up earlier: most noticeable here is the subconscious respect
for /ɑː/ in (ɑː/æ) words in spite of what one's conscious reaction
may be;   similarly, though [ɪn] is widespread there was much more
'[ɪŋ]-positive' and '[ɪn]-negative' response than might have been
expected;   and there was more favourable response to the back variant [ɑː] of (ɑː), and unfavourable response to regional forms of
(əʊ) than one had been led to expect.

In respect of the methodology, a number of points should be made, since various problems showed up. First, it is difficult to use this experiment to measure reaction to certain variants. When a variant is particularly stigmatised, it may be difficult to get examples of it in the 'comparative recorded material': for instance, none of my five speakers used a single [2] in the sentence I had intended to show concentrations of such. On the other hand, the occasional inadvertent use of [2] elsewhere is very relevant to the next point.

Second, the problem of extraneous variables is a very considerable one. It is quite impossible to produce a sentence concentrating on a particular variable without drawing in also examples of some other variable features, and it is almost impossible to hold all these constant i.e. always in their RP variant or always in their regional variant - and even if one could, it would not always be certain that informants were responding to the concentrated rather than the extraneous variable. These extraneous variables may be of differing importance: the odd example of a variant that does not attract much prestige or stigma (for example, /æ/ in *last* etc.) among a concentration of glottal stops might be of minimal importance, but one example of the latter in a sentence supposedly concentrating on [nʃ ~ ntʃ] which many informants cannot distinguish, may be crucial; so too may a particularly regional [o:] say in the last word of a sentence concentrating on (ɑ:/æ).

Third, content can be important. There were signs that some informants, in spite of having been told that a set passage was being read by all speakers, were influenced by the feeling that 'a nice person would not say that'. A 'neutral' passage, if such a thing is possible, would be preferable.

Fourth, with what should one compare a particular rating? Labov's method, which I followed, involves comparing the rating of a speaker's performance on a particular concentrated variable with that on the zero sentence: this is to cancel out the effect of underlying preferences for certain voice qualities. But, granting the necessity for this, I am not entirely convinced that the relation between the judgement of one speaker and that of a 'neighbouring' one is so completely irrelevant: hearing a concentration of one particular variant immediately after a concentration of another may surely affect one's judgement of the latter; so may hearing a particular type of voice after one of a different sort, perhaps.

Finally, what should be taken to indicate positive or negative response? Obviously 'higher'/'lower' judgements can reasonably be taken as positive/negative respectively, but what of the 'equal'? We noted that in some cases Labov included these with one of the other categories - with 'lower' in the case of someone rated low to

start with, for instance.   I felt that this could give an exaggerated impression of the degree of positive/negative reaction in some
cases;   and my findings show that a really positive response will
show up, even with Speaker 2 who was rated high initially (see the
findings with (ɑ:), (ɑ:/æ) etc.) and a definitely negative one
even with Speakers 4 or 5, who were rated lowest on the zero section
(see (t), (əʊ) etc.).   But there were a number of occasions where
it seemed very likely that some 'equal' responses to say Speaker 5
would have been 'lower' if it had been possible to get lower (see
(ook), where there was apparently more 'negative' response to
Speaker 1 though Speaker 5 used more regional variants), and it may
be that some more sophisticated method of classifying responses
should be attempted.

CHAPTER EIGHT

CONCLUSIONS[177]

1   TRADITIONAL DIALECT AND THE PRESENT SITUATION

If we assume that, some time ago at least, the majority of the population of the three biggest wool towns spoke dialects with vowel systems such as those outlined in Chapter 5, we may now compare these systems with the situation revealed by my survey of a random sample of the populations in the early 1970s, and see what sort of changes appear to have taken place or to be in progress. As in Chapter 5, we can deal in detail only with this one aspect of the picture of the change from traditional dialect to the speech of the present day: the stressed vowel systems.   Other topics will receive brief attention in the next section.

In (1945), J.A. Sheard suggested that various influences 'will probably result in the production of a standard West Riding dialect'.   My own findings would seem to indicate that such a situation is at least very nearly in existence: for the great majority the more localised features have now largely disappeared, and more or less the same sound systems operate.   These form a typically West Yorkshire 'accent' (see below), which is still quite distinct from RP and from other regional forms - though of course there is a good deal of variation within it, to the extent that different groups may be described as having different systems, and indeed some individuals may seem to use different systems at various times.

The *short vowel* system, as far as inventory, distribution, and realisation are concerned, is for the majority the same as emerges

---

177 Much of the material of this chapter has appeared in Petyt (1980) and (1982), but it is of course an integral part of this work.

from the various works examined earlier.   But, presumably largely
under the influence of RP, an extra vowel is being added to the
system of some speakers - by some of them consistently, by some only
in certain styles:

This can be regarded as a change in progress at the present time:
/ʊ/ is splitting into /ʌ/ and /ʊ/, as it did some centuries ago in
the South.   The change is presumably occurring because of pressure
from the Southern system, but as yet it has affected only a minority,
and it is not proceeding simply with 'time':   unlike say the change
[u:k] > [ʊk], where it is largely the case that younger speakers
use the latter form to a progressively greater extent, the split of
/ʊ/ is primarily 'class-led', from the top of the social scale.
While the split in one sense parallels an earlier development in the
South, in another it is less simple: in the South there was some
regularity in respect of which /ʊ/ became /ʌ/, but now, since various
new /ʊ/ words have resulted from other changes, the split seems
somewhat arbitrary (with results such as /pʌt/ - /pʊt/, /lʌk/ - /lʊk/
and so on) and speakers have to learn just which words are involved
in the change.

    As for the *long vowels*, where we saw two different West York-
shire systems at an earlier date, both have undergone changes;   but
the Bradford-type can probably be said to have spread at the expense of that of Huddersfield.

i:		u:		i:		u:		i:		u:
e:	(ə:)	ɔ:	∼	e:	(ə:)	ɔ:	→	e:	ə:	o:
	a:				a:			ɑ:	a:	ɔ:

Since long vowels and *diphthongs* are closely connected, we should
also note the changes that have affected the latter:

εɪ	ʊɪ		(εɪ)	(ʊɪ)		(ɪu)				ɪə	ʊə		eɪ		ɪə	ʊə
(aɪ)	ɔɪ	→	aɪ	ɔɪ		(εʊ)	ɔʊ	→	aʊ	ɔʊ	eə		→	εə	ɔ

(The dotted brackets around /aɪ/ denote that this was a marginal
member in one of the two systems summarised here.)

Of the long vowels, the /ɑ:/ of the Huddersfield-type system
has now all but disappeared, with a consequent 'strengthening' of
the /aɪ/ diphthong.   The new common system is now somewhat more
symmetrical in phonetic terms, due to emergence of the new /o:/
vowel, mid-back paralleling the mid-front monophthongal /e:/;   this
new vowel results from various changes (see below), but primarily
from many words with earlier /ʊə/.   /ə:/ has become an established
member of the system, with a correspondingly reduced role for /ə/,
and in some parts for /a:/ - these changes bringing the system more
into line with RP.

Among the front-closing diphthongs, /ɛɪ/ and /ʊɪ/ have, through
changes of incidence in the direction of RP, a now much-reduced role;
and /ɪu/ and /ɛʊ/ have virtually gone from the back-closing set,
while /aʊ/ has entered the system in a largely RP-like role, with a
corresponding reduction in the incidence of /a:/ and in some places
of /ɛə/.   Through another reduction in the incidence of /ʊə/, the
diphthong /ɔə/ has been added to produce a more symmetrical centring
set.

The long vowel and diphthong systems are by no means stable in
the newer states just described;   indeed, they are probably in a
greater state of flux than ever before.   As far as the pure vowels
are concerned, we can perhaps detect two separate developments in
progress, but society being what it is, there is a confusing of the
two.   First, there is a change proceeding largely with 'time':
increasing monophthongisation of /ɛə/ and /ɔə/ by younger speakers
to produce System A.   Second, there is the class-led development
towards a more RP-like System B.   Thus

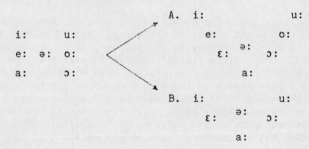

System A, which could be demonstrated in the /b - d/ environment
(bead/bade/bared/bard/board/bode/booed/bird), certainly seemed to
be in evidence among some of my youngest informants.   If, as is
my impression, the monophthongisation of /ɛə/ is also occurring

elsewhere in Britain, System B could be the incoming RP system.
This latter system involves the loss of West Yorkshire /eː/ and /oː/,
through a modification in both inventory and realisation in the
direction of the smaller long vowel and diphthong systems of RP:
/eː/ and /oː/ are diphthongised, in a front-closing and back-closing
direction respectively, while the start-points of /ɛɪ/ and /ɔʊ/ are
closed somewhat, resulting in a merger of /eː/ - /ɛɪ/ in [eɪ], and
/oː/ - /ɔʊ/ in [oʊ].   This development has been 'prepared for' by
the weakening of the /eː/ - /ɛɪ/ contrast, largely through a loss
of /ɛɪ/ words by change of incidence.   The /oː/ - /ɔʊ/ contrast is
of more recent origin; but while /ɔʊ/ is now of wider incidence
than /ɛɪ/, it has lost some of its incidence load, and the contrast
represents a 'closing of phonetic distance' between several groups
of words.   The distributions of the two phonemes are to a great
extent already complementary (for example before /l/ usually /ɔʊ/
occurs), and there are few minimal pairs.

The changes in progress in the diphthong system are:

(ɛɪ)	(ʊɪ)	→	eɪ	(ʊɪ)		→		ɪə	ʊə	→	ɪə	(ʊə)
aɪ	ɔɪ		aɪ	ɔɪ			aʊ ɔʊ	aʊ oʊ	ɛə	ɔə		(ɛə)

The front-closing and back-closing developments have been dealt with
above: they involve class-led changes 'from the top'; (/ʊɪ/ for
most speakers now has the same status as in RP, see Gimson (1970:92)
'of extremely rare occurrence within one syllable').   The centring
changes are not class-led; they involve the use of /ɔə/ in many
former /ʊə/ words, and the more recent monophthongisation of /ɔə/
and /ɛə/ by younger speakers already referred to.

The modifications of phonemic inventory just examined have contributed to what might be called the change from 'Yorkshire dialect'
to 'Yorkshire accent' (see below).   But very important in this
change, and in the modification of inventory, have been the very
many changes in phonemic *incidence* which have occurred and are still
occurring - almost always in the direction of RP (though not always
going 'all the way').   We cannot examine all such changes here,
and shall omit most changes which only affect one or two words, but
the major developments can be shown up.   This will be done in
diagram form - but of course it must be emphasised that the arrows
do not indicate 'phonetic change' in the sense of gradual developments, but rather, in the majority of cases, 'phonemic jumps'.

Let us look first at the changes that have already occurred for
the majority of the population:

Reductions in the load of close-centring diphthongs:

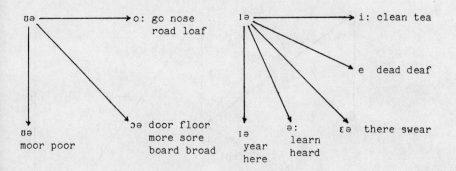

Changes involving the mid/low back area

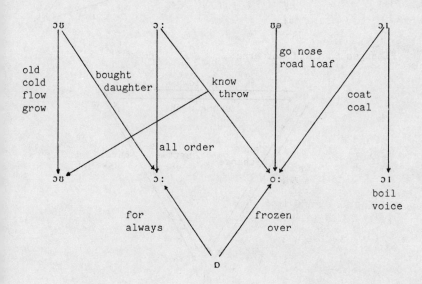

(The 'fork' from /ɔː/ in respect of words such as *know*, *throw*, *blow*, *crow*, *mow*, *sow*, *slow*, *own*, etc. indicates that they may either have joined the other set of 'ow' words under /ɔʊ/ e.g. *bowl*, *flow*, *grow*, *glow*, *owt*, *stow* etc., or have remained monophthongal, but closer - or, of course, they may vary between the two)

Changes in the back close area:

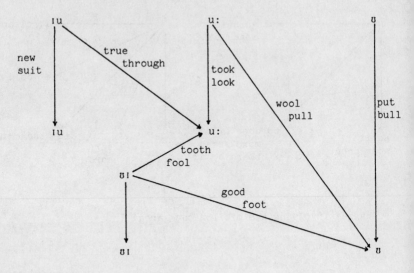

Changes in the front area:

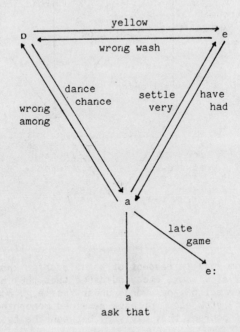

(Cont)

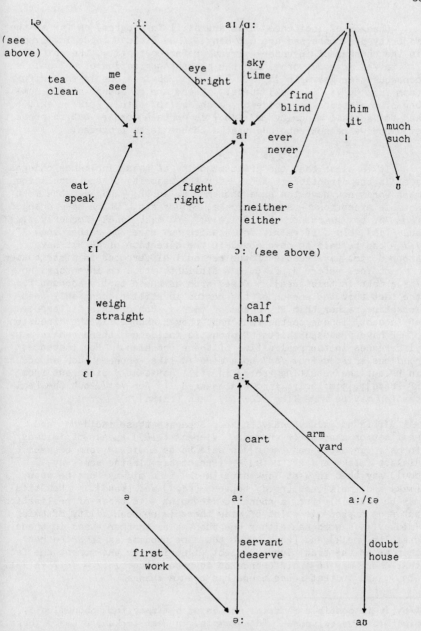

Changes of incidence which are still in progress as far as the
majority are concerned are not many, if we exclude those involved
in the changes of inventory already referred to (i.e. the shift from
/ʊ/ to /ʌ/ in some words, and the monophthongisation of /ɨə/ and
consequent merger with /ɔ:/).   The most obvious one is the shift
from /u:/ to /ʊ/ in (ook) words.   There are of course also a number of variations in incidence, such as /ɪŋ/ ~ /ɪn/, /e:k/ ~ /ek/,
and for a small minority /æ/ ~ /ɑ:/ in certain words; but on present
evidence we cannot conclude that a change is in progress.

    It is clear that the great majority of these incidence changes
are 'in the direction of RP'.   For the majority of the population
most words now have the same phonemes as in RP; and even the most
notable exceptions - such as *dance*, *chance* etc., which have changed
from /ɒ/ to /æ/ rather than RP /ɑ:/; and *much*, *such* (formerly /ɪ/);
and *flood*, *blood* (formerly /ʊɪ/) which now have /ʊ/ rather than RP
/ʌ/ - can be said to have moved in the direction of RP but have
stopped part-way because of the regional differences in distribution
(/æ/not /ɑ:/ before s, f, θ, n + sibilant, etc.) or inventory (no
/ʌ/ exists in this area).   Cases such as these partly account for
the fact that the speech of the region is still recognisably West
Yorkshire rather than RP.   And of course much of this difference
of 'accent' is due to the fact that though changes in the direction
of RP have produced shifts of phonemic incidence, there remain many
differences in the realisation of these phonemes.   For instance,
road has shifted from /ʊə/ to a more 'O-like' phoneme such as occurs
in RP,but the resulting [ro:d] is still noticeably different from
RP [rəʊd]; similarly, *find* has changed /ɪ/ for /aɪ/, but the realisation may be more like [fɑ·ɪnd] than [faɪnd].

    It is not always easy to keep separate these incidence and
realisation aspects of change.   Viereck (1966) speaks of 'midway
forms': in Gateshead [me:k] is said to be a midway form between
dialect (mɪək] and RP [meɪk].   (Presumably, in the same way, I
could say that in West Yorkshire [me:k] is a midway form between
[mak] and [meɪk], or [ro:d] between [rʊəd] and [rəʊd].)   Now this
may be plausible from a phonetic viewpoint - in terms of realisation
but from a phonemic point of view there is no possibility of being
'midway': a word has either one phoneme or another - and in these
examples [me:k] and [ro:d] have the same phoneme as in RP rather
than as in the traditional dialect (ignoring for the moment the fact
that there may be a difference of inventory too: /e:/ - /ɛɪ/ vs /eɪ/
etc.), and in that sense there has been a change[178].

----

178 It is possible that the notion of a midway form phonemically
might just be salvaged; for example, in West Yorkshire [mek] there is
the /e/ phoneme where dialect has /a/ and RP has /eɪ/ - perhaps /mek/
could be said to be midway in that it has a short vowel as in dialect
but a mid one as in RP?

2   DIALECT, ACCENT, STANDARD ENGLISH AND RP[179]

In everyday English the terms dialect and accent are often used
interchangeably, but most people, if they think about the matter,
would try to distinguish between them.   One way of doing this which
is commonly accepted among linguists, is seen in Trudgill (1974b:17):

'The term *dialect* refers, strictly speaking, to differences
between kinds of language which are differences of vocabulary
and grammar as well as pronunciation.   The term *accent* on the
other hand refers solely to differences of pronunciation'.

Related to these terms are the definitions of *Standard English*
and *RP*.   Standard English is linked to the notion of dialect: Abercrombie (1951:11) indeed defines an English dialect as 'any form of
English which differs from Standard English in grammar, syntax, and
vocabulary, and, of course, in pronunciation too, though a difference of pronunciation alone is not enough to make a different dialect'.   Somewhat differently, Trudgill speaks of 'the dialect known
as "Standard English"', but both agree that Standard English is that
particular form of grammar and vocabulary which is usually taught
in the educational system and is almost the only form regularly used
in written material;   it is also, with minor variations, 'the offic-
ial language of the entire English-speaking world and the language
of all educated English-speaking people' (Abercrombie).

Trudgill goes on to say that 'there is no necessary connection
between Standard English and any particular accent';   Standard English may be and is spoken with various accents.   However, there is
one British English accent which only occurs with Standard English:
this is RP.   Abercrombie similarly distinguishes between RP-speakers
of Standard English (whom he classes as 'without an accent') and
non-RP-speakers of Standard English as two of the three main
groups of English speakers, the third being dialect speakers.

Clearly, both these writers agree that RP is a matter of accent
only, whereas Standard English is one of dialect;   where they differ
is that Trudgill makes the point that Standard English is just one
dialect among many, and RP just one accent, while Abercrombie treats

179 I am ignoring here the old (and still unsolved) problem of what
'a dialect' is - and indeed whether there are such things at all -
and concentrating on the use of the term in a more adjectival sense
by which it is employed to describe features which depart from some
standard form of language.

them as somehow neutral and basic: it is only forms of English which
depart from these which he classes as dialects and accents respectivel

Abercrombie's approach is probably closer to that generally
accepted among the population at large, while Trudgill's might seem
more reasonable to linguists. But in essence their views of what
distinguishes 'dialect' from 'accent', and 'Standard English' from
'RP', are the same.

Both seem to agree too that Standard English is widely regarded
as the correct or prestige form of grammar and vocabulary, and that
RP, while perhaps not so widely regarded as the only 'correct' pronunciation, is certainly a prestige one. RP is distinctively British, but it is not identified with a region of Britain but rather
with a particular social class. Accent in Britain has been more important than in many countries because whether one did or did not
use RP, which was generally acquired by the 'public school class', has
acted as a passport or a bar in certain social or professional circles

It would seem reasonable to conclude from the above that all
matters of pronunciation are matters of 'accent', while grammar and/
or vocabulary must also be involved before we can speak of 'dialect'[180]. But the use of the non-technical term 'pronunciation'
when defining two technical terms is perhaps unfortunate. It seems
to be being used to cover the whole area that might be in the pro-
vinces of both *phonetics* and *phonology*, but I think that to arrive
at a more satisfactory definition of 'dialect' and 'accent' we
should distinguish these, and indeed make some finer distinctions.

Certainly I would be prepared to grant that 'pronunciation' in
the sense of *phonetic realisation* is a matter of accent differences:
such as Yorkshire [ka:t] vs. RP [kɑ:t], [ro:d] vs. [rəʊd] 'road',
[rɔʊd] vs. [rəʊd] 'rowed', and so on. But in these last two examples
we are obviously involved with *inventory* as well as realisation, so we
are in the area of phonology rather than simply phonetics. Another
example of an inventory difference would be Yorkshire [kʊt], kʊm] etc.
corresponding to RP [kʌt],[kʌm]; surely this would generally be accepted as a matter of West Yorkshire accent, occurring as it may in a
speaker using Standard English dialect. What of *distribution* and
incidence, which also involve phonology rather than just phonetics?
Yorkshire [pɪnʃ]/RP [pɪntʃ],West Country [kɑ:r], [kɑ:rd]/RP [kɑ:],
[kɑ:d], which are matters of distribution, would probably be accepted as differences of accent rather than of dialect: so too would

180 This seems explicit in Abercrombie and implicit in Trudgill,
though the latter could possibly argue that his definition allows
'accent' to cover some but not all matters of pronunciation.

some differences of incidence, such as Yorkshire [dans], [paθ]/RP [dɑ:ns], [pɑ:θ], or the widespread [-ɪn]/[-ɪŋ].

But would distributional differences such as Yorkshire [wɪdə]/ RP [wɪdeʊ] or Yorkshire [tlɪp], [dlas]/RP [klɪp], [glɑ:s] be said to be matters of accent?   And this question arises much more often with matters of incidence: are such Yorkshire/RP differences as [raŋ]/[rɒŋ], [spɛɪk]/[spi:k], [kɔ:f]/[kɑ:f], [bɪət]/[bi:t], [li:t]/ [laɪt], [rʊəd]/[rəʊd], [bʊɪt]/[bu:t] etc.etc. merely matters of accent?   Is a person who says [wɪəz mɪ kɔɪt] 'Where's my coat?' or [ðəl bi: ə fɛɪt təni:t] 'there'll be a fight tonight' just using a different accent from RP?   Abercrombie sayd that 'a difference in pronunciation alone is not enough to make a different dialect'; now it is true that a person speaking the above examples might else- where show differences of grammar and/or vocabulary, but in these utterances only pronunciation differences show up: are they diff- erent in accent or dialect from [wɛəz maɪ kəʊt], [ðəl bi: ə faɪt tənaɪt]?

One cannot help feeling that some such differences of pronun- ciation are too great to be classed as matters of 'accent', that they are really 'dialect' - and it may be due to a popular feeling of this sort that the two terms have not been kept separate. 'Acc- ent' does not refer simply to pronunciation in the sense of real- isation (i.e. phonetics); it also covers *some* parts of phonology in the sense of inventory, distribution, and incidence - but espec- ially with the last of these it seems that we have to draw the line between accent and dialect somewhere within it.

Having reached this position myself, I accidentally found that workers on the *Linguistic Survey of Scotland* had reached it before, but that over 20 years later their suggested solution is still not widely known.   Catford (1957) discusses 'Scottish accents' and 'Scots dialect', and says that accents 'differ from RP chiefly in phonetic (allophonic) details' - matters which I would call 'realis- ation', such as [e:], [o:] for RP [eɪ], [əʊ] - and that 'considered as systems of sounds they do not differ widely from RP or at least for the most part *can be brought into a fairly simple relationship with the RP sound system*'.

For example, in matters of inventory, Scottish accents have only /ʊ/ where RP has /ʊ/ and /u:/, but since the relationship is simple (RP /ʊ/ and/u:/ correspond to Scottish /ʊ/), this can be counted as a matter of accent.

But 'Scots dialects may have sound systems which are quite differently constituted from that of RP, and invariably have a

lexical distribution of phonemes which cannot be predicted from RP
or from a Scottish accent.   This difference in distributional predictability...distinguishes the relationship between accents from
the relationship between dialects'.   Thus, matters of inventory
and incidence, unless a regular relationship can be established,
are sufficient to make a difference of dialect rather than simply
one of accent.

     Let us examine the *LSS* distinction, using West Yorkshire ex-
amples.

RP	/ʌ/	/ʊ/	/eɪ/		/əʊ/	
W Yorks	/ʊ/		/ɛɪ/	/e:/	/ɔʊ/	/o:/

- in these three cases today we can say that the relationships are
regular (W Yorks /ʊ/ will always correspond to RP /ʌ/ or /ʊ/;
RP /eɪ/ to W Yorks /ɛɪ/ or /e:/; and so on[181]; so these inventory
differences are matters only of accent.

     Turning to incidence:

     laugh pass path dance branch craft laughs laughed etc:

RP   /ɑ:/

W Yorks   /æ/

- here the relationships are regular and predictable: in a certain
set of environments RP /ɑ:/ will correspond to W Yorks /æ/ - so
this too is accent.   But things are very different in this next
set of examples:

	light	right	like	find	neither	me	beat	eat	feet
RP	————/aɪ/————				/aɪ/~/i:/		————/i:/————		
trad W Yorks	/i:/	/ɛɪ/	/aɪ/	/ɪ/	/ɔ:/	/i:/	/ɪə/	/ɛɪ/	/ɪ/

- in these cases there is no predictability between RP and this traditional West Yorkshire variety, and therefore these would be classed
as differences of dialect.

_____

181 Of course in the past the /ɛɪ/ and /ɔʊ/ sets included items not
in the RP /eɪ/ and /əʊ/ sets.

Catford's proposal comes very close to satisfying my intuitive feelings about how much difference in pronunciation is possible before we talk of a difference in dialect rather than simply in accent.   However, I have some doubts about 'distribution' (in *my* sense, which he does not discuss - his use of the term is for what I would call 'incidence'): would [wɪdə], [fɒlə], [barə] etc. generally be regarded as differences only of accent?   The relationship 'RP final unstressed /əʊ/: W Yorks /ə/' is certainly regular and predictable, so it 'should' be accent.   But does the feeling that the [ə] pronunciation is substandard, in a sense which say [paθ] is not, make it seem that a difference of dialect is involved? Moreover, I do not think it is necessary to define 'accent' and 'dialect' in terms of 'relation to RP'; RP can be treated as one form among many, and the definition of accents and dialects in general, throughout the English-speaking world rather than just in Britain, can be in terms of regularity of relationship.

Having now drawn a somewhat different line between 'dialect' and 'accent' from that usually accepted, we must consider how the definitions of Standard English and RP are affected.

Standard English can still, I think, be classed as a dialect; but it will now be taken to involve not only vocabulary and grammar but also some matters of phonology.   In particular, I think there is such a thing as 'Standard English incidence': [wɪəz mɪ kɔɪt] is not Standard English (though no vocabulary or grammatical differences are involved), since the incidence of two phonemes is 'dialectal', in the sense of not being in a regular relationship (W Yorks /ɔɪ/: St. E. /əʊ/ is not regular and predictable); however, [weəz mɪ kɔːt] *is* Standard English, pronounced with a West Yorkshire accent.

RP is still of course a type of pronunciation of Standard English, a matter of accent - but I take certain aspects of pronunciation to be matters of Standard English nowadays rather than of RP/non-RP.   Throughout the world, 'educated English-speaking people' share a great deal as regards phonemic incidence; some variation is possible, but unless it is in a regular and predictable relationship it will result in a different dialect, rather than just an accent of Standard English.

3   THE INFLUENCE OF STANDARD ENGLISH AND RP ON WEST YORKSHIRE
    SPEECH

It is surprising to find that very little attention appears to have been devoted to this type of subject.   Papers in the liter-

ature with promising-looking titles turn out to be disappointing:
for example, Abercrombie (1951) really only deals with definitions,
as discussed above; and Kolb (1968), though the author has great
experience in English dialectology, just looks in detail with a
philologist's thoroughness, at three items: *gate*, *oven* and *shovel*,
and makes no attempt to tackle the general question.

    In my previous chapters, I have tacitly accepted the common
distinction between Standard English (vocabulary and grammar) and
RP (pronunciation), and when dealing with matters of phonology or
phonetics I have spoken of 'the influence of RP', or 'changes in
the direction of RP', or 'more RP-like forms', and so on.   But I
have now suggested a somewhat different line between 'dialect' and
'accent', and consequently a correspondingly different view of what
is covered by 'Standard English' and 'RP'.   With these new definitions in mind, I think we can draw the following general conclusion
from the findings reported in Chapters 6 and 7:

Dialect has largely disappeared as far as the great majority of the
urban population of West Yorkshire are concerned.

It should be borne in mind that the types of features I regard as
matters of 'dialect' are

- vocabulary: it is clear that very few items now in common usage
are regionally specific and worthy of inclusion in a 'dialect
dictionary'; the vast majority of words would be accepted as Standard English.

- grammar: though a fair number of non-standard features of grammar
were recorded during my survey (and are described mainly in Chapter
6 ii), they are far fewer than many of the traditional dialect
grammars describe as existing in the area; most of them occurred
only a handful of times; and they are mainly restricted to Classes
IV - V.   It would appear then that Standard English grammar has
had considerable influence, and is still 'working down' through the
population.

- phonemic incidence: in Chapter 6 ii we noted a number of instances of incidence such as I would wish to label 'dialectal' - but
most of these were heard from only one or two speakers.   Most incidence has now come into line with what is generally found throughout the English-speaking world.   In particular we may note that
in the case of all the items quoted in the example on p.338 of differences between RP and 'traditional W Yorks', the incidence is now
as in RP as far as the great majority of speakers are concerned.
But I have now suggested that it is 'Standard English incidence'

that has exercised influence rather than RP in particular (though
the latter is of course one exemplification of this).

Most members of the West Yorkshire population, I therefore
maintain, speak a form of language approaching Standard English.
Certainly some non-standard features do survive, and may help to
identify a person as coming from this area, but most have now given
way before the influence of Standard English.

*What remains to identify most speakers is their West Yorkshire 'accent'
rather than their 'dialect'.*

- 'accent' covering features of realisation, and also those features
of inventory, distribution, and incidence where these are in a
'regular' relationship with those of other accents of Standard English, including RP.

What grounds are there for saying that the main influence on
traditional dialect has been that of Standard English rather than
that of RP?

On the one hand, like features of vocabulary and grammar, phonological features which I have now defined as matters of 'dialect'
or of Standard English - for example, incidence features, such as
[fli:] *fly*, [fɛɪt] *fight*, [fɪnd] *find*, [ɔ:ðə] *either*, [ɪəd] *head*,
[tɛɪtʃ] *teach* etc. etc. - have now virtually disappeared from the
speech of the majority.

On the other hand, however, features of 'accent', which is the
province of RP, are still quite widespread.   In matters of realisation, we saw that the majority still use regional variants such as
[e:], [o:], [a:], and so on; in inventory, the absence of /ʌ/ and of
/h/, and the presence of /ɛɪ/ besides /e:/, and /ɔʊ/ besides /o:/,
though giving way to some extent (the latter two partly because of
shifts of incidence), are still common - for here the relation to
other accents is 'regular', as it is with the incidence feature of /æ/
in *grass*, *path* etc., which is almost universal in the area.

In respect of these latter examples of accent features, it is an
interesting possibility that English as a world-wide medium is responsible for the different treatment of some West Yorkshire forms.
/æ/ in the words in question is probably commoner in English as a
world-wide medium than /ɑ:/, and here RP in spite of its prestive has
therefore made little impression; but /h/, /ʌ/, and the lack of the
/ɛɪ/ - /e:/ and /ɔʊ/ - /o:/ contrasts are widespread features of the
English-speaking world as well as of RP (as is too, for instance /ʊk/
in (ook) words) - so here West Yorkshire is giving way.

Of course, RP, as the prestige British accent, does have some
influence: we did see evidence, for example, that a more RP-like
realisation of (ɑː), (eɪ), (əʊ) has been adopted by some sections of
the population; and that /ɑː/ in *grass*, *path* etc. commands some
prestige even if few people adopt it; and so on.   But generally
these are features of the minority whereas those discussed above
have affected the majority.

Wakelin (1972b:156) spoke of a need to investigate 'in what
sectors of the community local dialect is primarily being modified
and in what order the dialect characteristics disappear, i.e. which
are the most stable, which the most easily lost'.   This work has
offered some evidence on which answers to these questions can be
attempted.

With regard to the first question, we have seen that in West
Yorkshire (as in other areas, insofaras evidence is available) the
sectors of the community leading the modification of local dialect
are the middle classes, with the working classes, especially those
I have included in Classes IV and V, being more retentive but still
having made considerable changes from the traditional dialect.   We
have also seen that often the women in any class are somewhat ahead
of the men.   It is true that some changes that are taking place at
present seem to be working down through age-group sectors of the
population, rather than through the class-system - but some of these
(such as [ɛə > ɛː], [t > 2] are not modifications of local dialect in
the direction of a wider 'standard'; those which are, like [uːk > ʊk],
also involve social class and are led by the middle classes.

In reply to the second question, we can say that local features
seem to disappear in the following order:

- first 'dialect' features - and possibly within this category:
  first, vocabulary; and second, grammar and phonemic incidence. We
  may note that such features are frequently the object of overt
  pressure in the educational system, which has some effect on the
  majority.   We should also note that these effects have been felt
  even on rural dialects - see Orton (1962:18): 'So strong is the
  pressure of the standard language upon (dialect speakers), so
  willing are they to accept variant forms, and so ready are they
  to modify their own pronunciation not only with strangers but also
  with people outside their own intimate circle that their spoken
  words often occur in three or four different forms'.

- second to go are 'accent' features: inventory, distribution, realisation, and some cases of incidence.   Generally these are not
  the object of overt pressure in the schools, and this may be one

reason why only a minority are affected.   These features, which
may remain after vocabulary, grammar, and incidence have come into
line with Standard English, may define some sort of 'Regional
Standard'.   Many people for example are recognisably Northern
(from the Yorkshire/Lancashire industrial belt), but they may not
readily be pinned down more precisely.   Other people may be recognised as from a smaller region - say West Yorkshire - but can be
identified no further.   (This is my own experience, and one that
was reported to me by several informants and other sources).

- last to disappear, I suspect, are 'tone of voice' features.   I
have not felt capable of tackling this subject, so this is only a
hypothetical suggestion which is not based on findings reported in
this work.   I merely record that I have observed examples of
speakers who have no 'dialect' features and who have modified
their inventory, distribution, realisation, and incidence so as
to come completely into line with RP 'accent' - but who nevertheless 'sound' as if they come from West Yorkshire and whom I have
later been able to confirm as doing so.

4   VARIATION AND CHANGE

This work is intended to be descriptive rather than theoretical:
its main concern is to present findings (which I consider to be interesting in themselves) rather than to build linguistic theories.
Others may interpret my facts for this purpose if they wish.   But
since variation and change are topics central to my subject, I should
perhaps attempt briefly to examine how my findings related to the
approaches to these problems which were current at the time I carried out the research (the early 1970s).

a)   Linguistic Variation

I showed in Chapter 2 that it had been demonstrated that the
term 'free variation' was largely an erroneous one which simply avoided the problem, and that methods have been developed by which
variation can be quantified and correlated with other factors, both
linguistic and non-linguistic, as I have done in Chapter 6.   I now
turn to the place of variation and its treatment within linguistic
theory.

What we may term the 'traditional approach' to linguistic
description (going back to Hermann Paul and the Neo-grammarians, but
also to be seen either explicitly or implicitly in de Saussure, the
Bloomfieldians, and the transformationalists), was to concentrate

on the individual speaker as the homogeneous object of study[182] –
and thus to equate 'structuredness' with homogeneity and to treat
heterogeneity or variation as merely an uncomfortable but theoret-
ically unimportant fact.

So the traditional treatment of variation was, essentially, to
'pretend it isn't there' – to abstract something homogeneous from
the actually occurring heterogeneous data.   We can see this approach
in dialectology, in those works which concentrate on the 'extreme'
system: the set of the 'most traditional' dialect features that
still occur, however infrequently, is described as 'The Dialect
of –'.   Even in recent years there have been examples – such as
Sivertsen (1960), or in our area Sykes (1961);   very few members of
the populations of London or Huddersfield use the phonology described, and hardly any of those few do so consistently, but the variation between these systems and more RP-like ones, both within
the community and within the individual, is deliberately ignored.
My own experience suggests that while it may be legitimate to describe a traditional system, this is so artificial in the light of
the present situation that certainly it is *not* reasonable to label
this 'The Dialect of –'.

Beginning around the mid-1960s, there was a growing acceptance
of the fact that variation is the *norm*, and that variation is not
incompatible with regularity and structure: there may be 'structured
heterogeneity', both within the individual and within the community.
Furthermore, this view not only fits the synchronic facts, but also
makes possible a more reasonable theory of linguistic change.   Let
us briefly examine some of these approaches, which accept that variation should be recognised and accounted for.

Several linguists, of various theoretical persuasions, have
treated the variants which occur essentially in terms of 'interference' or 'dialect mixture'.   For instance, dialect descriptions
such as those of Wolck (1965) on Buchan, or Viereck (1966) on Gateshead, have suggested that certain variants are 'midway forms' between
the traditional dialect and the standard language.   And some generat-
ivists have spoken either of a speaker of dialect A confronting dialect B and imperfectly learning a rule of the latter because of the
influence of his own dialect;   or of a speaker having internalised

---

182 Some have pushed this to extremes: for example, Bloch (1948),
recognising that variation occurs within the individual as well as
between them, says that the object of description must be the same
speaker using the same style on the same occasion.   It seems somewhat ironic that 'the greatest degree of abstracting away from data
variation has been advocated by the empiricists' (Bailey, 1973b:5).

the rules of dialects X and Y in his competence but his performance
reflecting a sort of tug-of-war between them; or of a speaker aiming at different targets according to his conceptions of his addressee's grammar; and so on.   And some Creole scholars have suggested
that where a Creole is in contact with the standard form of the same
language, the 'basilect' (the Creole) and the 'acrolect' (the standard) may give rise to a 'mesolect' - a form somewhere between the
two but identical with neither.

This type of model has a certain appeal, and could be applied
to the sort of situation seen in the West Yorkshire towns.   For
example, it might possibly be held that the contact between West
Yorkshire [bʊət] and RP [bəʊt ~ boʊt] has given rise to the compromise [bo:t].   But on the one hand, we have noted the problem of drawing the line between phonetics and phonology when speaking of midway
forms; and on the other the implied 'three variant' situation
('acro-/meso-/basi-' in creolist terms) is probably simplistic (see
below).

Whereas the 'interference' model implied, initially at least,
two discrete systems, the two models best known in the 1970s did not.

First, there was the approach which produced *Variable Rules*.
This was the model of Labov and his followers.   Labov held that
'variation is...an inherent property of linguistic systems' (Labov
et al., 1968:12), and that this variation is a part of structure and
can be stated by rule: 'linguistic structure includes the orderly
differentiation of speakers and styles through rules which govern
variation in the speech community' (Weinreich et al., 1968:187).

In (1969) Labov developed the notion of 'variable constraints'
which differentiate the frequencies with which a rule applies according to two types of factor: first, the grammatical and phonological features of the environment (a hierarchy of constraints can
be established, each outweighing the effect of those below it in the
hierarchy); and second, the extralinguistic factors such as age,
sex, ethnic group, social class, style and so on.   Information such
as this is built into a 'variable rule': for instance, such a rule
for describing the use of the glottal stop in West Yorkshire might
be:

$$x \ /t/ \longrightarrow [2]$$

where x = the 'function of' a specified hierarchy of linguistic constraints: _#C, _# #, _#V,_ L, V _ V, and the non-linguistic factors
of age, class, sex, style and town.   Wolfram (1969) and Trudgill
(1974a) are examples of works adopting this model.

My own findings could certainly be expressed within this model:

it is satisfactory as a descriptive device.   But its proponents
make much stronger claims about it: Labov held that such variable
rules are part of the native speaker's competence, and Trudgill too
believed that the individual has internalised all the rules of the
'speech community' (see below).   And when one considers the implications of these claims, they seem to me to be unsupportable.   For
example, if age is an important covariable of some rule (as it is
say in West Yorkshire for /t/ > [ʔ]) we presumably have to assume
that individuals "know" in some sense the various values of the 'age-
function' for the different groups.   Now if, as is so in such cases,
the variable is involved in linguistic change, these values will
continually be changing as the actual members of the age-groups
change (so too, of course, will those of class, sex, and other
groups - but leave that aside).   Are we to assume that the matrix
of values the individual has 'in his head' changes as he grows
older?   And suppose just the youngest group start to use a completely new variant of some variable; this view would imply that
even the oldest group acquire this variant (in their competence),
but that they just do not happen to use it.   And even if there is
no question of change in progress, are we to suppose that the individual is somehow 'counting' how many instances of variant X he
uses in particular environments, in order that he may keep the group
averages right (even if no other members of the group are present)?

     Such problems force me to conclude that though variable rules
may be a reasonable means of describing what occurs in the *community*,
it would be nonsense to envisage them as part of an individual's
knowledge.   In other words, they can be part of a linguist's
grammar, but not an individual's.

     The main alternative to the Labov view came from creole scholars
De Camp (1971) suggested that in a 'post-creole' situation (where
there has been a breakdown of the former rigid social stratification,
and a spread of education), there is no sharp creole/standard cleav-
age in language, but rather a continuum of speech varieties between
these two extremes; and (though the competence of the 'ideal
speaker-hearer' may span the whole continuum) the performance of
any actual individual in regard to the span within this which he
commands will depend on the breadth of his social contacts.   The
difference between this and the usual creolist model referred to
above, as Bickerton (1973) emphasises, is that it is not possible
to divide varieties into three discrete systems - acrolect/mesolect/
basilect; some variables may show more than three variants, some
fewer - there is no specifiable set of discrete varieties.

     Two notable features of this model may be emphasised.   First,
the individual speaker is given greater prominence than in other

models.   Individuals even of the same age, education, income etc.
can differ in speech because of differences of personality, experience, aspirations, and so on.   Now if we examine individuals'
speech we find that there is indeed a *continuum* of differences,
whereas putting them into groups according to sociological criteria
and then producing average scores gives an artificial impression of
discreteness.   Bailey (1973a,b) and Bickerton (1973) for this reason rejected the whole notion of 'dialect' as a group phenomenon.
Second, another aspect of the continuum view is the notion of
'implicational relations'.   For instance (using my own examples),
if a West Yorkshire speaker uses the [ɑ:] variant of (ɑ:/æ) say in
grass, he will certainly use the [ʌ] variant of (ʌ) in *cut*, but the
reverse need not be true.   Within a particular variable there may
be implicational relations between certain categories of words in
which it may occur: with (ɑ:/æ), if a speaker has [ɑ:] in *trans-*
or *plastic*, he will certainly have it in *grass* or *path* (but not
necessarily the reverse); if he has it in the latter, then certainly
he will have it in *father* (but perhaps not vice versa);   if in
father then in *half* and *calf*; and so on: see De Camp (1971),
Bickerton (1971, 1973), Bailey (1973) etc. for further examples.

My own experience in examining a fairly large amount of data
from a representative sample makes me feel that this model has points
which ring true.   For instance, I did find that in respect of numerous features there is a continuum of individual performances
rather than discrete groups (see p.109);   I can be almost positive
that there is no group within the community such that the linguistic
behaviour of all its members will fall within a certain range, and
that of all non-members will be outside this.   To 'average the
individuals' to produce group scores (as I did) can indeed give an
erroneous impression of discreteness if such 'findings' are not
interpreted with care.   A continuum of individual 'lects' (Bailey's
term for a particular combination of linguistic characteristics) is
probably a truer picture of what actually is found in a community
than a number of 'dialects', however large.   Also, I found evidence
of implicational relations, some examples of which I have given
above.   Another piece of evidence in this direction is that I noted
down as surprising (before the notion of such relations had appeared
in print) the form [geʔɪŋ] *getting*: intuitively I felt that the
use of [ʔ] would 'imply' that of [ɪn] (though not vice versa);
apparently then these implications are not categorical, but the
breaking of them produced something 'unexpected'.

While finding myself in sympathy with the above points, I
nevertheless feel that this model has not had the same large-scale
testing on actual data as that of Labov, and so it cannot yet be
accepted unquestioningly.

b)   Linguistic Change

Does variation always imply change?   Labov clearly believes
not: in (1966b) he made clear that both stigmatised and prestige
features may be either stable or in process of change; in Labov
et al. (1968) he said of 'rules with inherent variability' that
'some...represent sound change in progress, others are relatively
stable'; and in Weinreich et al. (1968) as one of the 'general
principles for the study of language change' he sa:d that 'Not all
variability and heterogeneity of language structure involves change,
but all change involves variability and heterogeneity'.

On the other hand, some proponents of the last model discussed
in the preceding section hold that variation is simply a stage in
linguistic change: Bickerton (1971) attacks Labov's notion of
'inherent variability', and maintains that it can be demonstrated
that linguistic change has three phases: categorical (Rule X),
variable (Rule X ~ Rule Y), categorical (Rule Y) - so variation is
simply a developmental phase between two categorical ones.

Probably only detailed and long-term diachronic investigation
can decide the point, and I am not convinced that Bickerton's asser-
tions have sufficient such foundation.   My own findings could be
interpreted as supporting either side.   On the one hand there are
cases of variation where the age-graph does not so clearly suggest
a change in progress as it does with say (ook), (t), or (ɔə), and
where it could be taken that the situation is relatively stable.
This is so with both stigmatised features like h-dropping, and prestige features such as the use of [ʌ], or [ɑ:] in (ɑ:/æ) words.   On
the other hand, since the traditional dialect descriptions of the
area give no indication at all of /h/, /ʌ/, or 'Long A', it could
possibly be argued that the present variation is a sign that change
is in progress, however slowly.   And it may be noted that Bickerton's colleague Bailey admitted that some 'rules may freeze in mid-
course' (1973b:84), thus offering a sort of compromise view.

Turning now from the relationship between variation and change
to theories of the latter - many people would accept that Labov
made important contributions in this area.   A major innovation was
his suggestion that we can view linguistic change in progress by examining the performance and attitudes of different age-groups in
respect of certain variables, and also the clues to be drawn from
differences between styles and between social groups.   His first
important paper (1963) examined a particular change in progress and
drew attention to the importance of social factors: 'social meaning' was attached to some variants, and this led to change as speakers identified with certain groups.   Another paper (1966b) dealt

with the special role he believed was played by one social class in
New York, the Lower Middle Class: being insecure socially and linguistically they were hypersensitive to the social significance of
variants, and so played a key part especially in the adoption of
prestige features. Another (1965), based on both his rural and
urban data, attempted to uncover the main factors in the mechanics
of linguistic change. This was expanded on in Weinreich et al.
(1968): as 'empirical principals for the theory of language change'
five problems were identified: 1) the 'constraints' problem - one
goal is to determine the set of *possible* changes and conditions for
change; 2) the 'transition' problem - to determine the mechanism
of the spread of a change from one language-state to another, where
'transitional dialects' and 'bidialectal' speakers and stylistic
differentiation may be important; 3) the 'embedding' problem, with
two aspects: the embedding of changes in the linguistic system
(for instance, in New York a change in (oh) is linked to developments of (eh), (uh), (ay) etc.), and also in the social system,
where the social significance of certain features is obviously important - the two being interlocked; 4) the 'evaluation' problem -
finding the subjective correlates (prestige, stigmatisation etc.)
of objective developments; 5) the 'actuation' problem - the reasons
behind a particular change starting to take place, which is the most
difficult to tackle and where most explanations offered are likely
to be after the fact: it is suggested however that change starts
when one variant spreads through a subgroup and thus attains social
significance.

     Most of the points made by Labov were suggestions based on the
data he examined. My own findings sometimes support them - but
not always: for example, I found no evidence of the 'hypercorrection'
of the Lower Middle Class that he considered important, presumably
mainly in the 'transition' stage. On the other hand, one of the
'constraints' suggested is that where a two-phoneme system is in contact with a merged one-phoneme system, except in very special circumstances the direction of change will be towards the latter: here
the breakdown of West Yorkshire /ɛɪ/ - /eː/ and /ɔʊ/ - /oː/ in contact with the more standard merged /eɪ/ and /əʊ/ does seem to be in
line with this (whereas the fact that the opposite may seem to be
happening with West Yorkshire /ʊ/ in contact with /ʌ/ - /ʊ/ is
probably not a fair counter-example since the former is not a merged
system - it is the latter which is split). The claim that any
change is 'embedded' in and has consequences for a wider system is
supported by my findings that there are considerable similarities,
at both phonemic and phonetic levels, between the developments of
the /ɛɪ/ - /eː/ pair and those affecting /ɔʊ/ - /oː/; and similarly
with /aɪ/ and /aʊ/; and the suggestion that 'actuation' is due to
one variant acquiring significance by being associated with some
sub-group is perhaps exemplified in our area by [ʌ]: this has acquired some social significance as a prestige form, having been

generalised only 'down to' the middle middle class, and is now
spreading further; we may expect that, if ever it becomes fully
generalised (i.e. the change is complete, with a shift from 'variable' to 'constant'), it will lose social significance, as in the
South.   It would seem probable that a prestige feature (like [ʌ])
enters the community through the more formal speech of the higher
classes, and a stigmatised one (like [ʔ]) through the less monitored
styles of the lower classes; then 'transition' starts.

        Another approach to linguistic change which influenced me was
that of Samuels (1972).   One of his main concerns was to demonstrate
that in the past insistence on a single cause or mechanism of change
had been a big drawback.   He maintained that in any of the three
levels of language - phonology, grammar, and lexis - there are three
main causes of change.   Two of these are internal.   First, variation: this is a matter of the idiolect, of 'parole' or the spoken
chain.   Two factors are of particular importance: inertia (the
well known principle of 'economy of effort', which explains the
majority of what are known as 'conditioned changes'), and stylistic
factors (careful and forceful variants will differ from those of
careless or relaxed styles, and the generalisation of either of these
is probably the main mechanism of 'isolative changes').   Of course,
different variants are constantly being produced; if one is accepted often enough it ceases to be a matter of 'parole' and becomes
one of 'langue', the system.   Here we link to the second main cause
of change: systemic regulation.   Where relations are, as it were,
disturbed by changes due to variation, balance has to be restored -
by processes described as 'push-chains' and 'drag-chains'.   These
internal causes are assisted by a third, external, one: diversity
and contact: the isolation or separation of groups accounts for
diversity, whether 'horizontal' (geographical differences) or 'vertical' (social differences), while contact with another type of language makes new variants available and often results in imitation,
hypercorrection, prestige and stigmatised features, and so on.

        It seems to me that Samuels's theory is not incompatible with
the views of Labov.   My own findings provide no arguments against
it, and indeed some of them seem to fit very easily into this framework.   To adapt one of Samuels's examples which is of particular
relevance, the phonemic split of /ʊ/ in English: in some areas of
Britain variants arose in the spoken chain such that [ʊ] occurred
after labials, and unrounded [ʌ] after other sounds (i.e. this was a
'conditioned' change of the 'least effort' type); in other areas
[ʊ] remained in all environments.   Then, due to contact between
dialects and incorrect imitation of unfamiliar forms (i.e. external
factors), the distribution came to be overlapping rather than complementary, with the possibility of both rounded and unrounded

variants in a labial environment.   There was no 'systematic' reason
for the split, neither pressure towards pattern congruity nor an
excessive functional load, but once it had occurred the /ʊ/ - /ʌ/
contrast was then built into the system and the reduced load of /ʊ/
was strengthened by another purely mechanical change - the many new
shortenings of /uː/ as in *good*, *foot* etc.   These developments did
not of course affect our area, which is only now beginning to experience the split solely via external factors (i.e. contact with prestige forms - with resultant uncertainty, hypercorrection, and so on).

    The third view of linguistic change I had in mind during the
period of my work was that of Bailey and his associates, which was
in a sense just a new and more complex version of an old theory.
In 1872 Johannes Schmidt had tried to explain resemblances between
separate branches of Indo-European by his famous 'wave theory':
linguistic changes spread like waves from some focal point, over
varying areas.   Bailey (1973a, 1973b etc.), building on the 'implicational relations' model (see above), proposed a modern version of
this: waves of change pass through a speech area - either through
geographical or through *social* space, and may be slowed down by
barriers of either kind, i.e. those of age, sex, class etc., as well
as those of geography - in such a way that a particular wave, say
affecting feature X, will gradually cover the area already affected
by the wave affecting feature W, and so on.   Thus a change in feature
X will imply a prior change in feature W, but not vice versa.

    These implicational relations may hold either between quite
different sound changes (for instance, those implied in our (ɑː/æ)
and (ʌ) variables: a person who changes from [æ] to [ɑː] in *grass*
will certainly have changed from [ʊ] to [ʌ] in *cut*, but not vice
versa), or between the different environments of change in the same
variable: a change in one environment implies a change in 'heavier-
weighted' environments, and so on.   Diagrammatically:

Environments: a   b   c   d

            0   -   -   -   -   - = no change
    stages
            1   x   -   -   -   x = variable change
      of
            2   +   x   -   -   + = categorical change
    change
            3   +   +   x   -

And building in the geographical/social 'spread' at the times of
these stages:

Time 0   Time 1   Time 2   Time 3

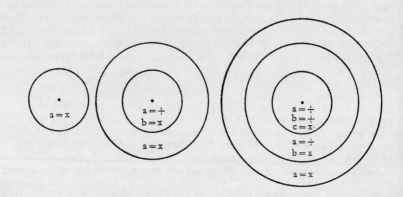

- here the smallest circles represent the social/geographical area
where the change has progressed to the 'stage' corresponding to
the 'time'; in the areas represented by the outer circles the change
will have only reached an earlier stage at this same time. Bailey
held that if we look far enough we shall find examples of all the
various stages postulated (see Bailey, 1973a:158).

For the most part this model does not seem to me to be incompatible with those outlined above; indeed, there are some obvious
similarities (for example, between the 'implicational relations' of
environments and Labov's 'hierarchy of constraints') - though one
obvious difference is that Bailey's model implies that variability
(x) is simply a phase in the historical development from one categorical state (-) to another (+), whereas Labov holds that variability may be inherent and need not imply change.

My main doubts about this model are that the evidence on which
it is based appears to be largely anecdotal rather than the result
of large-scale surveys; and that it, or at least the exposition of
it, is an over-simplified picture of what actually occurs. For
example, it is implied that change at any one point in social or geographical space proceeds by one environment at a time: thus, Stage
1) env a - variable, env b and c - no change; Stage 2) env a -
categorical change, env b - variable, env c - no change; and so on.
But surely Labov's findings and my own (say for the environments in
which /t/ > [ʔ]) show that there may be variation at the same time
in environments a, b and c - though the change may have gone further (i.e. there are more glottal stops) in a than in b, and in b

than in *c*, and so on. (In fact in a slightly later work (1973b:73)
Bailey said 'All the environments of a rule become variable before
the oldest becomes categorical' - but then immediately gave one of
Bickerton's examples which contradicts this in favour of the above
view.)

It will have become clear that my own findings have not led me
to come down strongly in favour of any one of the models for handling variation or change which I have briefly examined in this section: indeed, I have found various pieces of evidence that could
be interpreted as supporting several of them. But two general conclusions I would draw. First, like most of the writers referred
to here, I reject the old view of language as basically a homogeneous system 'où tout se tient', with dialectologists, stylisticians
etc. being merely in the nature of scavengers who tidy up trivial
matters of 'parole': variation must be seen as part of the core
rather than the periphery of linguistic science. Second, though
it is not yet clear whether variation always implies change, the
Saussurean dichotomy of 'synchronic' versus 'diachronic' is artificial and should be abandoned: synchronic variation and diachronic
change cannot be kept completely separate.

5   THE WEST YORKSHIRE 'SPEECH COMMUNITY'[183]

On the basis of evidence from his various evaluation tests,
Labov (1966b:500) concluded that New York speakers, in spite of
differences in performance, were in fact aiming at the same ideal;
and that 'New York is a single speech community, united by a common
set of evaluative norms'. Trudgill (1974:133) went somewhat further than this, and claimed that 'speakers of Norwich English belong
to a particular speech community which has very many common linguistic features...not shared by any other speech community'; and
he went on to set up a common framework, a 'diasystem' of rules
which are supposed to generate all types of Norwich English, and
stated his belief that 'members of the Norwich speech community can
be said to have internalised this diasystem...The diasystem can be
said in some sense "to exist".....'

---

183 In this section I used my findings to attack the notion of a
'speech community', particularly of the sort Trudgill proposed for
Norwich.   It should be noted that in recent years Trudgill has abandoned his view of 'a single grammar for the English spoken in the city
of Norwich': see especially Trudgill (1982:175).   Trudgill has in
fact reached a position very similar to that outlined at the end of
this section.

Trudgill's evidence appears to be that all Norwich speakers
can, for any variety of Norwich English, 'faultlessly imitate it for
humorous or other reasons', and 'assign fine sociological meanings
to different types of pronunciation'; i.e. his claims are based
on a) imitative ability, and b) evaluative norms (as were Labov's).
He admits that one could, as 'an intellectual exercise' write a
diasystem for *any* two varieties of English, say Yorkshire and Australian, but insists that his Norwich diasystem is essentially
different from this: the differences between Yorkshire and Australian are so considerable that a common underlying system would be
too abstract to be 'meaningful', and speakers could not perform
faultless imitations of each other; but the Norwich system is
claimed to have psychological reality, as part of the 'native speaker's linguistic competence'.

Before discussing this viewpoint, let us briefly refer to one
or two of its consequences. Trudgill says that because some Norwich speakers distinguish between the vowels of *nose* and *knows*, and
because there is a continuum from those who always distinguish them
to those who never do so (some Middle-Class speakers), it is unreasonable to set up two separate systems, one with two vowels, the
other with only one; rather, the deep-down system has two vowels,
but it just happens that some speakers always apply the rules which
merge them. He would presumably claim that the latter are able to
'make this distinction...*without error*, if they wish to for humorous or other purposes'. A similar case is made out in respect of
the vowels of *boat* and *boot*: 'two underlying phonological elements
are "kept apart' in the subconscious linguistic knowledge of speakers
because a small phonetic distinction is sometimes made between
sets of items which they perceive as phonetically "the same", and
because the elements are involved in two distinct sets of stylistic
alternation: *boat* /uː/ ~ /ʊ/, *boot* /uː/ ~ /ʉ/'. An important difference however is that this time it is the lower classes who apparently
perform the feat of applying more rules so that these separate underlying elements are usually realised alike.

How tenable is this notion of a 'speech community'? It seems
dubious, on two sets of grounds:

(i) THE EVIDENCE ON WHICH IT IS SAID TO BE BASED. This we have
seen to be of two main types:

a) *The imitative abilities of members of the community:* Members
of the community are said to be capable of faultlessly imitating various subvarieties, which outsiders presumably could not do. But the
evidence for this appears to be anecdotal. Trudgill, for instance,
does not seem to have tested this ability systematically with all
his informants. And anecdotal evidence can be countered by exper-
iences tending to the opposite conclusion: a number of my informants

said they could *not* imitate a 'broad Yorkshire' accent, and others
who attempted to do so did not do it 'faultlessly' - and surely the
finding that the /oː/ and the /ɔʊ/ sets are not clearly distinguished
now could be claimed to indicate that it would be artificial to set
them up as distinct in some common diasystem.   On the other hand,
I have come across people from other parts of the English-speaking
world who could imitate a broad Yorkshire accent better than some
of the more RP-like informants in my sample - which of these would
be said to belong to the 'West Yorkshire speech community'?

b) *A common set of value-judgements*: The evaluations by other in-.
formants of different variants are said to indicate that they are
united in their norms.   However, none of the evaluation data,
whether directly-expressed opinions, self-evaluations, or subjective
evaluations of tape-recorded examples, has ever produced 100 per
cent agreement on which variants are preferred or aimed at;   this
is clear in Labov's and Trudgill's work as well as my own survey.
Certainly the evidence of the latter does not seem to support the
idea of a united speech community: some informants seem to prefer
RP-like forms (e.g. [ʌ]) others seem to have a regional norm (e.g.
[ʊ]).   Moreover, there were signs that not all the evaluation
tests pointed the same way: it was clear, for example, that the
great majority had an [a] standard in words of the *grass, laugh,
bath* group (many of them said they disliked the 'long A' variant,
and that it was in fact incorrect).   But there were clear indications from the subjective evaluations that the [ɑː] form tended
to command prestige.   What is the evaluative norm in such cases?

(ii) THE PROBLEM OF DELIMITING A SPEECH COMMUNITY.   This delimitation problem has two aspects, as it were 'horizontal' and 'vertical'
- in terms of both geographical area and the social scale.

a) *Geographical delimitation.*   Whereas Norwich, where Trudgill
worked, is in a sense an isolated large town, the West Yorkshire
conurbation includes Bradford, Leeds, Halifax, Huddersfield, Wakefield, and numerous smaller towns.   In the past these towns were
more physically discrete, and there were probably some noticeable
differences of speech between them.   But nowadays they merge into
one another geographically, and such differences as I found between Bradford, Halifax and Huddersfield were largely of a 'quantitative' nature: in other words, it is not usually the case that
feature *x* occurs in Bradford but not at all in Halifax or Huddersfield, but rather that it is commoner *on average* in say Bradford
than in the others (though *some* Bradford speakers may not have it
at all, and some Halifax speakers may have it quite frequently).

In such a situation, what are the 'speech communities'?   Hardly
Bradford, Leeds, Halifax etc.   Are they smaller than these?   Surely not - this would be even more difficult to maintain.   Then

perhaps industrial West Yorkshire as a whole is a speech community?
Certainly it shares many features; but firstly, there are probably
also some well-marked differences between the ends of this geographical continuum; secondly, some places on the Western edge of
the area may in fact be more similar in many respects to neighbouring Lancashire towns than to Eastern of Southern parts; thirdly,
though there are some markedly different forms in rural areas, there
is no sharp urban/rural difference, and it would be difficult to
decide just who belonged to the 'industrial speech community'.

   b) *Social delimitation*. We noted that Trudgill set up separate vowels in *nose* and *knows*, claiming that all speakers distinguish
these deep down, though some members of the Middle Class never do so
in performance. Now to produce a similar diasystem for West Yorkshire it would be necessary to set up /o:/ and /ɔʊ/, which many
speakers distinguish at times - but some RP-speakers in the city
never do so, and would probably be *incapable* of doing so. On the
other hand, just as Trudgill claimed that all speakers really have
distinct vowels in *boot* and *boat* but that the lower classes usually
merge them, in West Yorkshire the diasystem would have to contain
/ʌ/ and /ʊ/ because even lower-class speakers may occasionally produce [ʌ], and anyway their evaluations show that some of them recognise its significance. However, [ʌ] is a minority phenomenon, and
many speakers produce some 'hypercorrect' forms; why should this
be, if they really have the distinction in their internalized system? Perhaps it would be more reasonable to have only /ʊ/ in the
diasystem, and to have rules for phonemic split which are more
likely to be correctly applied higher up the social scale. But
this would mean that RP-speakers who consistently and correctly distinguish /ʌ/ and /ʊ/ only do so at a relatively superficial level.

   Then perhaps the answer is that the RP-speakers in West Yorkshire are not really part of the local speech community; after all,
they are often not as good at faultlessly imitating a broad accent.
But is it realistic to exclude them? In many respects they are
only the end of a continuum, and they understand the local speech
perfectly well; *some* of them may even be able to imitate it.

   At the other end of the social scale we have a more serious
problem. We noted that Trudgill said it would be difficult to set
up a 'meaningful' diasystem for two very different varieties (such
as Yorkshire and Australian). Consider these two very different
varieties:

A.	light	right	like	find	neither	me	beat	eat	feet
	———————— /ai/ ————————				/ai/ ~ /i:/	——————— /i:/ ————————			
B.	/i:/	/ɛɪ/	/aɪ/	/ɪ/	/ɔ:/	/i:/	/ɪə/	/ɛɪ/	/ɪ/

With sufficient 'diasystemic incidence rules' such as Trudgill
employs for what amounts to 'phoneme swapping', it would probably
be possible to set up a diasystem which will incorporate both the
above - but I agree that it would hardly be 'meaningful'; it would
indeed be more in the nature of an 'intellectual exercise'. If we
take system B as basic, this would mean that the majority of West
Yorkshire speakers (who have A) have a deep phonemic incidence that
has to undergo considerable changes; but if we take the system of
the majority as basic, then the Bradford working-class informant
who had system B must have been applying an awful lot of rules to
produce his output (and he seemed to do it so easily!).

      Perhaps then the answer is that the West Yorkshire speech comm-
unity does not really include this eccentric individual. But he
in fact was one of at most two members of the West Yorkshire sample
who spoke the traditional dialect described by Wright and the SED
(see p.80 ff.) - could we really maintain that he is not a member of
'the West Yorkshire speech community'? Even a sample of the size
usually selected by modern dialectologists, could have failed to pick
up a single speaker of traditional dialect[184], but if they then
constructed a diasystem for an alleged speech community which excluded such speakers, this would surely be no less a distortion than
the description produced by a traditional dialectologist which is
based on an unrepresentative selection of 'pure dialect' speakers.

      A major problem with the notion of a 'speech community' is that
boundaries - linguistic, social, or geographical - are generally
imprecise, but this theory makes them precise: it postulates one
community with one set of internalised norms, another with a different set, and so on.

      But is such a notion needed anyway? Certainly not, of course,
in order to explain mutual intelligibility. Trudgill says he would
not regard a diasystem for Yorkshire and Australian English as a
reality; presumably Yorkshiremen and Australians are able to communicate because their separate systems are sufficiently similar.
The degrees of similarity between and familiarity amongst speakers
of different forms of English presumably contribute to the ease with
which they communicate - and this reasoning could of course be extended to different languages; Dutch and German speakers, or Polish
and Serbo-Croatian speakers may be mutually intelligible to some
degree without sharing a diasystem of any 'real' sort. So until the
evidence for some shared system is much stronger it is quite reason-

---

184 See Heath (1980:8), where he comments that not one 'pure' dialect speaker appeared in the random sample of 80 informants interviewed during his investigation of the speech of Cannock.

able to believe that different members of the West Yorkshire community have different systems or different sets of systems; they
are similar to and familiar with each other, and at times try to
adapt to each other, but they are not a united 'speech community'.

A P P E N D I C E S

A N D

B I B L I O G R A P H Y

A P P E N D I X   A

THE QUESTIONNAIRE

I   I'd like to start by asking you a few questions about yourself
and your background.

Were you born in (Bradford/Halifax/Huddersfield)?
    (If 'no')   How old were you when you came here?
    (If 'yes') Have you lived away from this area at all?
Where did your father and mother come from? Were they local
    people?
What school did you go to?
How old were you when you left?
Did you have any further education after that? Did you go to
    tech, or night-school?
What job did you go into?
Have you had any other jobs?
Is (last-named) what you are doing now?
Is that what you really wanted to do?
What did your father do?
    (Women) What does your husband do?

II   You know how we used to talk about 'social classes' (like
working class or upper class),

Do you think the business of 'social class' still exists in
    Britain?
What sort of classes do you think there are nowadays?
How do you decide what class a person belongs to? Is it by
    his money, job, education, birth, the way he dresses, or
    speaks...?
    (Or, if clue given in preceding answer: So you think that
    such classes as exist are determined mainly by money/
    education/occupation?)
What class would you say you belong to yourself?

III Now this is just a short list of words, just to hear the
different vowel-sounds round here.

IV   Now I'd like to ask you about some things you may have done,
or remember happening to you.

Do you remember, when you were a lad/girl and playing games,
how you used to decide who was going to start?   Did you
have a rhyme you used to say?
Do you remember playing any games then that don't seem to be
very common now? (Picking up response: How do you play
that?)
Do you remember, when you were at school any teachers you
were particularly scared of or hated?
Have you ever been involved in an accident, or just missed one?
(If 'no': Have you ever seen one?)
Can you remember anything very funny that's ever happened to
you?
Do you have any strong feelings about the number of immigrants
in (Bfd/Hfx/Hudd), and the West Riding towns generally?
What do you think of all the rebuilding that's going on in
town? Do you like it?

V   Now this is a longer list of words ([not to the more intelligent:] but they are all everyday words, and I don't think
you'll have any difficulty with them). If you find you are
getting dry, we can have a break. Just read them as you
would normally say them.

VI   Now if you've lived in this area all/most of your life, you've
probably come across people using the words 'thee' and 'thah'
Do you yourself ever use these words?
(If 'no') Why not, do you think?
What sort of people do use them?
Do you think they use them to just anybody, or
only to one another?
Do these words mean anything in particular if someone uses them
to you?
(If 'yes') Would you say 'thee' and 'thah' to your:
wife/husband
father
son/daughter
boss
a woman
somebody you've just met?
If you did use it to e.g. boss (if 'no' above), would it seem
a bit cheeky or even over-familiar?
Using 'thah' instead of 'you', can you think how you would say:
'You are a good lad'.
'You will not go'.

VII   Now I'd like to ask you a few questions about this part of the
      world and what you think about it.

      Are you proud of being a Yorkshireman/Yorkshire person?
      Is there anything you *don't* like about this part of the country?
      Do you think people down South have the right ideas about what
      Yorkshire is like?
      (If needed) What do you think they think about it?
      Do you like living in (Bradford/Halifax/Huddersfield)?
      Is this the side of town that you like to live on, or would
      you rather live in another part?
      Do you think that (Bfd/Hfx/Hudd) is a place where there is
      plenty to do in your spare time?
      (In Hfx/Hudd) If you/your wife/mother wanted to go some-
      where where she had a better range of shops, where would
      you/she go?
      Where would you go for a better range of entertainments?
      Do you have far to travel to your work?
      Do you take the local paper?   What other papers do you get?

VIII This is just a short set of words, words that sound quite
      similar; (you know, like 'principal'/'principle' or
      'council'/'counsel' sound just alike).   Some of these
      sound more alike than others.   Just read them in sets, as
      they appear on the cards.

IX   Now I'd like to ask you some questions about the way people
      talk round here.

      Do you think the way a person speaks is important for getting
      on?
      What do you think in general about the way people speak in
      this town or the West Riding generally?
      Is there anything in particular you *don't* like about it?
      Is there anything in particular you don't /didn't like to
      hear your children say?   You know, you said 'You don't
      talk like that, talk properly!'.
      (Alternatively, for younger informants): Can you remember
      anything your parents or your teacher used to correct in
      your speech?   You know, they said 'You don't talk like
      that, talk properly!'.
      What do you think about the way you speak?
      Have you ever tried to change the way you speak?
      Has anybody ever said to you, when they heard you speak, say
      when you've been away on holiday: 'I know where *you* come
      from'?

Were they right?
What do you think gave them the clue?
What sort of things do you think will give a Yorkshireman away?
Do you think that people in the South like the way we speak here?
Do you think people speak any differently in (other two) from the way they do in (Bfd/Hfx/Hudd)?
(If 'yes') In what sort of way?

X   Now this is a set of words that *I'm* going to read to you, because they are words that can have two or three different pronunciations. What I'd like you to do is to say, after each word, which is the pronunciation you use, number 1, number 2 or number 3 (there's no need to repeat the word). Also, if it happens in any particular case that you think 'Well, I know that number 3 is more correct', will you please say that as well. You take this set of cards, and I'll read from here.

XI   There's just one more thing I'd like you to read, and that's this short story. It's not very interesting, but it contains some of the words that we might say differently up here. It's not as long as it looks, because it's spaced out. You just read it at your own speed, as naturally as you can.

XII Now the only other thing is to go back to what we were saying a minute ago, about whether the way a person spoke could make a difference for getting on. On that card is a list of five jobs in what most people agree is the 'order of qualification' as it were from a speaking point of view. A BBC newsreader would obviously have to have a very good speech; a personnel-officer in a big firm might have to have been to a university and be able to talk well, dealing with directors and so on; a teacher in an ordinary school might have some accent but would have to be fairly well-spoken; and it is less important for an ordinary shopkeeper and least of all for a labourer.

Now, what I have done is to record on this little tape-recorder about two dozen sentences read by a number of different men of different jobs: they don't have those particular jobs, but they have a range of jobs. What I'd like you to do is,

at the end of a sentence to say what job from that list you
think the speaker could get, speaking as he did.   Now there
are not just five sentences, and the men don't have those
particular jobs, as I said, so there is no need to spread them
evenly: if you think they all sound like labourers, you can
put them all as labourers, or you could put them all as news-
readers if you want.

Now some people find they can't make anything of this, so just
listen to a few;   then if you can't tell much difference
we'll stop.
. . . .
Now then, what do you think you were judging by?

XIII Now there are just a few final questions, and then that's it.
     These questions are about yourself, to set you in relation
     to other people I've been talking to.   Of course, I keep
     all this anonymous, but if you do think any of these ques-
     tions are too personal, you must refuse to answer.   But
     I hope you'll understand that I'm only asking them because
     they might have some relevance to what I'm trying to find
     out.

     Do you belong to any church?
       (If 'yes') Are you a fairly regular attender?
     Either: Would I be right in guessing that you are in your
       (thirties etc.)?
     Or: On this card there are certain age-groups, referred to
       by letters;   would you mind telling me which letter you come
       under?
     Do you support any political party?   (If necessary)   Which?
     Is this house your own/your parents', or is it rented?
     How many children have you got?
     How many children are/were there in your family?
     Finally, and you don't need to answer this one if you'd rather
       not, but would I be right in guessing that you/your husband
       would come under group x on this card? (card with income-
       groups referred to by letters).
       (Early interviews: would you mind saying which group you/
       your husband comes under on this card?)

     Well, that's all the questions I wanted to ask *you*.   Is there
       anything you'd like to ask me - anything you couldn't see
       the point of, or that you want to come back at me on?

A P P E N D I X   B

VARIATION IN THE INTERVIEWER'S SPEECH

It has been seen in Chapter 6 that in many cases linguistic variation appears to relate to the social class, sex, age, or locality of various groups of informants. It has also become clear that the speech of individuals varies according to different situations which arise during an interview: these have been considered to be matters of 'formality of context', which produce different 'styles'. Now, it seems quite likely that variation could also occur in response to another aspect of the situation: the characteristics of the addressee, and particularly of course his speech.

Since all informants were interviewed only by me, it is not possible to test this hypothesis by examining *their* speech. But while listening to the tapes I noticed that my own speech seemed to show variation; some of this was obviously a function of such factors as speed and topic (which have been included here under the distinction between casual and formal speech) - but it seemed likely that some of it was in response to the speech patterns or social status of the informants. For example, my three pronunciations of *Huddersfield* [hʌdəsfi:ld], [hʊdəsfi:ld], [ʊdəsfi:ld] did not appear to occur randomly; rather, the first was more likely with middle class or 'well-spoken' informants, and the last with lower working class or 'broad' ones.

I therefore decided to listen again to a number of interviews, this time scoring my own performance on the variables. I selected three male Huddersfield informants who were all interviewed within a space of six days: one (Speaker A) was an RP-speaker of Class I, aged 40+; the second (Speaker B) was in Class III and aged 50+; the third (Speaker C) was aged 60+ and a member of Class V. All were good interviewees, with conversation flowing well. Though casual/formal differences were apparent in my speech, I decided to ignore this and simply to score the whole of my speech during the interview.

My findings were as follows. First, with certain features I showed no variation. One of these was (ɑ:/æ), where I used the 'Northern Standard' short vowel. The rest were a number of variables where the non-standard form is either stigmatised or associated with older people or 'dialect', and in these cases I used only standard forms; the grammatical variables (our) and (Meas); the use of word-medial glottal stops (VtV) and (VtL); the 'reduction' of the definite article to a glottal stop; the long-vowel variant of (ook); and the reduced forms of certain grammatical words:

(with), (too), (than).   With all of these I have at times used the
non-standard variants, but would probably do so now only in situations of considerable familiarity and informality.

Second, with (εə) and (ʊə) I did show some variation, but it
was within the 'standard' range, and only such as might be expected
from speakers of my age-group.

Third, with some features similar to those in the first group
referred to above ('dialect' or stigmatised features), I did produce a small number of non-standard variants: for example, with
(eɪC) I used 25% [ek] with Speakers B and C; with (-ow) I used
several [ə] variants with the same speakers, though the number of
instances was too small for percentages to be meaningful; with
Speaker C only, I used 20% and 14% non-standard variants of (was)
and (that).

Fourth, with the more common variables (mainly phonological
ones), where counts are more meaningful, I showed considerable variation.   Figures 41-44 show a number of variables where the non-
standard variant is not specifically Northern, whereas figures 45-
49 show some with more localised variants.   The informants' scores
in conversational styles (i.e. the total of casual and formal speech)
are indicated by the broken lines, my own by the continuous ones.

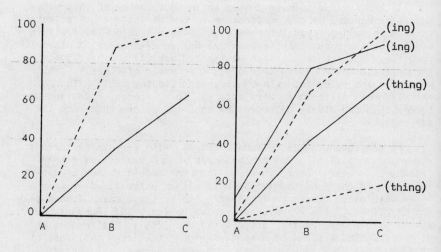

Figure 41:   (h) - % of h-dropping   Figure 42:   (ing) - % of [ɪn]

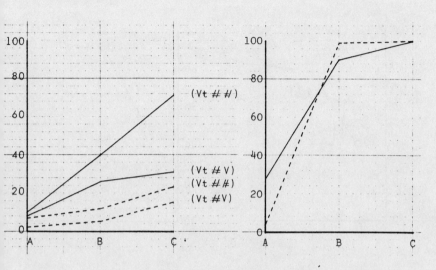

Figure 43: (Vt #) - % of [Ɂ]   Figure 44: (I) - % of [a]

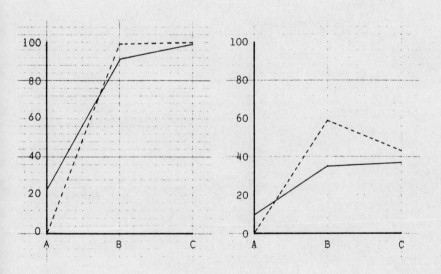

Figure 45: (ʌ) - % of [ʊ]   Figure 46: (ɑ:) score

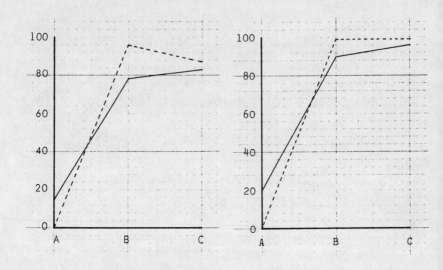

Figure 47: (eɪ) score   Figure 48: (əʊ) score

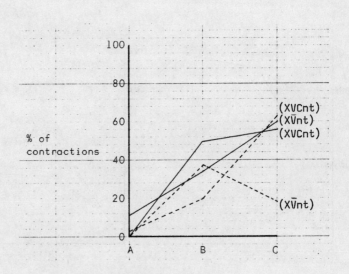

Figure 49 : % of Secondary Contractions

Obviously, my speech in conversation with Speaker A approached
the RP standard, while with B and C my use of non-standard forms was
much greater.   It is interesting to note that in respect of (thing),
(Vt#V), (Vt##), and to some extent with the contracted negatives my
use of non-standard variants was actually higher than those of
Speakers B and C;   now this may partly have been a result of my trying to create an informal atmosphere, but it could also be because
these variants (as was shown above) appear to be on the increase:
I was a good deal younger than Speakers B and C, and therefore my
scores were more typical of the younger age-groups.   On graphs
45-48 it is also interesting to see that my scores with Speakers B
and C were much closer to theirs than in say Figure 41:   h-dropping
had been castigated in my schooldays, whereas Yorkshire vowels had
not;   also, my scores increased in the order A - B - C, even though
with two of these variables Speaker B scored somewhat higher than
Speaker C.   My own variation presumably was governed by some general perception of the relative status of informants rather than
by their specific performance on variables.

The hypothesis that one's speech varies according to the addressee has certainly received some confirmation, but it must be
admitted that my performance may not have been entirely representative and natural.   I was concerned in the interviews to establish
a rapport with the informant and to encourage him to speak freely
and naturally, so some of my adaptation in speech was probably conscious.   But might this not be the usual situation - that one
subconsciously and consciously modifies one's speech in order to
create closeness with or social distance from the person one is add-
ressing?

A P P E N D I X   C

T AND V FORMS

'Most of us in speaking and writing English use only one pronoun of address: we say *you* to many persons, and *you* to one person.
The pronoun *thou* is reserved nowadays to prayer and naive poetry,
but in the past it was the form of familiar address'. (Brown and
Gilman, 1960:253).

Doubtless the above statement is true: most English speakers
know the *thou*-form only as an archaism. But there are areas of
England where relics of *thou*-usage survive in colloquial speech,
and West Yorkshire is one of these. A small section of the interview was concerned to examine how far this usage relates to the
ideas developed in Brown and Gilman's well-known article. The
topic was introduced as a light relief after one of the more arduous
linguistic tasks (and also in order to be seen to be interested in
'real Yorkshire' rather than 'all these ordinary words'). Virtually all my informants had heard such forms at some time, and
having established this I attempted to discover in what sort of
circumstances they would be used[185].

Before examining my findings, the point should be made that
the use of T forms in colloquial speech is a quite different phenomenon from that in prayer and poetry - a fact that would certainly
not appear from the above quotation. The person who may use *thou*
in both these contexts today has control over two separate systems
of usage, which differ phonetically, grammatically, and above all
semantically. In fact, speakers may not even associate the two,
as I found by asking my first few interviewees about [ðaʊ] - such
forms were taken to be 'religious', whereas the colloquial form is
[ða:] (though I shall continue here to use the term '*thou*-form').

Let us look briefly at the *thou* of prayer[186]. Phonetically,

---

185 The interviews did not stick rigidly to a fixed form of question during this section; this was found to be more appropriate,
since often the informant said he only used T forms occasionally,and
it would have been pointless and tedious to go through a whole list
of possible addressees with every such informant.

186 I do not write 'naive poetry', but I do pray; the usage I describe here is my own, but I do not think it is at all idiosyncratic.

the forms involved are [ðɑʊ], [ði:] and [ðaɪ]/[ðaɪn][187]; these occur
in any environment: there are no weak forms. Grammatically, *thou*
governs its own inflected verb-forms: main verbs have the termination *-est* [əst] e.g. 'thou goest', 'thou guidest' etc., but an exception is the verb *have* which shows the form *hast* - the same as
when *have* is used as an auxiliary: 'Thou hast the power' (Main),
'Thou hast redeemed us' (Aux) - we may contrast *doest* (Main) and
dost (Aux). Auxiliary and modal verbs seem to show a number of
patterns: *art*, *wast/wert*[188], *wilt* and *shalt* appear to have a
t-inflection (and note that the last two are the only members of
their paradigm to bear any inflection); *hast*, *hadst*, *dost*, *didst*,
canst, *darest* [dɛəst], *wouldst*, *shouldst* *couldst* and *needst* have
a *st*-inflection (and again, apart from *hast* and *dost*, they are the
only inflected members of their paradigms); finally, *must*, no doubt
for reasons of dissimilation or euphony, has zero inflection.
Apart from these morphological peculiarities, there is a difference of syntax in *thou*-language: forms with *do* + main verb seem to
occur virtually in free variation with the simple main verb forms
e.g. 'Thou dost look down from Heaven' ~ 'Thou lookest down from
Heaven' - whereas of course *do* + main verb usually has a special
function. Semantically, the *thou* of prayer now seems to be different from the T forms in any language I have come across, and certainly from the basically 'familiar' uses as described by Brown and
Gilman: however it may have originated, the *thou* of prayer now
seems to be a form of distance and respect rather than of closeness
and familiarity. In fact, in prayer the 'normal' patterns of T/V
usage seem to be reversed: until relatively recently, only those
denominations and sects which worship in a less formal manner and
seek to make God seem 'closer' tended to address him as 'You' - and
to one brought up in more traditional patterns of worship this seems
at first to be almost blasphemously *familiar*!

   Turning to the T forms of colloquial speech, we shall be concerned only with the three towns investigated in my survey. Elsewhere in the region there are various differences: for example, in
rural areas generally T forms are more commonly used, and in some
parts the phonetic shape of the pronoun is different from that found

187 The latter two forms are generally distinguished as attributive/
predicative, though there are also remains of the earlier situation
in which they were preconsonantal/prevocalic (see Strang, 1970:139).

188 These two forms appeared in the 16th century for 'thou were',
as new formations modelled presumably on *art* (see Strang, 1970:141;
Ekwall 1975:118)

in our towns (for instance, in one part of Yorkshire the subjective
form is [ðu:]).

Phonetically, the subjective form of the T-pronoun has three
shapes: [ða:], the emphatic form [ɪf "ða: dʊz ɪ2 fəst, ɑ:ɪl fɒlə];
[ða], the 'normal' form [ðal bi: ɪn trʊbl ɪf ða dʊz]; and [tə],
the 'inverted' form [dʊs tə wɒnt tə kʊm], [wɪl tə du:ʷ ɪ2]189.
The objective has two shapes: emphatic [ði:], [ɪf 'i: wo:ŋ2 kʊm, a
wɒn2 "ði:]; and unstressed [ðɪ], [al bre: ðɪ ɪf ða dʊŋ2 kʊm].
Likewise the possessive may be [ðaɪ] when stressed ["ðaɪ faðə wər
ə gʊd ən], or [ðɪ] when unstressed [a sɔ: ðɪ faðə jəstədɪ].

Grammatically, thou has either no or only one special verb
form¹⁹⁰, the one possible exception being the verb to be, which may
(see below) show the form art. Normally, thou takes the same verb
form as the third person singular pronoun: [ɪf ða dʊz,ðal kɒp ɪt],
[ɪf ða kʊmz wɪ mi:, ða wo:n2 mɪs mʊtʃ, bʊr ɪf ða go:z bɪ ðɪsen...].
This may also occur with the verb to be: [ðaz ə gʊd lad]; and it
also occurs in the interrogative: [dʊs tə wɒn2 tə kʊm],[wɪl tə kʊm],
[ɪs tə kʊmɪn], etc.   It may be noted that the do + main verb construction found commonly with the thou of prayer does not have the
same function in colloquial 'thou'-speech, where do works as in
Standard English: [ða "dʊz go: ɒn].

The thou form corresponding to you are is a variable one, and
I sought to gain more information on this by eliciting, from each
informant claiming to use thou forms on occasions, a translation of
'you are a good boy', at the end of this section of the interview.
A few did not know, which suggests they were not really thou-users
(or perhaps they were just unable to do it in this 'de-contextualised'
situation);   three gave forms for which I can find no support in this
area ([ðaʊst], [ði: ɪz], [ði:z]), which again probably indicates that
they do not in fact have command of the thou system;   but the majority gave one of three responses: [ða:z~ðaz ə gʊd lad], [ða:t~ðat ə
gʊd lad], or [ða:r~ðar ə gʊd lad].   The form [ða:z ~ ðaz] shows thou
taking the third singular verb is thus following the pattern of all
other verbs;   [ða:t ~ ðat] has the special form art as in prayer-
language;   whereas [ða:(r) ~ ða(r)] is presumably the form are extended from the V to the T form (I do not think it likely that this

_____

189 Wright (1892:117) says this form occurs in subordinate clauses
too, e.g. [ɪf tə dʊz ɪt].   I think I may have heard this, but certainly some people use [ða] here nowadays.   Samuels (1972:12) quotes
ME wiltu as an example of progressive assimilation; since most auxiliaries and modals end in dentals this is possibly the case with
'inverted' forms, but it would not apply to [ɪftə].

190 Brown and Gilman (1960:265) suggest that one of the reasons for
the disappearance of thou in English may be a general trend towards

---

form is basically *art*, with the /t/ becoming [r] as in [gerɒf] etc:
see p. 151).

The geographical distribution of the three forms among my informants was:

	Bfd	Hfx	Hudd	Total
ða:z ~ ðaz	9	3	2	14
ða:t ~ ðat	6	6	5	17
ða:(r) ~ ða(r)	1	1	8	10

(Not included here are one informant who offered both [ða:z] and
[ða:t], and was from Bradford, and one with [ða:t] and [ða:(r)], who
was from Halifax.)   The vestiges of earlier isoglosses seem to have
produced a situation where in passing from Bradford via Halifax to
Huddersfield one moves from a mainly [ða:z] area, through a more
[ða:t] area (this being the commonest form overall in my sample)
into a predominantly [ða:(r)] area.

In order to investigate the usage of T-forms in colloquial
speech I asked the following questions:

Do you ever use forms like 'thee' and 'thah'?

Exactly 50% of the sample claimed to have used *thou* forms on
some occasion; this proportion was virtually the same in each of
the three towns, and in Classes II - IV[191].   The age-groups figures
were fairly random, which might suggest that age is not a significant factor in the ability to use such forms; but it is of course
possible, and I would think it probable, that older informants had
done so with more frequency - but there was no obvious way to measure
this.   The only marked difference that showed up was between the
sexes: 73% of male informants claimed to be users, as opposed to
only 24% of females; this suggests that it may be perceived either
as more appropriate to men or as a rather substandard feature nowadays.

---

simplified verbal inflection.   In this area it has persisted in
spite of the loss of its own inflections.

191 Rather surprisingly, two of the three members of Class I claimed
to use it, but the 'genuineness' of this was suspect in the case of
the boy still at public school, and anyway the number in this class
is too small to give a reliable result.

What sort of people seem to talk like this nowadays?

Half-a-dozen or so informants responded by referring to individuals of their acquaintance and three mentioned specific places
where they recalled hearing *thou*, while two said 'mining areas' in
general.   Four said it was something that a 'proper Yorkshireman'
or a 'dialect-talker' would use ('Oh, no - I'm fairly broad, but I
don't "thee and thou" it!'), and two associated it with the 'uneducated';   a few said they did not use it because dialect is associated with lower standards.   However, a considerable proportion
(38%) of replies were such as 'further out', 'villages', 'outlying
areas' etc., which seems to indicate that 'thou'-speech is felt to
be more likely in rural areas;   and an even larger proportion (46%)
said that old people use it.

These replies seem to show that *thou* forms are felt to be
archaic and dying out, and as is common in such cases they hang on
longest in rural areas and are more likely to be heard among the
older generation.

With what sort of person would you use 'thee' and 'thah'?
(sometimes prompting: 'with your father/friend/boss/a woman' etc.).

There were a range of responses: 'with my mates', 'in the
country', 'in a bit of fun', 'to old people', 'when I'm imitating
a broad Yorkshireman', 'happen when I'm in a temper', 'on a farm'
etc. etc.   But I think the replies mostly fall into a few broad
categories: a large one is 'joking' or 'in fun', which accounted
for 17 of the 60 responses;   an equally large number referred to
'friends and/or relations' (18), and to these could perhaps be added
those indicating that it would be among equals: 'workmates', 'in a
pub' etc. (8).   The remainder referred to 'subordinates' (2), 'old
people' (2), 'only for imitation' (2), 'under emotion' (2), 'to
anybody' (1, but dubious).

How do these responses, and other incidental remarks, tie in
with Brown and Gilman's 'power and solidarity' theory?   Let us begin
with an earlier description of T/V usage.   The *English Dialect
Grammar* (Section 404) states: 'The pronoun of the second person
singular is in use in almost all the dialects of England to express
familiarity or contempt, and also in times of strong emotion;   it
cannot be used to a superior without conveying the idea of impertin-
ence[192].   This of course fits in well with Brown and Gilman's

_____

192   See also the discussion in Strang (1970:139): she says that from
1400 the number distinction was giving way, and from about 1600 the
'plural' was the unmarked form of address to a single person;   use of
thou marked the relationship as not belonging to the central type -
it might depart from this in the direction of intimacy, or in a
special case, of social distance - as with God.

findings about the present-day situation in a number of modern
European languages: it reflects the correlation of T/V usage with
the now predominant 'solidarity' dimension, with some traces of the
'power' dimension surviving. In this century, they maintain,
whether one says T or V relates to the 'solidarity' of the relationship: for example, one is solidary with one's friends or workmates,
and so a reciprocal T usage is appropriate, whereas one is usually
not solidary with say the boss, so here reciprocal V is more likely.
Last century, on the other hand, the 'power' semantic was more
relevant, and a person of superior 'power' (be it in terms of age,
wealth, authority, sex - in a particular sense of 'power'!) could
say T to an inferior but would expect to be addressed as V.

In previous work with an informant from a rural area not far
from the towns under investigation, I found confirmation that the
'familiar' force of *thou* is still felt in some places: this informant said it was not something he would use to his elders or bett-
ers - or to a woman; it was a form of address for friends and
equals (see Petyt, 1970:28).   There is a saying in the area 'to
"thee and thou"' (like *tutoyer* in French); and one informant in the
urban investigation recalled his grandfather saying 'tha'll not
"thee and thou" me, lad'.   Other informants too indicated that they
had similar feelings about *thou*-forms: they were in their 50s or
older, and they made remarks such as 'It would have been too familiar
to my father'; 'My father said it to me, but he'd've clogged me
(~ kicked me under the t'table etc.) if I'd said it to him'[193];
'You need to be more respectful to the boss'; 'I don't like to hear
it said to a woman - it would suggest you don't think nothing about
her'; 'Just to people you're friendly with - not to a stranger';
'It's mostly used among men'; 'You wouldn't use it to people older
than you'; etc.   Such responses seem to indicate that there are
still signs of the 'power' semantic: here the superior may say T
but expects V - for example, those cases where an informant said his
father or an older person or the boss could say *thou* to him but he
would reply with *you*[194].

It must however be admitted that this force of *thou* was felt
by only a minority of the informants interviewed.   Some others felt
that its use might be a sign of affection, rather than one of over-
familiarity; six indeed said that they (or at least somebody they

193 A typically dry Yorkshire reply was 'Oh, yes - I could have used
it to my father, if I had wanted a crack across the ear-hole'. There
is a similar quote in Brown and Gilman from a man converted to Qua-
kerism.

194 An interesting suggestion by a young working-class informant was
that the use of *thou* is governed by similar factors to those involved
with Christian names - a comparison that can also be found in the
T/V literature.

knew) would use it to the boss, since 'he talks a bit that way himself' - though one of these did add 'You'd have to think "would he
be offended?"', and four men who were among the few bosses in my
sample said that some people had used it to them in their 'boss'
capacity; six people thought they could say *thou* to their fathers,
and four thought it would be possible to say it to a woman.   Now,
to be sure, not all of these were regular users of *thou*-forms, but
some were probably quite familiar with them; so we must probably
conclude that many of the earlier restrictions due to the 'power
semantic' have now largely disappeared.

     Then what remains?   Quite a number of informants recalled
thou-forms being used to them by their fathers and other relations,
and many added 'in fun'; and we noted that a considerable proportion said they would use *thou* with friends or relations or workmates,
and a similar number said they would use it 'when joking' or 'in a
bit of fun'.   Surely there is here an indication that the 'solidarity semantic' is operating: one is solidary with one's family or
workmates, and when using an expression like [ɪs tə kʊmɪn ðən, lad]
or [ðad betə lʊk ʃaːp] for a joke, one is *creating* a friendly familiar feeling.   We may note too that some of those who believed they
could use T forms to the boss said 'He's a real Yorkshireman' or
'He talks a bit that way himself' - which may suggest that they have
solidary feelings for him[195].   On the other hand one informant said
'If they didn't know me, I think "thee" would be rude': in other
words, in such a situation there is no solidarity, so *thou* would be
inappropriate - if it occurred it would be taken in the 'impertinent'
or 'contemptuous' sense referred to in the *English Dialect Grammar*.

     Thus even though the survival of the T/V distinction in English
is only a marginal phenomenon, it seems to fit in quite well with
findings for France, Germany, and Italy, where in the past century
the 'solidarity semantic' has been gaining ground over the 'power
semantic', the result being a tendency to use reciprocal T in solidary relations, and reciprocal V in non-solidary.

---

195 Also it may reflect the development of the equalitarian ideol-
ogy that Brown and Gilman believe acted against the non-reciprocal
power semantic: the attitude may be 'If he "thou's" me, I'll "thou"
him'.

INFORMANTS' OPINIONS ABOUT THE AREA

A section of the interview was devoted to questions about the
opinions the informant held about the area.   It was hoped that this
would yield some speech data even from those who might not have been
able to say much in sections such as those on social class and on
the speech of this area.   Also it was thought that it might perhaps
yield findings of some linguistic relevance: for example, Labov
(1963) found that the greatest use of variants typical of Martha's
Vineyard was to be observed among those who were most proud of the
island way of life and their difference from outsiders - an 'identification' with their home area and a 'positive orientation to
Martha's Vineyard' led some speakers to be more retentive of certain features.   Perhaps similar feelings for West Yorkshire might
have similar results;   on the other hand, perhaps those with aspirations to 'get out' might use fewer regional forms;   and perhaps
there would be evidence of movement within the area which would tie
in with linguistic developments.

The first few questions were deliberately fairly general:

Are you proud of being a Yorkshireman/person?

There are various ideas, true, half-true, or mythical, associated with the word 'Yorkshireman', but the very fact that there is
such a word may be significant: there is no corresponding noun for
a person from say Surrey, and this may be because Yorkshire is a
county that attracts more pride and 'identification' - and perhaps
more antagonism - than most.

In response to this question:

- the overwhelming majority (85%) said that they were proud of being
  Yorkshiremen: 11 could be said to have replied 'Yes!' (e.g.
  'Very', 'I am that' etc.), including an RP speaker of Class I;
  61 gave a straight 'Yes';   and 16 'Yes?' (e.g. 'I suppose I am,
  really...' etc.).   All subgroups were represented in each category.

- 13 informants (6 men, 7 women, spread over the social scale) said
  they were neutral.

- only 5 said 'Not really' or 'Not particularly' - and only in the

case of one Class II woman does this appear to link to a lower
than average use of regional variants.   No informants at all
responded with a straight 'No'.

There does not appear to be anything here of more than general
linguistic significance.

*Is there anything in particular you dislike about this part of
the world?*

48 informants answered 'Yes', giving one or occasionally more
than one dislike.

The commonest alleged dislike was the 'dirt' ('muck/grime/smoke/
pollution' etc.): 15 responses; an equal number named the 'climate'
(sometimes more specifically mentioning the 'cold' or 'rain'); 5
spoke of 'industrial blots'; 3 of 'congestion' ('getting too built
up' etc.); 3 of 'slums' and 3 of 'decay' ('industry dying', 'demo-
lition'); 3 openly admitted to disliking 'immigrants'; and one
each said 'could be "softer"', 'some of these new buildings', and
'the way they talk here' (teenage girl, Class II).

The distribution of the 48 was as follows: 25 men, 23 women;
and by class and town:

	I	II	III	IV	V		Bfd	Hfx	Hudd
%	(67)	92	54	32	26		46	54	41

Leaving aside Class I (with only 3 members), people appear to be progressively more willing to express their dislikes as they are higher
up the social scale.   Now regional variants often become less frequent in the same way, but whether there is any connection cannot be
certain - it may simply be the case that people higher up the scale
tend to be more educated and willing to express themselves.   But
it is interesting to note also the overall figures showing the
highest proportion of 'dislikes' in Halifax, where our sample showed
the lowest usage of many regional variants; that the higher average
social class score in that town (see p.58) accounts for this is a
possibility, of course.

*Do you think that people down South have the right idea about what
things are like here?*

This question brought out the 'defensiveness' of many Yorkshire
people; of 106 informants:

- 84 said 'No', usually via stronger expressions;
- 5 said something like 'some have and some haven't';
- 15 were 'don't knows';
- only 2 said what amounted to 'Yes'.

(all but 2, both young, of these last 17 belonged to Classes IV and
V: such people are generally less mobile and so less likely to have
had much contact with Southerners).

Those holding that Southerners do not have the right idea about
Yorkshire were generally only too ready to say what the wrong ideas
seem to be.   They fall into two main groups:

- on the one hand, Southerners' impressions of the people of the
  area: 14 claimed that Southerners regarded them as 'thick'
  ('ignorant', 'gaumless', 'uneducated', 'slow', 'numbskulls',
  'backward', 'yokels');   12 said that the impression was that they
  were 'coarse' ('rough', 'uncouth', 'common' etc.);   3 that they
  were all 'broad spoken';   2 'hard-drinkers', 1 'gossips',
  1 'stubborn', and 1 'funny'.   Then there were a number employing
  a more visual imagery: 13 said the South saw them all as wearing
  'cloth caps', 6 'clogs', 3 'shawls', and 1 'scarves and rollers'.
  8 simply said that Southerners 'looked down' on them.

- on the other hand, Southerners' impressions of the environment:
  20 thought the South saw the North as one big industrial area:
  'dirty', 'mills', 'all built up', 'cobblestones' etc;   and 6
  specifically said 'like Coronation Street' (and another 4 reckoned that TV generally gave a wrong impression);   3 spoke of the
  impression of 'bleak moorland';   3 that of 'cold';   and 8 of a
  generally 'primitive' area.

(These remarks were amusing in the differences in where Yorkshire
people see Southerners as setting the 'border':   they are alleged to
think 'mud roads/the fog bank starts at Sheffield';   'there's only
wilds above Nottingham';   'they live in caves/back-to-backs after
Potter's Bar';   'savages start at North London;   they think we need
missionaries'.)

2 informants defiantly said that the South was soft: one old
man, a devout lay preacher, exclaimed 'The South are softies -
they're flayed to death of Yorkshire folk', and said that we should
set Freddie Trueman on them.

The general conclusion from these first three questions is that
the great majority identify strongly with Yorkshire, and though they
may have a few dislikes they will leap to its defence in the face of

criticism from outside.   There is little evidence of a 'striving to get out', such as might be expected to tie in with a rejection of local features of speech.

     The next few questions related to informants' attitudes to their own part of the area.

Do you like living in this town?

     Two-thirds of the sample (69 informants) answered with a straight 'Yes'.   Of the remainder 15 gave a less enthusiastic 'Yes?', 8 seemed to be 'Neutral', 6 were 'No?' (e.g. 'Not really', 'Not particularly'), and 8 were 'No' (though 2 qualified this by saying 'Not now' - since development, immigration etc.).

     The less-satisfied third comprised 22 women and 15 men; the percentages in each social class were (I 33), II 46, III 36, IV 33, V 32.

     It is doubtful whether any conclusions are possible, but it may be noted that some of those who are less regional in speech show higher proportions: for example, women, and people in Class II.

Do you think that Bfd/Hfx/Hudd is a place where there is plenty to do in your spare time?

     47 informants replied 'No' or 'No?'.   Almost 40% of these were young people (10+, 20+), but the number was fairly evenly divided between the sexes and the social classes.   Inhabitants of the largest town, Bradford, felt this deficiency to a much lesser extent (33%) than those in Halifax (50%) and Huddersfield (56%).

Do you get the local paper? (specified as 'Telegraph & Argus' (Bfd)/ 'Halifax Courier'/'Huddersfield Examiner').

     Only 13 informants did not take sufficient interest in the town where they lived to take the local newspaper.

Do you like living in this part of town?

     This question might have been expected to yield some evidence about the 'social ambitions' of various groups, but only 28

informants replied 'No' or 'No?', and there was little sign of any
correlation with sex or class, except that 43% of Class V showed,
not surprisingly, a greater desire than Classes II - IV (all around
23%) to get away from their present surroundings.

    The last three questions aimed to discover 'direction of move-
ment' within the area.

How far do you (does your husband/father) have to travel to work?

    The great majority of informants lived within a short distance
of their workplace, with only 24% overall travelling more than 3
miles.

- in Bradford there were 10 such, and 4 of these still worked
   within the town; of the remainder, 2 were 'reps' who travelled
   within West Yorkshire, and the other 4 worked in neighbouring
   towns such as Dewsbury or Wakefield.

- in Halifax 7 informants travelled above 3 miles, 2 of them just
   across the town; of the 5 working further afield 2 were employed
   in Bradford.

- in Huddersfield 8 worked more than 3 miles from home, 6 of these
   travelling outside the town.

(Hfx/Hudd informants only) *Where would you go for a better range
of entertainment?*

    The majority (18) of Halifax informants said they would go to
Bradford, with Leeds (11) the next most common choice; 3 said
Huddersfield, and one each named Nottingham, Blackpool, Harrogate,
Burnley, and Rochdale[196] .

    In Huddersfield, Bradford (17) and Leeds (18) were equally
popular; 4 named Wakefield, 3 Halifax, 2 Manchester, and one each
Batley, Sheffield, Harrogate, and London.

---

196 The total is more than 28 (the number of Halifax informants),
because some named more than one town.   (This applies to other
figures in this section also.)

(Hfx/Hudd informants only)   *Where would you (your wife/mother) go for a better range of shops?*

In Halifax, Bradford was again first choice (23) and Leeds second (13); 10 said they would go to Huddersfield, 3 to Manchester, and 2 to Keighley.

In Huddersfield, Leeds (17) was slightly more popular than Bradford (14); 4 named Halifax, 4 Sheffield, 3 Manchester, 3 Dewsbury, 2 Wakefield, and 1 Barnsley.

From these last few questions it would appear that, though it may be less the case now than in former times when the wool industry was more the dominant one, Bradford does act as a sort of 'regional centre' for people living in Halifax and, to a somewhat lesser degree, those in Huddersfield.   It is possible then that as the more localised features of speech disappear, Bradford may exercise most influence in a 'regional standard'.   However, the influence of the larger centre of Leeds would have to be considered too in any detailed investigation of this question.

INFORMANTS' OPINIONS ABOUT SOCIAL CLASS

Early in the interview I asked a number of questions relating
to social class. This had two main purposes: first, it might be
expected to yield speech data of a fairly formal nature, since this
was a serious subject as compared to some of those introduced later
in an attempt to elicit a more relaxed or emotional style; second,
it was hoped that it might yield information which would be helpful in deciding how to assess social class for the purpose of my
analysis, and which might also be of interest in other ways. For
example, if some subgroup within society was shown to be more class-
conscious than some others, this might go some way towards explaining why this group showed a lower proportion of non-standard features,
if such was found to be the case.

The questions did not all ask for simple 'Yes/No' answers, nor
did informants choose from a proffered list of possibilities: rather
they were left to answer in their own way. This had the advantage
of allowing more fluent speech and of not predisposing the informant to any set framework - but the disadvantage of producing responses not always readily comparable and classifiable.

(With the youngest informants I began by asking whether they had heard
such terms as 'middle class' or 'working class'; if these were unfamiliar expressions, the whole section was dropped.)

After some preamble, the first question was *Do you think the*
business of "social class" still exists in Britain? (or words to that
effect).

This question elicited a range of replies and elaborations, which
can reasonably be grouped as:

Yes! (e.g. 'Definitely', 'No doubt about it' etc.)
Yes
Yes, but less now than formerly
Perhaps
No? (I don't think so, really...)
No

If these responses can be scored in some way, and then the various
social groups can be given total scores, this might be illuminating.
Accordingly I rated 'Yes!/Yes' as 1, 'Yes, but less.../Perhaps' as ½,

and 'No?/No' as O; also included as O were 9 'don't knows', mainly
youngsters or old people who could not understand what I was getting
at.   The total for each group was then expressed as a percentage
of the total number of informants in that group, to give a crude
'class-consciousness' rating.

The scores for the social classes I used in my analysis are
given in the following table, subdivided by sex; those for the age-
groups are shown in Figure 50.

	I	II	III	IV	V
M	(83)	57	59	52	46
W	-	75	59	64	58
Total	(83)	65	59	58	50

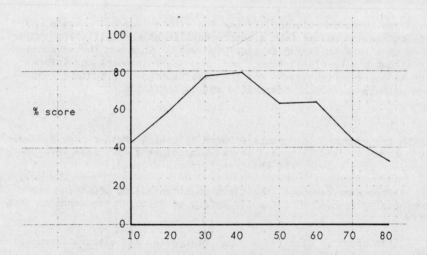

Figure 50:   Class consciousness - by Age

It would seem from these figures that, though the differences
are not great, there is some decline in class-consciousness towards
the lower end of the social scale[197] - but a majority do have such
feelings.   Women appear to be generally more class-conscious than
men; and among the age-groups the greatest amount of class-
consciousness appears in the early middle-aged groups, the lowest
among the youngest and the oldest.

---

197 This goes contrary to the view expressed by a few informants,that
it is the working class who are most conscious of such differences.

One is tempted to see some partial explanation here for some
of the differences observed in respect of linguistic variables:
there is a decreasing use of standard or prestige forms lower on the
scale, and women generally show more such forms than men; the lowest
use of many non-standard variants comes in the middle-aged groups,
the highest among the old and the young.   Could the greater class-
consciousness of higher classes and of women be significant?   Could
it be that in early middle-age one is most keen to get on, and so
most conscious of both social and linguistic differences?[198] .

What sort of classes do you think there are nowadays?

There was a high proportion of 'don't knows' in response to
this question: 49 (including the few youngsters with whom the whole
section was abandoned) out of a total of 106 informants.   It would
appear then that though a fairly high proportion of the population
believe that social classes of some sort do exist, a much lower
number are able to express what they mean by this.

The 57 replies were varied, and subclassification is difficult,
except into those who think in terms of a three-way strafification,
those holding there to be only two classes, and others.   The following table presents a breakdown in such terms:

	I	II	III	IV	V	Total
No. of informants	3	13	28	43	19	106
No. of d.k.	-	4	12	25	8	49
3-class system	2	6	8	8	3	27
2-class system	1	2	6	8	7	24
Others	-	1	2	2	1	6

It would appear that towards the upper end of the social scale informants are more likely to think in terms of a three-tier system (perhaps because they realise they are not at the top, but are quite sure
they are not at the bottom); the lowest class are most likely to
think in terms of 'us and them'.

---

198 A good example was a woman in her late 30s, of humbler background
and occupation herself, but qualifying as Class III on total 'score':
she said she thought she was Middle Class and liked to think she
could rise above her fellow-workers (in textiles) who were working-
class - and she was markedly 'speech-conscious'.

To give now some more specific details:

- those claiming there was a three-class structure mostly used the fairly neutral labels 'Upper/Middle/Working or Lower'; but two suggested, by calling the lowest group 'Poor', that they thought the divisions were mainly economic, whereas three suggested they were occupational: 'Managerial/Middle/Working' (2) and 'Higher/ Middle/Labour'. The most unusual reply was that of a public schoolboy: 'High Society/White Collar/Working'. Two inform- ants held that the three-class structure was now changing to a two - the lowest class being the one disappearing.

- those holding society to be two-tiered divided in various ways. The differences were roughly in terms of which two of the three referred to by the above they believed to exist: four said it was 'Upper' and 'Middle', four that it was 'Middle' and 'Working and sixteen that there was polarisation into 'Upper' and 'Work- ing'. (Of the first of these groups, three members used the neutral terms mentioned, while the fourth used the more economic 'Wealthy' and 'Comfortable'; of the second group, one used occupational terms 'White Collar' and 'Manual'; and among the last, a well-known 'Leftist' said the classes were 'Privileged' and 'Working', and four made occupational divisions: 'Employer/ Employed' (3), and 'Professional/Manual'.)

- other responses included one man who said there was 'Upper-Upper Upper/Middle/Lowest of the Low'; a woman who said there was 'Upper Class' and then 'various educational classes'; one who said there were a number of 'Standard of Living' classes; and one who just said 'occupational classes'.

It should be noted that I did not ask informants to give example of the sort of people they would assign to their classes, but some offered information of this sort - and even from such casual data it is obvious that although people may think alike in terms of numbers and names of classes they show considerable variation in who they think of as representative of such classes: for example, different informants claimed that 'Upper Class' means 'aristocracy', 'your Ted 'Eaths and folk like that', and 'doctors and such-like'!

How do you decide what class a person belongs to? Is it by his money...job...education...birth...the way he dresses or speaks... or what? (Or, if a clue had been given in the preceding answer: 'So you think that such classes as exist are determined mainly by money/education/occupation/etc?')

This again produced a considerable number of different response

but most can reasonably be grouped into a few broad categories:
for instance 'property', 'money', 'wealth', 'income', 'possessions'
etc can all be treated as referring to 'money'.   Quite a number of
informants suggested two or more factors: for example: 'education
and job':   these I class as two responses, under the appropriate
categories[199].

Four main factors recurred: Money, education, occupation, and
'background' - in that order.   Responses by members of class and
sex groups were as follows:

	No.of Inform.	d.k.	d.k. as %	No.of resps.	% Money	% Educ.	% Occ.	% Bckgd.	Other
I	3	-	-	5	20	40	40	-	-
II	13	3	23	18	39	22	11	17	11
III	28	1	4	44	39	27	9	9	16
IV	43	7	16	52	37	22	19	13	9
V	19	7	37	19	47	21	11	5	16
M	56	12	21	65	43	22	15	12	8
W	50	6	12	73	34	26	14	10	16
Total	106	18	17	138	38	24	15	11	12

The main differences seem to be that fewer women 'don't know',
and that they apparently consider money to be of less importance
than do men: the 'other' column, which accounted for more women than
men, usually refers to responses about what we may loosely call
'appearances'.   Figures for the age-groups show no sign of any regular pattern.

Responses to this question would seem to indicate that it is
correct to treat social class (as I did) as involving a complex of
factors, with income, education, and occupation being particularly
important.

What class would you say you belong to yourself?

Again there were quite a number of 'don't knows' (38) and also
a fair range of replies;   but the great majority were 'Middle Class'
or 'Working Class' or can be interpreted as such.

It is most interesting to examine how subjective responses
correspond to the class groups I set up more objectively.   For

---

199 Several informants mentioned that they thought the main determining factor was changing at present - from economic to educational.

example, of the three Class I informants one did not offer an opinion, but the others replied 'Upper Middle' and 'Between High Society
and White Collar' - which correspond fairly well to my assessments;
in Class II there was the largest range of responses: most were
obviously referring to 'Middle' (e.g. 'Middle', 'Middle Middle',
'Lower Middle', 'Professional', 'Old Order' etc.), but a few said
'Working' and one 'Lower Middle or Upper Working';   Class III had
the range 'Middle', 'Lower Middle', 'Middle Working', 'Working';
in Class IV a few said 'Middle' but most 'Working' - though some
modified this in some way (e.g. 'Foreman', 'Middle Working', 'Cul-
tured Working' etc.);   and in Class V only two claimed to be 'Middle'
the rest 'Working' or 'Lower'.   It is necessary however to realise
that not all used the same term in the same sense: some used 'Middle
as 'Ordinary', for example: a man in Class V who divided society
into 'Upper Upper/Upper/Middle/Lowest of the low' naturally thought
of himself as 'Middle', and a woman of the same class said she was
'Middle' but within two minutes spoke of being 'ordinary' and 'Working Class'.

Dividing the responses (excluding 'don't know') into percentages
claiming to be 'Middle Class' and 'Working Class', Figure 51 gives
the picture by my class groups, and Figure 52 breaks this down by sex

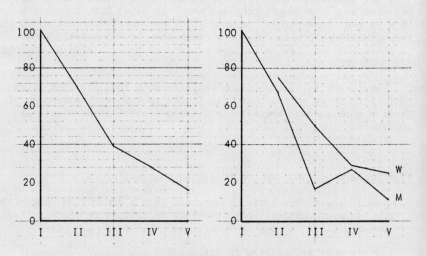

Self-assessment as Middle Class

Figure 51: by social class   Figure 52: by class and sex

There appears to be some confirmation from these self-evaluations for the more objective assignments to social classes that I made. One is also tempted to see a partial explanation for the fact that women ofen use more standard variants than do men of the same class - for women seem to have more of a tendency to see themselves as higher on the social scale than they really are. and so perhaps try to speak in a manner more in accordance with what they are aiming at.

No strong claims are made about the findings reported here: an investigation of opinions about social class was by no means a major aim of my survey, and the method adopted has numerous flaws. However some interesting possibilities have emerged.

BIBLIOGRAPHY

Abercrombie, D. (1951): 'RP and Local Accent'. *The Listener*,6 Sept.
    (1964a): *English Phonetic Texts*.   London: Faber.
    (1964b): 'Syllable Quantity and Enclitics in English', in
    Abercrombie et al. (ed.)

Abercrombie, D., Fry, D.B., MacCarthy, P.A.D., Scott, N.C. & Trim,
    J.L.M. (ed.) (1964): *In Honour of Daniel Jones*. London: Longman.

Bailey, C.-J.N. (1973a): 'The Patterning of Language Variation' in
    Bailey & Robinson.
    (1973b): *Variation and Linguistic Theory*.   Arlington: Center
    for Applied Linguistics.

Bailey, R.W. & Robinson, J.L. (1973): *Varieties of Present Day
    English*.   New York: Macmillan.

Barry, M.V. (1972): 'The Morphemic Distribution of the Definite
    Article in Contemporary Regional English' in Wakelin (1972a).

Baubkus, L. & Viereck, W. (1973): 'Recent American Studies in Socio-
    linguistics'. *Archivum Linguisticum*,NS 4.

Bickerton, D. (1971): 'Inherent Variability and Variable Rules'.
    Foundations of Language, 7.
    (1973): 'The Nature of a Creole Continuum'. *Language*, 49.
    (1975): Review of Trudgill (1974a). *Journal of Linguistics*,11.

Bloch, B. (1948): 'A Set of Postulates for Phonemic Analysis'.
    Language, 24.

Bottomore, T.B. (1965): *Classes in Modern Society*.   London: Allen
    & Unwin.

Bright,W. (ed.) (1966): *Sociolinguistics*.   The Hague: Mouton.

Brown, R. & Gilman,A. (1960): 'The Pronouns of Power and Solidarity',
    in Fishman (ed.).

Catford, J.C.(1957): 'The Linguistic Survey of Scotland'.
    Orbis, 6.

Crossland, C. (1899): 'The Vowel Sounds and Substitutions of the
    Halifax Dialect'. *Transactions of the Yorkshire Dialect
    Society*, Vol. I, Pt. II.

Crystal, D. (ed.) (1982): *Linguistic Controversies*.   London: Arnold.

Crystal, D. & Davy,D. (1969): *Investigating English Style*.   London:
    Longman.

De Camp, D. (1958-9):   'The Pronunciation of English in San Francisco'.
    Orbis, 7-8.
    (1971):   'Towards a Generative Analysis of a Post-Creole Con-
    tinuum' in Hymes (ed.).

Dyer, S. (1891): *Dialect of the West Riding*.   Brighouse: Hartley.
    (Republished in 1970: Wakefield: SR Publishers.)

Dyson, B.T. (1975):   'Notes on the West Riding Dialect Almenacs'.
    Transactions of the Yorkshire Dialect Society, Vol. XIII,
    Pt. LXXV.

Easther,A. (1883): *Glossary of the Dialect of Almondbury and
    Huddersfield*.   London: English Dialect Society.

Ekwall,E. (1975):   tr. A. Ward.   *A History of Modern English Sounds
    and Morphology*.   Oxford: Blackwell (originally: Berlin,
    Gruyter, 1914).

Ellis, A.J. (1889): *Early English Pronunciation; Part V: The
    Existing Phonology of the English Dialects*.   London: Teubner.

Ellis,S. (1976):   'Regional, social and economic influences on
    speech: Leeds University studies', in Viereck (ed.).

Fischer, J. (1958):   'Social Influences on the Choice of a Linguistic
    Variant'.   *Word*, 14.

Fishman, J.A.(ed.) (1968): *Readings in the Sociology of Language*.
    The Hague: Mouton.

Floud, J. (1962):   'The Sociology of Education' in Welford et al. (ed.).

Francis, W.N. (1968):   'Modal "daren't" and "durstn't" in Dialectal
    English'.   *Leeds Studies in English*, NS II.

Great Britain Office of Population Censuses & Surveys (1966a):
    Census 1961: Education Tables.   London: HMSO.
    (1966b): *Classification of Occupations*.   London: HMSO.

Gimson, A.C. (1962; 2nd Ed. 1970): *An Introduction to the Pronun-
    ciation of English*.   London: Arnold.
    (1964):   'Phonetic Change and the RP Vowel System' in Abercrombie
    et al. (ed.).

BIBLIOGRAPHY 397

Glass, D.V. (ed.). (1954): *Social Mobility in Britain*.   London: Routledge & Kegan Paul.

Grebenik, E. & Moser, C.A. (1962): 'Statistical Surveys' in Welford et al. (ed.).

Haigh, W.E. (1928): *A New Glossary of the Dialect of the Huddersfield District*.   London: Oxford University Press.

Hall, J.R. & Jones, D.C. (1950): 'Social Grading of Occupations' *British Journal of Sociology*, 1.

Harris, M. (ed.). (1950): *The Social Survey: A Handbook for Interviewers*.   London: Central Office of Information.

Heath, C.D. (1980): *The Pronunciation of English in Cannock, Staffordshire*.   Oxford: Blackwell.

Hoggart, R. (1957): *The Uses of Literacy*.   London: Chatto & Windus.

Honikman, B. (1964): 'Articulatory Settings' in Abercrombie et al, (ed.).

Houck, C.L. (1968): 'Methodology of an Urban Speech Survey'. *Leeds Studies in English*, NS II.

Hudson, R.A. (1980): *Sociolinguistics*.   Cambridge University Press.

Hymes, D. (ed.). (1971): *Pidginization and Creolization of Languages*.   London: Cambridge University Press.

Jones, D. (1960, 9th Ed; original 1914): *An Outline of English Phonetics*.   Cambridge: Heffer.
(1967, 13th Ed., revised by A.C. Gimson; original 1917): *English Pronouncing Dictionary*.   London & New York: Dent & Dutton.

Jones, W.E. (1952): 'The Definite Article in Living Yorkshire Dialect'.   *Leeds Studies in English*, 7-8.

Joos, M. (1959): 'The Isolation of Styles'.   *Georgetown University: Monograph Series on Languages & Linguistics*, 12.   (also in Fishman (ed.)).
(1962): *The Five Clocks*.   Baltimore: Indiana University, Waverley Press.   (= *International Journal of American Linguistics*, 28, 2).

Kolb, E. (1966): *Phonological Atlas of the Northern Region*.   Bern: Francke.

(1968): 'Die Infiltration der Hochsprache in die Nordenglischen
Dialekte'. *Anglia*, 86.

Kurath, H. (1939): *Handbook of the Linguistic Geography of New
England*. Providence: Brown University Press.

Labov, W. (1963): 'The Social Motivation of a Sound Change'.
Word, 19.
(1964): 'Phonological Correlates of Social Stratification'.
American Anthropologist, 66.
(1965): 'On the Mechanism of Linguistic Change'. *Georgetown
University: Monograph Series on Languages & Linguistics*, 18.
(1966a): *The Social Stratification of English in New York
City*. Washington: Center for Applied Linguistics.
(1966b): 'Hypercorrection in the Lower Middle Class as a
Factor in Linguistic Change' in Bright (ed.).
(1968): 'The Reflection of Social Processes in Linguistic
Structures' in Fishman (ed.).
(1969): 'Contraction, Deletion and Inherent Variability of the
English Copula'. *Language*, 45.

Labov, W., Cohen, P., Robins, C. & Lewis, J. (1968): *A Study of
the Non-Standard English of Negro and Puerto Rican Speakers
in New York City*. New York: Columbia University Press.

Laver, J.D.M. (1968): 'Voice Quality and Indexical Information'.
British Journal of Disorders of Communication, III.

Lehmann, W.P. & Malkiel, Y. (ed.) (1968): *Directions for Historical Linguistics*. Austin: University of Texas Press.

Lockwood, D. (1962): 'Social Mobility', in Welford et al. (ed.).

Marsden,F.H., (1922): 'Two Essays on the Dialect of Upper Calderdale'. *Transactions of the Yorkshire Dialect Society*, Vol.V,
Pt. XXII.

Martin, F.M. (1954): 'Some Subjective Aspects of Social Stratification', in Glass (ed.).

Milroy, L. (1980): *Language and Social Networks*.   Oxford: Blackwell.

Moser, C.A. (1958): *Survey Methods in Social Investigation*.
London: Heinemann.

Moser, C.A. & Hall, J.R. (1954): 'The Social Grading of Occupations',
in Glass (ed.).

Moser, C.A. & Scott, W. (1961): *British Towns*.   London: Oliver
& Boyd.

Orton, H. (1962): *Survey of English Dialects: (A) Introduction.*
    Leeds: E.J. Arnold.

Orton, H. & Halliday, W.J. (1962): *Survey of English Dialects:*
    (B) The Basic Material. Vol. I. The Six Northern Counties
    and the Isle of Man. Leeds: E.J. Arnold.

Orton, H. & Wright, N. (1975): *Word Geography of England.* London:
    Seminar Press.

Orton,H., Sanderson, S. & Widdowson, J. (1978): *Linguistic Atlas*
    of England. London: Croom Helm.

Owen, C. (1968): *Social Stratification.* London: Routledge &
    Kegan Paul.

Palmer, F.R. (1974): *The English Verb.* London: Longman.

Patchett, J.H. (1981): 'The Dialect of Upper Calderdale'. *Trans-*
    actions of the Yorkshire Dialect Society. Vol. XV, Pt. LXXXI.

Peacock, R.B. (1869): *A Glossary of the Dialect of the Hundred of*
    Lonsdale. London: Asher & Co.

Petyt, K.M. (1970): *Emily Brontë & the Haworth Dialect.* Leeds:
    Yorkshire Dialect Society.
    (1980): *The Study of Dialect: an introduction to dialect-*
    ology. London: Deutsch.
    (1982): 'Who is really doing dialectology?' in Crystal (ed.).

Pickford, G.R. (1956): 'American Linguistic Geography: a Socio-
    logical Appraisal'. *Word,* 12.

Putnam, G.N. & O'Herne, E.M.(1955): The Status Significance of an
    Isolated Urban Dialect. *Language,* Dissertation 53.

Quirk, R. & Greenbaum, S. (1973): *A University Grammar of English.*
    London: Longman.

Rohrer, F. (1950): 'The Border between the Northern and North
    Midland Dialects in Yorkshire'. *Transactions of the Yorkshire*
    Dialect Society, Vol. VIII, Pt. L.

Samuels, M.L. (1972): *Linguistic Evolution.* London: Cambridge
    University Press.

Sheard, J.A. (1945): 'Some Recent Research in West Riding Dialects'.
    Transactions of the Yorkshire Dialect Society, Vol.VII, Pt.XLV.

Shuy, R.W., Wolfram, W.A. & Riley, W.K. (1968a): *Field Techniques in an Urban Language Study.* Washington: Center for Applied Linguistics.
(1967 = 1968b): *Linguistic Correlates of Social Stratification in Detroit Speech.* (Michigan State University, 1967).
     =   *The Study of Social Dialects in Detroit.*
(US Office of Information: Final Report, 1968).

Sivertsen, E. (1960): *Cockney Phonology.*   Oslo: Oslo University Press.

Smailes, A.E. (1953; 5th Ed. 1966): *The Geography of Towns.* London: Hutchinson.

Strang, B.M.H. (1970): *A History of English.*   London: Methuen.

Sykes, D.R. (1961): 'The Vowel Sounds of the Huddersfield Dialect'. *Transactions of the Yorkshire Dialect Society.* Vol. XI, Pt. LXI.

Trudgill, P.J. (1971): *The Social Differentiation of English in Norwich.*   Unpublished Ph.D. Thesis, Edinburgh.
(1972): 'Sex, Covert Prestige, and Linguistic Change in the Urban British English of Norwich'. *Language & Society,* 1.
(1974a): *The Social Differentiation of English in Norwich* London: Cambridge University Press.
(1974b): *Sociolinguistics.*   Harmondsworth: Penguin.
(1982): 'On the limits of passive "competence": sociolinguistics and the polylectal grammar controversy', in Crystal (ed.).

Vachek, J. (1964): 'Notes on the Phonematic Value of the Modern English [ŋ] sound' in Abercrombie et al. (ed.).

Viereck,W. (1966): *Phonematische Analyse des Dialekts von Gateshead-upon-Tyne, Co. Durham.*   Hamburg: Cram, de Gruyter u. Co.
(1968): 'A Diachronic-structural Analysis of a Northern English Urban Dialect'. *Leeds Studies in English,* NS II.
(ed.) (1976): *Sprachliches Handeln-Soziales Verhalten.* Munich: Fink.

Waddington-Feather, J. (1970): *Yorkshire Dialect.* Clapham: Dalesman.

Wakelin, M.F. (1972a) (ed.): *Patterns in the Folk Speech of the British Isles.* London: Athlone.
(1972b): *English Dialects.*   London: Athlone.

Weinreich, U., Labov, W. & Herzog, M.I. (1968): 'Empirical Foundations for a Theory of Language Change', in Lehmann & Malkiel (ed.).

Welford, A.T., Argyle, M., Glass, D.V. & Morris, J.N. (ed.) (1962):
    Society: Problems and Methods of Study. London: Routledge &
    Kegan Paul.

Wells, J.C. (1973): *Jamaican Pronunciation in London*.   Oxford:
    Blackwell.

Wölck, W. (1965): *Phonematische Analyse der Sprache von Buchan*.
    Heidelberg: Winter.

Wolfram, W.A. (1969): *A Sociolinguistic Description of Detroit
    Negro speech*. Washington: Center for Applied Linguistics.

Wolfram, W.A. & Fasold, R.W. (1974): *The Study of Social Dialects
    in American English*. New Jersey: Prentice-Hall.

Wright J. (1892): *A Grammar of the Dialect of Windhill in the West
    Riding of Yorkshire*. London: English Dialect Society.
    (ed.) (1905a): *English Dialect Dictionary*. Oxford: Frowde.
    (1905b): *The English Dialect Grammar*. Oxford: Frowde (in
    Vol. VI of EDD; also separately).

Wright, J.T. (1966): *'Urban Dialects: a Consideration of Method'*.
    Zeitschrift für Mundartforschung, 33.

Yates, F. (1949; 3rd ed. 1960): *Sampling Methods for Censuses and
    Surveys*. London: Griffin.

Young, M. & Wilmott, P. (1957): *Family and Kinship in East London*.
    London: Routledge and Kegan Paul.

In the VARIETIES OF ENGLISH AROUND THE WORLD (VEAW) series the following volumes have been published and will be published during 1985/86:

G1 LANHAM, L.W. & C.A. MACDONALD: *The Standard in South African English and its Social History*. Heidelberg (Groos), 1979.

G2 DAY, R.R. (ed.): *ISSUES IN ENGLISH CREOLES: Papers from the 1975 Hawaii Conference*. Heidelberg (Groos), 1980.

G3 VIERECK, Wolfgang, Edgar SCHNEIDER & Manfred GÖRLACH (comps.): *A Bibliography of Writings on Varieties of English, 1965-1983*. Amsterdam, 1984.

G4 VIERECK, Wolfgang (ed.): *FOCUS ON: ENGLAND AND WALES*. Amsterdam, 1985.

G5 GÖRLACH, Manfred (ed.): *FOCUS ON: SCOTLAND*. Amsterdam, 1985.

G6 PETYT, K.M.: *'Dialect' and 'Accent' in Industrial West Yorkshire*. Amsterdam, 1985.

G7 PENFIELD, J. & J. ORNSTEIN-GALICIA: *Chicano English: an Ethnic Contact Dialect*. Amsterdam, 1985.

T1 TODD, Loreto: *Cameroon*. Heidelberg (Groos), 1982.
Spoken examples on tape (ca. 56 min.)

T2 HOLM, John: *Central American English*. Heidelberg (Groos), 1982.
Spoken examples on tape (ca. 90 min.)

T3 MACAFEE, Caroline: *Glasgow*. Amsterdam, 1983.
Spoken examples on tape (60 min.)

T4 PLATT, John, Heidi WEBER & Mian Lian HO: *Singapore and Malaysia*. Amsterdam, 1983.

T5 RICKFORD, J.: *Guyana*. Amsterdam, 1986. n.y.p.